Abandoned Children

SUNY SERIES IN MODERN EUROPEAN SOCIAL HISTORY

Leo A. Loubère, Editor

Abandoned Children

Foundlings and Child Welfare in Nineteenth-Century France

RACHEL GINNIS FUCHS, 1939-

Department of History
University of Arizona

State University of New York Press

ALBANY

For Mindy and Daniel

Published by
State University of New York Press, Albany

©1984 State University of New York

For information, address State University of New York
Press, State University Plaza, Albany, N.Y. 12246

Library of Congress Cataloging in Publication Data

Fuchs, Rachel Ginnis, 1939-
    Abandoned children.

    (SUNY series in European social history)
    Bibliography: p. 326
    Includes index.
    1. Foundlings — France — History — 19th century.
2. Abandoned children — France — History — 19th century.
3. Child welfare — France — History — 19th century.
4. France — Social policy.   I. Title.   II. Series.
HV847.F7F8   1983   362.7′044   83-425
ISBN 0-87395-748-2
ISBN 0-87395-750-4 (pbk.)

Contents

Tables

Figures

Maps

Illustrations

Preface

Several years ago, while reading Victor Hugo's *Les Misérables* I became intrigued by Gavroche and wondered how typical he was. Did parents in nineteenth-century Paris really ignore and neglect their children? Were young children left to wander the streets, take care of one another, and eat and sleep whatever and wherever they could? And were there really no state or private welfare agencies to take care of such children? I was also fascinated by Fantine's virtual abandonment of Cosette. What actually could a poor, unemployed, single mother do with a child whom she could not support? I was shocked that nobody seemed to provide for the care and nurture of abandoned waifs. Thus, I began my search to find out what really happened to unwanted children in France, and I soon realized that neither Gavroche nor Cosette was typical. In fact the misbegotten and abandoned were very numerous, and a state apparatus developed to provide for these babies who essentially were nobody's children.

Children are fundamental to every society and culture. How families and societies care for their young is one indication of the nature of the culture. The social fabric of a society is strained when there are large numbers of children who are unwanted and abandoned. Concomitantly, child abandonment and care for those so abandoned speak directly to a society's fundamental attitudes about the nature of the family and the relationship between the family and the state. Unwanted or abandoned children can survive only through their support by a family or by some system of social welfare. Any child who lives beyond birth does so only through his or her dependency on another human being. When mothers or fathers do not, for whatever the reason, accept responsibility, someone else must do so in order for the child to continue to exist.

Child abandonment was a serious problem in nineteenth-century France, and the problem was most acute in Paris, the nation's largest and fastest growing city. The number of abandoned children is astonishing. As many as one-fourth of all newborn babies and half of all illegitimate newborn babies in Paris were abandoned each year at the state-run, and only, foundling home in that city. In a country like France, where the law precluded adoption and where the state assumed responsibility for the material well-being of its citizens, what were the child's chances of survival? What price did society exact from the child in repayment for life?

These questions have particular importance for understanding the functioning of the working-class elements of society, for often the breakdown of traditional bonds reveals more about the binding forces within a culture than does an analysis of its norms. Since the 1960s and 1970s the new interest in social history has coincided with historians' recognition that any picture of the functioning of society that leaves out the poor is, at best, incomplete and, at worst, distorted. The "inarticulate" poor—field hands, domestics, semiskilled day laborers, and factory workers—constituted the greatest majority of the population of Europe at least through World War I. Historians have begun to seek ways of analyzing and understanding the lives of this large segment of the population and have sought to assess the impact of urbanization and industrialization on these social groups.

Most historians of the working classes, of the family, of childhood, and of social welfare have recognized the importance of child abandonment in understanding the functioning of society and have devoted brief attention to the phenomenon. Unwanted children have always been a problem, and different societies at various times have found ways of dealing with such offspring. Abandoned children were not, in one sense, an aberration in society, because they represented an acceptable means of coping with unwanted or illegitimate babies. The children were designated as *enfants trouvés*, or *enfants abandonnés*—both terms are equivalent to the English word "foundling." At mid-century, they were collectively referred to as *enfants assistés*—children aided or succored by the state; at the end of the century, they were designated as "Pupilles de l'Assistance Publique," often shortened to *assistés* or *pupilles*. Whatever the term used, the number of "foundlings" was so large in the nineteenth century, especially in Paris, that they threatened to alter cherished French perceptions of the sanctity of the family—first by their existence and, even more, by their survival beyond childhood. Indeed, *enfants assistés* became so much a part of the social and economic fabric of France that they constituted an integral component of the lower classes throughout the century and a vital part of the life of many rural communities.

The state's response to the problem of child abandonment was unique. French social policy with respect to abandoned children was fashioned and re-fashioned to create a docile, economically useful and politically

xii

neutral, family-oriented underclass out of a segment of the population that officials believed would otherwise be an economic drain and a potentially dangerous criminal or political threat. As Jacques Donzelot has suggested, the state aimed to preserve the children by direct surveillance. The children, in turn, by their labor, would repay the state for the costs incurred in caring for them. The state had devised a system that, on paper, assured that the children abandoned in Paris were at least given a chance for survival. Sending the children out to foster parents proved to be the most cost- and labor-efficient method of maintaining the thousands of children abandoned each year. This system provided not necessarily the best care for the children, but the cheapest, and the one with the most diffuse allocation of responsibility. To inculcate approved values, the state relied on the socialization and training of these children by foster parents.

Analysis of public welfare for the foundlings of Paris provides detailed information on family life among the poor. Official arrangements for abandoned children reflect French rural lower-class life and society-wide attitudes toward children and the poor. An examination of state policies toward abandoned children illuminates nineteenth-century French attitudes toward unwed mothers, illegitimate children, working-class and middle-class families, and the peasantry. In a broad sense, a study of abandoned children delineates the politics of social welfare as it affects the family and explores the interaction between the public sphere and the most private sphere—the family.

During the nineteenth century the state took an increasing interest in all children and their parents. The immorality and crime of the working classes and the resultant state expenditures for the care of their unwanted offspring permeate the writings of social commentators and public officials during the first three-fourths of the nineteenth century. State authorities condemned child abandonment and often tried to curtail it, if for no other reason than to limit expenses. At the same time they felt it was the duty of the state to care for the unwanted children. As the century progressed, the state was becoming more centralized, rationalized, and bureaucraticized. State provisions for abandoned children reflected a change in the whole culture. By the last quarter of the nineteenth century, attitudes changed. While still concerned with the proliferation, immorality, and criminal tendencies of the working classes of the day, social reformers no longer strove to curtail abandonment, but felt that the state, by means of social welfare programs, could do a better job of creating ideal working-class citizens than could biological parents. Doctors, social workers, teachers, juvenile judges and lawyers, and state officials became involved in the internal functioning of working-class families. Their roles were manifested in the lives of the wards of the state, the abandoned children. Social welfare for abandoned children was one aspect of the state's efforts to protect and control an underclass of the population—those whose families evaded responsibility for them.

The problem of child abandonment and public responsibility for the care of the children is terribly complex, convoluted, and virtually intractable. The weakest members of society were, at their most vulnerable time of life, cast off by their parents. Twentieth-century sensitivities are outraged if children are neglected and left to die. If the state, or other agency, does not act to protect and aid the children it is open to criticism. On the other hand, once the state begins to move its bureaucratic and social welfare apparatus to provide for the children it is open to a charge of excessive interference in the private sphere of the family. It is easy to criticize the state for failure to act at the beginning of the century as we would have liked it to, and then, when the state does actively engage in social welfare, condemn it for invading the privacy of families. At the outset, the state did assume financial and moral responsibility for the abandoned. It gradually developed a governmental apparatus to care for them. In so doing, France was unlike any other country of the century in attempting to look after the welfare of its citizens. At the same time, however, faced with a shortage of money and staff, with a large segment of the population mired in poverty, and handicapped by the state of medical science and current attitudes toward children, France's social welfare provisions for the children were flawed. There were enough defects in the system that there could be unethical collusion, evasion of responsibility, and consequent neglect of the children. It is not the task of this study to criticize the state for its failure to act decisively, according to twentieth-century standards at the beginning of the century, nor praise it for its involvement in child care after mid-century, nor condemn it for intrusion into family life at the end of the century. No system is perfect. Policies and provisions for the welfare of the children rested upon dramatic alterations in general nineteenth-century state policy, medical knowledge, and predominant attitudes.

Despite the historian's efforts at objectivity, no study of children can be entirely value-free. Culturally and temporally biased assumptions underlie much of the analysis despite all efforts to maintain a lack of bias. A twentieth-century American moral stance presupposes that the welfare of mothers and children should have been uppermost in all policy decisions. A corollary of this assumes it is proper for the state (or some

xiv

public agency) to take control over the problem of child abandonment and that economic considerations (the foremost being finance) should have been subordinated to the moral-ethical. Children hold a special place in many modern hearts. It is difficult—almost impossible—to eliminate these moral constraints.

A study of the children, of the women who gave them up, and of the state-paid foster mothers who took them in leads to a better understanding of the changing position of women and children in both the family and in nineteenth-century French society. In particular, it affords a glimpse of relationships between the mothers (both biological and foster) and the children. The mother was a central figure in the family, and the family was not always the nurturing refuge from the hard world. By current standards, many family members were indifferent and even abusive to one another. The material conditions of life for lower-class women exacerbated the conflict between their role as worker and that of mother. Available state social welfare programs profoundly influenced the ways in which they resolved this conflict.

In focusing on child abandonment from the perspective of the state, of the foster family, of the mother, and of the child, some sense of the interrelationships between children, the family, and the state can be achieved. To this end both quantitative and qualitative sources have been invaluable. Quantitative sources primarily include the previously untapped records and documents of the Hospice des Enfants Assistés, the only foundling home in Paris. Of the numerous record books and dossiers of the children abandoned at the Hospice, the *Registres d'Admission* proved the most complete and yielded by far the most important raw data. These registers included such information as date and place of birth of the child; date, place, and mode of abandonment; baptismal record; name of the child; description of the child's clothes when abandoned; name, address, occupation of the mother; father's name (if known); the name and place of residence of the woman to whom the child was sent to wet nurse and the date sent. If the child died within the Hospice, this information also appeared in the *Registres d'Admission*. From these *Registres*, I randomly selected 150 abandoned children per year for each of twelve sample years: 1820, 1825, 1830, 1835, 1840, 1845, 1850, 1855, 1860, 1865, 1870 and 1873. (1873 was the latest year open to researchers in 1977, so that year was sampled instead of 1875.)

The Annual Reports of L'Assistance Publique (Public Assistance) constituted the major source of aggregate quantitative data concerning the entire population of abandoned children of Paris. These reports include fiscal and demographic data on all the children who came under the jurisdiction of l'Assistance Publique, as well as any changes in the provisions for them.

Qualitative sources include public records, minutes of meetings, debates, and numerous letters and memoranda of all involved in the care of the children. The most valuable source was the collection of the complete correspondence, from 1818 to 1906, between the administrators of the Hospice and of l'Assistance Publique with the field representatives of the administration in Saint-Calais in the department of the Sarthe. This includes all memoranda sent from the representatives—requests for money and clothes for the children, requests for the return of undisciplined children to Paris, extra remuneration for the sick and infirm children, reports of conditions of the children with the wet nurses and foster parents, information from and about the doctors, and any and all problems concerning the abandoned children which may have arisen within this jurisdiction. I have combined the demographic and descriptive material to present as complete a picture as possible of the abandoned children, the working-class mothers who abandoned them, the wet nurses and foster parents who cared for them, and the state's social welfare activities regarding them—these unwanted offspring of France.

A study using the varied sources that I have consulted would not have been possible without the cooperation of many archivists and librarians at the Archives de la Ville de Paris et Département de la Seine, the Archives Nationales, the Bibliothèque Nationale, the Archives de la Préfecture de Police, the Bibliothèque de la Ville de Paris, and the Bibliothèque de l'Hôtel de Ville. I am particularly grateful to Mme. Florence Greffe and the staff of the Archives de l'Assistance Publique for their generous help. Mme. Greffe also graciously secured permission from the family of the late Dr. Albert Dupoux to enable me to use some previously published material. I owe special words of appreciation to Mme. Demeulenaere-Douyère of the Archives de la Ville de Paris et Département de la Seine. Not only did she grant me access to all the records of the thousands of abandoned children of Paris and advise me of the most valuable record books, but she also was considerate in enabling me to work comfortably with the century-old material.

Closer to home, the staffs of Indiana University and Purdue University libraries provided much assistance. I especially wish to thank Ruth Rothenberg and her talented searchers at Purdue University's Interlibrary Loan department who spent much time and effort in locating and obtaining materials. The editors of *Law and Human Behavior* and of Plenum Publishing Corporation kindly gave permission to use materials from an earlier article.

From the inception to the completion of this study, I have benefited from the generous encouragement and help of many people. Herbert Moller first awakened my interest in social history many years ago. Over the past few years, some very special people have combined good friendship with professional discussion of my work, and I wish to specifically thank them. William B. Cohen gave his constant encouragement, advice, and direction; I am deeply indebted to him. I am grateful to M. Jeanne Peterson for her questions, for her understanding, and for her critique of an earlier draft. Anne Lee Bain scrutinized the penultimate draft with the sharp eye and pencil of a very skilled editor. Her suggestions were invaluable and she taught me much about writing. Lester Cohen critically read the manuscript and helped me think clearly about some important issues. George Alter, James Diehl, Theresa McBride, George Sussman and Dena Targ have each read the manuscript, or chapters of it, in one of its many draft forms. To them, and to the anonymous reviewers for the press, I am grateful for all criticisms and suggestions. Naturally, I take all responsibility for any errors.

Cynthia FitzSimons deserves a special praise for patiently and painstakingly typing the manuscript and for taking such a helpful interest in the book. I am grateful to Daniel P. Bailey, Catherine Christie, and Daniel M. Fuchs, who cheerfully helped me prepare the index.

Norman, Mindy, and Daniel Fuchs gave me unwavering support and encouragement throughout the research and writing of this book. In addition, they helped compute tables, design the graphs, edit, proofread, and comment profusely. My two children, Mindy and Daniel, deserve more than these words of appreciation. At times, during the research and writing they must have felt almost abandoned themselves. This book is dedicated to them.

CHAPTER ONE

Social Problems and Social Welfare Until the Restoration

Social welfare programs in Europe became established in the late nineteenth century, although public involvement in the care of the indigent, the insane, and the abandoned originated over the course of centuries. The gradual evolution of attitudes, policies, and procedures provided the necessary foundation on which to construct the new programs. Procedures for dealing with child abandonment and provisions for these unwanted children in nineteenth-century France were in keeping with French tradition; they were the culmination of attempts, since the 1100s, to deal with problems of abandoned children. The nineteenth century differed from previous ones in that the responsibility for foundlings devolved upon the central and departmental government, replacing the jurisdiction of private charity and local officials. Governmental intervention and responsibility increased accordingly. To comprehend the treatment of abandoned children, the issues raised regarding their care, and the conflicts they engendered in the nineteenth century, the fate of unwanted children before the landmark decree of 1811 which regulated state provisions for abandoned children, needs to be understood. That decree provided the framework for the ensuing century.

Medieval and Early Modern Child Welfare

Frère Guy took the first initiatives in caring for the poor and the abandoned of society in 1180 in Montpellier, when he founded the first hospice or shelter for the sick and *les enfants exposés*. Newborns, anonymously deposited in a prototype of what was later called a *tour* (a revolving cradle located in a windowlike aperture in the building), were entrusted to wet nurses or foster parents until three or four years of age;

1

they then were returned to the hospice, where they stayed until they could earn a living—in medieval France, roughly age seven.[1]

In this twelfth-century hospice, abandoned children and sick adults cohabited in the same institution, often in the same room, a practice that continued until the nineteenth century. The church endorsed a type of *tour* and, by implication, the preservation of the mother's anonymity. From the twelfth to the twentieth century, church officials accepted the ease and secrecy of abandonment as an alternative to infanticide; conversely, state officials sought to discover and record the name and civil status of the mother and thus make abrogation of parental responsibility more difficult. The *tour* thus came to represent easy abandonment and became a focus of conflict between church and state in the nineteenth century.

Paris had its own quasi-hospice equipped with a prototype of a *tour* since the Middle Ages. Near Nôtre-Dame

a large stone shell was placed . . . like a washbasin. . . . It was a permanent cradle, destined to receive abandoned children, who were furtively carried there during the last hours of the night and who were entrusted to the church, which thus filled the role of universal mother . . . and received the friendless orphans. In Paris, more than elsewhere, the number of these poor little creatures given to the hands of charity was always considerable, and Sunday, during the service, the women who accepted babies displayed them [in order to solicit charity] at the entrance to the church in a sort of vast cradle where people placed alms. The babies were called "les pauvres enfants trouvés de Nôtre-Dame."[2]

After receiving these children, charitable women consented to wet-nurse them, either free of charge or for a nominal salary, paid in part by the religious order of Nôtre-Dame. Charitable women established a house near the cathedral on the Place de Nôtre-Dame, called "la Couche" or "la Crèche," which received the infants until they could be placed. This Maison de la Couche was simply the residence of the person who assumed responsibility for taking in the infants; its location changed with the philanthropic woman in charge. Since it was traditionally incumbent upon the local nobles, *seigneurs hauts justiciers*, to pay for the care of foundlings within their jurisdiction, they contributed toward the payment of the women at la Couche and of the wet nurses with whom the babies were placed.[3]

The origins of the nineteenth-century system for care of abandoned children can be seen in this system in twelfth-century Paris. Infants were received, a wet nurse was found, and, until such time as the infants were sent to a wet nurse or foster parent, they stayed in a refuge in Paris. And at age three or four they returned to a church-run charity hospital until they could be apprenticed. There are no mortality figures for the early centuries, but it seems reasonable to suppose that infants left in the shell-shaped cradle of stone, deprived of a wet nurse or a mother's milk, did not have a long life expectancy. The financial system for the support of abandoned children did not encourage local nobles to take an interest in the children's survival and some probably saw their own advantage best served if the children did not survive to place a drain on their pocketbooks. [4] On the other hand, these patrons' social prestige may have depended in some measure on such public acts of charity. For some it may have been an inexpensive way of enjoying the esteem of society.

From the twelfth to the sixteenth century, little change occurred in the care and treatment of unwanted babies. In the mid-sixteenth century, however, as part of Francis I's consolidation of power, the monarchy began to take an active part in foundling care. By a series of edicts, the administration of each hospital was removed from Christian charitable control and placed under a commission composed mainly of laymen empowered by the crown. This administration had to account annually to the royal officers of the locality in which the hospital was located, although spiritual administration—that is, surveillance, correction, and nursing—remained under the auspices of the church chapters of each institution. [5]

In Paris, while the religious orders at Nôtre-Dame continued to receive unwanted children without families, the Hôtel-Dieu (the general hospital) across the square from Nôtre-Dame also accepted some sixty to seventy infants per year. Infants came under the care of the Hôtel-Dieu when pregnant women died there in childbirth, when mothers who had been ill there died, when mothers who gave birth there had no means of support for their offspring, or when infants were left at the doors of the hospital "in a poor and piteous state . . . in great danger of being devoured by pigs and other beasts . . . [and dying] for want of human milk." [6] Wet nurses were virtually nonexistent and the infants were fed with cows' or goats' milk in a wooden bottle or by a rag soaked in the milk. Infants shared rooms with the sick, and as many as a dozen children sometimes slept in one bed. The children usually died within eight to fifteen days.

Due to the high mortality rate at the Hôtel-Dieu, Francis I held an investigation into conditions there, and in January 1536, to remedy the deplorable situation, the sisters of Francis I founded a hospital to receive foundlings. They named it the Enfants Dieu, but, because the children

3

were dressed in red clothes as a sign of charity, it became known as Enfants Rouges. This hospital was to receive "healthy little children who were abandoned by their fathers and mothers, ill or deceased, at the Hôtel-Dieu of our good city of Paris."[7] A decade later, the crown supplemented the care of parentless, but legitimate, children by authorizing the establishment of Hôpital de la Trinité, intended as a shelter for "poor children begging and living on charity."[8] Private charity and church funds alone did not suffice to pay for the care of the children in these two new institutions, Trinité and Enfants Rouges; in 1552, therefore, the Parlement de Paris imposed an annual tax on the sixteen Parisian *seigneurs ecclésiastiques justiciers*, obligating these Church officials to provide for the maintenance of the abandoned children and poor orphans from their respective jurisdictions. Even with the addition of these two new institutions and the added financial support, places were limited. Those admitted were chosen by chance; most of the others remained on the streets and died of cold and hunger. Some of them lived to become beggars, thieves, or circus acrobats.

The charters of the two new institutions, moreover, permitted Enfants Rouges and Trinité to receive only legitimate, older children. Indeed, from the fourteenth century to the present, public officials have distinguished between poor orphans (presumed legitimate) and abandoned children—*enfants abandonnés* or *enfants trouvés* (presumed illegitimate). Although the specific appellations have shifted somewhat since the sixteenth century, the concept has remained the same. *Pauvre orphelins* were the result of misfortune, but *enfants trouvés* represented vice, depravity, and crime. Differences in provisions for these two categories of children reflected this differing attitude toward them. Illegitimate children suffered discrimination; they were excluded from orphanages, and they were shown little pity. Any succor given them or kindness shown them supposedly encouraged vice, which officials of both church and state understandably did not wish to do. The only refuge for illegitimate babies was, therefore, la Couche, at least until the late eighteenth century. Paris did not yet have any hospice or hospital expressly designated for newborn foundlings, whose care continued to depend on the insufficient and precarious aid obtained from alms and other charity.[9]

Since illegitimate children were undesirable elements in society, what did women do with infants whom they chose not to keep, either from shame, dishonor, or abject poverty? Once pregnant, a woman could employ several strategies. Although concrete evidence is lacking, quite likely women were aware of abortifacients, and some probably attempt-

4

ed abortion. Those women who did not, or for whom abortion failed, had recourse to one of several forms of infanticide. They could either kill the baby outright, leave the infant on the roadside or in a doorway, or kill it by willful neglect. Infanticide had always been sacrilegious, but an edict of Henri II in 1556 equated it with homicide and thus made it a capital offense. To curtail both infanticide and illegitimacy (illegitimate children were those most often abandoned or killed), the edict obliged a pregnant, unmarried woman to declare her condition to the local magistrate, who was in turn to question her as to when, where, and by whom she was made pregnant. These *Declarations de Grossesse* (Declarations of Pregnancy) were primarily designed to prevent infanticide and shame women out of conception outside of marriage.

As an alternative strategy to infanticide, a mother could sell her unwanted child. There was a large market in babies, but not, as today, among childless couples willing to spend great sums to circumvent adoption procedures and waiting periods. A wet nurse whose former charge had died was willing to pay the small price demanded for an unwanted child. She could then pass the purchased child off as the one who had died and continue to receive payments for her nursing services. Mothers also sold their children to beggars and jugglers, to "people who practice witchcraft, and finally to the seekers of . . . the elixir of long life, who have their mysterious drugs and who would like to mix them with the still pure blood of children." [10] There seems to have been no civil or ecclesiastical law prohibiting the sale of children. Finally, a mother could abandon her child either by paying a midwife to get rid of it or by giving birth at a Hôtel-Dieu and leaving the child.

The Edict of 1556 requiring a Declaration of Pregnancy from unwed pregnant women and its supplemental measure, the Ordinance of Moulins of 1586, aimed to reduce infanticide, abandonment, and the sale of infants by curtailing cohabitation and resultant illegitimacy. Women facing humiliation, embarrassment, and public scrutiny by making such a declaration might, it was hoped, think twice before engaging in extramarital sex. The edict and the ordinance firmly fixed financial responsibility for the illegitimate children on the local nobles within whose jurisdiction the children were born. Knowledge of where the pregnancy and birth occurred was therefore important in fixing financial liability. The declarations also aimed at finding the father and making him pay for child support, or marry the mother, and thus reduce the expense borne by the community and local notables for the illegitimate children within their jurisdiction. Implementation of the ordinance was sporadic, and it fell into disuse in the eighteenth century. In the nineteenth century, the provisions of the Ordinance of Moulins reappeared, in spirit, when officials of public assistance needed to know the place of birth, since the maintenance of the abandoned child was the responsibility of the department in which the child was born.

Attitudes toward abandoned children from the sixteenth to the mid-nineteenth century remained similar. Illegitimate children were unwanted and unwelcome; those whose financial responsibility they were, whether parents or public officials, sought to avoid that responsibility. Their attitudes may seem harsh, inhumane, and particularly careless to us, but they were in keeping with society's attitudes toward children in general. Prior to the seventeenth century, children were not central to the family; mortality rates among infants were high, and children who lived past the weaning stage took their place beside adults. Children were not the objects of emotional attention, certainly not among the poor. Part of the lack of early emotional attachment, which also tended to preclude later parent-child bonds, may lie in the shadow of death that hovered over infants of all classes. And the nature of rural poverty also helps account for the lack of succor. In fact, children of the rural poor often had to live away from home—either with a wet nurse when very young or to do an apprenticeship or domestic service when they were older. Given such attitudes toward legitimate children, affective ties to illegitimate offspring would be surprising.

During the late sixteenth and especially in the seventeenth century, attitudes began to change, at least among the upper and middle classes. By analyzing paintings, children's dress, games, and attitudes toward childhood innocence, Philippe Ariès has shown that the child was no longer considered an inevitable loss. The belief that a child's soul, too, was immortal followed. Portraits of children became numerous and commonplace as did family portraits centering around the child. Artists also began painting pictures of children who had died at an early age. Furthermore, in the seventeenth century a new moral climate of childhood's sexual innocence, decency, and modesty prevailed. [11] Although these ideas probably did not filter down to the rural poor to any great degree, some patterns of behavior may well have begun to change even among the peasantry by the end of the seventeenth century.

These new attitudes toward children reflect what Jean-Louis Flandrin has called the "Christianization of morals in the seventeenth century" [12] brought about by the Counter-Reformation. The moralists of the Counter-Reformation saw the family as one of the privileged places of Christian life, extolled the virtues of married life, and condemned concubinage. The attitudes toward illegitimate children reflected this condemnation of children born of adultery or relations without benefit of marriage by the clergy. Only married couples were deemed suitable to bring up children, for they had the ties of kinship that permitted children to become integrated into society. Catholic charity of the Counter-Reformation, both to prevent infanticide and to protect the innocent infant, fostered the care of illegitimate foundlings.

As part of the "Christianization of morals" and of the Counter-Reformation's revived religious fervor, the Catholic Church took a renewed interest in Christian-inspired charitable works.[13] The reasons were many. The worsening economic conditions of the late sixteenth and early seventeenth centuries led to rioting and pillage by a desperate populace. This dearth and disturbance helped create a new concern for the problems of poverty on the part of notables and Church officials. They feared the activities of the poor and desired to reform the poverty-stricken and supervise their moral condition. Charity thus took the form of institutionalization of the poor and abandoned so their moral state could be monitored. This century saw the beginning of what Michel Foucault called the "Great Confinement"—a movement to withdraw the undesirables from society and to use institutions as effective apparatuses for the control and isolation of its deviant members.

Seventeenth-century charity had a religious aspect as well. In the belief that all individuals had a natural right to whatever was necessary for their existence, charity became an obligation for a good Christian. The rich gave to charities as a mode of philanthropy and took pride in having plaques designating their donations for all to see. The Church presented charitable acts as a road to salvation. The creation of the Hôpital des Enfants Trouvés in Paris by Vincent de Paul and the Ladies of Charity* was but one example of a more altruistic form of institutional and religious charity in the Counter-Reformation in France.

The new notions of charity and the new elevation of the place and innocence of children converged in the seventeenth century—and led to new sets of problems. Granted, the strictures on illegitimacy may have reduced the number of illegitimate births, but children born out of wedlock were wanted neither by the mother nor by society. The Catholic charity of the Counter-Reformation promoted the care of illegitimate foundlings in order both to prevent infanticide and to protect the inno-

* The Ladies of Charity (*Dames de la Charité*) were a group of approximately five or six secular women of wealth who devoted their lives to doing charitable works, including caring for abandoned children. The widow Louise de Marillac was especially prominent among them. The Sisters of Charity were a religious order of nuns who ministered to those within the Hospice des Enfants Trouvés.

7

cent infant. What was to become one of the major hospitals of Paris had its beginnings in 1638 when Vincent de Paul visited the Maison de la Couche and rallied the Ladies of Charity to the cause of the abandoned child on the basis of the innocence of childhood.[14]

The number of abandoned children in Paris grew dramatically in subsequent decades. Some observers saw a direct relationship between the number of abandoned children and the amount and extent of aid available through public charity.[15] Unrecorded infanticides probably diminished as aid for abandoned children increased. In Paris alone there were 372 abandoned children in 1640; forty years later there were 890; and in 1690 there were 1504. This represents a four-fold increase in fifty years. These increases necessitated new physical quarters, and in 1643 Vincent moved the reception place for the children from the old Maison de la Couche to a complex of thirteen buildings in the Faubourg St. Denis. The greater numbers also brought a need for more funds. Initially, from 1641 to 1644 financial support came from Louis XIII and Anne of Austria, but subsequent funds came from the women of the court, to whom Vincent pled the cause of the foundlings, as unfortunate, innocent babies who would die without their charity.[16] The local nobles, who had been responsible for children abandoned within their jurisdiction, in the case of Paris, paid directly to the hospitals. To support the ever-increasing expense of the hospitals, an act of *Parlement* dated May 3, 1667, increased the charges made upon the nobles by fourteen percent,[17] which they probably sought to avoid by any means possible.[18]

Toward the end of the seventeenth century, the increasing numbers of abandoned children and declining contributions from the local nobility and people of charity led to a change in the nature of the institution. In 1670 it was incorporated into the central organization of the Hôpital Général of Paris, which elevated the foundling home to the status of a public utility similar to the hospitals for the sick and poor.[19] When in 1674 the privileges and roles of the special local nobles of Paris were abolished and the money paid in taxes for the assistance of the children was thereby lost,[20] a sum was levied on the royal domain lands to replace the taxes paid by those notables. (Religiously inspired donations continued to supplement "public" income.) The secular state, in the person of the crown, had now become involved with abandoned children. Financial aid from the crown did not mean that the king determined procedures or policy in either the operation of the Hôpital or with regard to child abandonment in general. This task belonged to the Catholic order of Sisters of Charity (nuns) and, after the death of Vincent de Paul, to the administrators of the Hôpital Général. Incorporating the Hôpital des

Enfants Trouvés within the larger organization assured it a constant administration and source of funds not dependent upon the church or private charity. Hence, the emerging absolutist state financially subsidized this branch of welfare, although private charity helped administer it.

The Eighteenth Century

Echoing a general movement toward centralization of state government, the eighteenth century witnessed the expansion, consolidation, and centralization of institutions for receiving and maintaining the increasing numbers of unwanted children. Abandonment was becoming a social problem of great magnitude and the state eventually assumed responsibility. At the beginning of the eighteenth century, there were three facilities in Paris for the care of abandoned children and orphans: La Trinité, which continued to accommodate older legitimate orphans; the Hôpital des Enfants Rouges, which still admitted and cared for older children whose parents died at the Hôtel-Dieu; and the Hôpital des Enfants Trouvés (including the Maison de la Couche), which welcomed newborns of unknown parentage and maintained them there only until they were sent to a wet nurse in the countryside or died. Most often, of course, these abandoned infants did not survive.

In 1714 the directors of the Hôpital Général established another facility for parentless children. This institution, known as the Maison du Faubourg St. Antoine, was designed to receive sick or infirm abandoned children as well as children who returned from the wet nurse or foster parents in the country. Since surviving abandoned children only stayed with their foster parents until they were between four and seven years of age, this institution in Paris was deemed necessary to receive these children when they returned from the country. In later years it received all children orphaned or abandoned who were between two and twelve years old, and it became known as the Hospice des Orphelins. It ceased existence in 1838.

Although these four hospitals specifically housed abandoned children and orphans, some young children continued to be housed in institutions together with men and women who were indigent, old, sick, incurable, and infirm. Adults and children alike slept in attics, four or five to a bed, where they froze in winter and suffocated in summer. The precise number of children who were housed in these institutions is not known; estimates range from one hundred around the beginning of the eighteenth century to over eight hundred at its end.[21] Despite the multiplicity and expansion of institutions, greatly increasing numbers of abandoned children were left at the Hôpital des Enfants Trouvés in Paris. Admissions to the Hôpital grew from 312 in 1670 to 7,676 in 1772, a twenty-five-fold increase. [22]

The increase in the population of Paris played only a small part in the growth of the numbers of abandoned children. Although from 1711 to 1777 the number of baptisms in Paris increased eleven percent, the number of abandoned children in Paris increased by one hundred percent. [23] Flandrin has pointed to high fertility rate throughout the seventeenth and first half of the eighteenth century. By the second half of the eighteenth century, however, the fertility rate ceased to be so high, both among the peasants and in the urban population, [24] but abandonment steadily rose during the second half of the eighteenth century. Child abandonment in the eighteenth century clearly relates to factors other than the population explosion prior to 1750. This substantial increase represents in part an increase in illegitimacy. Other factors in the growth of admissions are (1) an increase in poverty, (2) increased shipments of babies to Paris from the provinces, and (3) the great ease of abandonment of a baby at the Hôpital des Enfants Trouvés in Paris.

Illegitimacy rates in Paris and in all of France more than doubled from the middle to the end of the eighteenth century, burgeoning from one to two percent before 1750 to five percent of registered births by 1800. Causes of the rise in illegitimacy* have been discussed by others, [25] but this positive relationship between rising abandonment and rising illegitimacy suggests that most abandoned babies were illegitimate. By a series of intricate computations, Claude Delasselle has posited the percentage of illegitimate children at between seventy and eighty percent of all children abandoned. Conversely, about one-fourth of the abandoned children were legitimate; thus, the increase in illegitimacy may only account in part for the increase in abandonments.

Economic conditions—as suggested by the increasing price of grain—also correlate to child abandonment. Delasselle has shown that "when wheat prices began to climb in 1723, the number of aban-

---

* There are two schools of thought on the reasons for the increase in illegitimacy: either more people who were having children were not marrying, or more people who were not marrying were having children. The first reason can be supported by a decline in the marriage rate among a group of people, and the second can be supported by an increase in the birthrate among this "bastardy prone sub-community." See Peter Laslett, Karla Oosterveen, and Richard M. Smith, *Bastardy and Its Comparative History* (Cambridge: Cambridge University Press, 1980), p. x.

donments broke all restraints . . . and continued to rise."[26] When wheat prices declined, so, temporarily, did the numbers of children abandoned. Even before the spectacular rise in prices and abandonments of 1723, the numbers of abandoned babies reflected grain prices. There was a rapid jump in abandonments in 1693-94, reflecting the jump in the price of grain from 10.78 in 1691 to 34.88 in 1694.[27] Similarly, the bad winter of 1709 when the price of grain went from 11.89 to 41.04 is reflected in a sudden rapid jump in the number of children admitted to la Couche of Paris.[28] The percentage of abandonments, however, always fluctuated less drastically than that of grain prices.

The nature of the poverty, and its effects on the people involved, adds some color to the picture of poverty as a cause of child abandonment. In eighteenth-century France, most poverty was rural; children could be in some circumstances maintained—and retained—more easily in the countryside than in the cities when times were harsh. Most authorities agree, therefore, that poverty was the prime motive for abandoning legitimate children. Many members of the rural poor, who always lived on the brink of destitution, were able to survive in good times. An economic disaster, such as a period of several years of high prices and grain shortages, was sufficient to push them over the line to indigence. Indeed, there were two types of poverty in the Ancien Régime, "structural" and "conjunctural." Those suffering from "structural" poverty were too poor to support themselves even under ideal economic situations. A mother in abject or "structural" poverty, suffering malnutrition, would have had insufficient milk with which to nurse her baby and would have had to feed the infant by allowing it to suck on a rag dipped in water or milk, neither of which would be clean. In abandoning the child, the mother at least spared herself the sight of watching her baby suffer from and die of starvation. Those who experienced "conjunctural" poverty were the ones who when times were normal could survive, but who could not save against harder times. If there were a "conjuncture" of unfavorable events, such as illness, unemployment, or a rise in bread prices, these people had to take drastic measures, or charity, in order to survive.[29] Though it has not yet been proved, families living on the brink of poverty in the eighteenth century probably divested themselves of a new baby, in the face of "conjunctural" poverty, in order to survive. These crises occurred frequently in the eighteenth century. Rural mothers, in times of economic stress, sent their children to the Hôpital des Enfants Trouvés in Paris. Birth control methods were either too little known or practiced among the poor to have eased the problems of poverty and child abandonment.

The increase in the number of abandoned children in Paris is in part due to rural families sending their unwanted offspring to the capital city. Rural children generally arrived in Paris because either the parents themselves could not care for them, or the provincial hospitals where the children had been deposited did not have the financial resources to provide for foundling care without help from local nobles, who generally assumed little responsibility for the abandoned children within their jurisdictions. Most abandoned infants, whether sent by their parents or by the hospitals, owed their delivery to the activities and itineraries of *meneurs*, people who made a living from transporting and arranging wet-nursing services for abandoned children.

Midwives who assisted women in giving birth often offered for a small sum to ship the infants to Paris, thus providing the link between the parents and the *meneurs*. *Meneurs* transported the infants in baskets or boxes on their backs or on the backs of donkeys—often three to five to a box or basket. Frequently the basket was open and the child exposed to the elements; if the basket were closed, there was the danger of suffocation. *Meneurs* traveled along set routes, and the journey could take up to a week. A rag soaked in wine often was the infant's only nourishment. There are no records of the mortality rate en route, but it is probable that it was exceedingly high. When an infant died on the way, a *meneur* jettisoned it on the side of the road and then replaced it with another unwanted child from the next town in which he stopped. The nuns at the Hôpital des Enfants Trouvés in Paris paid the *meneur* according to the number of infants who arrived alive.

The wholesale shipment of children from the countryside to Paris gives credence to the idea that child abandonment was not solely an urban phenomenon. The rural character of the problem is apparent from the decrease of about thirteen percent of the numbers of children abandoned in Paris each of the two years—1773 and 1779—in which city authorities promulgated and enforced decrees forbidding the transport of children from the provinces to Paris.[30] In 1779 a national decree stipulated that unwanted children should be brought to the nearest hospital, which had to accept the child; transportation of children to the capital was expressly forbidden. If local revenues were insufficient, the public treasury was mandated to contribute. The need for such decrees and the *meneurs'* regular, lucrative employment testifies to the ease of abandonment.

For abandonment to serve as the state's acceptable alternative to either abortion or infanticide, it had to be easy, and its ease contributed to its increase. Authorities accepted all Parisian children brought to the Hôpital des Enfants Trouvés in Paris. Until the late eighteenth century all babies from the provinces were also accepted whether they arrived from the provincial institution or on the back of a *meneur*. For the parents, abandonment was equally easy. Women in Paris could leave their child at the Hôtel-Dieu, or directly at the Couche or Hôpital des Enfants Trouvés. Children found on the streets, in doorways of merchants, or on the porches of churches, where they were deposited during the night, were picked up in the morning and brought to the Hôpital. From the later eighteenth to the end of the nineteenth century, it was rare for a child to be left exposed on the streets. Most entered the Hôpital from the Hôtel-Dieu, in shipments from the provinces, or directly from a parent. No questions were asked of the parent, no identification of mother, father, or child was necessary, and no report was required. Easy abandonment was a logical, socially acceptable alternative for mothers who could not or would not keep an unwanted child. But why would they not keep the child? What were their motives?

The alternatives open to mothers of illegitimate children were few. Mothers could, of course, keep their children and risk incurring the dishonor and shame that accompanied birth out of wedlock, especially when not followed by marriage. Given the strictures of the Counter-Reformation Church against concubinage and illegitimacy, such children were a continual embarrassment, and the mothers' dishonor was held up to all. Mothers could not necessarily count on aid from their own parents, for many families put the honor of the family above the welfare of errant daughters. Thus, for unmarried mothers who could not work at home and earn enough to maintain their own shelter—and very few unwed mothers could—child abandonment was almost the only way to give bastard infants a chance to survive. A possible alternative was sending infants to wet nurses; since most were not expected to live, this did not usually demand a lot of money. Few unwed mothers, however, were willing to spend any amount on wet-nursing services, given the ease of direct abandonment at a hospital.

Provisions For Care of Abandoned Children

The general format established for handling the infants after admission during the course of the eighteenth century continued until the end of the nineteenth. When newborns arrived at the Hôpital des Enfants Trouvés, nuns washed, changed, warmed, and placed an identification number on the child and noted any distinguishing marks or clothes in the *Registre d'Admission*. They then took the infants to the resident wet nurses in the Chambre des Nourrices. In mid-eighteenth century, there were seven or eight wet nurses in residence to feed the almost two hundred nursing infants there at any one time.[31] Needless to say, not all infants could have been regularly breast-fed. Manuals, letters, and instructions from doctors on how best to feed infants with the milk of cows and goats support this conclusion. From the Chambre des Nourrices, the infants went to the Chambre des Pouparts, where, if they survived, they awaited their departure to the wet nurses in the provinces.[32]

The wet nurses in the country were recruited by the *meneurs*, who brought the wet nurses from the countryside to Paris for inspection and placement of infants and then transported both the nurses and their charges back to their provinces. In theory, regulations for the selection and behavior of wet nurses were reasonably strict. They had to present to the Sisters at the Hôpital des Enfants Trouvés

> a certificate from the *curé* or from a trustee of their parish attesting to their morality, their religion, their capacity to give milk, and the age of their last child or of their last nursling. The allocation of children among them was made by the Sisters of the Hôpital, after an examination of their milk. No one was allowed to receive more than one infant at a time. The Sisters gave them, with a layette, a *bulle* containing information communicated to the *curés* of the parish where they lived, because the local surveillance of the wet nurses and their nurslings was in their sphere of duties . . . . When the children fell sick, the local surgeons cared for them and sent their statements to the *curés*, who sent them for settlement to the surgeon of the Hôpital des Enfants Trouvés.[33]

Practice did not, however, conform to the rules. Frequently, the wet nurses did not come to Paris; the *meneurs* instead took the babies to women whom they had selected. As a result, there was no inspection of the women and no supervision of the infants' travel to the countryside.

The *meneurs*, interested only in a profit, were greedy and unscrupulous in their exploitation of the wet nurses to the detriment of both the women and abandoned children. *Meneurs* frequently failed to pay the wet nurses or to deliver the clothes for the infant until many months after payments or clothes were due. Hôpital authorities instructed the *meneurs* to visit each infant placed in their district twice a year and to give an exact accounting as to deaths, the numbers of children, and the payments to the wet nurses.[34] This visitation by the *meneur*, sometimes accompanied by a Sister of the Hôpital, aimed at correcting the flagrant abuse of not reporting deaths. *Meneurs* and *curés* often failed in their duty of reporting deaths, for payments stopped on the death of an infant.

While admissions of abandoned babies to the Hôpital des Enfants Trouvés increased during the eighteenth century, the number of wet nurses remained constant or decreased. [35] This shortage of wet nurses probably caused the worst abuses of the system: sending the children to nurses who were unhealthy, who had no milk, or who had more than one baby to feed. The major reason for this shortage was low pay. Nurses preferred private bourgeois parents as clients because the middle class paid more, and paid more promptly. Hôpital salaries were always lower than those paid by private patrons; the institutions were slow to issue the payments, and the *meneurs* were slow to bring them to the nurses. Furthermore, the church inadvertently abetted abuses by *meneurs*. The *curés* often did not want the abandoned children within their parish and refused to give the women of their parish certification to nurse. In addition to an antipathy to abandoned children because they were not native to the parish, local officials believed that these children were the fruit of debauchery and crime and might inherit some of these characteristics of their parents. [36]

In theory, during the first two-thirds of the eighteenth century children were to stay with wet nurses or foster parents until age four; then they were to be brought back to the Hôpital for education. The state always tried what it felt was the least expensive means to maintain abandoned children, and housing the older children at la Couche was generally cheaper than paying wet nurses. The Sisters of Charity at the institutions took care of the children without charge as part of their charitable religious duties, and supplemental income from the authorities was minimal. The children who returned lived either at la Couche, at the Hôpital des Orphelins, at la Pitié, or at Salpêtrière (asylums for the old and incurably ill men and women).

By 1761, authorities changed their minds as to the most economical means to maintain the older children. They decreed that children aged four to six stay in the provinces with their foster parents. From age six to twenty-five the children and young adults would live with laborers, merchants, artisans or bourgeoisie who requested them and who agreed to give them education and employment similar to that which they gave their own, biological children, whether it be in the household, in the trade, or in the fields. The families were paid until the abandoned children turned sixteen; at that age the young adults theoretically could at least support themselves and were likely to be economically useful to the families with whom they lived.

Despite this regulation, Parisian institutions continued to house the abandoned children who returned to Paris. The children served in the chapels and in funeral processions; it was the mark of status, wealth, and piety to have many children follow one's coffin, and the hospitals favored this custom. The families of the rich paid the hospitals for the honor and privilege of having the orphans and abandoned children in their funeral parade.[37] It must have been quite a spectacle to see the children from particular institutions all dressed alike in the color of their institution—red for Enfants Rouges, blue for Saint-Esprit, and gray for the Hôpital des Orphelins—in a funeral procession.

Those within institutions spent most of their time on religion—about five hours per day. The children were also to learn reading, writing, and arithmetic, but as was customary at the time, this secular education received less emphasis than religious training. On the eve of the Revolution, only twenty-four of the eight hundred girls housed at Salpêtrière, for example, knew how to read. When the children were not occupied with religious instruction, they spent their time on manual tasks; the girls made linen and knitted. The institutions sold this handiwork, and all profits went to the institutions. Discipline was strict. At Salpêtrière rooms were small, conditions dirty, and the children sat for eight hours on benches without backs. Their food was meager, and they lived in dormitories among the old, sick, and dirty women—often four or five to a bed. There they stayed until age twenty-five, when they were turned loose in Paris, untrained for a job. Frequently the girls who left Salpêtrière at age twenty-five and failed to find an adequate job became prostitutes. The boys at la Pitié did not fare any better. When they were released many could not find an adequate job or apprenticeship, or they ran away from their masters and led a life of vagabondage.[38] Prostitution and vagabondage were the two life styles most feared by middle-class authorities, not only out of moral abhorrence but also in the belief that the cycle would repeat: abandoned children who grew up to be vagabonds and prostitutes would themselves abandon their children. By the end of the eighteenth century authorities viewed the institutionalization of children in Pitié or Salpêtrière with disfavor, not because of harm to the children but because of the potential harm to society upon their eventual release from the institutions.

State Assumption of Responsibility

By the end of the eighteenth century the church, local nobility, and local governments were not coping adequately with the enormous social problem that the some seven thousand babies abandoned annually represented, and with the delayed problems posed by those of them who survived to adulthood. In response, the philosophy of social welfare in general and toward abandoned children in particular began to change.

In general, the state took over because private charity had failed to care for the needy. The charities were in a financial crisis in part due to the lack of donations. In the Counter-Reformation, donations to charity had become an important aspect of religious revival and securing salvation, but by the time of the Enlightenment, these religious motivations for charity were declining. The spreading religious indifference—or de-Christianization—cost the charities their support and their raison d'être at the same time that traditional municipal charity was being eroded as a viable institution because its fiscal base was inadequate. Furthermore, the years 1760 to 1789 saw the beginning of the notion of a modern, national, secular, state-supported system of public assistance. The secular reformers insisted that the care of the poor and abandoned was not the duty of the church or private charity but of the state. Secular reformers were less concerned with saving souls than with saving bodies, people who could in return work for the greater prosperity of the state and community. [39] Social welfare, or caring for the poor, abandoned, incurable, or indigent, became a social responsibility of the entire national community. Assistance became public assistance, not private. [40]

The Revolution dealt the final blow to religious and private charity. By the abolition of feudal rights and privileges, and by the nationalization of the lands and wealth of the church and clergy, the Revolution cut the economic underpinnings of the system of charity in general and of the treatment of abandoned children in particular. At the same time, it declared the right of all needy persons to public charity and assistance. Public funds replaced private and ecclesiastical donations and support. New sources of revenue had to be found and new administrative procedures had to be established for social welfare in general and for abandoned children in particular.

The Revolutionary period saw the emergence of more positive attitudes toward abandoned children and, hence, a new policy designed to benefit them. The Committee on Mendicity of the Convention studied the situation of abandoned children. In 1790 it reported their conditions as deplorable and stated that it was the duty of the state to care for these children, to see that they had a chance for survival, and to make them useful citizens by training them for positions where they would be most useful—for example, in the military, in agriculture, and in the colonies. [41] To this end, all of the hospices and hospitals in France were instructed to receive abandoned children. The state and the national treasury would reimburse the institutions for the cost of the children's maintenance. The

Constitution of 1791 "proclaimed for the nation the task of raising the abandoned children" and a law of June 28, 1795, charged the nation "with the moral and physical education of *enfants trouvés*," who were thereafter designated *orphelins*. Indeed, the use of any "other appellation" was "forbidden,"[42] For the first time, the prejudice against *enfants trouvés* (presumed illegitimate) was mitigated, but only in law. Euphemistically, in a new egalitarian and national spirit, all *enfants trouvés, enfants abandonnés*, and *orphelins* were called *enfants de la Patrie*.

Under the new state-supported assistance the administration was centralized, and the financial basis decentralized. In 1801 the state created a Conseil Général des Hospices and an Administrative Commission of hospices. The Conseil Général represented the deliberating power and the Commission the executive power. This system, under the general jurisdiction of what later became the Ministry of Interior, continued until the establishment of l'Assistance Publique in 1849. In 1801 all charity "hôpitaux," those that took care of the needy, changed their names to "hospices." Thus, the institutions that admitted abandoned children were henceforth called hospices.

The first move of Revolutionary officials to give local authorities financial responsibilities for caring for foundlings was enacted in 1790 when the National Assembly considered a decree that in its Article 7 stated that "aid accorded to particular parishes, hospitals, hospices, Hôtel-Dieux, [and] Hospices des Enfants Trouvés will no longer be furnished by the public treasury as of January 1, 1791. Their needs will be provided for by the respective municipalities and departments." Thus, the principal of local jurisdiction in the matter of assistance to abandoned children was set down. A year later, the decree of March 29, 1791, authorized the public treasury to reimburse, every three months, the expenses borne by the hospices for *enfants trouvés*.[43] But the monetary crisis worsened, and in 1795 the Directory issued a decree to place the financial responsibility for the care of abandoned children more precisely. In effect, it said that the abandoned children were the responsibility of the municipal administration of the *arrondissement* in which the hospice was located. The national treasury was to cover the expenses of those who were brought to hospices that did not have sufficient financial resources to care for the children otherwise.

Since funds were insufficient all around, fiscal liability shifted; the decree of October 17, 1801, placed the financial responsibility for the abandoned children on the department budget. Furthermore, the guardianship of abandoned children was given to the administrative commissions of the hospices who received them. These were the first of many acts that made the care of abandoned children a departmental responsibility.

The nationalization of church property, as well as the small—therefore crowded—and insalubrious state of old buildings, resulted in some changes in the institutions in Paris. The reports of the Committee on Mendicity of 1790 pointed out that in the Hôtel-Dieu, which had served as a maternity hospital, women both before and after giving birth were lodged three or four to a bed.[44] Furthermore, by the end of the eighteenth century over eighty-five percent of the children born at the Hôtel-Dieu went directly to the Hospice des Enfants Trouvés. To facilitate abandonment the Committee on Mendicity recommended that the maternity hospital and the refuge for abandoned children be located in one, much larger building or be placed next door to each other. The sudden availability of convents and monasteries made this idea practical. After 1795 the abandoned children were housed in the old convent at Port Royal, and the women about to give birth were cared for in the neighboring building of the former Institut de l'Oratoire on the Rue d'Enfer. In 1814, the functions of each building were exchanged.[45] (With many improvements and developments, the building at the Rue d'Enfer, now Rue Denfert-Rochereau, still houses the abandoned children.) In keeping with the philosophy that all in need had a right to assistance, and that admission of abandoned children was a mode of assistance, all were admitted.

Policies, Codes and Decrees

The procedures set forth in the *Code de la Maternité de l'an X* (1801) were followed throughout the nineteenth century.[46] Accordingly, a mother, upon giving birth in the maternity hospice, could specify that she wished to surrender her baby to the state. The child would be admitted as an abandoned child and be enrolled on the *Registres d'Admission des Enfants Trouvés.* Article 2 of the Code stated that, *"enfants trouvés* are first enrolled on a register, ordered by date and by number, and the series is repeated each year"—that is, the first baby admitted on the first of January of a given year received the number "1" and each succeeding child admitted is numbered in order of admission. "The register contains, besides the names and ages of the children, if they are known, their sex and all other information or indices that can establish their identity" (Article 3).

The procedure was similar for those abandoned directly at the

19

Hospice* or on the streets of Paris. For admission of children abandoned in the streets, "the police court magistrate or another police officer is required to give an account of the place of abandonment, and in fact to prepare a report of the status of the child . . . of his apparent age, external marks, clothes, and other indices which would shed light on his birth" (Article 8). After such a report was made, the child was admitted and enrolled on the *Registres d'Admission*. When an infant was brought into the Hospice by a parent (or a *meneur*), "the porter sounds a bell to call the maid, who takes the child from the hands of the person who brought the baby"; the attendant then took the infant to the reception office where, it was "enrolled in the register. . . . A copy of these reception transactions is sent, each day, to the prefect of police" (Articles 9-10).

Article 13 of the Code reaffirmed the policy for return of children to their parents. It stated that a mother who abandoned her child would receive no further news of the child, except when she presented herself to reclaim the child, paid the cost of raising him or her, and gave an additional thirty francs. Only after a mother had settled this bill was a search for the child made. If the child had died, twenty francs was returned to her, the remaining being kept for "le droit de recherche" (Appendix A, Article 21). This practice continued through the nineteenth century.

Thus, during the Revolutionary era, an attempt was made for state and public welfare to provide for all abandoned children, but in the early nineteenth century the state assumed completely the responsibility for the care and guardianship of unwanted children. The decree of January 19, 1811, (see Appendix A) codified procedures, practices, and institutions that had evolved through the centuries and set forth rules that lasted until 1904. The decree incorporated late eighteenth-century innovations in the care of abandoned children and specified state philosophy and policy toward them. It laicized charity toward them, established the right of abandoned children to public assistance, and encouraged the existing practice of anonymous abandonment of unwanted children at the hospices. Abandoned children and poor orphans became wards of the state. The responsibility for caring for unwanted children and for children whom parents were unable to keep permanently shifted from the mother and private religious charity to public welfare through open admission to the hospices, anonymous, nonpejorative conditions of place-

---

* The word Hospice with a capital "H" hereafter refers specifically to the Hospice des Enfants Trouvés.

ment and guardianship, and fixing financial responsibility firmly within departmental government.

Admission to a hospice was to be free and easily available to all. The decree therefore required that a hospice for abandoned children be established in each *arrondissement* of France (Article 4). A mother no longer had to send her unwanted child a great distance to the hospice in Paris and pay for the services of a *meneur*. A mother, midwife, or other person could bring the child to the local hospice, and the child would be admitted at a *bureau ouvert* (reception office). Pregnant women could still obtain admission to the Maison d'Accouchement, give birth there, and send the infant directly to the Hospice des Enfants Trouvés. The establishment of free hospices throughout France represented the state's recognition of the problem of child abandonment; making abandonment easy implied societal acceptance of this practice.

By the earlier Civil Code of 1804 research into the paternity of the child was forbidden. Several speculative explanations have been offered for the decree forbidding research into paternity. It may have been an example of Napoleon's male chauvinism and, as such, been intended to protect bourgeois seducers; it may have been to protect the property rights of legitimate children; it may have been to discourage false naming of a father; or it may have been feared that naming paternity would encourage paternal infanticide or even murder of the mother. Whatever the reasons, this decree exemplified the prevailing attitude that the pregnancy of an unmarried woman was her own fault, but that society had an obligation to care for the results of such women's mistakes.

An Administrative Commission and the Conseil Général des Hospices (set up in 1801 as part of the Ministry of Interior) ran the hospices. The staff of each hospice included an appointed lay director, doctors, and surgeons. Appointment to the Hospice des Enfants Trouvés in Paris carried little status, and doctors often sought to escape from that assignment.[47] The church was involved only in that there was a chaplain or priest in residence in each hospice, and the nurses or women who cared for the babies were nuns of the Order of Sisters of Charity.

Article 3 of the decree of 1811, the most controversial article of this legislation, stipulated that, "in each hospice destined to receive the abandoned children there will be a *tour* where they can be left."[48] Forms of a *tour* had existed prior to 1811 but only in some hospices. The decree of 1811 both required them in all hospices and regulated their structure. The *tours* were wooden cylindrical concave boxes, approximately 55 cm in diameter, which were in a windowlike aperture in the wall of the hospice and served as cradle-turntables. One half of the cradle was exposed outside the hospice. The cradle swiveled so that a person could deposit a baby in the half facing the street and then turn it so that the baby went inside. A person would then sound a bell to alert the nun on the inside that a baby had been deposited. The *tour* was deaf, dumb, and blind. The total anonymity of the mother and baby was thus assured, unless the mother or her messenger put some identifying tag or note on the clothes of the infant.

1) The *Tour* at Provins. It is on exhibition at the Musée de la Grange-aux-Dimes. From A. Dupoux, *Sur les pas de Monsieur Vincent: Trois cents ans d'histoire parisienne de l'enfance abandonnée.* Paris: Revue de l'Assistance publique, 1958.

Although this anonymity was deemed necessary to prevent abortion and infanticide, many Frenchmen believed it encouraged—or, at least, did not discourage—immoral behavior. Reformers engaged in a conflict between making abandonment easier in order to prevent abortion and infanticide and making in more difficult in order to prevent immoral behavior. Because the *tour* was the physical instrument of that anonymity, it therefore continued to be controversial, to generate much debate, and to be the focus of much criticism throughout the nineteenth century. The decree of 1811 stipulated that each hospice for abandoned children in France should be equipped with a *tour*, but the *tour* at the Hospice des Enfants Trouvés in Paris was not opened until 1827 and was closed in 1862, in part because of just this sort of controversy.

The decree of 1811 stated that the hospices must admit all unwanted children, both legitimate and illegitimate, without discrimination, but it abandoned the earlier revolutionary egalitarianism and established three categories of children committed to public charity: *enfants trouvés, enfants abandonnés*, and *orphelins pauvres* (Article 1). By the terms of Article 2, *"enfants trouvés* are those who, born of unknown father and mother, have been found in some place or other, or carried to the hospices destined to receive them." This appellation was given to those deposited in the *tour*, as well as to those found on the street or on doorsteps and to all of unknown parentage. Since the penal code punished, by fine and imprisonment, abandonment of babies outside the hospices,[49] most *enfants trouvés* were those left in the *tour*. Indeed, there was also debate as to whether the use of the *tour* itself violated the civil and penal codes.[50]

The *enfants abandonnés* were those whose mother or father was known and who were at first raised by them or by another person and later abandoned (Article 5). In practice, for a child to be considered an *abandonné*, only the name of the mother needed to be known. A child need not have remained with the mother for more than a few minutes after birth to be considered in this category, as long as the mother's name was given. Children born in the Maison d'Accouchement and surrendered within hours or days of birth were *abandonnés*. Article 6 stipulated that *"orphelins* are those who have neither father nor mother nor any means of existence." A "mean of existence" included relatives who would take them in. All three categories of children were readily admitted and became the responsibility of public charity, without distinction in care.

The responsibility of the state went one step further when these children were admitted to a hospice: they became wards of the state (Articles 15 and 16). The conditions of placement with foster parents and the education of these children was set forth in detail by the decree (Articles 7-10). As in the past, when a newborn was received in the hospice, it was listed in the *Registres d'Admission*, given a number, and all identifying names, marks, and clothes were noted. The child was washed, changed, and his number was affixed to him by means of a necklace, which became his identifying tag. The infant was put in the nursery of the

23

hospice, and was fed by bottle or by resident wet nurses until such time as the baby was sent to a wet nurse in the country. Transferral to a licensed wet nurse was done as soon as possible (Article 7). Weaned children were also sent to the country. The children received a layette and remained *en nourrice* or *en sevrage*—that is, with a foster mother— until six years of age (Article 8). As the child got older, payments to the wet nurse decreased. At age six, the child was placed with foster parents, whenever possible with a farm or artisan family. The pension paid to the farmer or artisan decreased each year until the child reached the age of twelve, at which time payments stopped. Twelve years was judged to be "the time at which the male children, able to serve, will be put at the disposition of the minister of the Navy" (Article 9). The motive behind this entire decree was to produce a Navy for France, and to repay the state for the debt incurred in raising the abandoned children. Actually this article was never put into practice. Children aged six to twelve who were weak, infirm, or disabled and who could not be pensioned to a foster family were to be returned to the hospices and occupied in the workshops at tasks that were appropriate to their age and physical capacity (Article 10).

The decree stipulated that children at age twelve were to be placed in apprenticeship. The boys who were not needed in the Navy were to be placed among the laborers or artisans; the girls among the housekeepers, seamstresses, or other workers, in the factories or with manufacturers (Article 17). The contracts of apprenticeship "did not stipulate any sum either in favor of the master or of the apprentice, but it guaranteed to the master the free services of the apprentice until he was twenty-five years old; the apprentice was guaranteed food, clothing, and shelter" (Article 18). The "guarantee" was almost meaningless since there was no surveillance or inspection of children in apprenticeship. Those children who could not be put into apprenticeship due to an infirmity were to be placed in the hospices and workshops established for them. Thus, the fate of the children once admitted was prescribed by law from birth to age twenty-five. Articles 13 and 14 did set up a system of inspection and medical care, without specifying who was to pay this expense. At the beginning of the century these articles were honored more in the breach than in the observance.

Financial responsibility, although fixed in the decree, was a matter of intense debate and was subject to change throughout the century. According to the decree, expenses were to be shared among the hospices, the departments, and the central government. The hospices were responsible for all expenses engendered by the children within the institution. The hospices had to furnish the layettes, "and all the internal expenses relative to the sustenance and upbringing of the children" (Article 11), including the salary of the wet nurses who lived there. It was not specified in the decree where the hospices were to get their funds, but a major source of funds still came from donations and bequests.[51] The earlier decree of October 17, 1801, which was never abrogated, imposed upon the departmental budgets the expenses for which the hospices did not have sufficient funds.

The state paid a fixed sum. Article 12 stipulated that "an annual sum of four million" francs for all of France was to be designated to help defray "the payment of the monthly salary of the wet nurses and the payment for board of the *enfants trouvés* and *abandonnés* over age six." If that sum proved insufficient, the funds were to be "provided by the hospices from their revenues or from the allocation of the funds of the communes." The obligations of the departments were not spelled out by this decree, and Article 12 was later rescinded by budget enactments of March 25, 1817, May 13, 1818, and July 18, 1819.[52] This post-Restoration legislation put expenses related to the upkeep of the children in the country—that is, the monthly payment of the wet nurses, the cost of transport, the payment for board for children over six—at the charge of the departments with the concurrence of the communes. The major expense of caring for abandoned children was thus placed on the departments. The state continued to set aside an annual sum for the upkeep of the children, but the proportion of the national budget in relation to total aid was substantially reduced. By 1869 the amount paid by the state was equal to one-fifth of the expenses for each department, and the state also paid the cost of inspection and surveillance. Funds were always declared to be insufficient, and hospice administrators constantly had to seek ways to increase revenue and limit expenditures.

Conclusion: Child Abandonment by 1815

Children, whether legitimate or natural, were secondary to the economic and social survival of working-class mothers. The characteristics that Ariès has ascribed to childhood and the child's role in the upper-class family *before* the sixteenth century seem to have prevailed among the urban and rural poor families of the later, more modern, period. Many children were not the objects of affection and attention. Impoverished mothers could not afford to expend emotional or physical time and energy on nurturing their offspring. Legal adoption for unwanted children did not exist, but an institution for them did. Population growth, an increase in illegitimacy, deepening poverty, ease of abandonment, and a general insouciance toward children who posed an economic burden all contributed to the skyrocketing increase of abandoned children and the social problem they presented during the eighteenth century.

Child abandonment cannot be considered merely an urban phenomenon, although Paris bore the brunt of the social problems and most of the expense in one form or another until then. The traffic in babies from the country to the capital and the obvious need to establish hospitals in all areas of France testify to the problem's national dimensions. The capital's large number of abandoned children was due in part to its size and in part to the facilities available there. The Decree of 1811 represents the culmination of the gradual recognition of the scope of the problems as well as a gradual shifting of responsibility for abandoned children from the Church to the state.

This shift from private religious charities of the seventeenth century to the assumption of state responsibility for the increasing social needs of its citizens in the late eighteenth century is fundamental to the transformation of social welfare prior to the nineteenth century. Although Christian society abhorred and condemned child abandonment, such children existed. Infanticide and abortion were both sacrilegious and criminal, and no one could intentionally allow these unwanted children to die. Catholic charity made gestures to save the children.[53] But during the eighteenth century economic conditions worsened, the general and illegitimate population increased, and the transport of children from the provinces to Paris became more widespread. As a result, the number of abandoned children in Paris increased twenty-five fold. Despite expansion, consolidation, and administrative changes, the facilities for the unwanted children became increasingly inadequate. At the same time that the social problem of abandonment grew, religious charity and the local nobility upon whom the care for the children was incumbent could not meet the financial or social task of caring for the children. Most of the children died in infancy and many of those who reached adulthood became prostitutes or vagabonds, thus becoming a further drain on society and often contributing additional *enfants abandonnés*.

By the end of the eighteenth century, religious charitable fervor had declined; at the same time, social reformers of the Enlightenment had come to believe that the nation or public community in its largest sense had the collective responsibility and a social debt to see that the indigent and abandoned of society had a right to life and care. Hence, charity became a public duty rather than a religious privilege. In the early nineteenth century, this shift from church to state was thus complete, since the social problem presented by these thousands of abandoned children could not be ignored. The Decree of 1811 gave the Ministry of the Interior and local departmental governments full control over child welfare in general and abandoned children in particular. It did not, however, create a new apparatus for coping with the problem of abandoned children; the procedures that had developed over the centuries had already been established. State officials merely codified time-honored practices, such as anonymous abandonment at an institution and shipment of babies to rural wet nurses by *meneurs*. The business of caring for abandoned children was nationalized since it could no longer support itself even with state subsidies. In essence, the Decree of 1811 regulated the entire process of child abandonment as well as the fate of the abandoned children throughout the nineteenth century. During the course of that century some new rules and regulations were enacted, some specific practices and procedures were changed or modified, but the decree remained essentially intact until it was superseded by the Law of 1904.

Despite state assumption of social and financial responsibility for unwanted children, the condemnatory attitude on the part of state officials toward child abandonment continued, and the reluctance of bureaucrats and reformers to pay for the children's maintenance also remained. The children whom the parents did not want were unwanted by the state as well. Public officials sought the least expensive means to handle the problem. At the same time, the state advocated policies that would ensure the best chance of inculcating and developing the social obligations of the family to reduce, insofar as possible, the need for—and the expense of—public child care.

CHAPTER TWO

Attitudes and Public Policy Toward the Family

French social welfare policy evolved from attempts to limit the number of those dependent on welfare in the beginning of the nineteenth century, to efforts to increase social programs and the influence of the state in family life at the end of the century. Social welfare for children precluded, for different reasons, both familial adoption and orphanages; the abandoned children became wards of the state, and authorities found wet nurses or foster parents for them. As it evolved during the century, the system resolved two potentially conflicting aspects of nineteenth-century French attitudes and policies toward abandoned children: state responsibility and socialization by a family.

On the one hand, as a heritage of the ideals of the French Revolution, the state, in theory at least, assumed responsibility for the welfare of all its citizens, including the weakest and most vulnerable—the abandoned children. Napoleon then gave the state the legal and financial responsibility for raising these children to become economically and militarily useful, law-abiding citizens. On the other hand, French authorities viewed the two-parent family with a lactating mother as the best means to keep the infants alive, and, for the children who lived, state officials regarded the family as the proper socializing agent, the unit of social control, and the most effective arena for instilling moral virtues. The nineteenth-century French system incorporated both these attitudes.

The state did not take direct responsibility for raising the children, but farmed them out to foster parents. Foster parentage was one of the least expensive ways of maintaining the children and keeping them out of public view and out of trouble in the cities. By sending the children to foster parents, state and local governments assumed financial respon-

28

sibility but still utilized the two-parent family for the proper socialization of the young. Furthermore, the household or family was the crucial unit in the economy and in society. It was reasonable for family-less children to be placed with families where they would be economically helpful and also socially educated. Throughout the course of the century, and especially in the 1880s, the state—through the Ministry of Interior and the Paris Bureau of Public Assistance—gradually assumed more responsibility for the abandoned children by the continual intrusion of state officials in the regulation and supervision of their lives.

With this broad outline of attitudes and policies toward abandoned children as a guide, the nineteenth century can be divided into four time frames. In all four periods, society criticized child abandonment and the mothers who rejected their children, but the degree of condemnation varied. Specific attitudes and the design and implementation of public policies also differed. The first third of the century, in which the system was just developing in the aftermath of the Decree of 1811, had easy, open, free, and unrestricted admission to the foundling homes for all abandoned children and little or no inspection and control in the countryside. The second period, roughly the years of the July Monarchy (1830-1848), was characterized by strenuous efforts to control child abandonment by various measures aimed at reducing expenses, improving the morality of the mothers, and strengthening the cohesiveness of the family. The 1850s and 1860s, the third period, shared the attitudes toward morality, the family, and state finances with the two preceding decades and witnessed further, more stringent measures to reduce the number of children abandoned. At the same time, especially during the 1860s authorities made greater efforts to see that those who were abandoned survived and thrived. The final period, the one that embraced the most marked changes in governmental policy and state control, encompasses the last third of the century. Improvements made in the care and treatment of abandoned children in the previous half-century reached fruition; the 1880s in particular experienced rapid advancements in hygiene coupled with changes in public attitudes and the growth of elaborate and comprehensive social welfare programs. For the first time, "economy" did not take precedence over the survival and well-being of the children and, to a lesser extent, the mothers who bore them.

Adoption, Orphanages, and Foster Parentage

Since authorities viewed the family—whether intruded upon by the state or not—as the proper unit for raising the children, legal familial adoption would seem to have been the ideal solution for raising the thousands of abandoned children of France. But familial adoption remained extraordinarily rare. Its rarity was due in part to the other newly pervading view, which held the state legally, morally, and financially responsible for its indigent and neglected citizens, a responsibility that legal adoption would have nullified.

There are other reasons as well for the absence of adoption in France.* The French saw legal familial adoption not as a means of providing a warm, loving home for a parentless child but as a means of providing heirs for childless couples without relatives. Few childless couples, however, wanted to adopt. Families with children had no desire to adopt, for then the biological children would have had to share the inheritance with any adopted child. Furthermore, the French also believed that inheritors should be blood kin or close familial relations by marriage. The only common forms of adoption were those by relatives of orphaned children; such adoptions were arranged by the family council, consisting of three members from the mother's and three from the father's side. Since the identities of all abandoned children remained secret, they were unable to claim relation by blood or marriage to prospective adopting families. In addition, most abandoned children were illegitimate; such children were socially unacceptable for adoption since people viewed them as carrying the stigma of their illegitimate birth and the consequences of the mothers' immoral behavior; most thought these children would inherit the vices of their mothers. The children of unwed mothers were, therefore, seen as potentially immoral, criminal, deviant, or subnormally intelligent. They were the pariahs of society.

The rare instances where people sought to adopt an abandoned child, involved couples who had no living relatives and wanted male heirs, and aging widows who wanted girls to take care of them. Authorities refused the requests on the grounds that the abandoned children's biological mothers should have the right to reclaim them at any time.

The underlying attitude preventing adoption involved the sanctity of the biological family. Lineage and blood relationships for descent were of utmost importance both to the middle-class families who might otherwise have adopted a child and to middle-class bureaucrats who made the laws. The bureaucrats tried to foster concepts of lineage on the working classes, from whose ranks most of the abandoned children came. Despite

* Legal family adoption, as it is known in the United States, involving the assumption of all legal parental rights and responsibilities, was also unknown in England until 1926. The reasons for the absence of adoption in England and other countries would be interesting to explore more fully.

a mother's ability under the law easily, freely, and anonymously to abandon her baby at the Hospice des Enfants Trouvés, authorities almost always knew her name, occupation, and address, especially if she gave birth in the Maison d'Accouchement. They respected the secrecy of the information, believing that a mother should always have the right to reclaim her child if she so desired, could repay the state for its care, and assure the child's legitimization. Thus, the state refused to break up the biological unit of mother and child, and the potential biological family, by allowing a child to be adopted by a nonrelated family.

State law, therefore, stipulated that no minor could be adopted unless the living parents consented to it. Furthermore, the state required a child's birth certificate for adoption. Authorities could not simultaneously protect the anonymity of the mother and provide a birth certificate. The family name and biological family ties were so important that the idea of providing a fabricated birth certificate giving the names of the adopting parents as the natal parents, as is done in the twentieth-century United States, never entered the discussions. Furthermore, when the mothers abandoned their babies, they did not sign papers permitting adoption. Indeed, they frequently stated that abandonment was temporary—until such time as they would be able to get their children back. In fact, few sought and reclaimed their children. Neither biological parents nor middle-class couples clamored for these children; only foster parents were willing to take them—and they were subsidized.

The notion of parentless children in Europe conjures up images of Oliver Twist and the Dickensian orphanages. That may have been the British picture, but it was not the French. State and church authorities, reformers and bureaucrats all considered and rejected institutionalization of children in a foundling home or orphanage as an alternative to foster parentage. They rejected orphanages on the grounds that they were a financial burden to the state as well as detrimental to the life and well-being of the children.[1] The church and private philanthropists did not volunteer to establish orphanages for the abandoned children since the foundlings were wards of the state and, hence, a public responsibility.

Because most children were abandoned within their first weeks of life, orphanages in any traditional form were not practical. Feeding thousands of foundlings would be a major problem if they were cared for in an institution. Artificial feeding was a possible, but not a good, solution. Mortality among the babies fed milk from a cup, spoon, little pot, or bottle was exceedingly high in this era lacking pasteurization and refrigeration. A staff of wet nurses to breast-feed infants in an institution

31

was also possible, and newborns, during their brief stay at the foundling home, were fed by wet nurses. But throughout the century authorities found it extremely difficult to recruit lactating women willing to nurse the abandoned babies at the foundling home. Thus, orphanages for so many thousands of newborns was not logistically feasible until 1894, when artificial feeding became safe and sanitary. In that year a new foundling home was established to provide care for babies until they were weaned; those children were safely fed by bottle with sterilized milk. By that period, the number of foundlings had been reduced substantially due to extensive aid to unwed mothers. Even after the advent of artificial feeding, moreover, the weaned children went to the countryside to live and work with foster parents. They did not stay in orphanages, because institutions could not provide the familial socialization thought necessary for raising children.

Foster parentage was preferred over orphanages for all children once they were weaned for several reasons. Fiscal reasons were foremost. State authorities calculated that, per-capita and per-diem, payments to foster parents were much less than it would have cost to keep children in an orphanage. The scale of payment to foster parents decreased as the age of the child increased; children over seven years of age cost the state very little, and those over twelve cost nothing. Bureaucrats and reformers also rejected orphanages for older children because they feared the institutions would breed vice among the children. Even when the children in orphanages worked, authorities believed that the children in a group would encourage one another's natural inborn vices and would not learn the proper moral precepts so important for the creation of a hard-working and docile social group. Individual placement with foster parents in the countryside appeared to be a reasonable solution.

Authorities also saw positive values for employing foster parents. Placement of the children in the countryside was beneficial to the economy of the nation in counteracting depopulation of the countryside and migration to the cities. Sending the abandoned children to the countryside, where most stayed, was an attempt to minimize the net exodus from the countrysides, repopulate it, and thereby increase agricultural labor and production. It was a relatively inexpensive way to achieve these goals. Foster parentage also served the economic and labor needs of the foster parents themselves. If foster parents could not use the child's labor, administrators moved the children to foster parents who did need the labor. Foster parentage seemed to be the ideal solution for all—the state, society, and the foster parents—except, perhaps, for the children.

French social policy was predicated on the idea that abandoned children were potentially deviant. It was the role of the state to bring them up to be decent, productive, and law-abiding citizens, and at the lowest cost possible. France developed an elaborate administrative apparatus to provide foster-parent care of the children from birth until they reached maturity (an age that was often redefined in the course of the century). The state devised a system that, on paper, assured that the children abandoned in Paris were given at least a chance for survival and sometimes gave them much more than that. The care the children received was not necessarily the best possible, but it was the cheapest. In every way, the situation for the abandoned children matched what bureaucrats thought the lives of the poor should be like. In the second quarter of the century, social policy attempted to limit those dependent on welfare. This took the form of discouraging the abandonment of children and committing those abandoned to poorly supervised foster parentage. After 1850, and especially in the last quarter of the century, it took the form of increased state social welfare programs and the influence of doctors and state officials on family life.

Foundations of the System, 1811-1830

During the first third of the century, the system of social welfare for abandoned children began to take form. The Bourbon monarchy was restored to power in 1814, and the subsequent years saw relative social quiet after an era of revolution and war. The government experimented with forming policies and procedures, many of which lasted a century. Free from external wars, with relatively sound public finance, with an administrative structure remaining from the reign of Napoleon, and with no major social or economic upheaval during the first third of the century, the government accepted the changes wrought by the Revolution and Napoleon. Perhaps because of the Revolution and Napoleonic reign, the French national government played a dominant role in social welfare—a role the federal government of the United States did not play until a century later. National economic policy was one of a balanced budget and lowest possible expenditures. Policies toward abandoned children fit the economic and social framework of the Bourbon Restoration.

The French government institutionalized and regularized the procedures both for mothers who sought to divest themselves of unwanted children and for the children themselves. Faced with ever-increasing numbers of foundlings, the Administration Générale des Hôpitaux,

Hospices Civils et Secours à domicile de Paris, Bureau des Enfants Trouvés et Orphelins, and the officials of the division of the Ministry of Interior in charge of abandoned children gradually began assuming authority and seeking implementation of the Decree of 1811. For example, the instructions of 1819 and of 1823 from the Administration Générale extended the arm of the administrators in Paris to all Parisian foundlings even after they were placed in the provinces with wet nurses. These instructions regulated the mode of transportation to the countryside, provided for field representatives or agents of the Administration in the provinces where the children abandoned in Paris were sent, supervised the appointment of doctors and medical service for the abandoned children, and set the salaries for the wet nurses.[2] Although successive administrators during the century modified and expanded these rules and regulations, the general structure remained.

The period prior to the 1830s was one of complete, open, unrestricted, and anonymous admission of children to the foundling home. As such, it was the heyday of the *tour* in the provinces (the Parisian *tour* was not opened until 1827). There was little debate and little in the way of legislation or new regulations. While the government accepted its responsibility, no one seemed to care about the expense of maintaining the children, about the welfare of either the children or their mothers, or about the social problems that child abandonment exemplified. Perhaps many were unaware of the foundling problem. Since about sixty percent of the abandoned children died within the first twelve months of life, cost of care also may not have been perceived as a problem. One later critic of the system even went so far as to suggest that the Administration preferred unqualified wet nurses as a money-saving measure, to avoid prolonged payment for their services.[3] Indeed, the high infant mortality rate was almost accepted, and the wet nurses earned the sobriquet "angel makers." The laissez-faire practices toward child abandonment of the first third of the century also led to a rapid rise in the number of babies abandoned. In Paris, the numbers of abandoned peaked in 1831, when 5,667 foundlings appeared on the *Registre d'Admission.* For the early part of the nineteenth century, in fact, between fifteen and twenty percent of all live births in the Department of the Seine became abandoned children by the time they were a few days old.[4]

The July Monarchy and the "Social Question": Theory

The 1830s witnessed the first major attempt to contain child abandonment and other forms of perceived social deviance while restricting the role of state institutions. The recession of 1826 to 1829 in part contributed to efforts to restrict the number of children dependent on state aid in the 1830s. Furthermore, after the Revolution of 1830 (and perhaps as a result of it), authorities feared a growing urban malaise and worried about the potential for working-class militancy and the spread of radical ideas. In seeking to remove the causes of social deviance they became concerned with the larger "social question"—the problem of poverty with its concomitant depravation, immorality, and crime. Child abandonment was an integral part of this larger social question. The birth of illegitimate children and their subsequent abandonment were seen as symptoms of the perceived immorality and potential dangerousness of the urban masses. Pressure from reformers and the constant threat of popular disorder led authorities to seek social reform.

Social economists were influential in leading the discussions about the ills of society, of which child abandonment was a part, and were instrumental in affecting policy. Specific attention to unwed mothers and child abandonment originated in their analysis of the "dangerous class." They believed that almost all forms of social deviance, including child abandonment, arose from segments of the poor and uneducated working population and the unemployed "floating population." In 1840 the social economist H. A. Frégier identified the inherent danger posed to society by this group:

> The poor and vicious classes always have been and always will be the most fertile crucible for all categories of wrongdoers; it is these classes that we designate more specifically as the dangerous classes; for, even if vice is not accompanied by perversity, simply because it is allied to poverty in the same individual he is an apt object of fear on the part of society; he is dangerous. [5]

In analyzing the danger posed by the laboring population, social economists studied the origins of *misère* (extreme poverty) and the influence of industrialization and urbanization on morality.

In looking for the sources of criminal or dangerous behavior, social economists posited a relationship between *misère* and deviance or immorality. They then looked for the roots of *misère* in an urban economy. Although they felt that industrialization had led to the poverty of some, it also improved the conditions of other workers. Therefore, since they could not explain *misère* by the economic system alone, social economists affirmed the moral origins of poverty. *Misère* was the result of moral weakness, lack of religion, decline of family ties, and relaxation of personal hygiene. To these middle-class reformers, not only were the

35

impoverished immoral, but they were dirty as well! Cleanliness was obviously next to godliness and morality; it was also one of the attributes the middle class wanted to instill in the working classes. The system was not at fault, only the laziness, depravation, drunkenness, and lack of foresight in providing for the future that were prevalent among the working classes. These moral defects led to poverty. Add passion unchecked by reason or education, and the poor had one short step to take from *misère* to deviance and immorality.

Charity, the social economists argued, only rewarded debauched behavior. In the eyes of one notable reformer, Baron Joseph de Gerando, charity encouraged poverty and immorality; it often created the problems that it hoped to alleviate.[6] Blindly accepting abandoned children was charity, and charitable care for them carried no punishment for the parents—that is, the mothers—responsible. Therefore, the state should limit its obligations to all abandoned children, for such charity would only encourage more vice, sexual license, illegitimacy, and the abdication of family responsibility. Rather, the government should make provisions for the moral rehabilitation of the unwed mother. The possible culpability of the father in producing illegitimate and, hence, abandoned offspring was never mentioned.

In sharing a general belief in the contagion theory of crime and deviance, social economists felt that an illicit union of man and woman not sanctified by legal marriage would contaminate and corrupt the impressionable young in their charge. It would in turn produce juvenile delinquents who would become a menace to society. The other major source of contamination of the young by the example of vice was the modern factory, which mixed men and women, boys and girls, honest and dishonest in an environment where they worked, and often lived, together. These social economists were ambiguous about the impact of industrialization and urbanization on morality and deviancy. In this instance, the economic system could indeed have pernicious effects. This negative view of factory labor had great import for the lives of the abandoned children and greatly influenced state policies for adolescent foundlings during the remainder of the century.

Moral economists reversed the relationship between poverty and immorality held by the social economists. Rather than moral weakness leading to poverty, moral economists believed that poverty led to immorality and vice. Alleviate the poverty, they said, and vice would decrease, although they did not specify how they planned to achieve this.

The opposition liberals united in the Société de la Morale Chrétienne and the resurrected Académie des Sciences Morales et Politiques of the

Institut de France. Their philosophy emphasized the moral leadership of the educated classes and the private initiative in charitable enterprise. Philanthropists of this type assumed that men and women were perfectible and that the educated classes had a duty to aid and guide the less fortunate. This emphasis on rehabilitation of the immoral and indigent through education by the more fortunate was a separate issue from charity per se and, in practical terms, meant establishing policies and programs to combat immoral habits.

Philanthropists concentrated on reinforcing the family structure, for the family represented the principal bulwark against social disorder. Philanthropic societies assisted couples living in concubinage to procure the necessary marriage papers, encouraged factory owners to give workers a holiday on Sunday so the poor could spend a day with their families, promoted the construction of hygienic and pleasant family dwellings for the legally married, and fostered the practice of *secours à domicile* (home aid) to families in need.

Church spokesmen were particularly active on the "social question" during this period. Social Catholicism, led by Frédéric Ozanam, was conservative and paternalistic, moved by a sense of moral obligation. During the Orléanist period, young priests and laymen were principally concerned with the reasons for poverty, the alleviation of *misère*, and greater social justice. Social Catholicism, along with social and moral economism, held that the family, rather than the individual, must be the ultimate unit in a healthy society, and both deplored what they perceived as the breakdown of family ties. While a university student, Ozanam founded the Société de Saint Vincent-de-Paul, which became the best known of the Catholic social welfare groups. In commemorating Vincent de Paul, the patron saint of abandoned children, the society's name further underscores the centrality of the problem of child abandonment to social welfare in the 1830s and 1840s.

Child abandonment loomed in the forefront of the "social question." The rapid growth of the foundling population and the increasing expenses that accompanied that growth gave an immediacy to the philosophical and moral precepts of the theorists and philanthropists. During the 1830s, the overriding themes of debates and discussions were reducing the numbers abandoned and limiting expenses of the state, departments, and communes.[7] In the 1830s government officials thought that the best way to cut expenses was to restrict the foundling population by repressing child abandonment. Governmental restrictions would alleviate taxpayers' fear that the practice was "threatening to absorb the greatest portion of departmental resources" and at the same time reassure reformers of the state's commitment to curb the immorality of the mothers.[8]

The lack of morality of the women who abandoned their children was a primary social and religious focus of the arguments in this period. The social economists who believed in the inherent immorality of all felons thought of the women who abandoned their children as criminals. They saw the abandoned child as the fruit of seduction, debauchery, libertinage, frivolity, and lack of foresight on the part of the mother, coupled with her laziness and lack of maternal sentiments—in sum, a *dépravation des moeurs* (corrupted morality). In nineteenth-century thought, women who married, had children and stayed home were "angels"; conversely, women who bore illegitimate children were dubbed "sinners." The mother who chose to rid herself of her child only wished to divest herself of this "product" and regain her life of libertinage and disorder.[9] If abandonment became more difficult, women would be forced to plan and take responsibility for their actions.

Those who emphasized immorality as a prime cause were at pains to argue against those who cited *misère*. "It is wrong," they argued, "to reduce the problem of *enfants trouvés* to a question of finance. Bad morals are the source of the evil; to combat the evil without improving morals is a senseless attempt. Mendicity, vagabondage, and ignorance of the *classe pauvre*, are the causes of the increase in the numbers of abandoned children."[10] The social economists of the *Journal des Débats* recorded the view that "work is abundant. Abandonment among the working classes cannot have extreme poverty as an excuse—it is laziness and libertinage."[11]

Some believed that fear of shame and dishonor which could accompany an illegitimate birth was a motive for the further "immoral" act of abandoning the child.[12] If a woman were living with her family, either in Paris or in the provinces, she probably had to hide the pregnancy as long as possible. Once her condition became apparent, the honor of the family probably drove the mother-to-be to seek the anonymity of a city, give birth there, and then resume a life unencumbered with the reminder of her "fault." Given the reprobation and scorn with which society regarded an unwed mother and her bastard, the honor of the family left the unwed mother no alternative.[13] Two Catholic writers, Alphonse de Lamartine and the Abbé Adolphe Henri Gaillard, stand apart in not condemning abandonment of an illegitimate child as immoral. They felt that the mothers' shame led them to take such a drastic step, and society had the duty to help alleviate that shame.[14]

Since most of the abandoned children were illegitimate, the reformers attacked illegitimacy and child abandonment in the same breath. Having a child out of wedlock seemed immoral, in part only because it often resulted in abandonment of that child. A mother who kept and nursed her illegitimate child was not considered immoral by some bureaucrats and reformers, but just the opposite—virtuous, a redeemed sinner. A married woman who abandoned her legitimate child was both an immoral and unnatural sinner. In the minds of nineteenth-century men, maternal love was "natural." Mothers who abandoned their children were therefore "unnatural."

Reformers differed as to the reasons for the mothers' immorality. They frequently mentioned the growth of big cities, industry, and the increase in population, especially that of workers in the cities, as contributing causes of an increase in immorality. [15]

> Public morals are profoundly relaxed in the big cities and in the neighboring countryside; they are especially so in the industrial cities where a very great number of workers of both sexes live together in one place. Relationships are established between the industrialists and workers, between the heads of the workshops and the girls whom one calls comrades [*compagnonnes*], between the masters and the domestics. Among most, there is a difference in the matter of religion, as well as the omission of all principles of morals in the relations between the two sexes; that is the natural explanation of the fact of the abandonment of newborns. [16]

Big cities and industrial centers were viewed as corrupting influences; working classes in the cities were considered immoral as well as dangerous by the bourgeoisie. Reformers felt the processes of urbanization and industrialization would lead to an increase in abandonments since they involved rural out-migration with a suspected breakdown of family ties. When people moved out of their village and away from families, it was feared that there would be no familial or social restraint on their behavior, with resultant promiscuity, illegitimacy, and child abandonment. They felt that city life was synonymous with alienation for many of its inhabitants, and that such alienation would lead to asocial or deviant behavior such as child abandonment. Urbanization and industrialization may well have led to the dislocation of the working-class family and the disruption of normal familial patterns, which resulted in illegitimacy and abandonment, but this possibility cannot be proven. [17] The economic arguments did not deny the immorality of the mother, but they asserted that child abandonment was primarily caused by two social ills. In the words of two social critics, "debauchery created the illegitimate children; extreme poverty produced the abandoned

39

children." [18] Both *Le Courrier Français* and *Le Constitutionnel* of 1835 suggested in editorials that, if work that paid a living wage were available, morals would improve and the well-being of the "difficult" classes would also improve; the family spirit would be revived. [19] The editors of these journals believed that money should be spent to improve conditions among the workers—the conditions that existed at the time favored vice. The aim of both papers was to attack the cause rather than the symptoms.

The voices of those raising economic arguments were small in comparison to those pointing to immorality and what that sin meant for the national treasury. The debates and varying attitudes toward illegitimacy, toward child abandonment, and toward the causes of such deviant behavior reflect the pervading opinions about crime, deviance, the working classes, and social welfare of the 1830s and 1840s. Reformers viewed the family structure as the primary bulwark against social disorder [20] and sought to strengthen it by reducing the ease of abandonment, which authorities assumed would thereby reduce illegitimacy and foster legitimate unions with concomitant family ties between parents and children. General social policies of the July Monarchy were an attempt to contain deviance in general and child abandonment in particular while minimizing the role of state institutions. But, despite these considerations of higher morality, religion, social reform, and social welfare, the real nucleus of the arguments of the 1830s and 1840s was public expense and the threat to the public budget posed by so many abandoned children destined to prostitution or vagrancy if they survived. [21]

The "Social Question": Reality

The dual themes of money and morality, not the welfare of the children, dominated the debates on the practical measures these philosophical positions and state aims suggested. There was hardly a word about what was good for the children. They were seen as the costly by-product of immorality and vice, not as defenseless, precious infants who—alone through no fault of their own—needed love and care. In seeking new ways to limit abandonment and to reduce the budgetary line, officials focused on three specific, hotly debated policies: *déplacement*, temporary aid to unwed mothers, and the closing of the *tours*.

Déplacement, or the moving of abandoned babies from the department in which they were abandoned to wet nurses in other jurisdictions, was first proposed in 1827 and reached its peak in the early 1830s; the practice rapidly declined and ended by 1837. This enforced geographic separation of mother and child severed contact between them and was designed to discourage abandonment by mothers who wanted to be near their children but have the state pay the expenses of raising them. Advocates of this measure told stories of mothers abandoning their babies in a *tour*, and leaving an identifying mark on their children. These mothers presented themselves at the Hospice as wet nurses to try to care for their own children. If that ruse failed, some mothers then sought out the wet nurses to whom the children were assigned to negotiate an exchange. Rather than sympathizing with the plight of women so desperate for aid that they resorted to this subterfuge, authorities sought to end this practice; no one gave any thought to welfare for the women as a solution to the problem.

Similarly, the welfare of the child was not at issue in *déplacement*. The measure died because of its ineffectiveness in significantly reducing abandonment (fewer than twenty-five percent of the mothers whose babies were destined for relocation reclaimed them), the trouble and expense involved in transporting them, and the large public outcry in the provinces against it. The measure did not die because it was judged detrimental to the well-being of the children; the effects on them from changing wet nurses and foster parents were rarely considered and, when mentioned, were not deemed important. Parisian foundlings had, of course, been transported to wet nurses in the provinces as a matter of routine since the eighteenth century, which may have contributed to the official lack of concern about such procedures. In any event, although *déplacement* in law pertained to all of France, it was not an issue in Paris. But other measures were.

Paris officials led the nation in instituting a form of aid to dependent children, or "temporary aid to unwed mothers to prevent abandonment" as it was less euphemistically, and more accurately, called. A decree of the Conseil Général des Hospices de Paris in January 1837, declared that "pregnant women will be admitted to the Maison d'Accouchement only if they will nurse their child for several days there and then take their child with them when they leave."[22] The Fondation Montyon, a private charity to aid and encourage women to keep their children, was established for that purpose. This initial attempt to provide some support for women in the Maison d'Accouchement who wished to keep and nurse their babies but who were financially unable to do so affected very few women. It was only in operation a short time, and women still gave birth in large numbers in the Maison d'Accouchement and then deposited their infants in the Hospice across the street. As an experiment in aid to unwed mothers, this combination of hospital order and charitable support provided a concrete model for those who debated hotly, in the 1830s and again in the 1850s, the advisability of aid to unwed mothers.

Ironically, even though authorities and social reformers viewed the family as the proper instiller of moral virtues, they disagreed as to whether or not children should remain with the *un*wed mothers. Some administrators favored "temporary aid to prevent abandonment" on the grounds that the presence of a child would be a reminder of her "fault" and would keep the woman moral in the future. They also argued that such a temporary aid program would cost the taxpayers less than paying foster parents; this was the key to their argument. Others, primarily some doctors and liberal Catholics, disagreed. They argued that temporary aid, when awarded, was too short in duration; it was insufficient to keep the mother and child fed, housed, and clothed. Furthermore, they felt that if an unwed mother kept the child, all could see that she was a "fallen woman" and she would thus be prey to further immorality or neglect of the child. Despite objections, temporary aid to unwed mothers, designed to prevent abandonment, began in Paris in 1837, took hold briefly in 1852, and then became a permanent part of social welfare in later decades.

Nothing more symbolized official approval of child abandonment and the idea of unlimited public support for unwed mothers and their forsaken children than did the *tours*. Moreover, no issue related to child abandonment generated as much intense debate as did their very existence. Supporters of the *tour*, mostly Catholics of all political persuasions, praised it for preserving the honor, and pride, of a woman forced by a sexual mistake or poverty to abandon her child. It also safeguarded the honor of her family, equally important to them as the honor of the unwed mother herself. These social reformers looked at abandonment as a preferable alternative to abortion and infanticide and felt that the possibility of anonymous and legal abandonment prevented infanticide or exposure of an infant in an isolated place. The baby passed from the arms of the mother to the arms of a solicitous attendant without undue exposure.

Reformers and social critics of both the July Monarchy and the Second Empire felt that closing the *tours* and thereby restricting admissions would save the government money that otherwise would have been spent in support of the abandoned children. The words that appeared in the *Journal des Débats* are echoed in much of the literature: "The closing of the *tours* seems a harsh measure; it is, however, the only one that can heal the ill that threatens to devour all the resources of the departmental budgets."[23]

Opponents of the *tour* believed that closing the *tours* would reduce immorality, promiscuity, and social disorder by making child abandonment less easy. *Tours* signified easy abandonment and invited loose morals by encouraging mothers to have illegitimate children and abandon them. [24] They argued that if not for the existence of easy surreptitious abandonment, these babies would never have been abandoned and many mothers would have refrained from sexual licentiousness in the first place. Furthermore, many of those who did get pregnant would have married if not for the existence of the *tour* as a place to leave the unwanted child. One prominent social critic stated that not only did the *tours* encourage abandonment and the abdication of parental duties, but they also served as an alibi for infanticide. He argued that when accused of infanticide, a woman could always say, "I put my child in the *tour*." [25] There was no way to check the veracity of her statement, but it seems unlikely that she would have resorted to infanticide if a *tour* were handy. The opponents of the *tours* won the day. Many of the *tours* in France were sealed shut by the late 1850s; the one in Paris did not completely cease functioning until 1862.

Further Efforts to Restrain Abandonment, 1850-1870

The debates of the July Monarchy reverberated and resounded in the Corps Législatif of the Second Empire. From 1851 to 1853, a special Commission of the Corps Législatif continued the discussion of the causes of child abandonment and the relative morality of the mothers. Authorities held high regard for the honor, dignity, and sanctity of the bourgeois family, but their attitude toward the families of the poor, especially those unsanctioned by legal marriage, was ambivalent. The oft-stated beliefs of authorities and reformers during the July Monarchy and Second Republic were so much alike and the similarities so striking that they do not bear repeating in detail.

Aside from creating l'Assistance Publique of Paris in 1849 which assumed administrative and decision-making control over the children abandoned in Paris, no new legislation had been passed either by the July Monarchy or by the Second Republic. In response to ever-increasing numbers and greater knowledge of the problem, however, the legislators of the Second Empire perceived the need for new legislation; they renewed the debates on ease of abandonment, temporary aid to prevent abandonment, and the existence of the *tours* that their predecessors had discussed. The Commission of the Corps Législatif was divided between those who wanted to prevent child abandonment and those who saw it as the duty of the state to aid and succor the forsaken babies.

The debates of 1851-1853 differed from those of the 1830s in one significant respect; a group of liberal Catholics admitted a need for the *tour*, argued strenuously for it, and stressed the importance of unrestricted abandonment at a Hospice. Since the French Revolution took the protection of women and children out of the hands of the church, some liberal Catholics insisted that the state do its charitable duty. Alphonse de Lamartine, the foremost spokesman for this point of view, insisted that women had to have some alternative to infanticide, abortion, or keeping the unwanted child. If she gave the child up to charity, both she and the child would have a chance for a better life. [26]

In many ways Lamartine was the ideological descendent of Saint Vincent-de-Paul and represented a general tendency in French Catholicism toward children: to protect them from possible infanticide and, at the same time, to allow the mothers a chance to redeem themselves. Saint Vincent-de-Paul believed that the state should have final responsibility for the care of the foundlings as opposed to their certain death or exploitation by the unscrupulous. [27] Lamartine would have agreed with his predecessor in that view, and they also shared a similar view on the *tours*. The *tour*, said Lamartine, was a perfect example of Christian charity—it had the cradling "arms to receive, but not the eyes to see, nor the ears to hear." [28]

Liberal Catholic reformers, in speeches reminiscent of social economic ideology of the 1830s, accepted the contagion theory of morality. But, unlike the social economists, they believed in the inherent innocence of the child, even a child born of an unwed and hence immoral woman. They also differed from the social economists of both the 1830s and 1850s in arguing that the presence of the child would not be a moralizing influence on the mother. Indeed, liberal Catholics affirmed that separating mother and child was in the best interests of both. Without a child around, the mother could find employment, be redeemed, and possibly marry. A child would make its mother's subsequent life of virtue difficult to achieve. In the Second Empire, as in the July Monarchy, social critics extolled the virtues of gainful employment and legal marriage. Separation also benefited the child. The "immoral" mother could corrupt the innocent child both by her example, in exposing the child to a supposed succession of lovers, and by her milk, in transmitting not merely nourishment but also her soul—her vices and her virtues. By vices, the reformers meant more than a disease, like syphilis, although that was certainly transmitted as well. [29] The liberal Catholics lost this round in the debates, and the 1850s witnessed even more restrictions on abandonment and Hospice admissions than did the earlier period.

Opponents of the *tours*, and of any official sanction for child abandonment (which the *tours* symbolized), comprised all other segments of the reform movement and the bureaucracy. In seeking to decrease the foundling population, opponents of the *tours* favored "temporary aid to prevent abandonment." Their moral and social arguments matched those of the earlier decades, and, as in the 1830s and 1840s, the bottom line was to reduce expenditures at all levels of government—national, departmental, and communal.

The majority of the Legislative Commission members held that the only Catholic doctrine that should apply was that of individual responsibility. The mother should assume responsibility for her sexual indiscretion and accept both emotional and financial responsibility for raising her child. Abandonment would turn her "fault" into a crime. The *tour*, by sanctioning abandonment, made the child the responsibility of the community and of society, not of the mother, and thus served to undermine the family. In opposition to the methods of strengthening the family advocated by the liberal Catholics, the majority of the Commission members argued that the process of raising an illegitimate child would redeem the unwed mother and might even lead to marriage with the child's father. Some Commission members did recognize, however, that not all mothers could afford to raise a child without welfare or charity, so they advocated financial aid to "worthy" women. Reformers were not, however, united in the idea of aid to unwed mothers, since such aid would not only subsidize public scandal and reward immorality but also provide a dangerous example for other young women. State aid, therefore, might not be the deterrent to immorality that others had hoped.

By the 1860s, after a minimal program of aid to unwed mothers had been in effect in Paris for about ten years, opponents of such temporary aid became more outspoken, arguing that the working-class mothers would not be able to support their children or give them the necessary attention after financial assistance ceased. In language and attitudes foreshadowing those of the 1880s, these opponents believed that the children would suffer much deprivation. Like the liberal Catholics, they argued that to hope that fathers would be encouraged to marry the mothers of their illegitimate offspring was an illusion. The mere presence of a child, they argued, would make it hard for women to marry other men, and would instead encourage seducers. It would also lead employers, in the face of adverse public opinion from the shame of illegitimacy, to refuse unwed mothers work. [30]

Despite opposition, advocates of aid to unwed mothers won the day.

During the Second Empire all *tours* were either closed or were carefully guarded by police to discourage abandonment, and temporary aid to unwed mothers became national policy. The Corps Législatif neither agreed on nor passed any legislation dealing with the foundling problem. The Imperial government carried out reform of the foundling system primarily by administrative action. In many cases the state merely enforced regulations already on the books, thereby increasing its repressive measures concerning child abandonment and extending its power and control. This activity contrasts sharply with the policies and actions of the 1830s which aimed at changing social behavior without an increase in the power of the state, merely by restricting admissions of abandoned children.

The most repressive measures of this regime related to admissions to all the hospices for abandoned children. Most of the *tours* closed. The one in Paris had a watchman posted at it during 1852-1853 to prevent anonymous abandonment, but public outcry in favor of keeping it open was so strong that it was not closed officially until 1862. The unenforced policies of the 1830s—aid to unwed mothers to encourage them to keep their babies and the requirement of interrogation and a certificate of birth for admission during certain hours of the day—were resurrected in 1852 and enforced. Further deterrents to abandonment were added, including the regulation that all women who gave birth at the maternity hospital had to keep their child with them for nine days before leaving the hospital with the infant. The admissions office increased its hours of operation from six to ten a day, and police roamed the streets in the vicinity of the Hospice to prevent surreptitious abandonment. If mothers succeeded in abandoning their infants, they had to pay the accumulated cost of upkeep before they could reclaim or even get news of their child. (This measure, instituted in the 1830s as a deterrent and never rescinded, was now enforced.) The immediate effect of enforcing old measures and establishing tough new ones was a sharp decrease in the number of children abandoned in Paris, from roughly four thousand to only twenty-three hundred per year. This sharp drop was short-lived, but the numbers of children abandoned never again reached their pre-1850 levels.

Beginning of Concern for the Children, 1850-1870

The 1850s and 1860s also showed the first signs of any official concern for the abandoned children themselves.[31] While officials of the 1850s took even more stringent measures to keep admission down, they made efforts to take better care of those who were admitted. L'Assistance Publique and public welfare expanded to take care of the abandoned children up to age twenty-one. This action complemented the prevailing attitude of the Second Empire that the foundlings should be "made useful to the state" to repay the state for raising them. [32] But since children rarely reached an age at which they could begin working and paying the state back, the "social economy" aspects of this concept could not be achieved. Hence, at the same time that a new interest was taken in supervising the older child, a concomitant interest in saving lives arose.

To reduce infant mortality, to increase governmental authority and medical influence in the countryside, and to augment a dwindling rural agricultural labor force, the state made a number of incursions into the foster-parent families during the 1850s and 1860s. Both the number and powers of the inspectors increased, and they became part of the regular national departmental bureaucracies. The number of doctors paid by the government to provide medical care to the abandoned children also increased, and their duties and payments were enlarged. Furthermore, in the 1850s, in response to growing official concern with health, education, and occupations, the government increased its efforts to have the abandoned children vaccinated, to give them a secular and religious education, and to provide proper apprenticeship or wage-earning positions, primarily in agriculture. To these ends, officials instituted more stringent requirements for wet nurses, raised payments to foster parents, supplied bonuses to foster parents who kept the children for long terms or sent the boys to school, augmented the children's clothing allotment, and increased the number of specified inspectors' and doctors' visits.

Having taken care of the problem of regulating and limiting admissions of abandoned infants, public officials began to concentrate on the older children. Most officials, reformers, and legislators seemed to believe that "almost all abandoned children . . . carry the most dangerous instincts in their hearts," [33] and authorities therefore aimed at controlling this corrupt and pernicious influence in society.* While many stressed the value of education in combating the detrimental effects of illegitimacy, others were convinced that most abandoned children who survived to adulthood would inevitably became prostitutes or felons. [34] Regardless of

---

* There is something curiously correct about the notion of "dangerous instincts in their hearts." Although reformers rendered the idea in language that is now archaic, the idea itself is similar to current thinking about the "battered child" syndrome. In psychological terms, abandoned children are hurt in some crucial way that is never completely overcome.

sion, whether with foster parents or placed elsewhere. Prior to 1852, all direct authority of any administrative agency over abandoned children ceased once they had celebrated their thirteenth birthday. In 1852 l'Assistance Publique of Paris extended its control and supervision to children up to age twenty-one.

Neither reformers nor officials of l'Assistance Publique saw juvenile detention centers in Paris as the ideal milieu for older abandoned children, and they did not want to house them in the Hospice, because they feared that the teenagers would corrupt the younger children.[35] Under Napoleon III, furthermore, scores of articles, books, and speeches discussed and deplored the depopulation of the countryside with the concomitant shortages in agricultural production and the growing number of young urban workers, who might tend to be insurrectionary.[36] Therefore, older abandoned children needed to be kept in the country. With the cooperation of the state, religious orders established the first rural institutions, *colonies agricoles*, for children whose conduct made them difficult to place with foster parents or a patron.

Although the motives that led to these new protective policies and procedures for abandoned children may not always have derived from interest in the children's welfare, the effect was to decrease infant mortality and to prevent children over age twelve from being twice abandoned, the first time by their parents and the second by the government on their thirteenth birthday. Certainly some of the concern arose from a general desire to protect the children, and from a budding sentimental and nurturing view of childhood which flowered in the 1880s. Empress Eugénie expressed these sentiments as early as the 1850s, when she donated money so that abandoned babies might be reunited with their natural mothers. Secular philanthropic societies for the protection of children also proliferated in the late 1850s and 1860s, undertaking to introduce more advanced educational practices and modern methods of childrearing among working-class families. Child protection agencies and private philanthropy agitated for legislation to prevent child abuse, exploitation, vagrancy, and prostitution. This type of interest in older as well as younger children, which began in the 1850s, may have been due to the creation of l'Assistance Publique in 1849, to the repressive measures of the Second Empire, or to a new, more fundamental concern for the welfare of the children. Whatever its basis, the concern lasted, indeed grew, throughout the remainder of the century, albeit for different reasons and with different results.

The Third Republic: Mothers and Children 1870-1904

Initiatives in the care and treatment of the children which had begun during the Second Empire reached fruition in the early decades of the Third Republic. The 1870s and 1880s witnessed a change in attitudes in which the importance of children was reaffirmed, stress placed on the value of doctors and science in raising infants, and adolescence was recognized. Obedience to authority became the prime virtue that both authorities and parents wished to inculcate in children. Increased education of children was seen as the key to social progress. The Third Republic supervised and educated children by exerting influence of the state in almost every facet of their lives through intermediaries—doctors, teachers, psychologists, social workers, juvenile judges, legislators—who regulated education and the rights of parents such that the government and its "tutelary complex"[37] gradually usurped parental authority by protecting children at home, at work, at play, and in school. Officials and reformers viewed the state as protector of the weak, the victims of society—the children. For the first time during the nineteenth century, abandoned children and the mothers who relinquished them were seen less as social deviants and more as victims of society. New attitudes toward abandoned children were part of new attitudes toward children in general.

As Jacques Donzelot has argued, there was an "increased attention to the problems of children, a consistent revision of the old attitudes of repression or charity, the promotion of a boundless educative solicitude more concerned with understanding than with the application of judicial punishment, replacing charity's good conscience with the search for effective techniques."[38] The predelinquent, or the child in danger of being a delinquent such as an abandoned child, was defined. Then an infrastructure of prevention was erected around him and an educative machinery set into motion.

The importance of children was affirmed and reaffirmed from the 1870s to the 1890s. A recrudescence of literature, both for and concerning children, began in the late 1860s and increased rapidly in the 1870s and 1880s. Many novels as well as learned works of which children were the subject were published each year. The books stressed parental and state authority over children, obedience of children to that authority, scientifically based methods of childrearing, and the proper moral behavior of the children. Children were to be supervised and well mannered at all times. These views, especially those of scientific management and organization, echoed larger themes in intellectual life.

49

Attitudes toward children also reflected the increasing concern with France's lack of population growth. The defeat of France by Germany in 1871 poignantly brought home the issue of depopulation of the country. At the same time, demographers recognized and published information that the French population was stagnant. Children from birth to age nineteen averaged about one-third of the entire population during the Third Republic, and authorities began to recognize them as a sizable social group. This percentage, however, was declining. Children under nineteen represented thirty-seven percent of the population in 1852, thirty-five percent in 1891, and only thirty percent in 1948. While people in traditional rural areas, where children represented farm hands, continued to have many children at least up until World War I, families in the cities frequently had only one child. The proportion of the population of Paris under nineteen years of age in 1891 was only twenty-seven percent.[39] This figure cannot be taken entirely at face value, since many of the newborn of Paris were sent to the countryside to be wet nursed. Nevertheless, the ideal family of the bourgeoisie, as illustrated by Jacques Droz's *Monsieur, Madame, et Bébé*, had only one child. Many governmental authorities saw France's declining population as evidence of family limitation predominantly by urban parents, who seemed to prefer "producing" quality offspring through education rather than quantity through fecundity.

Social theorists searched for reasons for the military defeat, and many doctors and reformers looked to the biological conditions of the French populace for possible explanations. The military defeat and declining birth rates were seen as evidence of the degeneracy of the race. Within this context, legislators, government officials, physicians, and social theorists aimed to increase the population, both by encouraging families to have more children and by protecting those already born from succumbing to death in infancy and young childhood. Since infant mortality rates for abandoned babies were considerably higher than those for the population at large, foundlings were a prime target for state protection. Rather than seeing the abandoned children as drains on the economy, as had been the view in the 1830s and 1850s, authorities in the 1880s perceived infant deaths as symbols of France's inferiority, and their survival as a hope for France's future.[40] Since authorities encouraged population growth, they felt obliged to nourish, protect, and then control these children by various social services in accordance with the age of the children.

Specific attitudes toward all children varied with the age of the child, according to the three perceived stages of childhood.[41] From birth through age six, the period known as *petite enfance*, the child was completely dependent on adults. In the next stage from seven through thirteen years of age, that of *enfance*, the child attended school and was quasi-dependent. From age fourteen to adulthood (usually perceived as attained at marriage or around age twenty-one), the state of *jeunesse*, the child was almost totally independent, either working or attending school—according to the socioeconomic group of the family.

Petite enfance was further divided into two stages, from birth to age two, and from two to six. For the infants under two years old, wet nursing flourished until World War I. Artisan and working-class mothers frequently sent their nurslings to wet nurses who lived in rural France, where the infants stayed, usually for one to two years. In these cases mothers had little contact with their children. The middle- and upper-class mothers often hired a wet nurse from the countryside to nurse an infant in the baby's home in the city. These wet nurses sent their own babies back home as soon as they got a position in a bourgeois home.* Some authorities have seen the lack of maternal nursing of biological babies as evidence of maternal indifference toward children; others have suggested that wet-nursing was rooted in maternal concern. Artificial feeding was neither safe nor sanitary until the end of the century, and doctors claimed that breast-feeding an infant, even by a wet nurse, was preferable to feeding a child cow's milk by a bottle. In addition, working-class families experienced a poverty squeeze when their children were under five; mothers with such young children found it difficult to be wage-earners outside the home, and sending an infant out to a wet nurse was necessary for economic survival of all of the family. Bourgeois women frequently employed a wet nurse in their home upon the advice of their doctors, but in those circumstances, mothers could supervise the wet nurse's feeding and habits. Wet nurses themselves nursed another's baby because they needed the income. Wet-nursing, therefore, seems to represent less an attitude of indifference toward children and more an economic or medical necessity, despite the higher than average mortality rate for babies sent to wet nurses. [42]

Doctors, equipped with their new scientific knowledge of pasteuriza-

* The wet nurses' own children either had been weaned and thus were left with their family in the countryside, or else the wet nurse in the home of a bourgeois woman would put her own child to feed with another nurse. This frequently resulted in malnourishment or even death for the child. The Roussel Law of 1874 was an attempt to prevent the wet nurses' own children from suffering as much as it was intended to prevent excessive mortality of urban children given to a wet nurse.

tion, the germ theory of disease, and pediatrics, felt it desirable to influence the family and assume a greater role in the lives of infants. They saw the infants as having special needs and instructed mothers to carry out scientifically determined schedules and amounts of feeding, to weigh infants periodically on home infant scales, to have separate beds for infants, and to reduce or eliminate the practice of swaddling. Doctors also sought to be summoned for consultation whenever a child was ill.

Authorities and parents were preoccupied with the health of the children from age two to age six and with teaching morality and obedience. Doctors looked after the health of the bourgeois children by working directly with the mother—the doctors prescribed and the mothers acted. Doctors influenced the health of working-class children by their educative surveillance as consultants in the Instituts de Puériculture and Écoles Maternelles, which had begun to proliferate toward the end of the century.

In *enfance* children joined groups of peers their own age, and went to school, where teachers and other professionals exerted authority over the children *in loco parentis*. The evolution of attitudes toward children of this age group was affected by the growth of cities and of factories and by the interest in childhood as a separate stage with its own special needs. Within this larger framework rural, bourgeois, and urban working-class society exhibited three different types of attitudes. In rural, traditional society, children worked and played in groups with their own hierarchy, rules, and rites. But, by the end of the nineteenth century, this gradually gave way to school and to adult society's codification of the games and organizations of childhood by control of after-school and leisure time. Bourgeois children from six to fourteen engaged less in mutual education with peers than did children of rural parents and spent more time with their families, especially their mothers. They were to imitate and emulate adults. Parents chose and imposed their children's acquaintances upon them, and their mother was to see that they did their homework, had their lessons prepared and their notebooks in order. The family and schools complemented each other.

For urban working-class children, factories vied with the schools for the children's time, just as in rural areas farm work vied with school. Despite compulsory education, urban working-class children sometimes did not go to school until parents had an extra income provided by several child workers. By the end of the century, however, attitudes changed, in part due to laws for compulsory education. Parents began investing in their children by sending them to school regularly and for more years. After, or in lieu of school or work, children organized themselves into peer groups, and often wandered the streets as *gamins*. [43] Authorities viewed these children as a potentially dangerous group of neglected or delinquent youths that needed to be supervised and they became preoccupied with child abuse, neglect, and juvenile delinquency.

For children of all social groups in this age bracket, doctors, psychologists, and teachers observed, guided, enriched, and molded the children through the family, schools, and organized leisure (clubs, sports, and *colonies de vacances*). Primary and secondary schools stressed conformity and discipline.

Youth, or adolescence, which began at age fourteen or the end of compulsory education and usually lasted until marriage (age twenty-four to twenty-six for women, twenty-five to twenty-eight for men), was the third stage of childhood. Adolescence was "constructed" in the 1880s and 1890s by the middle classes when their own children began staying in school longer, often became more knowledgeable than the parents, went to work at a later age, and remained in a dependent state for a longer period. The middle classes were chary of the adolescents of the urban working classes. The awakening of sexual desire was seen as one of the greatest dangers facing the young people of all social groups, and parents and society as a whole expressed concern over the sexuality of adolescents. In general, parents, educators, and officials hoped to encourage children's obedience to the adult world through long periods of work on farms, in factories, or in schools. Youths did not always accept this subordinate role; they often rebelled and were frequently accused of being disrespectful of authority.

Attitudes were not uniform toward rural, urban working-class, and bourgeois youths. Rural youths were expected to, and did, spend much of their time at home working on their family farm or in the trade of their fathers. Marriages were endogamous, and people usually married those in similar occupations. These youths were socially and culturally isolated, usually pursuing no education beyond age fourteen. Urban working-class youths spent their adolescence in apprenticeships, or, more frequently, in paid work. They, too, usually ended schooling at age fourteen.

Starting in the 1880s education was seen as necessary for girls as well as boys. Camille Sée best exemplified the new attitudes in the early 1880s by saying that France was not a convent, and women were not put in this world to be nuns. Education of all children was viewed as a force for progress.

The most striking aspect of attitudes toward children during the Third Republic was the emphasis on childhood, including adolescence, as a separate stage of life. Authorities saw children of all ages as needing expert nurturing, protection, and education. Equally striking was the shift in attitudes toward unwed mothers. As in the earlier decades, authorities viewed the family as the proper educative milieu for the children. Married parents who worked, who did not drink, beg, or cause their children to beg, steal, drink, or run loose on the streets, constituted a proper environment. But now single women could also provide the proper familial guidance. Unlike in earlier decades, very little rhetoric was devoted to the vices, debauchery, or immorality of the unwed mother. In fact, quite the opposite. She, like her abandoned child, was now considered society's victim rather than its criminal.

By the end of the century many moralists and reformers no longer castigated the unwed mother for her immorality but sought, instead, to understand her victimization, her plight, and her dilemma. Ernest Semichon best summed up the new attitudes when he referred to her as "the vehicle of seduction, and most often abandoned by her family and rejected by the world. But . . . there is one yet more guilty than she—the one who provoked her fall and caused her dishonor."[44] This is the first time even one reformer stressed that the man might have been as guilty or as immoral as the woman—but the woman still had to bear the problems. The unwed mother's choices were still few. Semichon presented a graphic description of her embarrassment and her dilemma:

A cruel battle between her honor and her maternal love rages within her heart. At the fatal moment, she must choose. She can not both keep her child and her honor. If she keeps her child and follows her sentiments of maternal love she would live dishonored. To keep her honor, she can not perform her motherly duties nor listen to the cries of her conscience; she would have to give up her child. But even if she kept the child, the evidence of her dishonor, and retained her maternal love, her womanly conscience, and her Christianity, wouldn't that just throw her into indigence? And wouldn't she then be forced by economic necessity to abandon the child?[45]

This statement shows an understanding of the mother's plight. It was only in the late 1870s and 1880s that writers stopped blaming the mother for lack of foresight and immorality and began to show this kind of concern and understanding for the woman who abandoned her child out of economic necessity.

Other reformers concluded that in cases of economic exigency both mother and child would fare better if the child were deposited at the Hospice. Some reformers even advocated reopening the *tours* in order to save the children. Much as the 1830s and 1850s were periods of intense debates over the *tours* and limitations on admissions, so were the 1870s. Rather than advocating closing the *tours* and controlling admissions, however, reformers in the 1870s proposed reopening the *tours* and allowing free unrestricted admissions. They argued that an unwanted child who was kept by an unwilling, impoverished, unwed mother would run a greater risk of disease and death than one abandoned at the Hospice. Dr. André-Théodore Brochard, a former inspector of abandoned children in Lyons and a leading outspoken critic of government care of abandoned babies, felt that newborns were sacrificed as simple budgetary entities; children were not considered "little ones worthy of compassion but numbers written in the budget." [46] He surmised that a mother even with aid could not afford to keep her infant. To be able to nurse her own child she must have the will and be well nourished or else she would not have sufficient milk. He described the mother's circumstance in some detail:

An unwed mother [who had received state aid to keep her child] arrives in her attic room, having several debts, completely without resources and unable to work. She must, with forty centimes a day, buy a cradle and the bedding, as well as that which she needs to eat, to warm herself, her soap, and even sometimes the water with which to wash the diapers of her infant. All must be bought in the city. This young girl, who needs good nourishment to regain her strength, does not even have anything to eat. In these conditions, it is impossible that she would have the milk [with which to nurse her baby]. Most often, the mother and the infant die of hunger. [47]

He added that the mother, not having enough milk herself and too poor to buy milk for her baby, ate bread or soup that she had to share with the baby, whose stomach became swollen from malnutrition. The baby could not be taken outside because she had no clothes for him. The program of aid to unwed mothers, which had been established in the 1830s and renewed in the 1850s, was badly administered and there was no inspection. The children died from exposure and malnutrition. Dr. Brochard's language and analysis differ greatly from those of prior decades and reflect the new attitudes toward the mother and child, as well as the desire to preserve lives.

Advances in medicine, technology, and hygiene during the 1880s contributed to changing attitudes and facilitated their implementation. Pasteurization, sterilization, the increase in knowledge of contagious diseases and the means of their transmission, and discovery of the waterborne source of typhoid fever were some of the major developments.

Chemical analysis of water became reliable only in the late 1880s, which explains the general indifference to polluted waters before that time. After the late 1880s, new scientific discoveries in the areas of hygiene and public health seeped, along with cleaner water, down to the countryside, with the obvious result of decreasing mortality and improving general hygiene.

A further development of this era was an increase in the power of scientific bureaucrats and administrators who believed in experimenting on institutional inmates, including abandoned children, in the hospices. Dr. Parrot, who was the physician in charge of the Hospice des Enfants Assistés in the 1880s, began a teaching and research clinic on the premises. This included the creation of dissection halls and performance of a large number of autopsies to uncover the causes of death and the nature of diseases.[48] The transformation of the Hospice into a major teaching and research hospital, which began in the early 1880s, reflects the influence of the technocrats and scientists on institutional reform and on social welfare in the last two decades of the nineteenth century.

In keeping with two aims of society—to preserve lives and to honor family ties, including those of an unwed mother with her child—policy makers of the Third Republic believed that as many mothers as possible should be encouraged and financially aided so that they could keep their children. To ensure that the children would receive proper care and would not be left to die from inanition, teams of pediatricians, social workers, and nurses counseled and taught the mothers about how to care for the children. Social welfare during the Third Republic provided extensive prenatal, delivery, and postpartum aid to unwed mothers, including financial and social service aid until the child was in school. If, despite such aid, a woman were unwilling, too impoverished, or too degenerate to keep a child, authorities believed such a child would fare better and have a greater chance for life if it were raised by the state and foster parents; consequently, all unwanted children were accepted at the foundling home. Thus, extensive aid to unwed mothers was combined with a complete and open admissions policy to the foundling home.

The MacMahon crisis, the new weight of the votes of the rural population, and the economic depression of the 1880s may all have contributed to changes that occurred at that time. Road conditions in the countryside improved greatly, and greater communication and travel resulted. The roads facilitated the travel of doctors and inspectors of foundlings, and thereby increased their influence and the spread of new ideas and policies.

As in the First Republic, the proper raising of poor, unwanted, and indigent children was seen as a function of all society. During the Third Republic the development and increasing sophistication of public assistance, social work, medicine, and psychiatry enabled society to fulfill its duty more thoroughly than it had in the past and made more complex the system of aid to, and therefore state intervention in, the lives of the families.

The Third Republic: Public Policy

These new attitudes toward abandoned children and their mothers and the advances in the biological sciences were combined in a series of programs and policies for the protection and education of the children. The first legislation to safeguard children was the Roussel Law of 1874 for the protection of nurslings and infants. It regulated the wet-nursing industry and sought to control abuses in order to reduce the high rate of infant mortality among all children sent out to wet nurse, including babies of bourgeois, artisan, and working-class parents. It was followed in 1877 by increased influence of doctors in the countryside. The number of doctors working for l'Assistance Publique went up; more importantly, the basis of reimbursement changed. Instead of paying the doctors for the number of abandoned children in their care, authorities paid them for the number of visits they made to a child each year and prescribed a minimum number of required visits. This spread new ideas in medicine to the foster parents in the countryside and at the same time increased medical supervision and the influence of other professionals over children. Regulations enacted in 1882, making primary school attendance not only free but obligatory for boys and girls until they were thirteen years old, constituted the major change of the century in terms of education of foundlings. As children's attendance in school lengthened, supervision by teachers and school psychologists employed by the state became more prominent in their lives.

In 1886, the debates of the early years of the Third Republic culminated in the re-establishment of completely unrestricted admission of children to the Hospice. Admission policy for child abandonment reverted to what it had been prior to 1837, with one exception: the *tour* was not re-established. Open, anonymous admissions at the Hospice made the *tours* almost irrelevant—except as a symbol. Impediments to abandonment set down in 1836 and 1852 had been observed more in the breach than in practice since the 1870s and were finally lifted in 1886.

Programs of aid to unwed mothers grew by leaps and bounds in the 1880s. Social reformers and legislators often coupled the aid to reduce infant mortality with that to prevent child abandonment. The results of these efforts can be seen in the law of 1904, which was a comprehensive statute to cover a number of measures instituted in the 1880s and 1890s to encourage maternal responsibility—in the belief that a child's best interest was served by remaining with the mother—and to insure healthy births. The law obligated each department to establish and maintain a Maison Maternelle, staffed by doctors, social workers, and female admissions officers, to give prenatal aid and advice, deliver the babies, and prevent abortion, infanticide, and child abandonment. Admission was open to all women upon demand during their last month of pregnancy, and aid was offered to unwed mothers and to married women without resources. The staff was expected to maintain contact with the mother following delivery, give medical care and advice, and provide the assistance necessary for women to keep their children. Mothers who wished to give up their infants were to be persuaded, and financially aided, to keep them for at least one month; during this time of "reflection," social workers were to continue the support necessary to prevent deprivation in the hope that the development of maternal ties and the promise of continued state assistance would mediate against child abandonment. By a law of October 24, 1919, the state, in another effort to reduce infant mortality and inculcate maternal feeling, provided a bonus to mothers who nursed their children, and, for those unable or unwilling to nurse, each department was to provide free sterilized milk at an Institut de Puériculture.

The most important, radical, and far-reaching governmental policy toward children was the much debated law of July 24, 1889, for the protection of the *moralement abandonnés*. By this measure, the state was enabled to deprive parents of their authority in cases of perceived immorality—vice, drunkenness, crime. Authorities presumed that such depravity resulted in unwholesome upbringing, neglect, or abuse of the children. The law defined the conditions under which fathers could be stripped of parental rights. It stipulated that the children of fathers and mothers who, by their "habitual drunkenness, their infamous and scandalous conduct, or their child abuse, compromise either the security or the health and morality of their children" become wards of the state with an official of l'Assistance Publique as their guardian.[49] It enabled police, social service, and medical authorities to determine which specific children should be taken away from their parents. This law, which proved difficult to interpret and enforce, was augmented by one in 1898 that gave power to a judge to confer the guardianship of children to l'Assistance Publique or to another third party. It prescribed punishment for parents who abused, beat, starved, or otherwise ill-treated their children. It ordered the devolution of paternal authority in all cases of "offenses or crimes committed by or against children." The government could transfer authority from a family found morally lacking to a body of notable officials—public assistance personnel, judges, social workers, and philanthropists.

These measures did not spring full blown from the head of the director of l'Assistance Publique; rather, they had their antecedents in the work of private philanthropic organizations of the 1860s, 1870s, and 1880s. Child protection agencies—such as the Patronage de l'Enfance et de l'Adolescence, founded by Henri Rollet; the Société pour l'Enfance Abandonnée et Coupable, created by Georges Bonjean in 1879; and the Union Française pour le Sauvetage de l'Enfance created by Jules Simon, and other private philanthropic agencies—agitated for legislation to prevent child abuse, exploitation of youths, vagrancy, and prostitution. [50] In fact, during the first decades of the Third Republic the care of neglected children (along with juvenile delinquents, unwed mothers, and repentant criminals) was shared by public and private institutions. This complete involvement of all sectors of the society in the protection of the children further exemplified the current protective attitudes toward them. Unlike the 1830s and 1850s, when all effort was made to keep the children with their parents, the 1880s made every effort to "protect" neglected and abused children from their families, even if it meant taking them away from their parents. The reformers were not purely altruistic in seeking to protect the children. Those *moralement abandonnés*, they feared, were the children roaming the streets of Paris, causing property damage, begging, and robbing. Gavroche in *Les Misérables* is the classic example of a *moralement abandonné*. It was the Gavroches of late nineteenth-century France whom the reformers wanted to take under a "protective" wing and send to *colonies agricoles*, thereby educating and training them to be law-abiding and useful citizens, repopulating the countryside, increasing agricultural production, and ridding the streets of major cities of juvenile delinquents.*

Conclusion: Responsibility

During the nineteenth century the state had on its hands many thousands of infants without a family, children who were regarded as potentially dangerous as they grew to adulthood. During the first half of

---

* Not surprisingly, parallel "child saving" movements occurred at the same time in the United States. For example, in the 1870s U.S. courts ruled that judges could remove children from families when they deemed that the child's welfare was threatened.

the century, except for attempts in the 1830s and early 1850s to curtail abandonment, the common practice of state and local officials was to exercise minimal responsibility. The government intervened as little as possible, farming the foundlings to wet nurses and then foster parents—literally hiding the problem in the countryside—and hoping that foster parents would inculcate familial values in the children. In the course of the century, however, attitudes gradually changed, and public policy evolved to reflect these changes.

Attitudes and measures taken toward restricting child abandonment, preserving the children who were abandoned, and supervising them for a longer period of time exemplify the general opinions about children and public welfare during the Second Empire. The principles had been established by the July Monarchy; the crisis of 1848 provided the impetus for their implementation. The concept of educating—both intellectually and spiritually—the working classes and their children, whether legitimate or illegitimate, and the idea of preserving the nation's youth for the well-being of the country originated in the 1830s and 1840s and grew to predominate in the 1850s and 1860s. With good reason, the Second Empire is usually considered paternalistic, repressive of individual freedoms, and increasingly bureaucratic—a state that exercised its police powers yet fostered efficient economic growth. [51] In keeping with these characteristics, all in some ways evidence of a fundamental concern for governmental and social stability, the idea of state welfare as the principal bulwark against social disorder received wide acceptance.

With the law of 1889 for the *moralement abandonnés* and with the new, child-oriented legislation of 1904, the state fully recognized and assumed full responsibility for aid and care for both mother and child. The system of foster parentage still prevailed and allowed for the children's socialization in a family environment, but the state employed inspectors and doctors who continually supervised and instructed the foster parent families. The Roussel Law of 1874 regulating wet nursing, the legislation for compulsory education in 1882, and the provisions for the *moralement abandonnés* in 1889 reveal the extent to which the state was then prepared to assume responsibility even for children who were not overtly abandoned by their parents.

Thus, by the end of the 1880s, governmental policies toward rejected children had undergone a reversal from that of the first half of the century. Toward the end of the century, while still maintaining the system of foster parentage for abandoned children, the government exerted influence and control in many areas of their lives. In the 1880s the family was removed from its pedestal as the all-important socializing agency. To middle-class bureaucrats, not all working-class families—whether biological or foster—could be trusted to raise law-abiding, hard-working citizens without help from "experts." The protection of children's health and lives, not the increased expenditures such protection would cost, was the overriding concern of the legislators. This concern was incorporated in the new law of 1904, which was allegedly "in the interest of the child." [52]

It took one hundred years for the avowed policy of the First Republic, that the state was responsible for the welfare of its citizens, to be put into practice by the Third Republic. Once the state had entered the realm of social welfare its influence grew. Its programs and policies gradually became intertwined with the family life of the poor. This presaged further extension of state responsibility for the general welfare of its citizens.

Attitudes and policies of state officials form only the public view of the problem—not the personal, human drama that created the need for public action. To that drama—the mothers, their decision to abandon their children, and the ways in which public policy affected maternal behavior—the next chapter turns.

CHAPTER THREE

Mothers and Their Babies

Women have always had methods of coping with unwelcome babies, and the availability of social welfare has been an important element in their deciding on a course of action. The character of such public programs, in turn, reflected attitudes held by social analysts and government officials. In nineteenth-century France, policies of social welfare were crucial to a specific female group—mothers who had children for whom they could not, or would not, care. Some mothers abandoned them. Who were they? Why did they do it?

Nineteenth-century officials and social reformers condemned the large numbers of women who abandoned their unwanted children "with deplorable ease"[1] and castigated the mother for her "unnatural act" of rejecting her child, an act they viewed as evidence of lack of maternal love. They saw these mothers' actions as contributing to the breakdown of the family and the lack of morality among the urban working classes. In their view, women abandoned their babies so they could resume their lives of promiscuity and irresponsibility.

Some novelists, however, were less inclined to condemn the "unnatural" woman who abandoned her child. They pitied the woman whom circumstances forced to abandon her child. Victor Hugo and Eugène Sue declared that some mothers gave up their children out of love, so that their offspring could have a better life than the mother herself could provide at the time. In Hugo's *Les Misérables*, when Fantine reluctantly leaves her small daughter Cosette with the Thénardiers, there is no lack of maternal love. Fantine feels that without the child she would stand a better chance of employment, and would thus earn enough money to get Cosette back and properly feed and clothe her. In *Martin, the Foundling*, Eugène Sue shows compassion for Bruyère, a sixteen-year-old turkey keeper and herself a foundling, who gives birth to an illegitimate child. Bruyère nurses her infant in secret twice a day, but the care she can give is insufficient and the child is wasting away. Claude, the benevolent gamekeeper who befriends Bruyère, suggests taking the child to the neighboring town, which had a foundling home with a *tour* and where the child would be "well cared for." Bruyère sobs and protests this abandonment. Claude declares,

> Oh, it would be utterly vain of me to endeavor to describe to you the utter agony with which she heard me make this proposal, or to paint to you the frightful despair of that young mother . . . [with] her sobs and heart-rending cries. At length, however, the safety of her son prevailed over all other feelings. I set out and she accompanied me nearly a whole day's journey on foot, by turns suckling her child and overwhelming it with tears and kisses. When at last it was necesary to part from the child, I feared that she would never have the courage to do so, but she at length resigned herself to it.[2]

Some twentieth-century writers agree with their nineteenth-century predecessors, looking upon child abandonment as evidence of a lack of maternal love. The modern writers, however, do not condemn the women. Edward Shorter says that mothers who abandoned their babies failed the "sacrifice" test. They put their own economic well-being ahead of the life and welfare of their infants.[3] They did not, or could not, allow their babies to take precedence over material objectives. He sees the incidence of child abandonment as a barometer of modern feelings of mother love. Elisabeth Badinter views child abandonment as evidence that mother love is not the predominant instinct in all women.[4] She feels that mother love is a gift which some women have and others do not. Both Badinter and Shorter assert that extreme poverty, or the pressures of economic deprivation led many women to abandon their children. In Badinter's words, "given the circumstances of their lives, the survival instinct dominated the maternal instinct."[5]

Abandoning their babies may have been the only acceptable choice available. On the other hand, mothers may have thought it was in their children's best interest. Although it was most unusual for a man to take responsibility, in the eighteenth century, Jean-Jacques Rousseau deposited his five illegitimate children at the Hospice des Enfants Trouvés and claimed that it was for the children's own good.[6] It is difficult to be accurate in discerning motives of the women who abandoned their babies; mother love is intangible, and motives are hard to assess. The women left no records of what went on in their hearts and minds.

Nevertheless, they did leave records at the Maison d'Accouchement where many in Paris gave birth and at the admissions office at the Hospice where they abandoned their children. The records contain personal information on the mother such as her occupation, home address, marital status, her place of birth, place of birth of her baby, and notes which she left with her child.[7] From these records, and from knowledge of the age, sex, and legitimacy status of each baby abandoned, a clear picture emerges of these mothers, the circumstances surrounding their decision to abandon, and the effect of public policy on this decision.

The Children Abandoned: Their Age, Sex, and Legitimacy

Most babies who were abandoned by their mothers were newborn—the incident of Bruyère abandoning her child of a few days is typical. During the nineteenth century most babies arrived at the Hospice within the first days of life (see table 3.1). Although the mean reflects an increasing number of older children entering the Hospice, the median indicates that more than half of the children were less than a month old when abandoned, even as late as 1870. Clues to the mothers' motives for abandoning these infants lie in the status of the children themselves, though—somewhat surprisingly—not in their sex.

Table 3.1

Age in Days of Children At Abandonment, 1820-1870

Year	Mode	Mean	Median
1820	0	16	0.9
1825	0	17	0.8
1830	1	41	1.2
1835	1	73	1.2
1840	1	428	1.4
1845	1	206	1.3
1850	1	240	1.6
1855	1	580	20.0
1860	9	380	14.0
1865	2	447	18.0
1870	1	710	26.5

Source: Computed from random sample of abandoned children from the *Registres d'Admission* of the Hospice.

There were an equal proportion of boys and girls abandoned, not more girls than boys as some have suggested. Marvin Harris has posited the similarity between the Parisian situation of child abandonment and the high rate of female infanticide found in other areas of the world.[8] Harris claims that more girl babies are ordinarily abandoned than boys. The reverse on the surface seems true for Paris: the data consistently show more boys than girls abandoned. This apparent greater propensity for the abandonment of boys over girls reflects the excess of male births over female at a ratio that varies usually in the range of 103-107 male births per 100 female births.[9] When the ratio of boys to girls abandoned is correlated with the sex ratio of live births in Paris, the apparent imbalance disappears. There was no significant difference in the number of boys versus the number of girls abandoned in Paris.[10]

A comparison of male births in the city of Paris with those in all of France reveals another phenomenon: a statistically significant greater proportion of reported live male births in the rest of the nation than in Paris (51.434 percent recorded born in France versus 50.840 percent in Paris).[11] This differential in the records may reflect underregistration of female births in the countryside or earlier registration and baptism of boys than of girls.

Fathers in the countryside reputedly preferred boys;[12] bells rang and horns blew when a male birth occurred, and parents rushed to baptize him. If parents in the countryside were cognizant of the higher postnatal mortality of boys than of girls, they may have felt a greater urgency to early baptism and registration of boy babies. Furthermore, the larger proportion of recorded male births in the countryside than in Paris may indicate a greater rural infanticide rate for baby girls over baby boys, as Marvin Harris and William Langer have claimed.[13] In Paris, on the other hand, parents may not have felt early birth registration important, perhaps because parents did not prefer boys. A male child's labor may not have been deemed as important in the city as it was in the country; indeed, the labor value of boys and girls may have been equal for the working classes in an urban mobile society. In Paris, with the nearby Hospice receiving all unwanted babies, there was no need for infanticide, and especially no recourse to gender-specific infanticide or abandonment.

For a variety of reasons, the oft-discussed preference for boys over girls is not reflected in the abandonment of children in Paris. The desire for male offspring may only have been felt by a father, only by fathers in the countryside, or only for legitimate babies. Since an urban mother was most often the one who abandoned an illegitimate baby, perhaps she had no preference for one sex over the other. A mother who abandoned her baby in Paris was probably in such a desperate situation that she could not keep the baby no matter what the sex.

The legitimacy of the baby might have been critical to the parents' lack of gender preference in abandonment during the nineteenth century. Since most abandoned babies were illegitimate, a preference for keeping a child of one sex rather than the other would not have applied. The proportion of abandoned babies who were illegitimate ranged from more than ninety-five percent at the beginning of the century to approximately eighty-five percent toward the end of the century (see table 3.2). Until 1890 legitimate babies were proportionally never more than twenty percent of all abandoned children, and for the first half of the century they constituted less than ten percent of the total.

Because children could be abandoned secretly, even furtively in the dead of night, the bastardy of the foundlings might seem problematic. But, when women abandoned their children in the *tours*, they almost always left a piece of paper attached to the child's clothing giving the name and date of birth. Despite the ease and possibility of completely anonymous abandonment (at least through 1852), mothers usually gave their own names as well. In the 1820s and 1830s somewhat over eighty percent of the mothers left their name at the time of abandonment. Under the more stringent attitudes of the July Monarchy, three-quarters of them did, and by the later years of the Second Empire and early Third Republic well over ninety percent left their names. [14] The increase in the percentage of mothers who revealed their identity corresponds to the establishment and enforcement of the requirement that the mother provide this information at the time of abandonment and is in inverse relationship to the existence and use of the *tour*. Strikingly, even prior to 1861 when the *tour* was available, authorities knew the identity of more than four-fifths of the mothers.

If the name of the mother was given and not that of the father, admitting officers of the Hospice assumed the mother was unmarried and the child illegitimate. If the mother was not named, she was neither presumed married nor single (her marital status was simply "unknown"). Until 1860 the children of unknown parentage were tabulated as illegitimate, but after 1860 they were listed separately. If the father was named, but his name differed from that of the mother and child, cohabitation without marriage was assumed, the mother was considered unwed, and the child was presumed illegitimate—a condition that occurs in the records in fewer than one percent of the cases. [15] Authorities considered an abandoned child legitimate only if the mother or father said so and gave the name (with a matching surname) of the other parent. Officials listed the child as legitimate under three other, very rare circumstances: if the name of the father matched both the surname of the mother and the baby, if either parent declared the spouse deceased, or if

Table 3.2

Hospice Admissions and Legitimacy Status, 1815-1900

Year	Number	Number Illegitimate	Number Legitimate	Percent Legitimate	Percent *Naturel Reconnu*	Percent Unknown
1815	5,080	4,832	348	6.9		
1816	5,080	5,104	363	6.6		
1817	5,467	4,482	297	6.2		
1818	4,779	4,659	398	7.9		
1819	5,057	4,748	353	6.9		
1820	5,101	4,725	238	4.8		
1821	4,963	4,847	193	3.2		
1822	5,040	4,951	165	3.5		
1823	5,116	5,030	183	3.6		
1824	5,213	5,034	206	3.9		
1825	5,240	5,175	217	4.0		
1826	5,392	5,152	264	4.9		
1827	5,446	5,186	311	5.7		
1828	5,497	4,995	415	7.8		
1829	5,370	4,803	435	8.3		
1830	5,238	5,150	517	9.1		
1831	5,667	4,368	614	12.3		
1832	4,982	4,325	478	10.0		
1833	4,803	4,463	478	9.7		
1834	4,941	4,466	411	8.4		
1835	4,877	4,441	351	7.3		
1836	4,972	4,191	453	9.8		
1837	4,664	2,894	143	4.3		
1838	3,207	3,132	222	6.6		
1839	3,354	3,423	205	5.7		
1840	3,628	3,522	176	4.8		
1841	3,698	3,896	199	4.9		
1842	4,095					

Table 3.2

Hospice Admissions and Legitimacy Status, 1815-1904

Year	Number	Number Illegitimate	Number Legitimate	Percent Legitimate	Percent *Naturel Reconnu*	Percent Unknown
1843	4,171	3,970	208	5.0		
1844	4,223	4,009	215	5.1		
1845	4,296	4,090	206	4.8		
1846	4,260	3,883	377	8.8		
1847	4,554	4,077	477	10.8		
1848	4,597	4,075	522	12.8		
1849	4,133	3,545	588	14.2		
1850	3,952	3,528	424	10.7		
1851	3,940	3,569	371	9.4		
1852	3,303	3,032	271	8.2		
1853	2,380	1,989	391	16.4		
1854	3,441	2,754	687	20.0		
1855	3,700	3,047	653	17.6		
1856	3,943	3,269	674	17.0		
1857	3,993					
1858	3,960					
1859	4,002					
1860	3,799	3,206	593	15.6	3.37	1.63
1861	3,768	3,227	541	14.4	7.33	1.26
1862	3,613	3,094	519	14.4	11.85	1.66
1863	3,469	3,001	468	13.5	11.79	2.02
1864	3,786	3,287	499	13.18	11.09	2.27
1865	3,942	3,384	558	14.15	11.24	1.83
1866	4,278	3,661	617	14.46	7.72	1.86
1867	4,469	3,765	704	15.75	9.33	1.54
1868	4,651	3,874	777	16.71	6.41	1.33
1869	4,260	3,443	817	19.18	5.14	1.22
1870	4,541	3,627	914	20.12	3.21	1.59
1871	3,423	2,809	614	17.93	5.15	2.54
1872	3,551	2,920	631	17.77	9.74	1.30
1873	3,336	2,647	689	20.66	7.76	1.68

Table 3.2

Hospice Admissions and Legitimacy Status, 1815-1904

Year	Number	Number Illegitimate	Number Legitimate	Percent Legitimate	Percent *Naturel Reconnu*	Percent Unknown
1874	3,146	2,562	584	18.56	5.41	2.00
1875	2,338	2,064	274	11.72	8.25	2.57
1876	2,260	1,901	359	15.88	13.00	3.51
1877	2,320	1,910	410	17.67	15.25	2.49
1878	2,760	2,285	475	17.21	16.46	2.38
1879	2,774	2,375	399	14.38	19.10	2.24
1880	2,730	2,324	406	14.87	16.64	2.82
1881	2,834	2,382	452	15.95	12.20	4.10
1882	2,746	2,019	457	16.65	13.55	4.68
1883	3,151	2,592	559	17.77	12.54	5.10
1884	3,128	2,602	526	16.82	8.57	6.44
1885	3,137	2,608	529	16.86	8.48	4.85
1886	3,257					
1887	3,472					
1888	3,724					
1889	3,552					
1890	3,621	2,796	825	22.78	3.70	1.27
1891	4,506	3,069	1,437	31.91		
1892	4,897	3,278	1,619	33.06		
1893	4,699	3,234	1,465	31.18		
1894	4,878	3,329	1,549	31.77		
1895	4,516	3,093	1,423	31.52		
1896	4,578	3,213	1,365	29.82		
1897	4,671	3,272	1,399	29.96		
1898	5,210	3,655	1,555	29.86		
1899	4,997	3,585	1,412	28.26		
1900	5,090	3,745	1,345	26.44		

Source: *Rapports Annuels,* 1852–. Unfortunately, the categories of "Naturel Reconnu" and "Unknown" were not considered prior to 1860.

Note: The increased proportion of legitimate children admitted after 1889 reflects the *moralement abandonnés* who were counted among the Hospice admissions.

a relative or priest attested that the child was a legitimate orphan.

Throughout the century, many of the legitimate abandoned children were orphans, but the relative proportion of orphans to all legitimate abandoned children shifted sharply from the 1820s to the 1870s (the only years for which complete data exist). In the 1820s, twenty-two percent of the legitimate abandoned children were orphans or had a mother in a hospital or prison; but, by the 1870s, not only were the number and percentage of legitimate abandoned children much higher, but three times as many (sixty-one percent) of them were orphans or had a mother in a prison or hospital. [16]

The first increase in the proportion of abandoned children who were legitimate occurred in 1832-1833 and was most likely due to the cholera epidemic, which decimated portions of the population (see table 3.2). Novelists have attested to its impact. As Rigolette in Sue's *Mystères de Paris* says, "After the cholera, I found myself alone in the world. I was then about ten years old." [17] Rigolette was taken in by neighbors. But what of the child without neighbors, friends, or family? Such a child, who lost one or both parents would probably have been brought to the Hospice.

Similarly, legitimate children arrived at the Hospice during the new conjunctural crisis, the agricultural shortages and economic depression of 1846 to 1850 sometimes called the "hungry forties." During these lean years, parents may have died, leaving an orphan who was brought to the Hospice. Families living on the brink of poverty (who in better times would have survived with all family members intact) may have found it necessary in times of economic distress to abandon a child so that the other members of the family could survive.

In 1853, the proportion of illegitimate abandoned children decreased from eighty-five to eighty percent, a proportion that remained relatively constant until 1890. This later shift in proportion of legitimate and illegitimate children is more difficult to explain than that for 1832-1833 and 1847-1850. At the first level of analysis the percentage of illegitimate abandoned children must be compared with the illegitimacy rate in the general population from which the abandoned children came—Paris and the department of the Seine. The illegitimacy ratio in Paris from 1816 until 1853 declined from almost forty percent to thirty-two percent—that is, about one-third of all births in Paris were illegitimate. In the department of the Seine the illegitimacy ratio decreased from thirty-six percent in 1816 to about twenty-four percent at the end of the century—that is, about one-fourth of all babies born in the department of the Seine were illegitimate (see tables 3.3a and 3.3b, and figures 1 and 2). To a very minor extent, this decline in the proportion of illegitimate abandoned children may reflect the small decline in the percentage of illegitimate children born in the area. The change in the legitimacy status of the population at large in the second half of the century was small. The fraction of legitimate births increased slightly as the century progressed, from sixty percent in 1816 to seventy-five percent in 1885, while the increase in the fraction of legitimate abandoned children doubled in the same period. Thus, a change in the make-up of the population of abandoned children cannot be explained solely in terms of changes in the population at risk. Other influences had to be at work.

Legitimacy status depended on what the Hospice authorities recorded. It may be conceivable that after the 1850s more mothers began naming their babies' fathers and claiming nonexistent marital ties or that Hospice authorities were more inclined to attribute legitimacy when in doubt. Both of these explanations are, however, unlikely, for there was no reason either for mothers or for authorities to change their procedures. Quite the contrary. Hospice administration officials specifically instructed their personnel to discourage abandonment of legitimate infants. Parents undoubtedly knew that abandonment of legitimate infants would not be easy, and they would not claim spurious legitimacy of their babies and thereby risk having the option of abandoning their children closed to them. Poor orphans with no family or other means of support were readily admitted to the Hospice, as were the offspring of widows too impoverished to feed their children. But rarely do the Hospice records show the mother to have been a widow. For a single woman to claim to be married was futile, and to name the father of the child was equally useless: the father could not be pursued and held responsible for breach of promise or for child support, and even research into paternity was forbidden by Article 340 of the Code Napoléon. Thus no father was legally or morally liable for a child he did not recognize. Therefore, it seems safe to assume that legitimacy figures were not inflated by the erroneous reporting by parents or Hospice authorities.*

In addition to the increase in the abandonment of legitimate children during times of economic hardship, most notably the 1840s and 1880s, several other changes account for the larger proportion of legitimate abandoned children after 1850. The explanation most likely lies in increasing official concern with providing for and monitoring the older child, usually legitimate and brought in by the police. Older children

---

* It is possible that the marriage rate increased and that more people were getting married or marrying younger. Both might have affected the proportion of legitimate children abandoned.

Table 3.3a

Relationship of Abandonment to Illegitimate and Total Live
Births in Paris (in percentages, 1816-1853)

Year	Proportion Illegitimate Births of Total Live Births	Proportion Illegitimate Births Abandoned	Proportion Total Births Abandoned
1816	39.31	55.0	22.72
1817	38.08	56.4	23.19
1818	35.07	55.4	20.18
1819	35.48	53.9	20.77
1820	35.68	53.5	20.52
1821	36.48	51.5	19.73
1822	36.28	49.7	18.75
1823	36.22	50.5	18.90
1824	35.47	49.2	18.09
1825	34.32	50.2	17.91
1826	35.04	49.3	17.99
1827	34.87	49.6	18.27
1828	35.39	49.5	18.57
1829	34.90	50.2	18.83
1830	35.01	48.0	18.48
1831	35.14	49.6	19.19
1832	35.14	47.3	18.75
1833	34.04	46.3	17.49
1834	34.31	44.7	16.98
1835	33.97	44.8	16.63
1836	33.28	46.1	17.18
1837	32.81	43.8	15.98
1838	31.23	31.2	10.78
1839	31.18	33.1	11.04
1840	31.94	35.5	12.01
1841	32.85	35.8	12.36
1842	32.86	37.9	13.08
1843	32.98	39.3	13.62
1844	32.65	38.4	13.22
1845	32.29	38.5	13.06
1846	32.03	36.3	12.76
1847	33.07	37.6	13.91
1848	32.91	37.7	13.98
1849	32.98	35.7	12.18
1850	33.69	35.4	13.34
1851	32.90	33.6	12.19
1852	32.62	27.9	9.92
1853	31.82	18.4	6.99

Sources: Computed from *Rapps. Anns.*, 1852–; *Annuaire Statistique de la France*;
France, Census Reports, 1855, 1-3, no. 27, pp. 436-437; Remacle, *Des hospices
d'enfants trouvés*; Lafabrèque, *Des enfants trouvés à Paris.*

Table 3.3b

Relationship of Abandonment to Illegitimate and Total Live
Births in the Department of the Seine (in percentages, 1815-1904)

Year	Proportion Illegitimate Births of Total Live Births	Proportion Illegitimate Births Abandoned	Proportion Total Births Abandoned
1815	36.0		
1816	35.3	53.5	19.87
1817	34.4	54.9	20.25
1818	31.6	53.7	18.09
1819	31.9	52.1	18.05
1820	32.3	51.4	17.93
1821	32.8	49.6	17.13
1822	33.5	47.8	16.29
1823	32.4	48.6	16.28
1824	31.7	47.0	15.43
1825	30.8	47.5	15.20
1826	31.2	46.4	15.12
1827	31.0	46.8	15.34
1828	31.4	46.5	15.51
1829	31.1	47.1	15.73
1830	31.1	44.8	15.31
1831	31.2	46.6	15.99
1832	31.2	44.2	15.53
1833	30.2	42.9	15.01
1834	30.4	41.7	14.05
1835	30.3	41.5	13.72
1836			13.22
1837			12.96
1838			8.67
1839			10.93
1840			10.22
1841			10.78
1842			10.23
1843			10.64
1844			10.22
1845			10.07
1846			9.79
1847			10.68
1848			10.74
1849			10.26
1850			9.57
1851	28.2	29.8	9.26
1852	27.9	24.4	7.41
1853	27.2	15.7	7.23
1854	27.2	20.0	6.11
1855	26.4	23.3	6.84
1856	26.2	22.9	7.18
1857	26.7		7.15
1858	26.4		6.67

73

Table 3.3b

Relationship of Abandonment to Illegitimate and Total Live
Births in the Department of the Seine (in percentages, 1815-1904)

Year	Proportion Illegitimate Births of Total Live Births	Proportion Illegitimate Births Abandoned	Proportion Total Births Abandoned
1859	27.0		6.24
1860	26.0	21.2	7.01
1861	26.5	20.0	6.22
1862	26.1	19.8	6.20
1863	26.4	18.3	5.77
1864	25.8	20.6	6.32
1865	26.7	19.7	6.59
1866	26.6	21.7	7.15
1867	26.0	22.2	7.47
1868	26.4	22.6	8.05
1869	25.8	20.3	7.88
1870	25.0	22.3	8.22
1871	24.5	26.9	7.04
1872	24.6	17.4	6.72
1873	25.2	15.8	6.20
1874	24.9	16.0	5.90
1875	24.2	13.2	4.56
1876	24.2	12.0	4.39
1877	24.2	12.0	4.56
1878	24.3	13.5	
1879	24.1	14.5	
1880	24.5	13.6	4.87
1881	23.8		4.73
1882	23.5		4.46
1883	24.5		4.97
1884	25.3		4.99
1885	24.6		5.22
1886	24.4		5.50
1887	24.4		5.81
1888	24.9		6.35
1889	23.9		5.93
1890	24.7		6.47
1891	25.1		7.63
1892	24.4		8.36
1893	24.3		7.97
1894	24.7		8.44
1895	24.6		8.16
1896	24.3		8.20
1897	24.9		8.37
1898	24.4		9.35
1899	24.7		9.10
1900	24.6		9.10
1901	24.8		9.11
1902	24.6		9.23
1903	24.5		
1904	24.5		9.59

Source: Computed from *Rapps. Anns.*, 1852–; *Annuaire Statistique de la France*; France, Census Reports, 1855, 1-3, no. 27, pp. 436-437; Remacle, *Des hospices d'enfants trouvés*; Lafabrèque, *Des enfants trouvés à Paris.*

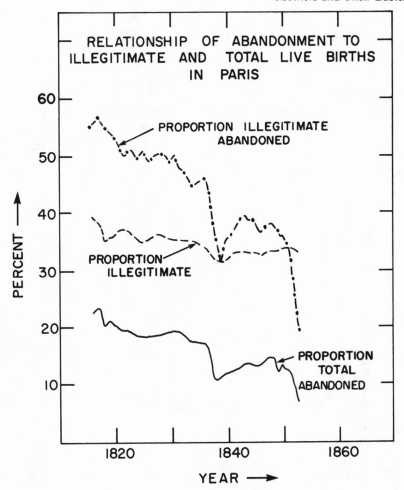

Fig. 1

began to be abandoned more frequently in the 1850s (see table 3.1), and the interest in the older child is certainly reflected in the proportion of legitimate children admitted to the Hospice after the 1880s (see table 3.2). In the 1890s, the proportion of legitimate abandoned children swelled to about thirty percent, and this increase is undoubtedly due to the admission of the *moralement abandonnés*.

If, instead of looking for the cause of a rise in the proportion of abandoned children who were legitimate, the reasons for a fall in the proportion of those who were illegitimate are sought, other possible explanations surface. Under the more rigid regulations of the Second Empire, fewer unwed mothers may have succeeded in leaving their infants at the

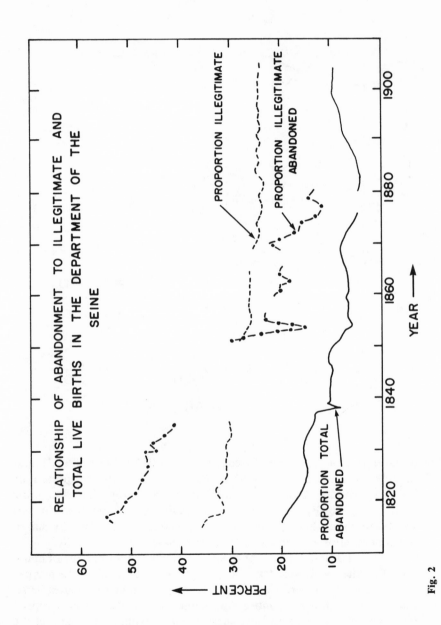

RELATIONSHIP OF ABANDONMENT TO ILLEGITIMATE AND TOTAL LIVE BIRTHS IN THE DEPARTMENT OF THE SEINE

Fig. 2

Hospice, and Hospice authorities may have turned away many who sought to abandon their illegitimate offspring. Temporary aid to unwed mothers to prevent abandonment, which was introduced in 1837, increased after 1852 and expanded in subsequent decades. Such aid may also have reduced the percentage of illegitimate abandoned children, especially since that aid was offered only to unwed mothers. People with illegitimate offspring were, in any event, much less likely to abandon their children as the century progressed.

Temporary aid to unwed mothers may also account for variations in the number of foundlings and the decrease in the percentage of total live births abandoned during the nineteenth century. The actual numbers of children abandoned at the Hospice des Enfants Trouvés in Paris show only slight variations during the entire century (see figure 3 and table 3.2). The numbers of foundlings fluctuated from highs of over five thousand per year to lows of between two and three thousand. The numbers did not steadily decrease or increase over the century; rather, the pattern is one of jagged highs and lows with appreciable lows in 1837, in 1853, and in the late 1870s. Although the spectre of some five thousand rejected infants per year in one city alone is rather striking, more significant than the actual number of children abandoned is the percentage of total babies born and subsequently abandoned.

The foundling home in Paris accepted unwanted children born in Paris or other areas of the department of the Seine; conversely, unwanted babies in the department of the Seine arrived at the foundling home in Paris. Therefore, calculating the percentage of live births in Paris and the department of the Seine who were abandoned is an accurate indicator of the abandonment rate (see figures 1 and 2). Until 1821, more than one-fifth of all babies born in Paris were abandoned at the foundling home. This proportion gradually declined to fifteen percent of live births in Paris abandoned in 1837. From 1838 to 1852 the percentage of live births abandoned was between ten and fifteen percent, and in 1853 the percentage of live births abandoned declined to under ten percent, where it remained for the rest of the century.

Although abandonment of fifteen to twenty percent of all babies born in Paris seems shockingly high, it pales in comparison to the percentage of illegitimate births abandoned. The ratio of illegitimate abandoned children to total illegitimate births reveals that about half of all illegitimate children born in Paris and the department of the Seine were deposited at the Hospice des Enfants Trouvés. After 1838 the number of all illegitimate offspring in Paris who were subsequently abandoned dropped to about thirty percent, and after 1853 to less than twenty percent. As discussed in the preceding chapter, something happened during the century and especially in 1837 and in 1853. Official policy, rules and regula-

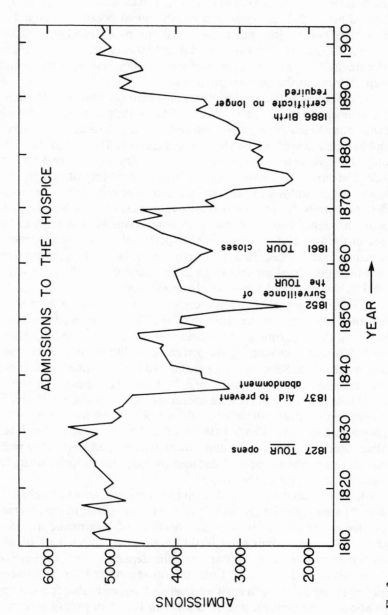

Fig. 3

tions, and admissions procedures constrained mothers' choices and affected the rates of abandonment both of legitimate and illegitimate children.

The Effect of Rules and Regulations on Abandonment

Throughout the century, mostly mothers abandoned babies at the Hospice des Enfants Trouvés, sometimes with the aid of an intermediary such as a midwife or priest (see table 3.4). While there were several means of abandoning a child that mothers could use, the choices available changed throughout the century due to modifications in the admissions regulations. In repeated efforts to reduce the number of abandoned children, and hence the expenses for the department, admission to the Hospice became increasingly difficult as the century progressed.

Despite the opening of the *tour* in 1827, during the first third of the century up to forty-five percent of the abandoned babies came from the Maison d'Accouchement.[18] As a result, the Decision of 1837 marked the start of restrictive measures in an attempt to limit abandonments and expenses. The Decision declared that "pregnant women will be admitted to the Maison d'Accouchement only if they will nurse their child for several days at the establishment, and take their child with them when they leave" (see Appendix B, Article 4). In the same year philanthropists established the Fondation Montyon, a private charity, to give aid to women in financial need at the Maison d'Accouchement who wished to nurse and keep their babies. The year 1837 also witnessed the beginning of a departmental program of aid to unwed mothers who did not give birth in Maison d'Accouchement and arrived at the Hospice intending to abandon their babies. There was no euphemism, such as "Aid to Families with Dependent Children," attached to this program. It was called "temporary aid to unwed mothers to prevent abandonment," or more simply, "aid to prevent abandonment" (*secours pour prévenir l'abandon*). The authorities were clear in their intent. The aid was not to help the mother and child but merely to reduce the numbers of wards of the state and hence expenses.

Officials offered aid to mothers who delivered their babies in the Maison d'Accouchement before the women left that hospital, and offered it to others when they arrived at the Hospice des Enfants Trouvés with their infants. There were two forms of such aid: one enabled the mother to keep the child with her, and the other helped pay the wet nurse if, for whatever reason, the mother could not nurse her baby. In either case, the aid was indeed temporary, lasting at most for four months,

Table 3.4

People Who Brought the Babies to the Hospice (in percentages, 1866-1900)

Year	Mother	Direct Abandonment			Wet Nurse	Indirect Abandonment*		
		Father	Midwife	Other[a]		Hospitals	Police	Other[b]
1866	81.3	3.0	—	15.6	—	—	—	—
1867	76.4	3.8	—	19.8	—	—	—	—
1868	56.1	5.2	21.3	16.4	—	—	—	—
1869	56.1	4.9	23.1	14.5	—	—	—	—
1870	44.9	4.1	23.2	26.7	—	—	—	—
1871	55.9	4.4	21.7	16.9	—	—	—	—
1872	50.7	1.4	23.8	22.8	—	—	—	—
1873	45.1	1.3	—	—	—	—	—	—
1874	39.6	1.6	19.2	—	—	—	—	—
1875	43.3	.6	—	—	—	—	—	—
1876	60.1	2.0	4.5	7.0	15.4	4.5	4.2	2.0
1877	57.9	3.1	2.3	6.7	14.1	6.8	3.7	5.3
1878	57.3	2.1	3.8	7.4	15.7	5.5	3.5	4.7
1879	66.0	2.4	4.5	6.3	9.0	4.4	2.3	4.9
1880	62.3	2.3	4.9	5.9	10.0	6.4	1.7	6.2
1881	62.0	2.8	6.8	9.2	6.5	5.5	1.6	6.1
1882	65.2	3.2	4.8	7.5	6.3	5.3	2.1	5.5
1883	65.3	2.9	4.4	6.9	8.3	4.6	2.5	5.4
1884	67.6	2.6	5.8	5.7	6.0	3.9	2.7	5.3
1885	68.0	3.3	5.2	6.3	6.8	3.7	1.1	5.6
1886	65.0	3.1	5.8	7.2	5.2	4.0	1.6	8.2
1887	63.1	3.9	5.9	9.9	2.7	4.4	1.3	8.8
1888	62.6	3.5	4.6	9.4	5.4	4.6	1.5	8.4
1889	66.1	2.6	4.3	8.9	5.6	3.8	1.2	7.4
1890	62.6	3.5	3.8	8.2	3.9	6.2	1.7	10.1

Source: Derived from *Rapps. Anns.*, 1866-1890.
   a: Includes police, wet nurses, priests, relatives, and friends, in that order of frequency until 1872. After 1875 includes only police and wet nurses.
   b: Includes priests, relatives, and friends.
   *Baby first left with an intermediary who brought it to the Hospice.

after which the mother was expected to work and provide for the child. If a mother wished to nurse the infant herself officials gave her a *demi-layette* which constituted the barest necessities in terms of clothes for the baby, and five francs per month for four months. If she chose to give the baby to a wet nurse, they gave her a *demi-layette* for the child, the first month of payment for the wet nurse, and money for transportation to the wet nurse. This was computed at 26 francs. [19]

Authorities did not offer aid to all mothers. When a woman went to the Hospice to abandon her child, she was interrogated by a *commissaire de police* (superintendent of police) of the City of Paris who was authorized to offer aid to a select few women. His instructions included several guidelines as to who should and should not be offered aid, and how much aid would be appropriate. If a midwife came to the Hospice with the baby of a patient and pleaded for aid for her client, the police were instructed not to honor her pleas. Married women were not to be offered aid since the needy among them could apply for assistance from the Bureau de Bienfaisance of the *arrondissement* in which they resided. There appeared a strict division of labor among social welfare organizations. With the local Bureau de Bienfaisance giving aid to married women with families, authorities of the Hospice did not deem it necessary to offer the married women assistance out of their coffers.

Only unwed mothers were offered aid, and not even all of them who wished it. Furthermore, the amount of aid was supposed to depend on the need of the mother. A domestic with wages of 250-300 francs per year was not to be treated the same as a poor day laborer who received less than one franc per day actually worked. [20] Police superintendents carefully evaluated mothers who personally came to abandon a child as to whether or not they should be offered aid. Mothers who could support themselves by their work or the work of their husbands or *concubinaires* (cohabitants) should not be offered aid. Nor should women in a state of indigence—that is, those who earned 60 to 75 centimes per day or less—be offered aid. For them, aid would not prevent abandonment, merely postpone it. If their babies went to a wet nurse, the mothers would not be able to afford to pay the wet nurse after the first month's payment ended. Such babies would then be abandoned, and the resultant expenses for the state would be greater than if the babies had been abandoned immediately. If indigent women wished to keep the children and nurse them, the five francs would not be sufficient. The police superintendents were instructed, however, that if an indigent mother was sincere in wanting to keep her infant and found abandonment repugnant, they should not deter her from keeping the baby. (If this were the case, why would she have come to the Hospice in the first place?) The prefect of police instructed his superintendents to exercise good judgment and economy in offering aid, because the administration could not aid all who asked for it. The superintendents could only recommend needy mothers for aid; they could not award it. Women only received the aid once a member of the Conseil Général des Hospices had visited her residence and verified need.

As a result of the combination of public aid to prevent abandonment, and the private charity of the Fondation Montyon, 2,407 women received aid in 1838, of whom slightly over half—1,272—received aid directly from the Fondation Montyon when they left the Maison d'Accouchement. [21] Of the total, only two-thirds were ever visited by an inspector. No records exist of the others; presumably they had left Paris, or inspectors were negligent in their duties. From 1838 to 1844, between 2,407 and 4,604 unwed mothers were given aid each year, either from public funds or by the philanthropy of Fondation Montyon. [22] This aid, even though minimal, partially accounts for the decrease in percentage of illegitimate children who were abandoned in Paris.

Another regulation that restricted the ease of abandonment was the required interrogation of the mother decreed by the Decision of 1837. Aimed at eliminating the anonymity of the mother and hence reducing the number of abandonments, this order specified that no child was to be admitted to the Hospice except upon a *procès verbal* conducted by a police superintendant. A police agent was stationed at the entry to the Hospice and intercepted each person who wished to abandon a child in order to complete the *procès verbal*. An admissions office was established at the Hospice which was open from 10 A.M. to 4 P.M. During those hours, the agent of the police would go to the admissions office with the mother, or the person abandoning the child, where he would interrogate her. While the questions posed to the abandoner in the admissions office varied somewhat according to the questioner, their essential nature remained the same. In effect, a birth certificate was required for admission. The abandonner had to supply specific information to the interrogator: first and last name, place of birth, and domicile of the mother; the names of her living parents, if any; other children in her household and other children previously abandoned, if appropriate; and the status of the father of the child. [23] The agent then was to inform the mother of the consequences of abandonment of the child and to suggest financial aid to mothers whom they thought deserved it. These questions, designed to intimidate the mother and restrict child abandonment, may not have been answered completely or truthfully. Nor did they always deter abandonment. When a mother contemplated giving up her child she had probably thought of all the answers to these questions and had weighed and rejected proposed alternatives to abandonment. But just in case she had not, Hospice authorities tried to dissuade her. Meanwhile, policemen constantly observed the *tour* to prevent surreptitious abandonment.

The restrictions imposed in the Decision of 1837 were in full effect for not more than one year, during which there were only forty-one abandonments via the *tour* and admissions to the Hospice declined by 1,457. The presence of police and of interrogators served to intimidate many of the less determined or desperate women. Public outcry, mainly by Lamartine and spokesmen of the Catholic Church, led to less severe enforcement of these measures after 1838. From 1839 to 1852, constant surveillance of the *tour* ended and the *tour* was available, unwatched, from the hours of 4 P.M. to 10 A.M.; during these hours admission of infants was without formality for those mothers who wished to escape the *procès verbal*.

Another regulation that affected the rate of abandonment resulted from the authorities' desire to prevent mothers from coming from the provinces to Paris to give birth and then abandon their children. Regulations of the 1840s specified the commune, *arrondissement*, or department in which a person was born as the responsible agency for giving charity and aid to the person in need. In the case of abandoned children, the *domicile habituel* of the mother at the time of parturition was considered the *domicile de secours*. Thus, the department of the Seine had financial responsibility for the abandoned children of mothers who gave birth in the Maison d'Accouchement and listed Paris as their address. To cut costs, therefore, Paris authorities attempted to restrict admission to the Maison d'Accouchement.

In 1845 Paris hospital authorities promulgated a regulation that required mothers to have lived in the department of the Seine at least one year prior to admission to the Maison d'Accouchement (unless there were a medical emergency or the mother were already in labor). This regulation did not take effect until 1852. In that year, they further ordered that for a pregnant woman to be admitted to the Maison d'Accouchement, she had to have a certificate from the *commissaire de police* and the Bureau de Bienfaisance of the *arrondissement* in which she resided, attesting that she was unable to afford to be delivered at home by a midwife and also that she had resided in Paris for at least one year. Furthermore, once a woman gave birth in the Maison d'Accouchement, she was required to stay there for eight or nine days (instead of one day after delivery), nurse her child, and then take her child with her when she left.[24] This reinforced the Decision of 1837, which had fallen into disuse. Authorities believed that if a woman nursed her child for several days, maternal ties of love would develop and the mother would not be so apt to abandon the child.[25] This rule probably affected the infant's age at time of abandonment more than it did the rate of abandonment.

In 1852 there were further restrictions placed on the abandonment of the child at the Hospice, which account for a further reduction of the rate of abandonments in 1852 and successive years. Although police agents still patrolled the Hospice and its grounds to prevent surreptitious abandonment, sought the identity of the parents who abandoned a child on the street, and brought children abandoned on the street to the Hospice, their intervention in daily abandonments at the admissions office in the Hospice stopped. Instead, the reception—or admissions—office, staffed by the director of admissions, the Superior of the Sisters of Charity, and the *économe* (steward) of the Hospice became central. The office was open from 6 A.M. to midnight. In order for a child to be admitted, the birth certificate and a response to an interrogation (similar to the one of 1837) was necessary.[26]

Mothers had to explain why they sought to abandon the child, and then the director of admissions encouraged them to keep their baby, and told them of the consequences of abandonment. He informed the mother that the destination of the infant would be unknown to her, and that only rare news could be obtained (upon payment of the *droit de recherche*). He then offered her aid, either in the form of financial assistance to her or direct payment of a wet nurse. If the mother refused all aid and she insisted upon abandonment, the child was then admitted—but only after "all proper means are taken to deter the abandonment."[27] Sometimes, "all proper means" included intimidating, harassing, and requiring the mother to sit in solitude and meditate upon her decision for up to several hours.[28]

A decree of 1852 prohibited midwives from abandoning a child at the Hospice. While this may have been enforced in the 1850s, by 1862 it was no longer. A memorandum from the director of the Hospice acknowledged that "children were brought by parents or midwives" and demanded that midwives supply the mother's name or the parents' names, as well as the name and address of the child.[29] After 1869 midwives came under further restriction—they had to submit a written declaration signed by the mother to the effect that the abandonment was made upon her request.[30]

In the 1860s authorities took two additional measures designed to decrease abandonments, but these seemed to have little effect; the rate of abandonment did not decrease—in fact, it increased slightly. In 1862 they closed the *tour* and henceforth the only mode of admission was at the admissions office of the Hospice or with the *garde de tour* who was basically a night watchman. Seven years later, in 1869 aid to unwed mothers became part of public assistance and payments to the unwed mother lasted until the baby was ten months old. At that time the mother was expected either to take the child back or pay the wet nurse herself. The maximum aid offered to a new mother would be the wages for the wet nurse for this ten-month period, which was estimated at 380 francs, and a layette which went to the wet nurse for the baby. The layette consisted of one set of woolen swaddling clothes and two sets of cotton swaddling clothes (similar to receiving blankets), six new diapers, two old diapers, four *béguins* (bonnets) of calico, four *chemises* (shirts), two bonnets of *indienne*, two *brassières* (undershirts) of *indienne*.[31]

The numbers of children abandoned and the rate of abandonment increased again in the 1880s and 1890s in part because of changes in the rules and regulations. In keeping with the change in attitudes in which the welfare of the mothers and children became of greater concern than saving money by restricting admission, authorities eased restrictions on admissions.

In 1883, the director of the Hospice established procedural policy for children presented for admission who did not have the required birth certificate.[32] During business hours, and if the mother was willing to pay the necessary fees, the admitting office called a carriage and made a search for the certificate. If it was late, or the mother could not keep the child even for a few hours while the search was made, the Hospice kept the child, waiving the requirement. When the identity of the child or the identity of the person who presented the child was in doubt, the would-be abandoner was taken to the superintendent of police of the *quartier* (area) who opened an investigation to determine the child's identity. The Hospice directors late in the century emphasized that any child in need of prompt aid was given it. "Humanity," said Peyron, "is our guide."[33]

Finally, in 1886, the directors of the Hospice lifted the requirement of a birth certificate,[34] which correspondingly decreased the role of the police. This resulted in increased abandonment. The administrators, however, continued to try to obtain birth certificates, posting notices stating that, although the birth certificate and responses to the questions were not required, the best interests of the child would be served by the mother (or other abandoner) supplying as much information as possible. In line with the new attitudes of the 1880s, the Hospice aimed to protect the health and life of the infant; administrators believed that immediate admission accomplished this and they admitted legitimate and illegitimate alike.

Thus, during the entire nineteenth century, fluctuations in the number of children abandoned and changes in the rate of abandonment (as depicted in figures 1 through 3) can be partially explained by variations in rules and regulations governing the ease of abandonment. The admissions restrictions and police presence, however, did not deter women from abandoning their children if they really wanted to.

The Mothers

Most of the mothers who abandoned their babies at the beginning of the century were single. By the end of the century, both the proportion of legitimate abandoned children was higher, and more of the children were older; but this does not necessarily mean that more mothers who abandoned their children were married. Older or legitimate children were frequently those picked up by police or whose mothers had died. Throughout the century, women who themselves brought their children to the Hospice and abandoned them there were predominantly unmarried.

The age of the mothers did not vary much from the 1820s to the 1870s (see table 3.5). Teenage pregnancies were not the problem here: in the 1820s, 12.8 percent of the mothers were aged twenty or younger at the time they abandoned their children, and, in the 1870s, 16.5 percent were under twenty-one. This might, in part, reflect a slight decline in the average age of menarche in France from fifteen and a half to fifteen. In Paris, between twenty-seven and forty-five percent of the female population reached puberty at age sixteen or older. Only 2.5 percent of the women in Paris who abandoned their babies were under eighteen and about fifteen percent were in the eighteen to twenty year age bracket through most of the century. Their pregnancies, almost immediately postmenarche, may correspond to teenage pregnancies in contemporary America where the age of menarche is twelve and a half. In nineteenth-century Paris, most mothers who abandoned their children were in their twenties (see table 3.6). The average age for mothers at the time of abandonment does not, moreover, differ significantly from the average age of marriage and the presumed average age of women upon the birth of their first child for the population of France as a whole. The average age for first marriage for French women during the first quarter of the century was about twenty-six, and in the last third of the century just over twenty-four.[35] In Paris, the average age at first marriage around mid-century was somewhat older—twenty-five years in 1851 and twenty-seven years in 1861.[36]

Table 3.5

Age of Mothers at Time of Abandonment, 1820-1825 and 1870-1873

Years	Range	Mode	Median	Mean	Standard Deviation
1820-1825	17-44	22	25	26	5.5
1870-1873	15-43	22	26	26	5.6

Source: Compiled from Archives de Paris, (AP) *Enfants Assistés, Registres d'Admission.*

The women who abandoned their babies were predominantly of marriage age. If their pregnancy had been the result of sexual misadventure and freedom that accompanied urbanization and the capitalist market economy, as Edward Shorter has suggested, then the age of mothers at time of abandonment should have been close to the onset of menarche, or soon after the women left home and were on their own.[37] Either teenage women were exerting restraint, were not being freely seduced, or the seduction of women was occurring in the eighteen to twenty-one year old bracket. Perhaps younger women just had less opportunity to become pregnant, or did not leave home until they were in their twenties. The predominance of women over twenty-one who abandoned their babies suggests the possibility that the women who became pregnant had a somewhat serious relationship with a man. The illegitimate birth and subsequent abandonment of the child may have been a result of the breakdown of family control, control that in earlier times or in a rural environment might have enforced marriage of the couple. But marriage

Table 3.6

Age of Mothers in 1869 at Time of Abandonment

Age of Mothers	Number of Mothers	Percentage of Mothers
Under 15	1	0.02
15-17	107	2.5
18-20	635	14.9
21-25	1099	25.8
26-30	959	22.5
31-35	537	12.6
36-40	285	6.7
41-45	128	3.0
46-50	486	0.5
Unknown		11.4

Source: *Rapps. Anns.,.* 1869.
Note: 1869 is the only year for which such complete data are available.

87

did not ensue for many women in their twenties and child abandonment was chosen as one of the alternatives to dealing with the unwanted pregnancy and live childbirth.

The occupations and socioeconomic status of the women often made keeping an illegitimate child difficult if not impossible. Virtually all mothers who abandoned their children were from the working classes (see table 3.7). Between one-fourth and one-third of all mothers who abandoned their children were *domestiques* (domestic servants). *Ouvrières* (workers) and *journalières* (day laborers), when considered together, represented thirty percent of the mothers in the 1820s; toward the end of the century this proportion first increased to forty percent and then dropped to twenty-five percent. The fluctuation in the percentage of workers can be attributed to the vague and general category of *ouvrières* and *journalières*. Many of the diverse occupations in the category of worker were associated with the garment industry—that is, vest, glove, shirt, and pant makers as well as shoe stitchers and makers of garment ornamentation and trim. The third most common single occupation was that of *couturière* or seamstress.

In novels of the time seamstresses often supplemented their meager income by taking lovers, and prostitutes claimed to be seamstresses. Fantine, in *Les Misérables*, was a type of seamstress—a *grisette* (a smartly clad young milliner). To her and other *grisettes*, having a lover meant having more food and clothing and a few luxuries; indeed, their lovers sustained them during seasonal unemployment. In Balzac's *Cousine Bette* another seamstress had a job on the side. In this novel a man of wealth says with some pride, "I set up, as they call it, a little seamstress, fifteen years old, a miracle of beauty."[38] But Rigolette, in Sue's *Mystères de Paris*, worked as a seamstress and took great pride in remaining virtuous. These women were not street walkers. There is no clear way of knowing how many mothers of abandoned children were prostitutes or women of "easy virtue." In 1844, 1866, and 1867, the three years for which complete data are available, only 0.08 percent, 0.12 percent, and 0.02 percent of the mothers admitted to working as *filles publiques* (regular, registered prostitutes).[39]

Not all prostitutes were *filles publiques.* Prostitution could be a seasonal or temporary means to supplement a worker's meager income. We need a new definition of the oldest profession—one that includes part-time work in the trade to augment income earned in a less infamous occupation. A woman could engage in occasional or clandestine prostitution and not call herself a prostitute. As Elizabeth Weston and Alain Corbin have shown, the garment trade "provided a large proportion of the prostitutes of Paris throughout the nineteenth century, and *couturières* constituted thirty percent of the clandestine prostitutes."[40] Domestic service was the occupation that provided the second largest

Table 3.7

Occupation of Mothers (in percentages, 1820-1876)

Occupation	1820	1844	1854	1866	1867	1868	1869	1870	1874	1875	1876	Average
Domestique	26.8	29.7	33.0	32.0	33.4	27.6	28.7	30.0	26.4	25.7	36.5	30.0
Ouvrière	22.8	13.9	18.0	16.5	13.2	10.0	17.6	11.6	34.0	34.5	12.8	18.6
Journalière	7.4	5.2	—	10.4	10.9	8.9	8.0	10.0	6.0	8.9	11.2	8.7
Couturière	15.4	13.9	10.0	13.8	15.3	19.8	17.8	23.3	11.9	9.8	15.5	15.1
Lingère	—	6.6	—	8.4	4.2	5.8	4.6	8.3	3.5	3.9	5.2	5.6
Blanchisseuse	4.7	2.2	—	6.4	4.5	4.9	4.4	5.0	3.0	3.2	5.4	4.4
Cuisinière	6.7	—	—	0.7	1.2	2.5	4.3	5.8	—	—	—	3.5
Fleuriste	—	—	—	2.4	1.7	—	1.5	—	1.4	1.7	2.0	1.8
Marchande	2.7	0.6	—	0.1	0.4	0.5	1.6	—	0.8	0.3	0.4	0.7
*Other**	9.4	0.7	—	0.9	4.9	10.2	3.8	4.2	8.9	9.5	8.7	6.8
Sans état	3.4	—	—	2.0	3.3	2.9	1.4	1.7	4.9	3.0	2.3	2.8
Unknown	5.1	26.9	39.0	6.2	6.7	—	6.7	—	—	—	—	—

Sources: Data for 1820 and 1870 compiled from the *Registres d'Admission* of the Hospice; data for 1844 derived from Boicervoise, *Rapport au Conseil général* (1845); and other data derived from *Rapps. Anns.*, 1854-1876.
*Includes women whose occupations ranged from rag-picker to teacher (*institutrice*) in relatively equal proportions, both under two percent.

source of prostitutes. Thus, some of the women who claimed to be seamstresses or domestics may indeed have been part-time or temporary prostitutes, especially during the months when they were otherwise unemployed. That some of the women who claimed to be seamstresses or domestics were occasional prostitutes does not preclude the earlier assumption that illegitimate abandoned babies of the twenty-five-year-old mothers were the offspring of premarital sex and failure of subsequent marriage and not of promiscuous behavior. Even in the case of prostitutes, Weston had concluded that prostitutes' children were often the result of special love relationships. [41]

The occupations of mothers who abandoned their children were representative of the entire female working-class population of Paris during the nineteenth century. [42] Roughly thirty percent of the women who abandoned their children were domestics, and domestics constituted almost thirty percent of the active female population. [43] *Couturières* alone represented on the average sixteen percent of the abandoners, and twenty percent of all female workers were employed in the garment trade. [44] The four percent descrepancy could be a yearly variation or could reflect the *lingères* or *journalières* who may have worked in the garment trade.

Women working in Paris were not necessarily born there. While almost all babies abandoned in Paris were born in Paris or the department of the Seine, the same cannot be said for their mothers. During the century most mothers were born outside the department, but their predominance decreased as the century progressed. In the 1820s, 93.6 percent of the mothers who abandoned their children at the Hospice des Enfants Trouvés were born in departments other than the Seine; by the 1860s, roughly seventy percent were Parisian immigrants from other departments (see table 3.8).

Table 3.8

Mothers' Birthplaces (in percentages, 1820-1869)

Year	Department of the Seine	Foreign	Other Departments	Unknown
1820	—	—	93.6	—
1856	14.0	7.2	68.8*	10.0*
1866	16.5	4.4	70.0	15.7
1867	13.3	5.6	70.7	10.4
1869	11.4	5.1	74.8	8.7

Sources: *Rapps. Anns.*, 1856-1869.
      *Estimated.

The decline in the percentage of mothers born outside the department of the Seine reflects the migration patterns to Paris. Between 1801 and 1817, the population of Paris rose from 546,856 to 713,966, an increase of thirty percent in less than twenty years. Although some of the growth was due to an increase in the number of children born, much was the result of immigration. Other periods of substantial growth in the population of the capital, due in considerable part to an increase in migration, occurred from 1831 to 1836, from 1841 to 1846, from 1851 to 1856, and then again just before 1881.[45] Generally, only one-third of the increase in population was due to births; the rest was the result of provincial migration. The periods of the greatest emigration from the provinces—the depopulation of the countryside that so worried officials of the July Monarchy and the Second Empire—occurred primarily before 1860. Only after 1861, however, are the data accurate enough for detailed analysis. During the last four decades of the century the percentage of mothers born outside Paris is only slightly greater than that for the population of the city as a whole. Presumably, the same was true before 1860. Even the birth places of the mothers reflect the birth places of most of the migrants to Paris—the Seine-et-Oise.[46]

Whether women who abandoned babies in Paris were those who had lived there for several years or were newly arrived, living alone, without benefit of family and community ties, and in Paris to seek the anonymity of the city in order to conceal their pregnancy and abandon their baby cannot be determined with any accuracy. Until 1852, however, many were probably new residents—women who got pregnant either in the provinces or shortly after their arrival in Paris. This speculation is based on the heavy migration to the city prior to 1852 and the lack of residency requirements for admission to the Maison d'Accouchement prior to that same year. In the 1820s, seventy percent of the abandoning mothers who were born outside Paris delivered their babies in that free maternity hospital.

A survey of 1844 bears out the notion that most women who abandoned their children in Paris were indeed recent arrivals. To reduce the numbers of children abandoned, the Conseil Général des Hospices authorized an investigation by which the director of the Maison d'Accouchement was instructed to question women who abandoned their infants there to ascertain how long they had lived in Paris. The director found that "almost two-thirds of the infants abandoned after their birth at the Maison d'Accouchement belonged to mothers who had come to Paris expressly to hide their pregnancy and to deliver their baby or who lived in Paris for only several months."[47] In 1845, therefore, a requirement of one year was instituted prior to admission to the Maison d'Ac-

91

couchement, but it was not immediately enforced. As the prefect of police complained, "access to the Maison d'Accouchement [is] entirely free to pregnant women without requiring . . . any proof of identity or residence."[48] Such "easy access" ended by 1853. Women thereafter were less likely to come to the capital from the provinces within months or weeks of expected delivery since they were no longer eligible for admission to Paris' maternity hospital. But whether the women were new arrivals or had resided in Paris for several years, many of those giving birth in the Maison d'Accouchement lived alone and had no close friends or family ties. On the baptism certificate for many of the babies who were born in the Maison d'Accouchement and subsequently abandoned, the godfather was the sacristan of the chapel in the hospital and the godmother a nurse.[49]

By the 1860s the majority of abandoned children in Paris were probably not the offspring of provincial women who came to the city for the specific purpose of giving birth and leaving the child. Only ten percent had been in Paris for less than a year (see table 3.9). These figures, though decidedly different from those of the investigation of 1844, may not be conclusive since the women of "unknown" length of residency grew larger each year. Given the residency requirement prior to admission, many women might have wanted to avoid telling the truth, which they could easily have managed by arriving at the hospital in labor and, hence, making admission with few questions asked almost certain. Hospital administrators, for their part, after admitting women in labor may have been less zealous about interrogating them postpartum, since any questions at that point would have had little practical value. In any event, at the beginning of the century most of the mothers who abandoned their children may have been new arrivals, but by the end of the century about two-thirds had allegedly lived in Paris for over five years.

When asked their place of residence, most mothers during the century simply listed Paris and gave no specific address. The data are more complete for the 1820s and 1870s, and during these years many mothers gave a street address. These generally proved to be addresses in the poorest and most populous working-class quarters of the city.[50] In the 1820s, 26.3 percent of the mothers resided outside of Paris and another 21.4 percent gave no specific address in the city; the remaining 52.3 percent provided addresses in the 3rd through the 8th and the 12th *arrondissements*; almost ten percent of all of the mothers came from the 12th *arrondissement*, and each of the other six *arrondissements* were the places of residence for 4.7 to 6.4 percent of the mothers. In 1835, the ratio of the population receiving relief to the general population for these same *arrondissements* ranged from one in six for the 12th and one in seven for the 8th to one in twenty for the 3rd—the most poverty-stricken areas of the city. [51]

Table 3.9

Length of Mothers' Residence in Paris prior to Delivery (in percentages, 1866-1874)

Length of Time	1866	1867	1868	1869	1872	1873	1874
Less than 1 year	13.2	10.0	9.7	9.3	9.2	8.1	9.6
1 - 2 years	15.8	14.0	12.0	18.2	13.4	6.1	7.8
2 - 5 years	17.1	20.2	19.8	24.8	21.6	23.0	14.7
5-10 years	19.4	16.0	11.8	11.9	15.2	17.1	8.7
More than 10 years	25.9	23.0	24.0	21.2	21.1	16.0	21.2
Unknown	8.3	16.2	22.4	14.6	19.5	27.0	37.9

Source: *Rapps. Anns.*, 1866-1874.

In the 1870s, only 5.5 percent of the mothers gave their residence as outside of Paris, and 16.1 percent simply listed the city as their place of residence. Of the others, most listed their address in the new 2nd, 5th, 6th, 10th, 11th, 14th and 18th *arrondissements* (see table 3.10). In 1860 Paris expanded to include contiguous areas in the department of the Seine; the twelve old *arrondissements* were renumbered, and new ones were added to make a total of twenty. But the street addresses had changed very little. The 2nd *arrondissement* (old 3rd) had a large percentage of domestics and employees; the 10th (old 5th) had a relatively high percentage of *ouvriers* (workers); the 5th and 6th (old 12th) housed many domestics; the 11th (old 8th) housed large numbers of day laborers and *ouvriers*; and the 14th and 18th were densely populated with *ouvriers*. [52] Generally, these were the new, populous, working-class areas of low income, low rents, and furnished rooms.

In the 1820s the mothers of abandoned children who worked as domestics resided throughout Paris; many lived in the old 12th *arrondissement*, as did most of the seamstresses. Adeline Daumard's study of the domestics of the 12th *arrondissement* shows them to be among the poorest paid in Paris. Their wages were 200 francs per year while those in the richer quarters often received wages of 300 to 500 francs. [53] In the 1870s the mothers who were domestics lived in all areas of Paris with marginally more in the new 10th and 18th *arrondissements*. These were not the wealthy bourgeois districts but, rather, working-class districts. This suggests either that some domestics worked for the poorest of those who could afford a servant or that they lived at home and traveled to work and, hence, were really *femmes de ménage* or charwomen. René

Table 3.10

Place of Residence of the Mothers, 1868-1870

Place of Residence	1868 Number	Percentage	1869 Number	Percentage	1870 Number	Percentage
1st *Arrondissement*	131	2.8	114	2.7	141	3.1
2nd *Arrondissement*	156	3.4	96	2.3	128	2.8
3rd *Arrondissement*	211	4.5	176	4.1	166	3.7
4th *Arrondissement*	280	6.0	173	4.1	188	4.1
5th *Arrondissement*	240	5.1	224	5.3	240	5.3
6th *Arrondissement*	285	6.1	272	6.4	231	5.1
7th *Arrondissement*	96	2.0	251	5.9	200	4.4
8th *Arrondissement*	113	2.4	242	5.7	176	3.9
9th *Arrondissement*	193	4.1	244	5.7	150	3.3
10th *Arrondissement*	404	8.7	309	7.3	240	5.3
11th *Arrondissement*	262	5.6	263	6.2	207	4.6
12th *Arrondissement*	185	4.0	168	3.9	262	5.8
13th *Arrondissement*	88	1.9	158	3.7	139	3.1
14th *Arrondissement*	333	7.2	100	2.3	164	3.6
15th *Arrondissement*	104	2.2	113	2.7	153	3.4
16th *Arrondissement*	60	1.3	140	3.3	137	3.0
17th *Arrondissement*	171	3.7	173	4.0	168	3.7
18th *Arrondissement*	216	4.6	271	6.4	203	4.8
19th *Arrondissement*	136	2.9	147	3.5	171	3.8
20th *Arrondissement*	123	2.6	121	2.8	152	3.3
St. Denis	160	3.4	79	1.9	91	2.0
Sceaux	92	2.0	38	0.9	67	1.5
Other Departments	118	2.5	78	1.8	83	1.8
Foreign	11	0.2	9	0.2	6	0.1
Unknown	483	10.3	301	7.0	738	16.2
TOTAL	4651		4260		4541	

Source: Material derived from *Rapps. Anns.*, 1868-1870.

Lafabrèque, director of the Hospice des Enfants Assistés in the 1870s, reported that domestics "did not live with their employers but had their own domicile, their own attic room where they returned each night. In the *grands quartiers*, their neighbors were the *valets de chambre*; in the *quartiers populeux*, the shop boys, the employees of commerce—all men who were more disposed to take advantage of this proximity than to preach reserve and good morals."[54] Theresa McBride, however, has convincingly shown that almost all servants did live in the houses of their employers, but on the sixth floor, underneath a mansard roof where they could be out of the master's sight but easily summoned.[55] In these crowded rooms, without light and ventilation, men and women lived together unsupervised, which may have promoted pre- or nonmarital sexual liaisons.

No matter what their precise age, place of residence, or occupation, domestic servants, seamstresses, or laborers probably experienced a sense of isolation and loneliness in the city. Without familial ties and supervision and with peer-group pressures for belonging, liaisons between men and women likely developed out of a sense of loneliness. Without birth control, without a family to enforce marriage, or without the economic resources to support a marriage, illegitimate children followed by infant abandonment ensued. The isolation and loneliness may also have made the women more vulnerable and easily seduced, often by their employers or neighbors.[56] Conclusive evidence is, however, lacking; the reasons for the high number of illegitimate births among this segment of the population must remain speculative, based on scattered documentation. The act of abandonment had no single, obvious motive or cause. Several factors are involved.

Motives for Child Abandonment

Women who abandoned their babies were in most ways typical of single, working women in the city of Paris. They differed from them only in making use of one particular form of social welfare—state acceptance of their child at the Hospice and state responsibility for the maintenance of that child. What women did to cope with an unwanted child depended to a great extent on public welfare programs available to them. Within their range of options, women chose legal, free child abandonment for a variety of reasons.

In their letters and notes which accompanied the infants, most mothers simply stated that "necessity made me do it."[57] Occasionally, a woman amplified that comment, such as by requesting that the baby be taken care of because "I am unable to nurse."[58] Both of these claims seem vague, but what a mother most likely meant by "necessity" or her inability to nurse, was that her level of income, her occupation, her marital status, or her poor health prevented her from keeping and nursing her baby. Several mothers said that they had a promise of marriage from a man, became pregnant by that man, and then the father of the child left them. The mothers also stated that, having no means of support, they were obliged to place their children in the Hospice des Enfants Trouvés. One mother's note, while lending credence to the theory that the midwives were regular transporters of babies to the Hospice, may have served as an excuse. This mother, an unmarried laundress who lived in Paris, requested the return of a daughter who was "snatched from [her] in the delirium that followed [her] delivery," [59] presumably by the midwife.

When a mother abandoned her child in person at the Admissions Office of the Hospice, she most often claimed indigence as the reason. In mid-century, three out of four mothers who abandoned their child did so for reasons of indigence. [60] Reasons given by mothers on notes and in person may indicate only the acceptable reasons—what the women thought the authorities would accept as valid or what might get them aid. Given the women's occupations, however, indigence as a motive for abandonment seems valid.

If mothers' claims that abandonment was due to dire poverty and if the nineteenth-century reformers' belief that *misère* (extreme poverty) was the motivating force behind abandonment are valid, the cost of living and price fluctuations in several grains should be correlated with the rate of child abandonment in Paris. The total number of abandoned children per year throughout the century is not meaningful statistically because of the rapid increase in the population at large of the department of the Seine and of Paris. Therefore, the number of abandoned children must be standardized in relation to live births in the department of the Seine. [61]

A plot of the ratio of the number of abandoned children to the live births shows a steady decline throughout the century except for three distinct breaks: in 1838, 1852, and 1870. The year 1838 was unusual due to the temporary enforcement of the order of 1837, and therefore must be omitted from the statistical analysis. Putting these gross features aside for the moment, it is of interest to examine the short term fluctuations that can be seen in figure 4 in order to test various hypotheses relative to the several factors that have been suggested as contributing to child abandonment.

To perform the analysis, least-squares fits of straight lines through the data in each of the three time periods (1816-1837; 1839-1851; 1852-1869) were made and the residuals were tested for possible correlations with the price index for bread, the price of grain (average mean), cost of living index in Paris, annual rainfall, and price of wheat (see table 3.11). [62]

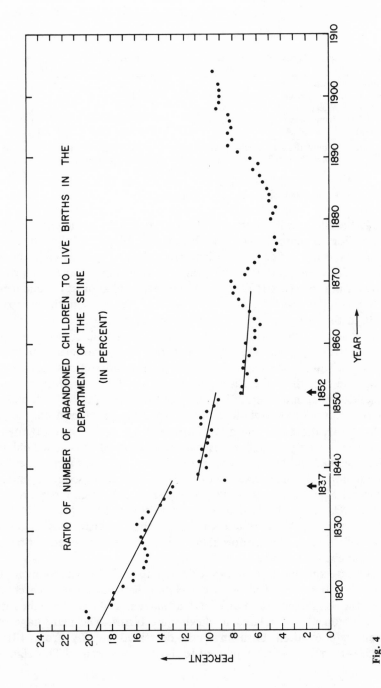

RATIO OF NUMBER OF ABANDONED CHILDREN TO LIVE BIRTHS IN THE
DEPARTMENT OF THE SEINE

(IN PERCENT)

Fig. 4

Table 3.11

Correlations: Economic Indices and Abandonment, 1816-1869

	1816-1837	1839-1851	1852-1869
Price of Grain	+0.71[a]	+0.65[a]	+0.30
Price Index of Bread	+0.67[a]	+0.27[b]	+0.34
Price of Wheat	+0.73[a]	+0.25	+0.37
Cost of Living	not available	+0.16	+0.38[c]
Rainfall	+0.18	+0.20	+0.076

Sources: Fourastié, *Documents pour l'histoire . . . des prix*; Labrousse, *Le prix du fro-ment*; Mitchell, *European Historical Statistics*; and Singer-Kerel, *Coût de la vie.*
[a]Significant at one percent confidence level.
[b]Significant correlation at the five percent confidence level.
[c]Significant at the ten percent confidence level.

In the fine details of the statistical analysis minor fluctuations can be seen. For the years 1816 to 1837 there is a positive correlation at less than a one percent confidence level between child abandonment and the price index for bread, the price of grain (average mean), and the price of wheat. For the years 1839 to 1851 there is a correlation at the one percent level with the price of grain, and a possible, but not significant, correlation at the five percent level between abandonment and the price index for bread. For the period of 1852 to 1869 the only possible correlation is one at the ten percent level between the rate of abandonment and the cost of living indices for Paris. In summary, after corrections for a general decrease over time, there is a strong evidence for a correlation between abandonment and economic indices for the years 1816 to 1837, and only weak evidence of correlations in the later years. Furthermore, the years 1846-1847, those of great crop shortage and crises in the economy (*disettes*), show only a small increase in the number of abandoned children. During 1837 and 1853, also years of *disettes*, there was a great decline in admissions of abandoned children. In 1854 and subsequent years, the number again increases but the increase may have been more a response to the relaxation of restrictions than a response to the *disette*. Economic fluctuations highly correlate with child abandonment only in the first part of the century; therefore there must have been other conditions that influenced abandonment.

While economic crises in France were important in abandonment, they were not the only variable. A correlation between abandoned children and the illegitimacy ratio of Paris was made in order to see if the rate of abandonment was related to illegitimate births. The percentage of illegitimate children born in Paris decreased slightly from 1816 to 1853—from almost forty percent to thirty-two percent.[63] This eight percent decrease in the ratio of illegitimate to total live births partially explains the fifteen percent decrease in the percentage of total births abandoned. The correlation with the residuals is +0.27. In the department of the Seine, where data exist for almost the entire century, the proportion of illegitimate births declines from thirty-six percent in 1815 to twenty-four percent by the end of the century. [64] The percentage of total births abandoned declined from twenty percent in 1816 to about six percent by the last years of the century. Furthermore, fewer illegitimate children were abandoned as the century progressed; that percentage declined from fifty-five percent to fourteen percent. The illegitimacy ratio decreased smoothly through the century. The rate of abandonment does not. After a sharp decrease in the rate of abandonment for the first twenty years, there was a slight decrease after two sharp drops. Increasing illegitimacy, as the reformers hypothesized, was not a factor in child abandonment since illegitimacy in fact decreased, and at a slower and different rate from that for child abandonment (see figures 3 and 4 and tables 3.3a and 3.3b).

Some officials blamed unscrupulous midwives for contributing to child abandonment by allegedly persuading mothers to give up their babies. [65] They accused midwives of taking advantage of the weak, confused, and dependent state of the woman at the time of her delivery. More than half of the mothers who abandoned their babies did not give birth in the Maison d'Accouchement or another hospital. They, therefore, gave birth alone or with the aid of a midwife, friend or acquaintance. To an unwed mother, a working woman alone in Paris without the support and counsel of parents, relatives, or friends, the midwife became very important.

Midwives had customarily been the ones who relieved the mother of her child and had the child carried to the Hospice. For this service, the midwife charged the mother a fee of 10, 15, 20, or even 50 francs. The amount she charged depended upon the degree to which the midwife could convince the mother of the difficulties of abandonment. [66] It is not known how many of the babies abandoned at the Hospice with only a note, or at the *tour*, were actually brought there by the midwife or upon her advice. A mother, after giving birth, would have been advised by the midwife that abandonment was a solution; the mother would agree to it, and the midwife or her agent would then take the baby and deliver it to the Hospice, with a handy profit made by the midwife.

Instructions in 1837 and Regulations in 1852 aimed to curtail this mercenary practice of midwives; they required that the midwife have proper authorization from the mother to have the baby abandoned. But it is probable that a mother alone, at the height of her distress and confusion, would take the midwife's advice. People in a state of medical or psychological distress become dependent on the person in charge and will often heed the advice of an authoritative medical figure, which the midwife certainly was.*

Far more important as reasons for child abandonment than either national or regional economic circumstances or medical advice, however, were the occupation and civil status of the women who abandoned their babies. A domestic servant, who was almost always unmarried, could conceivably keep and nurse her child if she lived in the house of her employer and if the employer both allowed her to keep the child and gave the mother time off to nurse. The conventional view among the bourgeoisie (from whose ranks her employer came), however, was that a woman who conceived and did not marry was engaged in vice, sin, and debauchery; as such she would probably lose her job and be out on the streets with her infant.

A factory worker, or any woman who worked outside her home, could not keep her child about her and nurse during the day. There were no flexible maternity leaves until the very end of the century and virtually no day-care facilities. The first *crèche* (infant day-care facility) was established in 1844, and within two years there were eleven in Paris—some of which soon closed. Each had fewer than twenty children.[67] They were run by private charity but encouraged by the Ministry of the Interior. They were not primarily located in centers of working-class population, and many excluded illegitimate children. The intent of the founders of the *crèches* was to provide care for children of married workers and thereby increase the availability and productivity of female labor.

A single domestic or working woman could not keep her child and maintain her job—unless she found someone to nurse her child in her absence. To do this she had to have enough money to pay a wet nurse and required enough food, rest, and time to nurse the baby herself after work. Given the long, difficult, and irregular hours of work, and the low income, few working-class women could keep a baby and still remain employed; nor could they afford to pay wet nurses.

Whatever their occupation, women on the whole received half the wages of men for equal work[68] and their wages were very low. Data for the 1830s puts women's wages at 75 centimes to one franc per day.[69] Jules Simon noted that in the 1850s and 1860s a woman could earn a maximum salary of 600 francs a year, and more likely it was 500 francs

* The French word for midwife is *sage-femme*, literally meaning wise woman, which is perhaps indicative of attitudes to midwives.

annually—slightly more than one franc a day.[70] In the 1860s expenditures for life in a garret or sixth-floor room cost roughly 300 francs per year: 100-150 francs for lodging, 115 francs for clothing and linen, 36 francs for laundry, and another 36 francs for heat and light. With a maximum salary of 600 francs a year, a woman would have about a franc a day for food, enough for an inadequate diet composed mainly of starches.[71] Allowing for periods of unemployment, however, her annual salary would be closer to 250-475 francs. Thus a working woman could barely cover expenses; she certainly could not afford food, clothing, crib and soap for the baby, nor a wet nurse.*

One and two decades later the unwed mother's situation was little better. Wages rose slightly during the century; wages for working women in Paris in 1876 were estimated at 2.80 francs a day (up from 2.12 in 1853) for some industries and 1.51 francs a day (up from 1.07) in other, smaller industries. In 1885, female cotton spinners in the department of the Seine earned 780 francs per year. Three francs and fifty centimes to 4 francs was maximum pay per day for women in the garment industry, but because of the seasonal nature of the work and long periods of unemployment this never equaled the 1,277 francs per year it should have.[72] The increase in wages in the 1880s did not necessarily raise a woman's standard of living because the cost of living in Paris rose rapidly before 1880.[73] At best, wages kept up with inflation and servants' wages, at least, paralleled the cost of living.[74] Textile workers' wages in the 1870s were estimated to be, at most, 3 francs 50 centimes per day.[75] With deductions made for no work on Sundays and holidays, she could get, at most, 87.50 francs a month. Allowing for two months' unemployment, her annual salary was approximately 875 francs. Her expenses were: 180 francs for the rent of a *chambre garnie* (a furnished room), 365 francs (a franc a day) for food heavy in starches, 100 francs for laundry, and 24 francs for shoes. She could, therefore, barely afford the 100 or so francs to provide necessities for the infant; she did not earn enough to pay a wet nurse 300 or more francs per year. Even with these relatively high wages and on this budget the money allotted for food and clothing was exceedingly low.

* In England, during the same time period, many mothers in similar circumstances sent their newborns to baby farms. They often paid a woman a flat fee at the very beginning for taking the baby. Many women who took such infants were not wet nurses and the babies frequently died. Furthermore, payment of a set fee when first sending an infant to a baby farm likely did not ensure the good care nor the longevity of the child. If a mother did not send her infant to a baby farm, the poorhouse or workhouse was an alternative. In England, after 1843, the main recourse for the poor, unwed mother was to be admitted with her infant to the workhouse, where few special facilities, if any, existed for the care of babies.

An unwed working mother could not afford to keep her child without a substantial program of aid to cover the entire salary of the wet nurse or to enable her to keep and nurse her own child. Doctors did not find the aid to unwed mothers (temporary aid to prevent abandonment) sufficient. The program provided a layette for the child and the equivalent of 40 centimes a day for the mother who kept her infant. This, one person estimated, was 10 centimes more than the price of a *cannette* of beer. [76] In 1837 aid was 5 francs a month for four months, and in 1870 was 380 francs for ten months. On this amount no mother could adequately lodge, warm, and feed herself and her infant. A nursing mother needed more adequate nourishment than the poor woman would afford. As a result, she had little milk, and the infant died of hunger and cold. [77] In situations when the programs of aid provided the salary for the wet nurse, such aid was temporary. Assistance lasted for one month in the beginning of the century and ten months toward its end. Even if the aid was sufficient while it lasted, the mother had no way to provide for the child once the aid stopped. At that point she stopped paying the wet nurse, the baby was considered abandoned at the wet nurse, and the infant then became a ward of the state. This particularly unfortunate consequence of state aid—unfortunate because those very maternal bonds that officials wanted to see developed made later abandonment more wrenching for the mother—partially explains the increase in the mean and median age of children at abandonment after the 1850s.

Mothers abandoned their babies not for lack of love but out of dire economic need. In their notes, they did not regard abandonment as permanent. A few even stated, "Please take care of this baby until I am able to take him back." [78] Even when the mothers abandoned the babies surreptitiously, they frequently left enough information on the children so that they might later be able to find their offspring and perhaps reclaim them. Throughout the century many mothers saw abandonment as a temporary expedient until such time as they could reclaim their children. It was the best alternative they had, the most socially acceptable solution to their problem—but not the only alternative possible.

Mothers' Alternatives

The most obvious and best possible alternative to child abandonment for an unwed mother, of course, was not getting pregnant in the first place. In an era when contraceptive techniques and devices were neither widely known or available, nor were those available—like coitus interruptus—safe and sure, avoiding pregnancy usually meant not engaging in sex. But, once a woman became sexually active and then pregnant, she had very few alternatives; none was as acceptable as abandonment.

Abortion was one possible choice. As Angus McLaren has argued, abortion must be considered a "back-up method of fertility control."[79] In arguing for the availability of the *tours*, proponents posed them as an acceptable alternative to abortion. Proponents assumed that women of the working classes were familiar with abortive techniques or abortifacients and knew one of the main sources of such information and aid, the midwives. Midwives had a lucrative business in attempting to remove the fetus by manual manipulation of the uterus. They also used instruments such as a needle, and attempted to rupture the uterus to provoke the expulsion of the fetus. They were also purveyors of herbal concoctions including some efficacious ones such as ergot.[80] Women sometimes summoned doctors when an abortion threatened their lives. Doctors condemned the midwives both for performing abortions and for carrying babies to the foundling home. In part, their invectives against midwives resulted from botched abortions and in part, coincided with their moves to take childbirth practices and general gynecology and obstetrics out of the hands of the midwives. Abortion, however, like contraception of the time, was neither sure nor safe; indeed, it could frequently result in permanent sterility or even in the death of the mother. Furthermore, abortion was a crime, punishable by a fine and imprisonment. Unless a woman wanted to conceal her pregnancy, she had little reason to resort to abortion when abandonment was safe, sure, and legal.

Infanticide was another criminal alternative to abandonment, perhaps even a last-ditch, back-up method to failed contraception and abortion. There is no way of knowing quantitatively how many mothers resorted to infanticide. An unwed mother had many ways to kill a newborn without fearing a charge of infanticide. She could, for example, starve, suffocate, or put the child on a cold floor to die of exposure.[81] It was generally impossible to prove willful neglect resulting in death. Conversely, a few mothers may have been accused of killing their newborns when such deaths actually resulted from sudden infant death syndrome. This erroneous accusation of infanticide probably occurred only rarely since the incidence of sudden infant death syndrome is now, and probably was then, very low. Many cases of infanticide probably could go undetected because the infant was declared stillborn. Legally, a declaration of birth was required within three days of a delivery, and all infants who died before a declaration of birth was made were considered "stillborn." Stillbirths were remarkably higher for illegitimate than for legitimate babies, a statistic that perhaps reflects instances of infanticide as well as the poorer health of many unwed mothers. The mothers' poverty, poor diet, malnutrition, long hours of work, and lack of education and prenatal care more likely accounts for most of this higher rate of stillbirth among illegitimate children. Moreover, since so many mothers showed an attachment for their abandoned infants by giving them a name, most mothers were unlikely to resort to any form of infanticide, especially when abandonment, at least until 1852, was so easy. What mothers did after 1852 is somewhat more problematic.

The number of both abortions and infanticides may have risen when abandonment was no longer easy and anonymous, but the data are limited and unreliable. The available data derive from cases of abortion or infanticide brought before the courts. Thus, only the number of cases prosecuted, not the number of occurrences, are known. Furthermore, most of the women accused of abortion or infanticide were acquitted, suggesting that society was reluctant to penalize or condemn such women. [82]

There seems to be only a slight relationship between restrictions on admission and reported charges of abortions or infanticides despite the more than tripling of the average annual number of prosecutions in France from 1825-1830 to 1861-1865 (see table 3.12). The average annual number of infanticides prosecuted increased by thirty percent in the 1836-1840 period, and by seventeen percent in the 1851-1855 period over the average annual rate in the previous five years. These were the decades of major restrictions on admissions. Considering reported abortion, infanticide, and involuntary homicide of newborns by the mother all together, the five year periods with the highest increase over the preceding ones are just those years when restrictions on admissions were the greatest—1836-1840 and 1851-1855. Nevertheless, when the average annual number of infanticides of the 1851-1855 period is compared with that of the next five years (1856-1860), the rate of increase is fifteen percent—hardly much less.

Reported prosecutions for infanticide, abortion, and homicide committed against infants increased each year until 1860, but the twenty-one percent increase in the five year period from just before until just after the new restrictions was less than the twenty-seven percent increase for 1836-1840. The rise in prosecutions is probably due more to the population increase and perhaps to the greater efficiency of the justice system rather than to the suppression of the *tours* or other restrictive measures. [83] The average annual number of abortions, infanticides, and involuntary homicide of infants by mothers declined after 1861. There are several reasons, all conjectural, for this: admission of abandoned children became less restrictive in the 1870s thereby giving women less cause to resort to outright killing of their babies; the later years of the Second Empire and the early one of the Third Republic may have been

Table 3.12

Crimes and Misdemeanors against Children (annual average in France, 1826-1875)

Time Period	Infanticides	Abortions	Homicides	Total	Percent Change	Destruction of Birth Certificate	Grand Total	Proportional Increase	Crimes Against People	Proportional Increase
1826-1830	102	8	10	120		0	120	100 (base)	1354	100 (base)
1831-1835	94	8	53	155	+22.58	5	160	133	1547	114
1836-1840	135	13	75	213	+27.23	9	222	185	1593	118
1841-1845	143	18	76	237	+10.13	8	245	204	1695	125
1846-1850	152	22	83	257	+7.78	4	261	218	1778	131
1851-1855	183	35	109	327	+21.41	4	331	276	1880	139
1856-1860	214	30	123	367	+10.90	2	369	308	1753	129
1861-1865	205	24	132	362	−1.38	27	389	324	1717	127
1866-1870	206	17	101	324	−11.73	100	424	353	1626	120
1871-1875	206	20	70	296	−9.46	119	415	346	1687	125

Source: Lafabrèque, *Des enfants assistés*, p. 49, and Rachel G. Fuchs, "Crimes Against Children in Nineteenth-Century France: Child Abuse," *Law and Human Behavior*, vol. 6, no. 3/4 (January, 1983), pp. 237-259.

times of diminished police effort in detecting and prosecuting such cases; parents may have exhibited new, more nurturing attitudes toward their children which coupled with state financial aid would have made them less prone to kill their babies; or, finally, contraception may have been better known and more efficacious, which resulted in fewer unwanted pregnancies that terminated in the killing of the fetus or offspring.

A different light is shed on the picture by comparing crimes and misdemeanors against children with the average annual number of crimes committed against people in general. Here the difference is striking (see table 3.12). Crimes against people barely increased during the century, going from an annual average in France of 1,354 per year in 1826-1830 to 1,880 in the period of 1851-1855 and declining after that five year period to the end of the century. Taking prosecutions as real rates of crime, crimes against adults increased and decreased in the same years as did crimes against children. Suppression of the *tours* and restrictions on admissions had relatively little effect. Yet, the proportional increase of crimes against children was greater than the crimes against people in general. This, in part, can be explained by restrictions on admissions of abandoned children which resulted in their death, and in part on an increase in prosecutions of such cases. The increase in prosecutions may have been the result of new attitudes toward protection of children. Mistreatment of children to the point of their death—such as beating, starving or freezing—was increasingly considered a crime as new concerns about the welfare of the children become more prevalent after 1880. New attitudes toward children can be seen in the consideration of the destruction of birth certificates (*suppression et supposition de part*) as a crime against children. Not only did authorities become more concerned with children's physical well-being, but they also wished to protect their identity and civil status so they would have a greater chance in life.

Regardless of the increases and decreases in crimes against children and the reasons for the rate change, the average annual number of such cases of reported child abuse in all of France is very low when compared to the four to five thousand children abandoned annually in Paris alone. Figures for the department of the Seine, available only since 1868, preclude any study of the impact of admissions restrictions on infanticide and abortion. From 1868 to 1883 the number of prosecutions for both crimes taken together averaged one hundred per year. In 1884 and 1885 the number of reported abortions increased to half again as many and remained at that level for the remainder of the century. The number of prosecutions for infanticides remained constant at around fifty.[84]

Unfortunately, the data on stillbirths prior to 1853 are unreliable. Of the infants who died within the first three days of life, reportedly one child out of thirty-five was stillborn in 1839, one in thirty-four in 1843, and one in nineteen in 1873. [85] The restrictions on admissions may have contributed to the higher incidence of stillbirths, but the better reporting of infant deaths also may have led to the larger ratio. Given the number of stillbirths, reported cases of infanticide, and reported abortions, either most crimes against children were not detected or most women did not resort to these alternatives to abandonment.

Keeping the child was, of course, an alternative to abandonment, and undoubtedly many mothers who could, did. But the socioeconomic status of the women who abandoned their children meant that raising their children was not feasible. Keeping the child would have been, at best, difficult and, at worst, impossible. The program of aid to prevent abandonment was evidently sufficient to enable some mothers to raise their children, but inadequate for many others. For those who could not possibly keep their babies—due to shame, dishonor, financial distress, or nature of employment—child abandonment was legal, safe, and easy. The ease of abandonment was definitely important in a mother's decision to give up her child—the rate of abandonment declined when it was made more difficult and when lengthy interrogations of the mother preceded acceptance of the child at the Hospice, and the rate increased when rules and regulations made it simple for her to divest herself of her infant. The attitudes and policies of social welfare directly affected mothers and their children.

How Mothers Abandoned Their Children

From 1811 to 1826, a mother could abandon her child in one of several ways. She could give birth in the Maison d'Accouchement and the baby would be sent to the Hospice des Enfants Trouvés directly across the street, usually the same day the child was born. All the mother had to do was to state her desire to abandon the child. Those mothers who did not give birth at the Maison d'Accouchement but at home or at the place of the midwife either abandoned the baby herself at the Hospice, or paid the midwife to deliver the baby to the Hospice. A mother could also abandon her child simply by leaving the baby on the street, on a doorstep, or in a church. This method was rare, since it was punishable by a fine and imprisonment; abandonment at the Hospice was free and easy enough to make abandoning the baby on the street unnecessary. There were no restrictions for abandonment at the Hospice during these years. All who were left there were accepted, with no questions asked.

During the 1820s, more than one-third of the babies abandoned came directly from the Maison d'Accouchement when they were one day old. Another half of the children were infants left at the Hospice with a note that generally contained the mother's name, the date of the child's birth, and the name given to the child. This name did not signify baptism, although babies born in the Maison d'Accouchement were baptized immediately after birth. For these "anonymously" abandoned children, whether the mother, the midwife, or someone else who wrote the note actually left these babies at the Hospice is not known.

In the early 1830s abandonment became even easier for women who did not give birth at the Maison d'Accouchement. About fifty-six percent of the abandoned babies were left at the *tour*, thirty-nine percent came directly from the Maison d'Accouchement, and five percent came directly from other hospitals. Even with the *tour*, more than ninety-five percent of all abandoned children came with both first name and surname as well as a birthdate. Hence, even though the *tour* guaranteed anonymity, most mothers chose to give their babies some identity. The general pattern continued through 1837, with as many as forty-five percent of the mothers who abandoned their children leaving them at the Maison d'Accouchement to be brought across the street by hospital authorities to the Hospice des Enfants Trouvés. After the establishment of the Fondation Montyon in 1837, however, only thirty percent of the mothers abandoned their children at the Maison d'Accouchement, a decrease on the average of ten to fifteen percent from previous years.[86] When the state provided the option of aid to dependent children, many women accepted it and chose not to resort to abandonment of the infant.

In 1852, the surveillance of the *tour*, the interrogation of the mother at the Hospice, and the requirement of a birth certificate prior to admission changed somewhat the way in which mothers divested themselves of their children. A mother who could not, or would not, supply a certificate of birth for her baby or submit to interrogation could still submit to surveillance and abandon her infant at the *tour* during the hours it was open. She could leave the child on the street; such children were admitted, but very few mothers chose to abandon their children that way (see table 3.13). Surveillance was effective in decreasing abandonment at the *tour* and in increasing the number of children left on the street: the number of children abandoned on the street doubled from 1851 to 1852. Nevertheless, those left on the street remained only a small fraction of those who had been abandoned at the *tour*. Evidently, mothers who might have left infants at the *tour* either chose not to abandon them, submitted to questioning at the admissions office of the Hospice, or abandoned them with some intermediary. The requirement of the Maison

2) *Le tour de l'Hospice des Enfants Trouvés rue d'Enfer.* A lithograph by Granpré, 1862.

d'Accouchement, first enforced in 1852, which specified that mothers must stay in the hospital eight or nine days, nurse their children there, and take the infants with them when they left, served to reinforce the state's regulations and alter the mode of abandonment of some mothers. This measure, drafted following the survey of 1844, was designed to encourage the development of natural maternal ties.

Maternal ties may have developed in some instances, and some mothers who had planned to abandon their children may have decided to keep them, but such tactics did not always succeed. A *marchande des sucreries* on the Champs Elysées told the *commissaire de police* the story that one day just after noon, an unknown woman approached her and asked her to take care of the woman's infant for two hours. The mother said she had to go to the *quartier des Invalides* to see someone she knew who could, perhaps, take her on as a wet nurse. The mother said that her infant was nine days old. The *marchande* took the infant and waited for the mother's return until mid-evening. She then assumed that the infant was abandoned and went to the police with the child and the package of

Table 3.13

Abandonment at the *Tour* or on the Street, 1838-1860

Year	Abandoned on the Street Number	Percentage	Abandoned at the *Tour* Number	Percentage
1838	41	1.3		
1839	22	.7	294	8.8
1840	46	1.3	551	15.2
1841	32	.8	677	18.3
1842	25	.6	738	18.0
1843	14	.3	723	17.3
1844	25	.6	698	16.5
1845	19	.4	776	18.1
1846	32	.8	657	15.4
1847	30	.7	698	15.3
1848	17	.4	621	13.5
1849	32	.9	565	15.4
1850	19	.6	527	13.3
1851	26	.7	565	14.3
1852	51	1.5	513	15.5
1853	74	3.1	81	3.4
1854	86	2.5	144	4.2
1855	75	2.0	174	4.7
1856	87	2.2	197	5.0
1857	85	2.1		
1858	69	1.7	data are	
1859	66	1.7	not available	
1860	64	1.7		

Source: Dupoux, *Sur les pas de Monsieur Vincent*, p. 215.

effects left with the infant, which were abandoned with the child. The police filled out a report, and the infant was given the name of DesChamps because it had been abandoned on the Champs Elysées. [87]

This story exemplifies many such incidents. After 1852, the average and modal age of abandonment increased; the data of 1860 suggest that women left the Maison d'Accouchement with their babies as required and then walked across the street and abandoned them. Furthermore, from 1855 to 1865 the percentage of abandoned children arriving directly from the Maison d'Accouchement declined by more than fifty percent—from thirty percent of all abandoned children in Paris to 11.5 percent. An increasing number of babies were admitted at eight or nine days of age, when priests or police brought them in after the mothers left the children either with these officials or with people who delivered the infants to such officials. Although the data on this type of abandonment are irregular or unreliable, indirect abandonment seems to have increased substantially in the 1850s and 1860s, particularly after 1862,

3) From *Le Boulevard* by Gustave Doré. This is one of six vignettes titled *Paris Nouveau* taken from *Le Boulevard. Journal littéraire et artistique.* Paris, 1862-1863.

when the *tour* in the Hospice des Enfants Assistés in Paris finally closed (see tables 3.4 and 3.14). During the hours when the admissions office was closed, an employee of the Hospice received the abandoned children. This employee's position, with the title of *garde du tour*, lasted until 1943. By the 1870s virtually the only mode of admission was at the admissions office of the Hospice or the *garde du tour*. Once the restrictions on interrogation eased in the 1880s, mothers could freely deliver their children in person again.

About one-third of the abandoned children were admitted when the mothers brought the child there directly, but the other two-thirds of the women still would not, or could not, submit themselves to the admissions procedures. Their children arrived at the Hospice via an intermediary such as a police officer, a priest, an employee of another hospital, or directly from the wet nurse when payments from the mothers stopped (see table 3.14). Still, it was the mother who most frequently brought the baby to the Hospice.

Increasingly, in the last quarter of the century, a mother or midwife

4)   *L'enfant dans le tour de l'Hospice des Enfants Trouvés* and *La réception de l'enfant par les Soeurs.* An engraving by Henri Pottin (1820-1864).
Note: In all three illustrations a woman and a man both are abandoning a baby. In actuality only the mothers usually brought the baby to the Hospice.

relied on the local parish priest, who in turn delivered the child to the Hospice. Perhaps the women felt that some secrecy might thus be ensured, or perhaps they were unwilling to face interrogation at the admissions office. The interdiction against midwives abandoning babies was not regularly enforced, especially after 1870, when new attitudes prevailed favoring unrestricted admissions. In 1870-1873, 13.7 percent of the babies were brought by the midwife. In the 1880s, Michael Moring, the director of l'Assistance Publique, stressed the interest of the child, and admission requirements of both the birth certificate and the interrogation of the mother were not enforced.[88] Unfortunately, post-1873 data were closed to scholars in 1977, and there is no way to know whether more mothers delivered their own children to the Hospice for abandonment. After 1889, and the law making the *moralement abandonnés* wards of the state, police increasingly brought the children to the Hospice.

Table 3.14

Mode of Admission (1870 and 1873 combined)

	Number	Relative Frequency (in percent)	Adjusted Frequency (in percent)
Mother (unspecified where or how)	55	18.2	19.8
Police	47	15.6	16.9
Curé	44	14.6	15.8
Midwife	38	12.6	13.7
Mother at admissions office	37	12.3	13.3
Direct from *Nourrice*	18	6.0	6.5
Hospital or from Hospice	16	5.3	5.8
Administration	5	1.7	1.8
Dépôt	4	1.3	1.4
Nourrice or *Curé* to Hospice	3	1.0	1.1
Father at admissions office	2	.7	.7
Midwife to *Curé* to Hospice	2	.7	.7
Mother and Father at admissions office	2	.7	.7
Uncle at admissions office	1	.3	.4
Friend or neighbor	1	.3	.4
Friend of Mother or *Curé*	1	.3	.4
Voie Publique	1	.3	.4
Left with a note	1	.3	.4
Unknown	24	7.9	—
	302	100.0	100.0

Source: Compiled from data in AP, *Enfants Assistés, Registres d'Admission*, 1870 and 1873.

Although more than ninety-five percent of the abandoned children were newborn, some mothers faced the problem of abandoning the older, or weaned, child. The manner of, and requirements for admission were the same as for the infants. Moreover, there were three additional ways in which a mother could abandon older children; as abandonment of older children became more prevalent toward the end of the century, these modes of abandonment were practiced more frequently.

The most common form of abandonment of a non-newborn was directly from the wet nurse where the child had been sent as an infant.[89] Sometimes the parent had been making regular payments, after 1837 often subsidized by the state, and then payments stopped or state support stopped. The wet nurse, or her representative, was frequently unable to locate the parent. Under such circumstances, the wet nurse generally refused to keep the child, so she notified the administrators of the Hospice, l'Assistance Publique or the Direction des Nourrices (a bureau in Paris that recruited wet nurses and placed children of artisan and working-class mothers with the wet nurses from the country). If a search for the parents or another relative proved fruitless, the authorities considered the child abandoned. Sometimes the wet nurse (or foster parent) agreed to keep the child and receive her payment from l'Assistance Publique; sometimes she sent the child to the Hospice, and another wet nurse or foster mother was hired. When payment was assumed by l'Assistance Publique in these instances, the child was considered as abandoned *sur lieu*. Data are available for the years only after 1873 when abandonments *sur lieu* constituted roughly ten percent of the total. [90]

A second method of abandonment for older children increased in use during the latter third of the century. Many older children were left *en dépôt*—that is, in "temporary custody" while the parent was in prison, in a hospital, or in complete destitution. These children were usually brought in by the police. [91] If the parent did not return for the child, the child was considered to be abandoned.

The third way for a mother to get rid of an unwanted older child was simply to run off—often with a man who did not want the child. [92] The child would be left alone in the apartment, or on the street, "waiting" for the mother to return. The record books, as well as novels, contain numerous cases of such abandonments. [93] In *Les Misérables* not only Gavroche and his *gamin* friends but also the two Thénardier boys serve as examples. From time to time the police rounded up such homeless urchins and brought them to the Hospice. Some days saw ten or more older children brought in to the Hospice at one time. [94] Often the children were brought in together with siblings. The children were kept *en dépôt* until a parent could be located who reclaimed the child. Occasionally a parent came to reclaim the child or children within a few days. More often, no parent was found, and the children were entered in the *Registres d'Admission* as abandoned.

Conclusion: Maternal Love

Nineteenth-century French society prescribed a definite role for women—motherhood. At the same time it established a system whereby those women who could not assume that role could relinquish their unwelcomed children to the state. These women, by abandoning their children, were not *femmes denaturées* (unnatural). Generally, they were unmarried women of 22 years of age, born outside the department of the Seine and residents of Paris. They were employed as domestic servants, workers or day-laborers, or seamstresses. Typical of other working-class women in Paris, they differed from them only in that they had an illegitimate child whom they did not keep.

Abandonment of an infant for single, working women should not be taken as evidence for lack of maternal love. Many had to work to support themselves. In the absence of family support or day-care facilities, a job and baby were incompatible for many single women. Moreover, their wages barely covered the meager necessities for themselves, let alone the additional expense of a child. They could not afford payments to a wet nurse. Even if they struggled to keep their baby with them, their long hours of work and inadequate diet might render them unable to nurse. Women who abandoned their babies failed the "sacrifice" test, but their occupation, wages, and marital status gave them little they could sacrifice. With survival at stake, abandonment was the preferred alternative to keeping the babies and watching them die of starvation. Abandonment could even have been an act of love for the children if mothers believed that their offspring would have a better chance in life as wards of the state. They probably shared the current beliefs that the state should, and could, care for its weak and destitute citizens.

Much analysis of maternal love is speculative. There is some evidence, however, that is directly relevant. Despite the assurance of complete anonymity for the mother while the *tour* was open, more than ninety-five percent of the mothers left their babies with a given first name, surname, and birthdate. A mother probably would not give a baby a name and make sure the authorities knew its date of birth if they were devoid of feeling for the child. Stong bonds of affection and attachment to a baby, of either sex, was a luxury she could not afford. She had neither the emotional nor physical energy for it. Abandonment was a realistic option for her.

Mothers exercised this option in varying degrees during the course of the century. Abandonment declined erratically. Some nineteenth-century commentators linked the rate of abandonment to the illegitimacy rate. In the nineteenth century the two did not rise and fall at the same time and at the same rate. In fact, the illegitimacy rate never increased during the course of the century in the department of the Seine; rather it steadily declined. Consequently, this decrease in the proportion of women who had illegitimate babies cannot be the dominant cause of the decrease in the proportion of women who abandoned their babies during the century.[95] Edward Shorter suggests that a decline in child abandonment signals an increase in modern feelings of maternal love.[96] Two external developments, however, influenced the decline in the rate of child abandonment—the increase of aid to unwed mothers to prevent abandonment and the imposition of state rules and regulations which limited mothers' options for abandonment.

State social welfare policies more than other conditions (levels of poverty being equal) influenced poor womens' decisions to abandon their children. Aid to unwed mothers, first introduced in 1837, reintroduced in 1852, and made a large part of social welfare since the 1860s coincided with a decline in abandonment. When offered sufficient welfare aid to keep their babies, many women may have chosen to do so rather than abandon them. Up until the 1880s, restrictions on abandonment were in effect during the same years in which aid to unwed mothers increased. This combination of state policies was a more powerful influence on the women than sentiments of mother love. In the 1880s, when restrictions on abandonment were rescinded, abandonment again increased. Aid to unwed mothers to prevent abandonment was sufficient to enable some mothers to keep and raise their children. For those who could not keep their babies, even with aid, child abandonment was legal, safe, and socially acceptable.

The Hospice offered facilities to receive and maintain these "unwanted" children. The state condemned abandonment but acknowledged that it was necessary to receive and raise abandoned children. When abandonment was easy, more women left their children; when abandonment was restricted, fewer women did so. Public charity took care of all of those who were abandoned. In actuality, by abandoning a child, the mother was sending her child out to wet-nurse via the Hospice. In this respect, the single mother was not much different from her bourgeois, artisan, or working-class sisters whose habit it was to send children out to wet-nurse; on the other hand, the mother who abandoned her child could not expect to see or hear of him again. The Hospice took over the parental role of providing for the child's welfare, albeit indirectly through wet nurses and foster parents.

CHAPTER FOUR

In the Hospice

Above the door of the nursery for newborn babies in the Hospice des Enfants Assistés in Paris is the following inscription: "Mon père et ma mère m'ont abandonné, mais le Seigneur a pris soin de moi" ("My father and my mother have abandoned me, but the Lord has taken care of me").[1] In this case the Lord was a trinity composed of the director of l'Assistance Publique, the director of the Hospice, and the budget of the City of Paris. After the children left the arms of their mothers, the hands of Hospice authorities received them. The Hospice was not an orphanage or foundling home in a strict sense but merely a way-station, a temporary shelter for the children from the time they left their mothers to the time they went to wet nurses or foster parents in the countryside—which was as soon as possible. The state, department, city, commune, and Hospice in which the children were abandoned bore the fiscal and legal responsibility for feeding, maintaining, and raising the children. The institution of the Hospice did not replace the family, which authorities viewed as the best milieu for child rearing. The Hospice was merely a place where state social welfare for children began.

The treatment Hospice personnel gave the abandoned children during their stay there may, on one level, have been the best care possible, with the restricted resources and the rudimentary knowledge of disease, hygiene, and medicine in the nineteenth century. On another level, however, state and Hospice personnel did not place the children's and mothers' welfare ahead of other (particularly financial) considerations. Economy dictated the quality of child care, and budgetary concerns were more important than humanitarian ideals, at least through the 1850s. Conditions at the Hospice remained roughly the same from 1815 until

117

the 1880s, with minor improvements in the 1860s. Yet, the children's lives were affected by their short stay in the Hospice, and the care they received while there did not materially improve until after 1860.

Functioning of the Hospice:
Administration and Admission Procedures

Sources of revenue and allocation of fiscal responsibility affected the nature of the administration of the Hospice and the care and treatment of the children within it in many ways. The Hospice had financial responsibility for all of its internal expenses. These included the cost of the building and all utilities, wages and food for all Hospice personnel, medical expenses, clothing and food for the infants, and wages and food for the resident wet nurses. The department and the state had responsibility for all external expenses, most notably the salary of the wet nurses in the countryside and all expenses engendered by the children after they arrived at the wet nurses' or foster parents' houses. Therefore, the fewer number of days a child remained in the Hospice, the less the expense borne by that institution.

The Hospice depended for its revenues largely on private philanthropy, much as in the seventeenth and eighteenth centuries hospitals and other charitable institutions had depended on the piety and charity of individuals. In this sense, the Hospice was very much in keeping with the tradition whereby private, well-to-do individuals gave to the needy poor either as an act of Christian charity or as fashionable philanthropy. People left money—sometimes "conscience money"—to the Hospice in their wills, and such bequests and donations comprised a substantial portion of Hospice revenues. Bequests were frequently earmarked for certain types of children, for children entering a particular occupation, or even for a certain child. If the children for whom the money had been intended had died, the funds could go into the general fund of the Hospice. [2]

Private foundations and charities also sponsored benefit theatrical performances to raise money for the Hospice. Joseph Bouchardy's play, *Les Enfants Trouvés*, a sentimental tale of abandoned children, Saint Vincent-de-Paul, and his need for money for the poor children was presented for the first time in Paris in 1843. [3] It probably aimed to raise money for the Hospice and the worthy children. In the play Vincent-de-Paul wanders from city to city in search of alms, which are always insufficient; the ministers of state, the bourgeoisie, and the peasants all say how these have been bad years for them financially and all have an excuse for not contributing to the care of foundlings. He is concerned that for lack of funds he will not be able to care for the children, and then, by implication, they will be out in the streets causing great anxiety among the bourgeoisie. In the play, however, the foundlings were always gentle, God-fearing, and educable children. The play seems to be a plea for Christian charity for the poor, deserving children. This type of private philanthropy, always insufficient, was supplemented by revenues from police fines and from the treasuries of l'Assistance Publique and the department of the Seine.

The director of the Hospice headed the administrative staff. He was not a medical doctor but an appointed administrator. The director was immediately responsible to the special division of the Ministry of Interior for Hospitals and Hospices, and to the Conseil Général des Hôpitaux et Hospices Civils de la Ville de Paris. After 1849 and the creation of l'Assistance Publique de Paris, the director of the Hospice was immediately responsible to the director of l'Assistance Publique, not to the Ministry of Interior. The director of the Hospice was the authority in all policies and practices pertaining to the internal functioning of the institution—from admission of the babies to the fate of the children deposited there. A steward, who during most of the century was the Sister Superior, assisted the director in his duties. A chaplain, clerk-treasurers, a bursar, copying clerks, and an office boy rounded out the administrative staff of the Hospice.

The actual care of the children rested with Sisters of Charity and young laymen and lay women who served as their helpers (*filles et garçons de service*). These personnel aides carried out the daily functioning of the institution. Their duties included everything from taking care of the laundry, to staffing the admissions office, supervising the *nourrices sédentaires* (wet nurses resident in the Hospice), and delivering primary health care to the children in the nursery and infirmaries. The medical staff associated with the Hospice consisted of one physician who from time to time was complemented by one or two surgeons. They, in theory, made their rounds daily with the assistance of two intern students (similar to current American residents in medicine) and four extern students (similar to American interns). Doctors were appointed to their position at the Hospice. Of all the Paris hospitals, appointment to the Hospice des Enfants Assistés had the least status, (although an appointment in Paris carried more prestige than did any post in the provinces). The medical personnel associated with the Hospice were frequently the same as those assigned to the Maison d'Accouchement, thereby linking obstetric and pediatric service in the nineteenth century.

Babies came into the hands of Sisters of Charity without any formality after abandonment in the *tour*, or during the hours when the admissions office was closed—usually from 4 P.M. to 10 A.M. daily. Babies did not pass quite so easily from the mother to the Hospice personnel when she came to the Hospice herself to abandon the baby, or when she had an intermediary bring the baby, during the hours when the admissions office was open. The abandoner was then ushered into the admissions office where she was first interrogated—sometimes by a Sister of Charity, sometimes by the director himself, sometimes by a clerk, and frequently by an agent of the police who had been on duty as regulations in mid-century had required.

When police and Hospice authorities could not deter the abandoner from leaving the baby, the infant was admitted to the Hospice. The child's name was recorded on the *Registre d'Admission* along with his or her date and place of birth, mode of admission, the date and time of admission, and any information gained from the interrogation. The degree to which all information was recorded depended on the orders from the director of admission and the thoroughness of the admitting officer and the clerk. At the time of admission, each child was given an identifying number. The first child abandoned in a given year had the number one, and each successive admitted child received a sequential number. For example, a child with the identity number of 1849/3650 was abandoned in December of 1849. After 1865 admissions officers kept records sequentially, without differentiating the year of abandonment. Throughout the century, giving a child a proper and accurate identity was of utmost importance.

Admitting officials showed great concern for the name recorded for the child upon abandonment. When a child arrived with a birth certificate or an identifying note that included a name, the child was registered under the given first and last name. From 1814 until 1831, however, the first and last name with which the child arrived remained a secret from the wet nurse, from the *surveillants* (supervisors), and from the child itself. It was recorded only in the *Registres d'Admission*. During those years, the admitting officer gave the child another name upon admission. With their penchant for orderliness, the officials named the babies abandoned at the beginning of the year with a name starting with the letter "A" and those abandoned toward the end of the year were given names beginning with letters toward the end of the alphabet.

The names assigned were not unusual. There were no Duponts, Lafayettes, or other famous names, and there were also no Trouvés or Exposés either.[4] In a circular in 1823, officials were enjoined not to use such facetious names. Until 1831, the secrecy of the child's true name was maintained for two reasons. One was to protect the family name of the mother and to preserve her anonymity—honor her supposed wish for concealment. The other reason was to prevent alleged abuses in the system. Some bureaucrats believed that a mother would abandon her child and then seek employment as a wet nurse: They "wished thus to avoid having the true name of the child be known by the wet nurse in order to hinder the ruse often employed by the unscrupulous parents who might otherwise succeed in raising a child supported by the state without losing that child from view."[5] After 1831, no pseudonyms were given; the abandoned child kept and was known by his or her given and family name. Secrecy for the mother was no longer deemed of paramount importance. Ease of record keeping and the desire to deter abandonments, coupled with the realization that mothers did not abuse the system to get back their children, may have supplanted the desire for secrecy.

When an infant was abandoned without any identity given and without a name, the *procès-verbal* was transcribed from the *Registres d'Admission* to the registers of City Hall, and the *officier de l'état civil* gave the baby a name. This name, according to official circulars of 1812 and 1823, "must not be the same for all *enfants trouvés* as is customary in many parts of the Empire."[6] The circulars urged that each name must be distinctive. They specified that an infant should receive two names; the first was considered as a baptismal name and the other a family name for the infant, transmittable to her own descendants. To guard against confusion, officials were told not to give the same name to several children: "We have too many children with the same name in the army, in prisons, as deserters"[7]—a statement highly indicative of where authorities expected the abandoned children to wind up! Furthermore, a name belonging to existent families should not be used. The officials were advised to modify several letters in order to obtain an infinity of combinations.

Circulars further stipulated that all names should be avoided which would be indecent, ridiculous, or suggestive of abandonment. Names in the history of past times, in botany, in the arts, and in the circumstances particular to the existence of the child, such as his traits, his coloring, the countryside, the place or the hour when he was found—all of these would be appropriate. An examination of the *Registres d'Admission* reveals that the surnames Trouvait, Trouvé or Trouvay (all names found in the 1977 Paris telephone directory) were not assigned although Dieudonné was. Other names taken from such diverse sources as streets or color or hair—for example, des Champs and Blonde—were used. In the granting of names, some humanity was shown toward the child; perhaps because no extra expense was involved in doing so. And it made police and army records more efficient.

Functioning of the Hospice: Initial Care of the Children

Once a child was properly enrolled on the *Registres d'Admission*, the child was immediately given an identification tag so that no switching of babies could occur. The tag guaranteed the child a proper *état civil*. Until 1818 there were two identifying signs attached to the child and to his clothing. The Sisters attached to the baby's bonnet a *parchemin* (parchment) on which the registration number, the Christian name and surname, the date of birth, and the date of entrance into the Hospice had been inscribed. This *parchemin* was green for the boys and white for the girls. Because it was merely affixed to the bonnet, it can be assumed that it soon disappeared, fell off, or become torn, crumpled, and unreadable. In addition to this paper each child received a band on his left arm which consisted of a paper on a *ruban de fil* (tape). On the paper was inscribed the year of abandonment (admission to the Hospice) and the identification number. [8]

On December 24, 1817, a decree of the Conseil Général des Hospices stipulated that henceforth all children received by the Hospice would receive a necklace affixed in such a manner that it could not be removed. It was of three millimeters thick silk cord (blue or green for boys, pink or red for girls) and was strung with seventeen olive shaped beads of bone. The ends were joined with a medal—a lump of lead or pewter about one inch in diameter and one-quarter inch thick. One side of the medal had a picture of Saint Vincent-de-Paul; on the other side, the word "Paris," the identification number the child received upon admission, and the year of admission were inscribed. Henceforth, the records referred to the child as the number *n* of the year *x*. [9] Except for a short period in 1843 and 1844, when earrings were used instead of necklaces, the custom of using an identity necklace prevailed for the remainder of the century. The only change noted in the records was that a medal of silver replaced one of pewter after 1850. [10] These necklaces were to be worn at all times, until the child was at least six years old. The same necklace was to fit both a newborn and a six-year-old child, and be relatively comfortable on both.

The purpose of the necklaces was twofold: to insure correct identification of each child and prevent the mixing up of babies (a humanitarian and bureaucratic gesture), and to insure that no wet nurse got paid for

5) Identification necklace worn by the infants. It consisted of a silk cord and a silver medal. From A. Dupoux, *Sur les pas de Monsieur Vincent.*

the wrong child or for a child who did not exist (an economic concern). An investigation of 1818 had shown that about eleven thousand children, some who had been dead for years and the others, who had never existed at all, were listed on the accounts from which the wet nurses were paid; these payments represented a loss of 300,000 francs per year.[11] The necklaces were to stop the "theft" from the government and to decrease expenditures. Such identification procedures did not entirely succeed in eliminating fraud. In 1847, Boicervoise, Administrateur des Hôpitaux et Hospices de Paris, found it necessary to issue a circular to the *préposés* (agents in the provinces) insisting that no payments be made to wet nurses without a certificate of life issued by the mayor; the mayors were not to issue the certificates without seeing the children with the

123

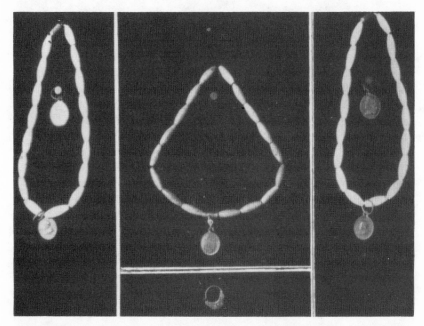

6) A style of necklace made of bone beads and pewter medal. Necklaces of silk
    cord were used more frequently than those of beads of bone. In the lower
    center of the picture is the earring used in the 1840s. From A. Dupoux, *Sur
    les pas de Monsieur Vincent.*

necklaces attached. [12] When the child died, the necklaces were to be sent
back to the Hospice. A few voices spoke out against the necklaces, arguing that it "was inhumane to show the children to all the world with the
stamp of their reprobation." [13] But most contemporaries considered the
necklaces necessary identification. [14] When identification procedures
were completed, the child was taken by a *fille de service* to the nursery
where he was undressed, washed, and dressed in warm and dry clothes
issued by the Hospice.

The infant's Hospice clothing consisted of a bonnet, short shirts, a
sleeved undershirt, and a *maillot* (swaddling clothes) "of good quality
linen or outer swaddling clothes of strong wool material." Dr. F. S.
Ratier, the Hospice physician in 1830, felt that such swaddling clothes
were indispensible in an institution of that genre. [15] Swaddled babies took
up less room and required less attention than freely moving ones. They
could be put two-to-a-bed and there would be little danger of swaddled

babies flailing about and hitting one another. Swaddling clothes also served to keep infants warmer in winter. But even Dr. Ratier noted that the application of swaddling clothes had a few inconveniences; specifically, the clothes were wrapped too tightly. He said it was difficult to impress upon some people the importance of keeping the child free from all compressions, restraints, or crushing. Even though doctors disapproved of total swaddling, and the practice was disappearing from middle-class homes during the nineteenth century, it persisted in the Hospice out of expediency.

If the attending physician was on duty at the time the children were admitted, he examined them after they had been registered and cleaned and dressed. If the children arrived at the Hospice at a time when the doctor was not on duty, the children stayed in the nursery until such time as the doctor and his intern made their rounds and examined them, usually the morning after admission. If the doctor declared the children healthy, they remained in the nursery; if they were ill or moribund they went to the infirmary. Many children merely passed through the nursery to be taken immediately to the infirmary. [16] If they had died between admission and examination, the doctor sent the children's bodies to the *amphithéâtre des morts* where he might later perform an autopsy. To be certain that each child was baptized, each morning all infants received the previous day were carried to the chapel where the chaplain baptized them. [17]

Older children were admitted in the same way as the infants. They were brought to the admissions office either by parents or by an intermediary such as a wet nurse, priest, relative, or usually the police. After registration and examination, Hospice personnel took them to dormitories rather than to the nursery. The Hospice had two dormitories for these older children—one for boys and the other for girls—and they were separated by a courtyard. The older children who had been abandoned stayed in the dormitories until such time as they went to foster parents—usually a matter of days. Many older children, however, were provisionally abandoned and said to be *en dépôt* until such time as the parents were located or were able to reclaim the children. The children at the Hospice *en dépôt* were usually those picked up off the street and brought in by police, or those whose parents were in a hospital or under arrest. If after several days, the parents could not be found and the children could not be reclaimed, their status changed from provisionally abandoned to definitively abandoned,and they went to foster parents or, if ill, to another hospital.

No children stayed in the Hospice for any significant amount of time.

The administrators aimed to get the children out of the institution and to wet nurses or foster parents as soon as possible. Most abandoned infants stayed in the Hospice for three days, at which time they went with a wet nurse to the provinces (see table 4.1). All but the sick soon left. The sick were placed in the infirmaries until they were well enough to be transported to the country or, more frequently, until they died. Until mid-century the median age at which infants, including those who had been in the infirmaries, were sent to wet nurses was, therefore, just five or six days, while most were sent to wet nurses at four days of age. In the 1850s, the more restrictive abandonment procedures led to a slight increase in the age of infants at the time of abandonment; the median age of children sent to wet nurses was from two weeks to a month old (see table 4.2). The higher mean age of one to two years for placement of children during the second half of the century reflects the greater proportion of non-infant abandonments (see table 4.1). Only those children who were *en dépôt* remained in the Hospice for more than a few days at any time during the century. Such a short stay was in their best interests, for conditions in the Hospice were far from ideal.

Table 4.1

Number of Days Spent by a Child in the Hospice
and Age of Child in the Hospice (in days, 1820-1870)

Year	Mode Age Abandoned	Mode Number of Days in Hospice	Mode Age Sent to Wet Nurse
1820	0	3	3
1825	0	3	3
1830	1	3	4
1835	1	3	4
1840	1	3	4
1845	1	3	4
1850	1	3	4
1855	1	5	6
1860	9	3	12
1865	2	1	3
1870	1	4	5

Source: Computed from data contained in AP *Enfants Assistés, Registres d'Admission.*

Conditions in the Hospice

The physical environment was cold, dirty and overcrowded, and the babies generally lacked adequate postnatal care. The *crèche* (nursery) where the nuns took the newborn abandoned infants was formerly the

Table 4.2

Age of Children Sent to Wet Nurses or Foster Parents

Year	Mean Age to Wet Nurse (Days)	Median Age to Wet Nurse (Days)
1820	21	5.5
1825	—	—
1830	39	6
1835	64	5
1840	264	6
1845	171	8
1850	227	6
1855	548	26
1860	381	20
1865	382	23
1870	721	33

Source: Computed from data contained in AP *Enfants Assistés, Registres d'Admission.*

chapel of the novitiate of the *Institution de l'Oratoire*. It was a large, vaulted room, measuring roughly ninety-five feet in length, thirty-two feet in width, and approximately twenty-two feet in height (equivalent to two floors). It contained eight windows and only one fireplace. The one wood fire kindled there "never brought the temperature in this large room above 11.5°C."[18] In December 1814, the doctors expressed dissatisfaction with the chilly temperatures and shortly thereafter two big stoves were installed. The nursery contained four rows of iron cribs, each draped with white curtains. There were eighty cribs at the beginning of the century, increasing to eighty-five in 1862. The *crèche* was always overcrowded, with no more than one-and-a-half feet between cribs. The cribs were mounted on small wheels and could not be rocked, "much to the great detriment of the nurslings."[19] The stability of the cribs was a mixed blessing since it was suspected that some infants had often been rocked so hard that they were rocked into insensibility.[20] In the Hospice, however, it was highly unlikely that anyone had time or inclination to rock the babies.

Cleanliness may have been a middle-class virtue, but reports of it in the Hospice for working-class babies were mixed. In 1830, Dr. Ratier, who was the attending physician of the Hospice, reported on the general cleanliness and hygiene in the nursery: "The most extreme cleanliness is a condition *de rigeur* in the rooms which received the children, in their cradles, their clothes, on the persons who take care of them and on the children themselves."[21] In 1860, however, the inspection and inquiry into the general conditions of the service of *enfants assistés* reported the

127

terrible conditions and *insalubrité* of the Hospice.[22] Little was done in the way of cleaning, modernizing or refurbishing during the thirty years between one report and the other. In 1864, in the aftermath of the investigation of four years earlier, the nursery was thoroughly cleaned and repainted for the first time in over twenty years. There is no record of any further changes in the nursery for another twenty years.

A room the size of the nursery, heated by only one fireplace and two stoves, could never have been warm in winter. Even on the occasions when the temperature may have risen above 11.5°C, the heat was not uniform in the room, and there must have been tremendous variations in the heat and cold, and great drafts due to the high ceilings. Such dramatic changes in temperatures were certainly detrimental to the infants, especially the weak and sickly, despite their wool swaddling. The nuns and their aides changed, warmed, and sometimes washed the babies on a cot or padded shelf placed in front of the fireplace and then put them back in their cribs.[23] No mention was made of a bathing area or a place with water for cleaning the babies regularly. Bathing did not have the same importance then as it does now.

There were, at the most, eighty-five cribs in the nursery and ninety cribs or beds in the infirmaries for a total of under two hundred places for babies to sleep. The average number of children present in the Hospice on a given day was three hundred. Thus, the healthy infants probably slept two in a crib.[24] Two persons, or more, occupying the same bed was a common practice in the nineteenth century. Such doubling-up may even have helped keep them warm, perhaps harmfully warm in the heat of summer.

Conditions in the infirmaries were no better than in the nursery and remained much the same from the beginning of the century through the mid-1870s.[25] The medical services of the Hospice were divided into three major sections: the medical infirmary, the surgical infirmary, and *Salle de l'Ophtalmie*. The infirmaries occupied the second floor of the central building. The *infirmerie de médecine* held thirty-seven cribs, and the *infirmerie de chirurgie* held thirty-two cribs. Both were served by one Sister and five *filles de service*. These were the statistics for both 1826 and 1876; there had been no change in fifty years. The medical and surgical infirmaries seemed to be similar to large hospital wards of roughly seventy-five feet by twenty-four feet, and the opthalmology ward was somewhat smaller. There could not have been much more than a foot of space between the cribs, hardly commodious conditions.

The *Salle de l'Ophtalmie* was referred to as the *Salle Verte*, because the curtains were of green calico, the walls painted over in green, and even the window panes were green so as to not tire the eyes of the infants afflicted with ophthalmia (an unspecified inflammation of the conjunctiva of the eyeball). It was believed that patients afflicted with this eye disease were particularly sensitive to light. Because doctors believed ophthalmia was very contagious, those infants afflicted were placed in isolation. They lay on individual beds or cribs with bandages over their eyes. [27] The Sisters did not seem to appreciate this color, because they felt that the colored light from the windows hindered their ability to judge the state of the infants. Why ophthalmia was so common is not known. It may have been the eye disease that infants got during the birth process. If gonorrhea bacteria were present in the birth canal, they could infect the babies' eyes, resulting in eventual blindness. This is the eye disease that doctors have been preventing since 1884 by putting a few drops of silver nitrate in the eyes of newborn infants.

Conditions in all three infirmaries left much to be desired. Money for the medical services proved insufficient and Hospice personnel were able to provide only basic medical or custodial care for the infants in the infirmaries. [28] Furthermore, personnel failed to maintain basic cleanliness in the infirmaries not only as we know it but even by nineteenth-century standards. In 1830, Dr. Ratier complained that the infirmaries "needed to be a little more frequently aired or better ventilated. The odor of the excretions of such a large number of children is sometimes painful to bear." [29] He recommended that vases of chlorinated water placed in the room might be sufficient to dispel the odor. It seems not to have occurred to the poor doctor that increased staff to attend to diapers and cleanliness might have provided a solution more attuned to the infants' well-being. Instead he proposed an olfactory cover-up. In 1838, two hundred or more orphans and abandoned children over the age of two were moved to the Hospice upon the closing of the *Hôpital des Orphelins*. The only change in the Hospice was the addition of one infirmary with twenty more beds, so that doubling children in cribs had to have occurred even in the infirmaries. "An insufficiency in the service in the infirmaries"—overcrowding and unwholesome air—resulted. [30] Reformers and the director of the Hospice, writing in 1837 and 1839, complained that the infants were placed too close to one another in the infirmaries. They wanted to institute changes so that there would be no more than twelve to sixteen cribs per room. [31] Thirty years later, Dr. Victor Hutinel commented on the situation in the early 1870s and echoed the complaint. He stated that "nurslings are placed side by side in cribs too close, the mildly ill alongside those more sick, [and, to compound these crowded conditions, the rooms all faced north and were] always sombre, and dismal."[32] René Lafabrèque's analysis of conditions in the Hospice in 1876 shows the same number of cribs in each infirmary as had been there in 1826. And, as Dr. Ratier had done almost half a century earlier, he criticized the conditions. He stated that "although infirmaries were large enough for the number of sick children housed there, there was a lack of ventilation. The disjointed floor boards served to collect the dust; the heating system is brutal and in no way is suitable for the needs of sick children."[33]

Despite the insalubrious environment, sick children received special treatment in the infirmaries. The examinations and treatments, however, varied little during the first three-quarters of the century.[34] Each morning the doctor and an intern made the rounds and examined the infants in the infirmary; they also examined those in the nursery to determine if any should be transferred to the infirmary. To facilitate examinations, the doctor requested that the infants be placed in the nude. A doctor or intern then examined the children, "to see their 'conformation,' the color of their skin, and their temperature and degree of firmness. In the 1830s he employed the techniques of tapping and of sounding; listened to the cries 'to which his trained ear is very sensitive'; tapped the abdominal region and glanced at the excreted matter; examined the oral cavity and the pharynx and terminated the examination by an 'exploration of the pulse.' "[35] Dr. Ratier complained, however, that the Sisters did not completely undress the children for the examination due to "a modesty laudable in principle."[36] Perhaps they did not completely undress the children because they were too busy or too tired or because it was just too cold in the building.

In the 1870s rather than "tapping" and "sounding," doctors conducted slightly more scientific, but not necessarily more thorough, procedures. According to Dr. Hutinel, since most of the sick children were nurslings, "the physician sat next to their cribs, examined them, weighed them, looked at their tongues, took their temperature, and at the same time dictated a brief, but precise observation." After the examination of the children in the infirmaries, during the entire century doctors went to the amphitheater "to perform autopsies on some of those who had died during the night," examining "all organs to amass data to serve for the history of *athrepsie* [cellular hardening and wasting away] and hereditary syphilis," the two most commonly cited "diseases" at the Hospice.[37]

Doctors frequently diagnosed a child admitted to the Hospice as suffering from hereditary syphilis although the children did not necessarily die from the disease itself. There is cause to question this diagnosis. Most children were abandoned within a day of two of their birth, and only in very rare cases do infants present these symptoms at the moment of their birth. Doctors may have been prejudiced in diagnosing syphilis. Since they believed an unwed mother to be engaged in debauchery and vice, they assumed a sickly child would have the common disease of such vices. Symptoms do, however, occur within the first two weeks of life, so for a child more than a week old the diagnosis may have been correct. The symptoms were obvious: "raised, flat plaques, scaly or damp, the color of copper, which appeared on the forehead, in the armpits, and around the parts of the genitals; there are grayish ulcerations in the corners of the lips, in the interior of the mouth, in the anus."[38] There is no mention of how doctors treated children with diagnosed syphilis other than by inadvertently hastening their death with artificial feeding.

Doctors attempted to treat *athrepsie*, the other commonly diagnosed ailment, by *bains de vapeur* (steam baths). First, they rubbed the entire body of the infant with *l'eau tériacale* (a stimulating liquid) and then completely wrapped the infant in flannel, which they then covered with a sticking plaster. Thus "dressed," the doctor placed the child in a steam bath. As Dr. Baron described it,

> Every morning, thermometer in hand, I put some fifteen of the newborns affected with hardening of the cellular tissue, in a steam bath, to which by conscience and by humanity I submit myself as well as them. These poor infants and I, get out of these sweating baths, red as boiled lobsters. These suffering skeletons of human forms let out cries.[39]

It seems doubtful that this treatment did any good, even as symptomatic relief. With this "boiling," the high mortality figures for such infants is hardly surprising. The use of *bains de vapeur* is the only described medical treatment in the Hospice records for abandoned children.

Doctors spent little time at the Hospice and certainly were not the only health care deliverers. Sisters of Charity and their aides carried out daily nursing care, both in the infirmaries and in the *crèche*. But throughout the century, in varying degrees, the lack of sufficient and adequate personnel by modern standards affected conditions in the Hospice and the treatment of the children.

Sisters of Saint Vincent-de-Paul headed the nursing service and *filles de service* assisted them. The duties of both Sisters and aides included feeding, changing, and cleaning the children. In 1830 there were three Sisters and eleven nurses' aides in the nursery, which housed from eighty to one hundred and fifty infants—or one member of the nursing service for every seven to ten children overall. This ratio was similar to that of

7) "L'Enfants et le Bain." Illustration by Noël Dorville for *L'Assiette au beurre*, no. 32, November 9, 1901. Issue was titled, "L'Assistance Publique."

London's Foundling Hospital a half-century earlier. [40] The entire staff was probably not on duty at one time. Given standard working hours in the nineteenth century it seems likely that there were two shifts a day, or that at night practically the entire staff slept and left the children unattended. If, however, there were three shifts per day, the effective care was one nurse for every twenty to thirty infants. (By comparison, U.S. regulations for infant day care in 1982 require one adult for every four children.) Two Sisters and eleven nurses' aides served in the infirmaries. For the sixty-nine beds in the infirmaries, not including those in the *Salle Verte*, the ration of nursing staff to children is slightly better than in the nursery; a ratio of 1:7, or allowing for three shifts, a ratio of 1:21. The general ratio of the total number of nursing staff to children in the Hospice during most of the century was 1:10. Assuming three shifts, the ratio was 1:30.

The nurses' aides were "for the most part, girls of the country—from the Auvergne and Brittany, specially chosen by the representatives of the Administration in the provinces. . . . They were assiduous, very devoted and necessarily unselfish in an institution where the *pensionnaires*, not ever having a penny, can not give a tip." There were reputedly women of good heart and intelligence. Dr. Ratier reported that, even though few in number, the Sisters and the aides handled the children with "sweetness, dexterity, and great zeal."[41] Female *enfants assistés*, predominantly those over the age of twelve who were not placed with an artisan or farmer in the countryside or who were sent back to the Hospice from the country due to illness or behavioral problems, further augmented the nursing personnel.[42]

Even though the nurses' aides supposedly had the virtues of devotion and kindness, because of the lack of care-taking personnel, children were neglected—especially those in the infirmaries. Observers were "surprised at the number of infants lying under blue curtains with their eyes hidden by a damp compress," for their diagnosed ophthalmia. "Despite the comings and goings of servants who hurry around their little beds, despite the active and well-meaning presence of the Sisters, who are admirable nurses, the child—at the moment when he had the greatest need to be cared for and pampered—is in a desperate solitude."[43] Again, "since the number of nurses is not large enough, this among other inconvenience prolongs the stay of the children in the bed, not without detriment to their health." In an attempt to "remedy" this problem, "the children are staggered eight to ten on a sort of *lit de camp* at some distance from the fire." There they could stay "for several hours" just "covered almost entirely with a thin sheet." Once they finally fell asleep, "after having cried more or less for a long time," only by lifting the sheet could anyone know of their existence—a long line of silent, sick children, solitary and alone.[44] Neglect, even by nineteenth-century standards, as much as inadequate diet and disease accounted for the high mortality rate.

Infant Feeding

Whether the children were ill in the infirmaries or well in the nursery awaiting departure for wet nurses in the countryside, adequately feeding the hundreds of abandoned babies at any one time in the Hospice presented enormous problems for the administrators. There is no more crucial barometer of the care of the children in the Hospice than an analysis of how and what they were fed. In theory, some thirty *nourrices sédentaires* (resident wet nurses) fed the one hundred or more children in the nursery but not the infants in the infirmaries, out of fear of infecting the wet nurses. Ironically, those children who were ill and most in need of good nourishment received milk of the most dubious quality and in the most unsanitary way.

Once a month, the director of the Hospice required each field representative or agent for specified rural areas of France to send a few wet nurses to Paris who remained in the Hospice as *nourrices séden-taires*. These women had to be married and ideally were either mothers of stillborn, deceased, or soon-to-be weaned children. If their babies were alive, they often brought them along. Upon the women's arrival in the Hospice, the doctor on duty examined them to ascertain if they were in good health and if they were producing milk. Those who did not pass the examination were sent back. The expenses for their trip were borne by the Hospice. The Hospice director tried to make sure that his field representatives sent good wet nurses—or, he accepted those not quite ideal in order to save the money of the return trip, and give the infants at least some minimal care.

The director constantly found it very difficult to recruit *nourrices sédentaires*. In a letter to a field representative at Saint-Calais, in 1847, the director stated that the "hospice does not have at this time sufficient *nourrices sédentaires*, and it is essential to increase the number. I ask you therefore to do all that you can to send me one or two who are in the desired condition by your first shipment. It is necessary that the milk be as young as possible. Let me know if you can satisfy my request." [45] There were many such letters, particularly since conditions at the Hospice were not attractive to women selling employment and their milk.

Until mid-century the wet nurses lived in the dormitories in the attic eaves above the nursery. Their quarters were narrow, and cold in winter and hot in summer. [46] There were thirty beds for them and thirty cribs for their own infants. In 1859 the Administration improved a few conditions for the *nourrices sédentaires* in order to induce more to accept the position. The "diet of the *nourrices* received a notable amelioration. Their ration of wine, which was only twenty-two centiliters was at this time increased to thirty-two centiliters and to the quantity of boiled beef, which the *nourrices* received each day, was added [a portion] of roast meat." [47] These improvements, and others, were spelled out in a letter asking the field representatives to send more wet nurses:

> Please look in your area for *nourrices sédentaires* whom we lack at the Hospice. Make a good choice so we do not have to send them back in one

month as we do for certain *arrondissements.* You know that the food for the
wet nurses has improved. Their wages have increased to twenty francs per
month, and, if they stay at the Hospice for some time and do their work
well, they would be rewarded with a bonus when they leave the Hospice.
Please consider this request as urgent.[48]

Even though it was extremely difficult to recruit married wet nurses to
stay in the Hospice, the Administration was reluctant to hire unwed
mothers as wet nurses because people believed that the "immorality" of
such women would be transmitted to the abandoned babies via the
nurses' milk. Therefore, they preferred married women of good morals
and of good health, and these women were the most difficult to recruit.
Married women were probably (and understandably) reluctant to leave
their husbands and farms to go to Paris to stay and nurse, unless they
were impoverished and needed both the money and the room and board
provided by the Hospice for *nourrices sédentaires.* In the winter, when
times were harder and the women could be spared from agricultural
work, the shortage of *nourrices sédentaires* was not as substantial.[49] By
1864 the director of the Hospice had again increased the salary for the
nourrices sédentaires from twenty to thirty francs per month. Still,
recruitment difficulties continued due to poor pay, the unwillingness of
wet nurses to leave their families in the country, the chance of nursing
sick infants (especially those with undiagnosed syphilis), poor working
conditions, and the constant changing of nurslings.[50]

In the early 1860s, for a variety of reasons (concepts of transmission of
morality were beginning to change, the Hospice was in a truly desperate
situation, the preservation of the lives of the foundlings was assuming
greater importance), the director, Eugène Ory, solicited unwed mothers
as *nourrices sédentaires.* He urged the field representatives, "to make
every effort to convince these women to come to Paris." He qualified his
request, however, by asking for "advance warning" and "assur[ance]
that, aside from their situation as unwed mothers, they still have
character traits which warrant our confidence."[51]

The situation must truly have been urgent, for in 1860, the number of
nourrices sédentaires ranged from fifteen to twenty-five, and not the full
complement of thirty for which there were beds. Furthermore, the administrator at the time felt that there should be forty. He knew that the
Administration was cognizant of the means to improve the conditions to
induce more to come; he urged them to take such measures. Aside from
using unwed mothers from the countryside and from the Maison d'Accouchement, Parisian young adults who had, themselves, been aban-

135

doned children, and who, as their mothers before them, had a child out of wedlock were taken on by the Hospice as *nourrices sédentaires*. Since they were wards of the state until they reached twenty-one, if they bore an illegitimate child they had little choice but to serve as *nourrices sédentaires* when asked to do so. The state had parental authority until the children were twenty-one.

If there were fifteen to twenty-five *nourrices sédentaires*, each one had to nurse four or five infants. Each wet nurse may also have had her own child to nurse; a wet nurse's own infant—unless already weaned, dead, or in the care of a relative or neighbor—came with her to the Hospice. A crib next to the bed of each *nourrices sédentaires* specifically for her own child attests to the presence of the wet nurses' own infants in the Hospice. Thus, a wet nurse most likely was nursing five to six infants, one right after another. Under such circumstances, no abandoned infant got enough milk, because the *nourrices sédentaires* could not possibly produce enough. The obvious solution was artificial feeding of cow's or goat's milk by bottle, even in the nursery. In fact, most sources confirm the existence of artificial feeding in the nursery when the "number of wet nurses was insufficient—in other words, almost always. [52]

While an attempt was made to feed all babies in the nursery by wet nurses, all infants in the infirmary were fed artifically; they were not nursed because of fear of contagion. Hospice personnel suspected most of the babies in the infirmaries of carrying syphilis. Artificial feeding was, in a sense, justified by the mode of transmission of that disease. Syphilis could be communicated from an infected mother to her child during gestation and birth. That child could in turn infect a wet nurse from contact between the mucous membranes in the child's mouth and the nipple of the wet nurse. The wet nurse could then infect her spouse and all other children whom she nursed or later bore. If a wet nurse did contract syphilis from an abandoned child, she was entitled to an indemnity—which represented an additional expense for l'Assistance Publique.

Indeed, almost all children in the Hospice were at some time during their brief stay fed artificially. In 1806 a diet was established for feeding all children. For those infants nursed by *nourrices sédentaires* the diet provided a supplemental feeding; children who were not nursed received the same diet with double the amount of milk. [53] All children under six months of age received one-half liter of milk (a full liter for those not nursed), fifty grams of bread for *panade* (a type of soupy bread and milk mixture), fifty grams of *vermicelle* (pasta), and forty grams of sugar.

In 1838 roughly the same diet was still being followed, although authorities recognized that there should be a difference between the diet of newborns and that of six-month-old children, and quantities of food were reduced. The recommended diet for infants under six months was: two-fifths liter of milk, thirty grams of bread for *panade*, twenty grams of *vermicelle*, and an unspecified amount of sugar. Authorities were unsure of the need for sugar in children of this age, and therefore left the amount of sugar up to the discretion and budget of the doctors and the chief officers of the institution. For infants under one month, officials proposed that they be given, as a further dietary supplement to the wet nurse's milk, an additional one-fifth liter of milk and thirty grams of sugar.[54] As with the 1806 diet, any child not serviced by a wet nurse was to have double the amount of milk (four-fifths of a liter). This recommendation was a frank admission that the number of wet nurses and the quantity of milk were insufficient enough to warrant further supplemental feeding; it was an equally candid acknowledgment that infants might be fed artificially for reasons other than illness.

By modern standards, the formulas proposed in 1838 do not seem unusual or particularly indigestible for an infant. The mode of feeding these formulas to the children was particularly noxious, however, since sterilization was unknown until the late nineteenth century. Dr. Ratier described the feeding in 1830 in a few words: "The milk, more or less cut and sugared, is given to the infants in a *gobelet*."[55] Given the shortage of nurses' aides and the number of children to feed, measurements may not always have been accurate nor time and attention given to feeding the babies. Furthermore, cutting the milk surely introduced unsanitary water, and, of course, unpasteurized milk from dirty hands on dirty cows was not so clean either. Besides, the milk mixture contained *fécules* (starch) and *crèmes de pain au lait*.[56] Dr. Ratier did insist that *bouillie* (pap or cereal) and fats not be fed to the babies under six months of age.

Hutinel's description of the situation in 1876 deserves to be quoted in its entirety. It was written after he, and other doctors, realized how existent conditions contributed to infant deaths.

Milk, contained in large jars, exposed to all dust, rested in an office situated in the center of the rooms where, from morning to night, it was contaminated by germs that dry sweeping would raise up several times a day. There was no sterilization, hardly any cleanliness. . . . When the infant cried, the nuns prepared something for her to suck upon made of a pinch of biscuit crumbs wrapped in a cloth rag poultice moistened by a sticky syrup exposed to all germs. Soon a rash appeared, a stubbornly virulent rash, then vomiting and diarrhea. Weight loss was hundreds of grams per day, and the drama of *athrepsie* or dehydration followed, slowly or rapidly, according to the season. In summer, an infant was transformed in twelve hours. In the morning, she

137

was pink and lively; at night, she was bluish, cold, and moribund; she had "turned," as the nuns said, who likened this development to fermentation. . . . I cannot . . . remember without sadness this period of my medical life. The light did not shine. Some years later, we discovered the causes of infant mortality; only a bit of cleanliness and some precautions were needed to reduce mortality in the same hospice by eighty percent. [57]

Milk that had been sitting out all day was fed to babies by a spoon, a cup, or a *biberon* (bottle). If fed by a spoon, it was probably the same one used for several children and was perhaps from the communal pot of milk mixture. The feeding took up much time on part of the nurses' aides. An infant who was fed by a cup probably shared the cup with several other babies, and, again, milk most likely sat in the cup for hours. (And an infant with just a sucking reflex probably got little nourishment with cup feedings, ingesting far more air than milk). A *biberon* was a baby bottle and, by modern standards, an acceptable mode of feeding a baby. In the nineteenth century, bottles were usually of glass, but were sometimes made of cylindrical pieces of wood, and the nipples were pieces of rubber stretched over the top. Wood absorbs and holds particles of milk. The *biberons*, though probably refilled for each baby, certainly were not sterile, may not even have been rinsed, and those of wood had absorbed sour and germ-ridden milk. As was said at the time, "the *biberon* and death go hand in hand." [58]

To counteract the fatal results of feeding of milk to an infant by means of a spoon, cup, or *biberon*, new ways were sought to feed infants. Doctors felt that the problem with such feeding was that the *biberon* came between the mammary gland and the mouth of the infant. The *biberon* was blamed as the intermediary responsible for the lack of success of artificial feeding. Therefore, it was believed, suppressing the intermediary and placing the nursling directly at the udder of the animal would solve the problem. The milk would always be at a constant temperature and sheltered from external air and all impurities and alterations. [59]

Dr. Boudard's *Guide pratique de la chèvre nourrice au point de vue de l'allaitement des nouveaux nés et de la syphilis constitutionelle* advocated placing the child directly at the udder of a hornless goat. [60] Not only was a goat better than a *biberon*, but a goat was also better than a mercenary wet nurse. He attributed the slow increase of the population of France both to mercenary wet nurses who fed the infants with a *biberon* and to the artificial feeding of *enfants trouvés*. A *chèvre nourrice* was excellent since the quality of milk could vary according to the diet of the goat, and the goat would come to love the child. Furthermore, whereas the vices of the wet nurse could be transmitted to the child, the goat has no social vices to transmit. There were those who claimed, perhaps tongue-in-cheek, that the traits of the animal would be absorbed by the infant: "It has been suggested that [Paul] Bert, who as an infant was nursed by a goat, owed to that animal some of his independence of mind, fantastic gaity, petulance and vivacity."[61]

In 1881 Dr. Parrot, the director and resident physician of the Hospice, established a model nursery to feed the infants afflicted with syphilis. It consisted of two rooms, each room with eight cribs and four beds for the *infirmières*. There was one nurse for two infants. Nurses were with the infants day and night. In the stable of the model nursery was a cow, an ass, four goats, a mare, and even dogs. In the eight-month experiment of this model nursery, eighty-six infants were fed there five times per day, from 7 A.M. until 8 P.M. and twice during the night. The mortality rate was the lowest for those nursed by the *pis d'ânnesse* (udder of an ass).[62] Not only was the mortality rate lower for those infants fed with the donkey milk, but a donkey was cheaper than a cow since it could nurse several infants at a time and would eat any grasses. The mortality rate for those fed by the udder of a goat was high for children under eight months of age; therefore goats were eliminated. Needless to say, the experiment was not controlled. Several years later it was determined that feeding an infant from the *pis d'ânnesse* had fatal results for the infant. In this model nursery, the higher ratio of *filles de services* and nurses to infants in and of itself may have substantially contributed to the decrease in mortality.

Dr. Marfan, the physician at the Hospice in the 1880s, claimed that infants fed with the *lait d'ânnesse* (milk of a donkey) often had serious digestive troubles. Cows' milk was not satisfactory for children under one month. A mother's milk was best; in the absence of that, the milk of donkeys was second. Newborn spyhilitic infants were initially given donkeys' milk, which was low in fats and relatively easy for a newborn to digest. After a few weeks, the infants ceased to gain weight, at which time cows' milk, diluted with water and supplemented with sugar, was given. As sterilization became wide-spread in the early 1890s, however, the model nursery was eliminated, and sterilized cow's milk and its derivatives became the staple diet. In 1897 the Pouponnière (Nursery) at Antony, a suburb of Paris, was opened, and all abandoned newborns were placed there and fed safely. The wet nursing of infants thus ended.

Experiments in feeding to improve the infants' health and reduce infant mortality were not the only measures that became successful only in the latter part of the century. Other changes also helped in the reduction of deaths in the Hospice by the 1880s, but not until many children who were cared for there had died.

8) "La crèche de l'Hospice des Enfants-Assistés" from *L'Illustration*, March 25, 1882.

9) "La crèche de l'Hospice des Enfants-Assistés" from *L'Illustration*, March 25, 1882.

10)   *Les Enfants Trouvés*. A lithograph by Marlet, 1831.

11)   La "Nourricerie Modèle" from *L'Illustration*, July 1887.

Death in the Hospice

Each day a child spent in the Hospice increased the chance of death. The mortality rate for abandoned children just during their brief stay in

141

the Hospice remained spectacularly high—twenty to thirty percent—for the first half of the century and decreased erratically thereafter to a fairly reasonable level by its end—two to five percent (see table 4.3 and figure 5). [63] In other words, prior to 1850 roughly one-quarter of all abandoned children at the Hospice des Enfants Assistés died during their short, three- to four-day stay. The mortality rate of children in London's Foundling Home in the early part of the nineteenth century was twenty-six percent—roughly corresponding to that in the Hospice, and in the eighteenth century more than twice that proportion of children died. [64] But the data are not precisely comparable between the London and Paris foundling homes. Children in the London foundling home appeared to be much older and reside there for much longer periods of time than those in Paris. These two differences would severely affect the mortality rate and render a true comparison virtually impossible. Furthermore, after 1834 in England, most illegitimate children went to the workhouses with their mothers and many died during their first year. High mortality for illegitimate infants was not unusual. In the three to six days after birth, all infants are most vulnerable, but the mortality rate for those abandoned in Paris is extraordinarily high, considering it applies to infants at risk for only about ten days. Indeed, the mortality rates in the Hospice during the first half of the century were already so high from other causes (and the children's length of stay was so short) that the rates were not appreciably affected by the cholera epidemics of 1831-1832 and the 1850s.

The stated causes of death at the Hospice were varied. Except for the higher incidence of *athrepsie*, diarrhea, and pneumonia, the causes were similar to those for the infant population of France during the same periods, just in greater numbers. *Induration*, or *athrepsie*, remained the most common cause of death throughout the century (see table 4.4). *Athrepsie* was not a disease but a general weakening and eventual death due to the nurslings' inability to assimilate or digest food. Infants became very thin and their tissue—both skin and internal organs—hardened. Physicians described it as the *endurcissement du tissu cellulaire.* Too much solid food too early in life or food with too high a salt content caused it. Doctors perhaps suspected its etiology, for Dr. Baron claimed that a prolonged stay at the Hospice without good wet nurses contributed to deaths from *athrepsie.* [65] Improper infant feeding was also the basis of the second most frequently cited cause of death, diarrhea.

Other causes of death not directly attributable to infant feeding (but certainly not ameliorated by the diet) occurred with lesser frequency and

Table 4.3

Mortality of Abandoned Children at the Hospice

Year	Number Admitted	Number Died	Deaths per 1,000	Comments
1815	5080	1447	285	
1816	5080	1465	288	
1817	5467	1562	286	
1818	4779	1354	283	
1819	5057	1367	270	
1820	5101	1473	289	
1821	4963	1294	261	Gradual substitution of
1822	5040	1221	242	cribs made of iron for
1823	5116	1333	261	those made of wood begun
1824*	5213	1189	228	in 1821.
1825	5240	1223	233	
1826	5392	1414	262	
1827	5446	1486	273	
1828	5497	1444	263	
1829	5370	1534	285	
1830	5283	1541	292	N.B. No significant in-
1831	5667	1556	275	crease in mortality 1831-
1832	4928	1391	282	1832, the years of cholera
1833	4803	1258	262	epidemic. Only 7 recorded
1834	4941	1230	249	deaths from cholera in
1835	4877	1081	222	1832.
1836	4972	1253	252	
1837	4664	1376	295	
1838	3207	765	239	
1839	3354	871	260	
1840	3628	897	248	
1841	3698	1048	283	
1842	4095	1171	286	
1843	4178	1092	261	
1844	4223	1120	265	
1845	4296	1130	263	
1846	4260	819	192	
1847	4554	946	208	
1848	4597	837	180	
1849	3671	686	187	
1850	3952	686	174	
1851	3940	800	203	
1852	3303	552	167	
1853	2380	262	152	Increase in *nourrices*
1854	3441	609	177	*sédentaires.* 8 deaths from
1855	3700	726	196	cholera, 1853. Epidemic
1856	3943	689	175	of dysentery and cholera,
1857	3993	812	203	Epidemic of measles, 1858.
1858	3960	1009	254	
1859	4002	886	221	
1860	3799	713	187	
1861	3768	707	204	

Table 4.3

Mortality of Abandoned Children at the Hospice

Year	Number Admitted	Number Died	Deaths per 1,000	Comments
1862	3613	524	145	Inspection, cleaning re-
1863	3469	409	118	modeling and increased
1864	3786	421	111	food and salary for
1865	3942	428	109	*nourrices sédentaires,* 1862
1866	4273	523	122	17 deaths reported from
1867	4469	468	105	cholera, 1865
1868	4651	442	95	
1869	4260	357	84	
1870	4451	743	167	War
1871	3423	617	180	War and Siege
1872	3551	252	71	
1873	3336	241	72	
1874	3146	210	67	
1875	2338	213	91	Epidemic of Scarlet Fever.
1876	2260	128	57	
1877	2320	178	77	
1878	2760	164	59	
1879	2774	156	56	
1880	2730	170	62	
1881	2834	195	69	
1882	2746	189	69	
1883	3151	218	69	
1884	3128	136	43	
1885	3137	98	31	
1886	3257	76	23	
1890	3621	136	38	
1895	4516	239	53	
1900	5090	101	20	

*For all the years the number admitted is the number of abandoned children according to Hospice records. However, from 1824 until 1867, the records are unclear as to whether the number dead represents *only* abandoned children who died, or includes the deaths of those left temporarily *en dépôt* as well. After 1867 the figures for the number who died represent only those officially abandoned who died and does not include children temporarily left at the institution.

Source: Compiled from data in AN F[20] 282[39-44] and *Rapps. Anns.*, 1852-1890.

varied in their prevalence during the century. Few children died of syphilis while in the Hospice, although in 1878 Dr. Parrot attributed more deaths to syphilis than to other diseases, and "pustules" cited early in the century as a cause of death may actually have been the symptoms of syphilis. The increase in deaths from pneumonia and croup— not listed in the 1810s at all but the stated cause of death from the 1840s to the 1880s in ten to twenty percent of the cases—is probably due, at least in part, to changing nosology. Some "coughing sickness"

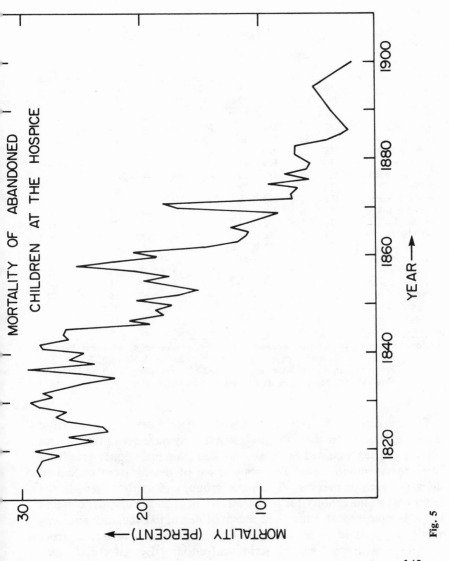

MORTALITY OF ABANDONED CHILDREN AT THE HOSPICE

MORTALITY (PERCENT)

YEAR →

Fig. 5

deaths early in the century may be buried in the statistics for "weakness at birth." Since pneumonia and diphtheria were associated with older children, moreover, the incidence of such lung and throat ailments points to the greater median age of abandoned children after mid-century. Dr. Parrot claimed that those who succumbed to pneumonia were likely to have been tubercular or syphilitic, and pneumonia also appeared as a complication of measles.

Table 4.4

Most Commonly Cited Causes of Mortality

| | 1814-15 | | 1816-19 | | 1841 | | 1878 | | 1882 | |
	No.	%	No.	%	No.	%	No.	%	No.	%
Induration (*athrepsie*)	707	25	1554	28	346	33	91	19	—	28
Diarrhea	587	22	964	16	540	51	—	—	—	—
Weakness at birth	378	13	725	12	—	—	—	—	—	—
Eye infection	126	5	629	11	—	—	—	—	—	—
Premature birth	207	7	481	10	—	—	—	—	—	—
"Pustules"	29	1	385	6	—	—	—	—	—	—
Ictère (jaundice)	104	4	341	6	—	—	—	—	—	—
Arrived moribund	179	6	326	6	—	—	—	—	—	—
Syphilis	38	1.5	86	1.5	—	—	118	25	—	12
Convulsions	22	1	86	1.6	—	—	—	—	—	—
Scrofula	8	.3	17	.2	—	—	—	—	—	—
Pneumonia (broncho-)	0	—	0	—	170	16	47	10	—	9
Smallpox	3	—	2	—	12	1	6	1	—	—
Measles	0	—	0	—	—	—	87	18	—	20
Diptheria and croup	—	—	—	—	—	—	50	11	—	9
Edema	—	—	—	—	—	—	26	5	—	—

Sources: Compiled from data contained in Dupoux, *Sur les pas de Monsieur Vincent*; deGerando, *Bienfaisance publique*; Parrot, "Clinique"; Steward, *Hospitals of Paris*; and mortality tables in AN[20] 282[35-44]. For the years 1814-1815 and 1816-1819 the percentages are the best possible estimations.

Certain causes of death were age-specific. Those who died from *athrepsie* were under three months old and may have been prone to this condition when admitted.[66] Those who died from pneumonia were from three to six months old. The appearance of deaths from childhood diseases—such as measles, diphtheria, croup, and scarlet fever—in the latter half of the century further attests to the presence of older children in the Hospice. Most other cited causes of death, like jaundice and convulsions, appeared as secondary symptoms of other diseases or from high fevers associated with all serious infections. "Eye infections" too, so prevalent as a cause of death early in the century, were probably symptomatic of other illnesses or of more general systemic infections. That *ophtalmie* was not listed as a major cause of death after 1841 is in part also due to fashion in diagnosis, as is the lack of pneumonia cases before 1841.

In general, the infants arrived at the Hospice in poor health which probably contributed to their early death. The meager diet and general physical condition of the mothers made it unlikely that the fetuses received adequate nutrition *in utero*, and the life-style of the mothers made it equally unlikely that they obtained any prenatal care. Unwed domestic servants, who spent all day in a kitchen without ventilation and all night under the eaves of a dirty, drafty room, which was hot in summer and cold in winter, could not have been in the best of health.[67] Hard manual labor also contributed to the poor health of the mother and of her unborn child.[68] Extreme poverty, malnutrition, and the weakened condition of the mother or previous attempted abortions in some cases compounded the mothers' problems and led to the birth of infants who were weak, premature, or already ill at the time of delivery. The deWatteville Investigative Commission of 1860 concluded that a principal cause of mortality at the Hospice was the infants' weakness upon arrival—a weakness that in part resulted from the poverty of the unwed mother.[69]

The deWatteville Commission cited several causes of mortality, but the prime one was the lack of proper feeding and the lack of mothers' milk or suitable wet nurses. In 1861 the commission charged to study the causes of mortality of *enfants assistés*, headed by Dr. Hervieux, concurred, citing only the age of the infant at abandonment as more important. There were eight causes of mortality:

1. Age of infant at abandonment.
2. Lack of natural feeding, that is, nursing.
3. Abuse of the horizontal position.
4. The bad condition in which one finds a great number of newborns upon their admission to the Hospice.
5. The administrative measure by which all women who gave birth in *Maternité* [also called the Maison d'Accouchement] must keep their infants with them up to and including the moment when they leave the Hospital.
6. The custom, which had existed, that all children stay in the Hospice until the scab forms around their smallpox vaccination.
7. The legal formalities to which most of those admitted are submitted—that is, long waits in the Bureau d'Admission, or trips to the Mairie for a *procès-verbal* or birth certificate.

8. The uncleanliness, lack of nurses and the lack of wet nurses in the *crèche* and infirmaries of the Hospice.[70]

Although all of the causes cited contributed to the high mortality rates, the last was the most frequent complaint of some reformers as well as some directors and doctors at the Hospice during the nineteenth century. There were constant complaints that fifteen to thirty wet nurses for the more than eighty-five to one hundred healthy babies were insufficient, and that crowded and unsanitary conditions in the nursery and infirmaries were life-threatening.

Hospice to Hospital

Improvements in the medical care at the Hospice des Enfants Assistés prior to 1860 were minimal. In the 1820s and again in the 1850s, Hospice administrators had worked to increase the number of *nourrices sédentaires*; at both times they succeeded at least temporarily. But the only other advance occurred in the 1820s when "cribs of iron were gradually substituted for wooden ones and thus separated the children from the incommodious insects that trouble the sleep so necessary to their age."[71] Indeed, in the first sixty years of the nineteenth century, the building was cleaned and repainted just once, in the 1830s.

In the wake of the investigation of 1860 into the mortality rate of children in the Hospice, several—still minimal— changes occurred. Not only was the building thoroughly cleaned and repainted once again, but some remodeling was done. The cleaning alone may have contributed to more hygienic conditions. The salary of and food for the *nourrices sédentaires* were also improved. The more nutritional diet may have led to the better health of and better milk from the wet nurses, and possibly the increased pay led to a less impoverished class of *nourrices sédentaires*. Better conditions for them certainly aided in attracting more wet nurses, and their augmented numbers probably contributed to the slight decrease in infant mortality during the decade. Substantial changes in Hospice care did not, however, occur until the 1880s. With the pasteurization of milk and other medical discoveries of the late 1880s and 1890s, the Hospice des Enfants Assistés became, by the end of the century, more of a pediatric hospital than a foundling home.

It was only in 1882 that Pasteur's germ theory of contagion and disease was accepted by the established medical profession in the state institutions, and that the director of the Hospice acted on this knowledge. Coinciding with the growth of new knowledge of diseases and with the establishment of experimental medicine, the Hospice des Enfants

12) Entrance to l'Hôpital Saint Vincent-de-Paul. 1977 photograph by Norman H. Fuchs.

Assistés underwent major structural changes in the 1880s. Three new infirmaries were added, and the existing ones were modernized in keeping with new ideas. In the 1880s six additional doctors were assigned to the institution, bringing the total number of attending physicians and surgeons to seven, with a complement of interns and externs.

With the Hospice's new infirmaries, the 1880s and 1890s saw two major changes—antiseptic disinfection and isolation of children with contagious diseases. Under the initiative of René Lafabrèque as the director of the Hospice, coupled with the energy and zeal of Drs. Parrot and Hutinel, the Administration established a quarantine station for new arrivals in order to avoid contamination of the children by illnesses not yet identified in the newly admitted. They isolated those with suspected cases of contagious diseases. In addition, within the infirmaries, they inaugurated the isolation of those infants with infectious diseases such as diphtheria, measles, or scarlet fever. To accomplish this they constructed a multiplication of rooms. The big rooms of the infirmary included isolation boxes containing two beds and separated from one another by glass enclosures.

Hutinel, as the doctor of the Hospice in the 1890s, began a large-scale,

149

13) Chapel of l'Hôpital Saint Vincent-de-Paul. 1977 photograph by Norman H. Fuchs.

regular disinfection program. He ordered the disinfection of the spoons and tongue depressors used to examine throats, stethoscopes, other medical instruments, and the bed linen and babies' clothes. Previously, the same instruments and clothing were used for many children, both for well ones and for those with differing diseases. It is hard to believe that before the 1880s these items were used from one baby to another without sterilization. Previous directors and doctors cannot be faulted for not isolating contagious diseases or for not sterilizing and disinfecting articles. They did not see the necessity.

14) Main building of l'Hôpital Saint Vincent-de-Paul which existed during the entire nineteenth century. Dormer windows on the mansard roof indicate the lodging quarters of the *nourrices sédentaires*. 1977 photograph by Norman H. Fuchs.

Another medical advance of the 1880s and 1890s was the pasteurization of milk and the concomitantly better knowledge of infant formulas. In these years artificial feeding became safe and sanitary, and the mortality rate of children fed by bottle was no longer exorbitantly high. The safety and practicality of artificial feeding meant that abandoned infants could be cared for in an institution for longer periods of time. The Administration of l'Assistance Publique had a building constructed in Antony, on the outskirts of Paris, specially designed for newborn abandoned babies. This Pouponnière, as it was called, opened in 1897. From that time forward all newborn abandoned babies deposited at the Hospice des Enfants Assistés were transported to the Pouponnière. There, infant-care personnel fed the babies from a bottle until foster parents were found for them and they were old enough to travel safely to the countryside. Henceforth, the Hospice des Enfants Assistés served as a pediatric hospital, eventually becoming the major pediatric medical center that it is today.

Conclusion: Budgets not Babies

Given the deplorable state of medical knowledge prior to mid-1880, it is not so surprising that so many babies died in the Hospice—rather, that

151

15) Courtyard of l'Hôpital Saint Vincent-de-Paul with inhabitants of the institution. 1977 photograph by Norman H. Fuchs.

any of them survived. Perhaps so high a percentage survived because they spent only a few days there. Hospice personnel sent them to wet nurses as soon as possible. What at first glance seems to have been quick distribution of children among wet nurses to save money, may upon closer examination have served the child's best interest. The lack of modern medical practices, the shortage of personnel, and the poor physical and nutritional conditions of the Hospice, to say nothing of emotional neglect, means that children could be no worse off with wet nurses in the country than in the Hospice.

16) Courtyard of l'Hôpital Saint Vincent-de-Paul with statue of St. Vincent in center. 1977 photograph by Norman H. Fuchs.

But the questions remain. Why the neglect in the Hospice? Why the lack of a sufficient number of nurses and *nourrices sédentaires*? Was it just a matter of economy? Officials knew about the high mortality rates, about dietary inadequacy and the problems of artificial feeding, and about overcrowded conditions and staffing deficiencies. They seemed to give less thought to the welfare of the children than they did to questions of economy. In the twentieth century, it has been customary to place the welfare of children above other considerations. This was not the case for abandoned children in nineteenth-century Paris. "Economy—that is now the watch-word of the service [des Enfants Assistés]. . . . Such is the consideration to which all other preoccupations except perhaps basic hygiene are sacrificed."[72] While economy may have been the key motivating force in the treatment of the children in the Hospice, at least until the 1880s, it was not always merely a heartless administrative philosophy; rather, it was sometimes a pragmatic response to the lack of public support for society's cast-offs and the resultant lack of funding.

Conditions in the Hospice were deleterious to the lives of the children in large part due to insufficient funds and the current state of medical knowledge. Even by early nineteenth-century standards, however, better care could have been taken of the children. Doctors of the time realized

153

that conditions were dirty and that the Hospice lacked wet nurses in both quantity and quality. To some extent authorities knew what to do to save lives—separate sick from well babies, keep things cleaner, and above all increase the nursing and wet nursing staff—but they could not, or would not, appropriate more money to alleviate the distress. Nevertheless, against terrible odds and under the worst conditions (including financial insufficiencies and inadequate medical knowledge) the French central government and Hospice authorities took responsibility for a difficult social problem and managed to save many newborns from immediate death in the Hospice by sending them out.

Despite the terrible conditions in the Hospice up to the 1880s about seventy percent of the abandoned infants survived the few days they spent there, and were expedited to wet nurses in the country. The Hospice and its staff did not function *in loco parentis* for children without their own family. When the state supplanted both the parents and the *Seigneur* in providing for unwanted children, it assumed what had been the legal, moral, and financial parental responsibility. Nevertheless, it was not the role of a public institution to raise the children. Government authorities hired wet nurses or foster parents to perform that duty for it. The family milieu of the wet nurse or foster parents was to be the proper setting for maintaining, raising, and educating the abandoned children. The state, theoretically, fulfilled its obligation to keep a watchful eye on their wards through placing the children with the families and following these children until they reached adulthood. This necessitated an elaborate administrative apparatus to recruit wet nurses or foster parents, to distribute the babies around the country, to inspect their charges and foster families, and to pay foster parents. Consistent with economy and with the notion that children were better off in families than in institutions, Hospice authorities wanted to be rid of the babies as quickly as possible. France was unique in assuming state responsibility for the children's welfare and in sending them from institutions to families. A bureaucratic structure developed to take the children and provide for their care after they left the Hospice.

CHAPTER FIVE

Spreading the Wealth

No one in Paris had both the desire and the ability to take care of the thousands of children deposited at the Hospice des Enfants Assistés each year, not the mothers who left them, nor the Hospice which initially received them. Hospice authorities hastened the babies into the homes of rural wet nurses. The children then stayed in the locale to which they were sent, ideally with the same wet nurse, until they reached the age of seven, or in many circumstances, until age twelve or older. The wet nurses were similar to foster parents, and it is useful to think of them as such. The state hired and paid them to maintain the children whom the biological parents could not keep.

Foster parentage resolved two potentially conflicting aspects of nineteenth-century French attitudes and policies toward abandoned children: state responsibility and proper socialization by a family. On the one hand, as a heritage of the ideals of the French Revolution, the state, in theory at least, assumed responsibility for the welfare of its citizens. These included the weakest and most vulnerable—the abandoned children. Napoleon then gave the state the legal and financial responsibility for keeping alive and raising these children to become economically and militarily useful, law-abiding citizens. On the other hand, French authorities viewed the two-parent family, with a lactating mother, as the means to keep the babies alive and, for the children who lived, as the approved socializing agent, and the most effective arena for instilling correct moral virtues. By this system, moreover, the state took financial responsibility and still utilized a family for the socialization of the young. Throughout the course of the century, the state gradually assumed more control and responsibility for the abandoned children by the continuous influence of state officials and state-paid professionals on their lives and on their foster parents.

By the time the state exercised rather complete control of and took full responsibility for abandoned children in the 1880s, the administrative apparatus for dealing with the problem had been in effect for almost a century. The practice of sending abandoned Parisian children to wet nurses in the countryside began in the eighteenth century, became structured at the turn of the century, and persisted throughout the nineteenth century. Sending the children out to wet nurses had long proved to be the most cost- and labor-efficient method of maintaining the four to five thousand children abandoned annually. It provided not necessarily the best care for the children, but may have been the best care possible under the circumstances for most of the century. It did prevent the children from receiving little or no care at all, and it got the children out of institutions and into homes, although with some of the poorest families and with initially inadequate supervision and inspection. The system also spread the responsibility—fiscal, medical, familial, and administrative. In effect, child-rearing for abandoned children was a shared enterprise by families and the state throughout the nineteenth century.

Fiscal and Administrative Apparatus

Fiscal responsibility for the children loomed foremost in the minds of the administrators. All expenses incurred by the children while they were in the Hospice constituted internal expenses borne by the institution. The Service Extérieur of the Service des Enfants Assistés bore fiscal responsibility for all other expenses: payments to the wet nurses and foster parents (by far the greatest expense), clothing for the children, payments to the doctors and inspectors, payments for medicines for the children and for doctors' visits in times of illness, extra payments to the foster parents if a child were infirm or incapacitated and could not work, and the cost of inhumation if a child died. Early in the century the Ministry of the Interior had supervisory control of these expenses; after 1849, l'Assistance Publique administered the distribution of funds and exercised supervisory jurisdiction of all Parisian children placed with foster parents.

Even though the children abandoned in Paris went to wet nurses in many other areas of France, none of the provinces, departments, or communes that received the abandoned of Paris had to pay for the maintenance of the children; in fact, localities usually reaped the benefits of the children's future labor and productivity and received added in-

156

come, spent in the local economy, from payments to the wet nurses. The department of the Seine and the city of Paris held fiscal and administrative accountability for the care of the children abandoned in Paris. A subsidy from the national or state government, prorated according to the needs of the department, completed the financial resources for the Service Extérieur des Enfants Assistés. The state, however, did not give each department as much as it needed or wanted. Until the late 1860s, legislation fixed the state subsidy at a specific number of francs per year. A promulgation of 1869 re-allocated fiscal responsibility prorating the subsidy to the departments from the national treasury at one-fifth of the total expenses of the Service Extérieur. Likewise, the Conseil Général des Hospices regulated the allocation from the departmental budgets so that it did not exceed one-fifth of the total expenses of the Service Extérieur. [1] The money came from general funds as well as from donations, foundation gifts, and legacies specifically earmarked for the welfare of the abandoned children. Proceeds from police fines and special allocations from departmental and communal budgets brought additional funds.

It is ironic that in a highly centralized state with a form of social welfare specifically regulated by ministerial decrees of a central government, the financial responsibility for abandoned children was decentralized. The national government would not, or could not, bear the entire expense, so it passed most of the burden for the maintenance of these children on to the departments in which they were abandoned. By doing so, state officials speculated that each department, in an effort to limit the expenses for the maintenance of abandoned children, would make child abandonment difficult, would endeavor to limit the number of abandoned children and, hence, the burden on state and local treasuries. This particular type of decentralization was not unique to the administration of welfare to abandoned children. From the Counter-Reformation (if not before), charity and welfare was of concern to the local magistrates, notables, and lords. It remained a local concern in the eighteenth century, when the largesse of the king supplemented local treasuries. In the nineteenth century, even though provisions for the insane, incurables, and abandoned children were set forth by national decree, the implementation of, and most of the funding under these decrees was left to individual departments. A subsidy from the state replaced the beneficence of the crown. Welfare for abandoned children thus differed little from other types of social assistance. Charity, obviously, began at home.

The administrative branch of the national government that bore the legal authority for all abandoned children in France was the Ministry of Interior, with a subdivision of that ministry solely for the service of *enfants trouvés, abandonnés, et orphelins pauvres* in all of France, including Paris. In addition, in Paris, a separate organization had the administrative responsibility for all of the hospitals, hospices, and social welfare institutions in Paris, including the Hospice des Enfants Trouvés *(*Assistés). This was the Administration Générale des Hôpitaux, Hospices civils et Secours à Domicile de Paris: Service des Enfants Trouvés et Orphelins de Paris (hereafter referred to as the Administration).[2] Administrative responsibility for the children abandoned in Paris and sent to the countryside rested with officials in Paris.

In 1849, legislators and officials removed the entire administrative responsibility for the *enfants trouvés, abandonnés et orphelins pauvres* of Paris from the Ministry of Interior and created a new metropolitan organization committed to social welfare institutions: l'Assistance Publique de Paris.[3] The state thus extended its power and control over the abandoned children by establishing a separate administrative apparatus just for their care; while creating more bureaucrats and administrators, it also increased the number of inspectors and medical personnel. During the era of paternalistic social reform of the Second Empire, l'Assistance Publique played an active role. Having taken stringent measures to control admissions of abandoned children, the authorities made efforts to take better care of those admitted. The Service des Enfants Assistés of l'Assistance Publique had specific authority for abandoned children, and the director of l'Assistance Publique was the legal guardian of all children abandoned in Paris.

Not only was it impossible for the director of l'Assistance Publique to exercise active guardianship over all abandoned children in his charge, but it was equally impossible for the Administration in Paris directly to control, supervise, and administer the regulations of the system wherever they sent the abandoned children. The administrative problem in the countryside was substantial. Responsibility was necessarily delegated. The Administration hired local agents, or field representatives, to whom it delegated authority in the specified *arrondissements* of each department in which abandoned children of Paris were sent. This field representative or agent of the Paris Administration had responsibility for recruitment of the wet nurses, getting them to Paris and back with the children, paying them, and supervising or inspecting the conditions surrounding the children after placement with the wet nurses.

The titles of the field representatives changed during the century in keeping with modifications in function and responsibility. They were successively called *meneurs, préposés, sous-inspecteurs,* and *agents de surveillance.* These titles indicate a shift in emphasis—from recruitment and transportation to representation, inspection, and surveillance—as the activity and police function of the government in the realm of social welfare and the lives of the children increased. Until 1819 the local contacts were *meneurs*; after that date the Administration superimposed field representatives called *préposés à la surveillance des enfants trouvés de la Ville de Paris,* or simply, *préposés.* Concomitent with the changes in attitude and public policy of the Second Empire, in 1852 the title of *préposé* was changed to that of *sous-inspecteur,* corresponding to the regulatory and police functions necessary under the restrictive abandonment decrees. The subsequent title changes to *agent de surveillance du service des enfants assistés de la Seine* in 1874 and to *directeur d'agence* in 1881 represented attitudinal and policy changes of the Third Republic as well as the growth and diversity of the welfare programs for the children abandoned in Paris. As Jacques Donzelot has discussed in *The Policing of Families,* there was a growth of state intervention and supervision of certain family members—those children who lacked biological families or whose families evaded responsibility for raising them.

From the eighteenth century through the first decades of the nineteenth century, a private entrepreneur called the *meneur* had the delegated authority in the countryside. *Meneurs* were in the profitable business of recruiting wet nurses, bringing them to Paris to get the babies, and returning the nurses and their charges to their local communities. They also delivered the trimestral payments to the wet nurses.[4] The Administration in Paris did not supervise or inspect either conditions at the wet nurses' homes or directly regulate the activities of the *meneurs* themselves. The *meneurs* recruited whom they wished, and the only constraint placed on them was the limit of five abandoned children per one hundred inhabitants in the commune. Mayors of the communes assisted the *meneurs* in recruitment. It was their duty to issue a *certificat d'allaitement* (certificate of qualification for nursing). There was no medical examination of a wet nurse until she reached the Hospice in Paris (and often only a cursory one then) and no supervision of the *meneur.* Consequently, there was nothing to stop collusion among the mayor, the *meneurs,* and the women of the commune to the economic benefit of all. The *meneur* maximized his profits by carrying farm and manufactured goods in the wagons with the wet nurses and the infants. Some mayors were reluctant to have many Parisian foundlings in their communes for fear that those who survived would grow up to be beggars, vagrants, thieves, or just generally indigent. To avoid the presence of these undesirable elements mayors could certify unqualified women—wet nurses whose milk was inadequate or who were likely to neglect their charges. These women would take an infant and collect wages for the first few months; then the infants would die. In this scheme, the women got some money, and the *meneur*, who got paid for each wet nurse he brought to Paris, benefited. Even some mayors received small sums from the *meneurs*—that is, "kickbacks"—for false certification. The *meneurs'* business was occasionally profitable enough that they subcontracted the job to others and lived a life of relative ease.[5] The only ones who lost were the babies.

An inspection of 1818 revealed just such abuses in the system. In an effort to prevent them as well as to consolidate control over the operation of the system in the country, the administrators decreed major changes in 1819. Rather than sending the children to foster parents where the *meneurs* happened to be, the Administration sent the children to specific communes in certain *arrondissements* of selected departments within an approximate two hundred kilometer radius of Paris. It designated certain *arrondissements* within each geographical area as administrative centers for the care of abandoned children of Paris in the countryside.[6] These were known as Agencies, or branch offices of the Administration des Enfants Trouvés (Assistés); there were roughly forty branch offices at any one time during the century. Initially, many branch offices were located in the same areas where the *meneurs* had served. This was reasonable since many of the Parisian children were already there as were known wet nurses and cooperative mayors. Furthermore, these areas had come to rely on abandoned children as additional income and labor.

A field representative or *préposé* of the Administration in Paris headed each branch office or agency. He was the delegated authority with responsibility for all facets of the children's care in his area; he supplanted the *meneurs* and usurped their powers.[7] *Préposés* enlisted the wet nurses in numbers stipulated so that the foundlings would not exceed five per one hundred inhabitants of any commune. They sent the wet nurses to Paris twice a month in shipments of ten to twelve in a wagon. Although *préposés* merely arranged for the transportation, *meneurs* were still used to deliver the wet nurses. *Préposés* kept extensive records for all children sent to their jurisdiction and disbursed payments to the wet nurses. In addition, they supervised and, in theory, evaluated the care that the abandoned children received from the foster parents four times a year, when they visited the foster parents to deliver the wages to the women.

This administrative position of *préposé* carried an indefinite term of service. The only requirement for the job was the ability to read, write, and keep accounts. The *préposé* did not need any knowledge of children, hygiene, or medicine. The administrators in Paris could remove an agent from office, or ask him to resign, if they judged that he failed to fulfill his duties adequately. Although some *préposés* were dismissed, removal from office occurred rarely and only for flagrant incompetence in recruitment and supervision of wet nurses.[8] Agents' salaries were based on the number of *enfants assistés* under their jurisdiction; it was calculated as one-twentieth of the total money distributed to the foster parents employed in their district.[9] Thus, the Administration offered the local *préposé* financial incentive for having as many children and foster parents in his jurisdiction as was legally permitted. Funds for his salary, like money for foster parents' wages, came from the Service Extérieur of the department of the Seine.

Two inspectors, named by the *préfet de la Seine*, supervised all *préposés*.[10] The duties of the inspector included checking the record books of the branch offices, the payments made to the foster parents as recorded by the *préposés*, and the warehouse of clothes for the children. The inspectors, like the field representatives, did not have to be doctors or even have knowledge about babies, children, hygiene, or medicine. Many were only minimally qualified. (Inspectors of livestock were better qualified than were inspectors of abandoned children, since the former had to have expertise in livestock raising.)[11] Inspectors were to visit the *préposés* and the foster parents without advance notice to see if the children were dressed properly, to examine the quantity and quality of the wet nurses' milk, and to advise on the continuation of nursing.[12] Since the inspectors were not trained medical men, and since they had so much territory to cover and no way of knowing which women had foster children, this instruction was meaningless. A *préposé* in Saint-Calais in the department of the Sarthe, even complained to the director of l'Assistance Publique that one inspector spent two days in the branch office going over the books, never once suggested visiting the children and never seeing one.[13] The inspectors functioned more like general accounting officers than child welfare officials.

The *préposé* of each branch office, after consultation with the Administration in Paris and the mayor of the area, appointed one doctor per commune as the health official for the *enfants assistés* and their wet nurses in the area. As such, the doctors assisted the *préposés* and headed the Service de Santé des Enfants Trouvés.[14] Consultation and approval procedures suggest recruitment of highly qualified physicians; unfortunately, this was not usually the case. The post had relatively low status, and the doctors were poorly paid. Many were very young and inexperienced, were recent *emigrés* (especially from Poland), or had lost earlier, more lucrative practices. [15] Since their appointments derived from the local *préposés*, many physicians may have been more interested in satisfying the field representatives to whom they owed their appointments than in tending to the needs of the children and foster parents.

Although the establishment of the field representatives had been intended to prevent—and did abolish—some abuses, the potential for enrichment at the expense of the children was inherent in the new system as well. Because of the cost incentives involved, doctors could assist *préposés* in recruiting unqualified wet nurses, in suppressing incidents of child abuse by foster parents, and in failing to report children's deaths. To counteract collusion between unscrupulous *préposés* and underqualified, self-serving doctors as well as to institute some checks and balances within the system to keep doctors honest and responsive to the Administration, a regulation of 1840 removed the jurisdiction for medical appointments in the local districts from the *préposés* and placed it with the Conseil Général des Hospices. Every three years the Conseil Général was to review doctors' qualifications and make new appointments. All doctors under sixty years old who had performed satisfactorily were eligible for reappointment. [16] After the creation of l'Assistance Publique in 1849, the *préfet de la Seine*, on the recommendation of the director of the Administration Générale de l'Assistance Publique de Paris, appointed the doctors to the Service de Santé des Enfants Trouvés and placed them in specific field offices. Thus, by 1850, the medical qualification of the physicians who cared for the abandoned children was, in theory at least, assured. Doctors could be removed in cases of gross negligence as reported by either the *préposé* in the district or one of the two inspectors of the Administration.

Doctors' duties included recruiting and selecting the wet nurses and vaccinating each infant during the first three months the baby was with the wet nurse. In order to ensure proper medical care of the children, doctors were to accompany the *préposés* in the inspection rounds every three months. During this visit doctors were to examine the children, administer aid to the sick, and furnish any necessary medicines. No child could be transferred from one wet nurse or foster mother to another without the doctor's consent, and his trimestral visit was to ensure that no exchange of babies had taken place, that no wet nurse was getting paid for an infant who had died, and that no child was obviously neglected or abused. Each year, the doctor in each district had to file a report on conditions under his jurisdiction.

At the outset, doctors' wages were set at three francs for each child in their authority regardless of age. In 1852, however, in an attempt to improve the well-being of the children and reduce infant mortality, the Administration Générale of l'Assistance Publique raised doctors' wages to six francs for each infant under one year and graduated payments of lesser amounts as the child got older. [17] The new wage scale was based on evidence that newborn children had the highest mortality rate and required the most medical care and concurrent supervision of their wet nurses. The Administration believed that, if the doctors received more for infants, they might exert more time and energy in their behalf.

Whether or not administrators paid the doctors more for infants, wages for the first three-quarters of the century depended on the number of *enfants assistés* under the doctors' supervision. Like the similar method of determining the wages of *préposés* and *sous -inspecteurs* (field representatives), the child-based payments were evidently supposed to serve as an incentive to increase the number of *enfants assistés* in their jurisdictions. Doctors could then increase their income by recruiting more wet nurses and foster parents, including, perhaps, some who were not fully qualified. Recognizing this possibility, the Administration shifted to a visit-based system in 1877, paying the doctors per documented examination of each child. The new regulations required, moreover, that the doctors visit each infant under one year old at least once a month. The Administration provided the necessary money to pay the doctors per visit. More children in each district still tended to translate into more fees for doctors, but the blatant incentives to recruit unqualified wet nurses and foster parents had been removed.

Mayors in each commune rounded out the administrative apparatus in the countryside. The mayor—traditionally the largest, richest, and most powerful landholder in the village—was almost invariably the local patron, the one person who "knew everyone." [18] The post was somewhat honorific, given by a *préfet* to a wealthy citizen in recognition of his financial status, [19] but it carried specific duties. Mayors completed all birth, marriage, and death certificates, and they provided the *certificats d'allaitement* for the women whom the field representatives selected to be wet nurses. Mayors also served as sources of information for doctors and field representatives in recruiting women in the commune for the position.

Recruitment of Wet Nurses

Placing the abandoned babies with wet nurses in the countryside was a major concern of Paris administrators and their field representatives in the provinces. It was also essential for the health of the infants

163

themselves. Recruitment of wet nurses was, therefore, a fundamental component in the distribution apparatus for the *enfants assistés*; field representatives, doctors and mayors all had a role in this important task.

The basic requirements for wet nurses did not change appreciably during the century. The women had to be married, of certifiably good morals, and have proof that the date of their last childbirth was from seven to fifteen months prior to requesting an abandoned infant. They had to have a crib for an infant and a screen for their fireplace.[20] The women also had to prove that they were able to raise and take care of children. Mayors frequently interpreted this last requirement to mean no more than the women were not destitute, overburdened with more than a dozen other children, or mentally incompetent. Fulfillment of these criteria enabled women to get a *certificat d'allaitement* or a license to wet nurse. The only exceptions to these requirements came in times of great shortages of nurses. Then, field representatives and Hospice authorities accepted unmarried women, especially those who had themselves been abandoned as infants.[21]

In 1852, authorities added restrictions and qualifications to the requirements for wet nurses. This led to greater influence of doctors and of the state on families paid by the government to raise the children who were wards of the state. For the first time there was an age requirement, although a liberal one: the women had to be between twenty and forty years old. This suggests that some women, both younger and especially older, were hired as wet nurses prior to the 1850s. Further, after 1852 no wet nurse was accepted unless her own most recently born infant was at least nine months old and weaned, and her milk was clean and abundant.[22] The women had to be certifiably without any infirmity or contagious diseases, such as syphilis. Each woman had to undergo three medical examinations before she could get a nursling.[23] The effect was to improve somewhat the quality of wet nurses and thereby the well-being of the babies.

Requirements for the wet nurses of abandoned babies were almost identical to those for wet nurses placed through the Direction des Nourrices in Paris, the agency that served as a registry and placement service for wet nurses hired by bourgeois and working-class families. The Police Ordinances of 1828 and 1842 set minimum requirements for a wet nurse in the private sector. She needed a certificate from her mayor testifying to her age, her good morals, the age of her youngest child, and the possession of a cradle and a screen for the fireplace. Furthermore, her own child had to either be weaned or given to another wet nurse for, like the wet nurses of foundlings, no nurse was permitted to nurse more than one infant at a time.[24]

The Roussel Law of 1874, hailed as a milestone in legislation for the protection of newborn infants, regulated the wet nursing industry as it applied both to wet nurses for abandoned children and wet nurses for the children of the Parisian bourgeoisie, artisan, and working classes. This law incorporated the rules and regulations for wet nurses stipulated by the Administration Générale des Hospices and by l'Assistance Publique for the wet nurses of the abandoned children of Paris in 1823 and especially of 1852, including the requirement for a medical examination of all prospective wet nurses. It did for all registry wet nurses and all babies what successive series of edicts had done just for the foundlings of Paris. In this instance, public welfare directives paved the way for legislation and regulations in the private sector.

Although the requirements for becoming a wet nurse became more stringent during the century, the mechanics for recruiting them did not appreciably change. Medical inspection of the women was a *sine qua non* of recruitment. Perhaps some women came to the *préposé* or the mayor seeking employment as a wet nurse, but the doctor in the commune had the duty to review her qualifications, and attest to the availability and age of a woman's milk and to her freedom from disease. He had to report to the mayor that she was eligible for certification. Communal doctors had the responsibility to seek out and recruit qualified women.

If the communal doctor deemed a woman qualified, then the doctor of the major city of the *arrondissement* from which she had been recruited examined her as to the quantity and quality of her milk and her freedom from syphilis.[25] Intended as a second medical opinion, the requirement of two medical examinations was regularized and specified for the *certificat d'allaitement* after 1832[26] The mayor attested to the *etat civil* of the woman and her fulfillment of moral, legal and physical requirements. His signature completed the *certificat*, which was necessary before the woman could obtain a child.[27]

Approval by the mayor was often a stumbling block in recruitment of wet nurses; mayors frequently refused to sign and deliver the necessary *certificat d'allaitement.*[28] Some mayors did not want as many abandoned children in their area as the law allowed, a maximum of five per one hundred inhabitants. For the mayor, money was not the issue since neither he nor the community had to bear the expense for these children. The mayors objected that the children who stayed in their commune (as most did) might grow up to engage in crime or become shiftless and indigent beggars, swelling the prison population or the welfare rolls. This fear, though exaggerated, was the typical middle-class prejudice against abandoned children expressed in the first half of the nineteenth century. The reluctance of the mayors to sign *certificats d'allaitement* appeared from time to time in the Sarthe; it may have been more widespread.[29]

After obtaining two medical opinions and the *certificat d'allaitement,* a woman had to undergo one more medical examination, by a doctor at the Hospice in Paris, before she could secure an infant. The resident physician examined her and attested to the quantity, quality, and age of her milk, her general health, and ascertained if she were indeed who she claimed to be and was the same woman for whom the *certificat d'allaitement* had been secured. [30] If the doctor at the Hospice found the woman inadequate or unsatisfactory in any way, he ordered her sent back on the next transport without a child, or, in rare instances, with a child already weaned. If she were sent away without a child, the expenses for her trip to Paris had to be paid by the *préposé* or *sous-inspecteur* in her home district. The field representatives had recourse only to the doctors who had recruited and examined the woman to assume or share the expense. Fixing the expenses for the return transport of unqualified wet nurses on the doctors and field representatives was designed to ensure that they only sent women who were suitable.

By regulation, the women who were wet nurses should have been examined several times and certified by the established criteria of marriage, morals, and milk. The process of recruitment was not, however, always as it was set forth on paper. Nor was it without its abuses, some of which resulted from the single, greatest problem: perennial shortages of wet nurses.

Throughout the century, the director of the Hospice in Paris, along with the director of l'Assistance Publique, complained constantly about the shortage of wet nurses. The field representatives failed to meet their quotas, which were based on the population of their districts and the number of wet nurses they had regularly supplied in the past. [31] Given this shortage of wet nurses for the abandoned babies, and the desire of Hospice administrators to transfer abandoned infants out of the institution as soon as possible, there is little doubt that officials accepted women of dubious qualifications. The abuses of the system grew out of the dishonesty of the officials, including the *préposés* with "elastic" consciences, greedy or fearful mayors, unethical doctors, and mercenaries among the women themselves. [32] The payment to the doctors and field representative based on the number of *enfants assistés* in their district abetted sticky-fingered officials in their recruitment of unqualified wet nurses.

To fill a quota, a *préposé* sometimes encouraged doctors to recruit as many women as possible. Whenever a *préposé* did not fulfill his quota, he received a reprimand from the director of the Hospice; after a *préposé* was reprimanded several times, the director reduced the number of wet nurses in the quota for the district. Although this move seems to be in keeping with the availability of qualified women, no *préposé* or *sous-inspecteur* wished to see his quota reduced, since his income depended on the number of wet nurses he sent to Paris. The wet nurses and abandoned babies were items on a budget, assets to the field representative. He did not have to pay for their upkeep; rather, he was paid for the numbers he was able to maintain within his jurisdiction. Therefore, some *préposés* were not terribly scrupulous about the quality of the women they sent or very worried about contributing to abuses in the system, especially if the women they sent were accepted by the Hospice—as almost all were.

Doctors were not always scrupulous in certifying women as wet nurses. Initial recruitment of the women was confined almost entirely to the doctors; they not only tended to do as the field representatives requested but undoubtedly found it easier to accept all the women who presented themselves than to search for more qualified ones. Directors of the Hospice and of l'Assistance Publique continually enjoined the doctors to be more active in seeking out women so that there would be enough qualified wet nurses. [33]

Field representatives sometimes sent wet nurses without sufficient milk or without a *certificat d'allaitement* to the Hospice. [34] Most often the milk of the wet nurse was too old; it had sometimes been fifteen to twenty-four months since the woman had last given birth and begun nursing. Women whose milk was old often had false *certificats d'allaitement*. For example, a woman who had had her most recent child fifteen months prior to her arrival at the Hospice had a certificate stating that her milk was seven months old. [35] There was another instance of a woman who had last given birth over two years prior to receiving a certificate claiming that her milk was six months old. She realized that her milk might not appear as young as the certificate stated, so in order for her milk to appear more mature she delayed her departure to the Hospice for six weeks! [36] Throughout the 1820s and 1830s administrators of the Hospice complained that women arrived either without signatures of both doctors and the mayor, or without certificates. [37]

Area representatives and doctors were not solely to blame for recruiting women with "old" milk. The administrators were inconsistent in whom they accepted. During the late 1820s and 1830s, when the numbers of abandoned children—and the shortage of wet nurses—increased, the enforcement of the requirements for wet nurses declined. The director of the Hospice, after consulting with the resident doctors, decided that, although milk less than one year old was desirable, they would accept women whose milk was as much as sixteen months old. By the 1850s, however, the doctors at the Hospice, in theory at least, refused

167

women who had no milk at all. [38] Of the women who arrived at the Hospice in the 1830s, about three-fourths were unfit but were accepted because there were no others. [39] The directors of the Hospice accepted less qualified women on the premise that a wet nurse with old milk was preferable to no wet nurse at all or to artificial feeding in the Hospice. Refusing the women delayed the departure of the infants from the Hospice, and a delay led to an increase in the chance of death at the Hospice. Although the risk of death for the infants who stayed in the Hospice was great, the chances for death were probably as high for an infant who was sent with a dry nurse. These later deaths, however, appeared on the record books of the field representatives and not on those of the Hospice. Administrators sought to protect their records—even at the expense of the children.

Whether a baby with an unqualified wet nurse had a greater chance of survival than one left longer in the Hospice is a moot point. Sending infants out quickly was certainly more economical for the Hospice, since the cost of maintaining a child there was borne by that institution, while the cost of a wet nurse was shared by the state, department and commune in which they were abandoned. Sending babies out to wet nurses as soon as possible was certainly financially advantageous for the Hospice; nonlactating nurses were almost as economical for the department and state. One critic even suggested that the administrators preferred unqualified wet nurses because with them the children would die and the Administration would avoid the prolonged payment to a nurse. [40]

The most flagrant recruitment abuse in the system was the traffic in abandoned children carried on by *nourrices voyageuses*—traveling wet nurses. These women made a living, or supplemented their income, by getting *certificats d'allaitement* from the doctors and mayor of their commune, going to Paris and getting an abandoned baby, and upon returning to their villages giving the baby to a woman who was old, ill or infirm, who had no milk, or who in other ways did not qualify for a *certificat d'allaitement*. The *nourrices voyageuses* kept the payment for the trip and also the first trimester payment, which was customarily paid in advance. In addition, she often kept some of the clothes intended for the abandoned baby. The unqualified, "dry nurse" would get the rest of the payments as long as the foundling lived and she kept the child. [41] Generally, babies in the houses of "dry nurses," soon perished, and the process began again. Both women benefited—the wet nurses who made the trip and kept the first payment, and the "dry nurses" who received successive payments. The only ones who lost were the babies, who had to be fed artificially, often with fatal results.

Traffic in foundlings was especially common in the 1830s. The Administration often enjoined the *préposés* and doctors to make sure that the women who received the *certificats d'allaitement* were the ones who kept the babies. The directors of the Hospice and of l'Assistance Publique often threatened the field representatives with a cessation of shipments of children to the districts where infant exchanges had taken place and a termination of their duties if the traffic continued.[42] A gradual diminution of the traffic in foundlings became apparent during the 1840s and the 1850s. The more structured system of inspection and stricter enforcement of the rules contributed to the decline of the abuse. The traffic in foundlings still existed in 1852 in some areas. The *sous-inspecteurs* were warned that the numbers of babies exchanged from one wet nurse to another and the number of *nourrices voyageuses* was so flagrant in one *arrondissement* of their jurisdiction that it had to stop or babies would not be sent there and the *sous-inspecteurs* would lose their jobs.[43]

Exchange of babies continued despite all threats and precautions. Even though Hospice personnel affixed a necklace as an identification tag on each infant, this was an inadequate preventive measure. Either the necklaces were removed after the babies left the Hospice or they were just ignored by doctors and local officials. This suggests inherent weaknesses of the system and duplicity on the part of all officials involved. Apparently the area representatives and doctors were less than careful in whom they certified, since the demand for good wet nurses exceeded the supply, and some doctors and women of the villages put their own pecuniary interests above the welfare of the babies. In general, before the 1860s children were not the objects of tender solicitous care either by their own families or by government officials who established policies. If children's welfare was not always foremost in the hearts and minds of their own biological families it is hardly surprising that the lives and well-being of the foundlings would assume importance to doctors, officials, and wet nurses.

Geographical Distribution of Wet Nurses

The difficulties in recruiting wet nurses in the districts where there were field representatives were so great that it raises questions about why the Administration chose those areas. They definitely were not chosen for their immediate proximity to Paris. Wet nurses for the abandoned children of Paris were geographically distributed in departments in the northern half of France, but not necessarily those contiguous to the

169

department of the Seine. The number of abandoned children in a particular department did not correlate with the proximity of that department to Paris. By the 1880s, the departments accepting foundlings from Paris lay in somewhat of a checker-board formation in the north-central quarter of the country and near Arras and Calais (see maps 1, 2 and 3). The development of communications and improvements in transportation stimulated the traffic of children to areas far from Paris.

Some departments, such as the Yonne, Nièvre, and Pas-de-Calais, received the bulk of abandoned children throughout the century (see table 5.1). After the advent and use of the railroad, those further away from Paris received more than double the original number (Pas-de-Calais, Côte d'Or and Nièvre); officials also used ones south and northwest of Paris, like Ille-et-Vilaine and Allier, which had not received abandoned children earlier in the century. The employment of wet nurses from more distant provinces after 1850 and from communes more than 300 kilometers from Paris, in part shows the impact of railroad transportation on the distribution of children to foster families. Indeed, the spread of abandoned children to provincial centers throughout the century follows patterns similar to the expansion of French rail lines.

Transportation facilities were far from the only reason for sending abandoned babies to particular departments and to specific communes or villages within each department. The tradition of wet nursing and the importance of it to the economic structure of the areas made recruitment in certain places easier. Wet nurses came from geographical locales where families needed either the income from government subsidies, or the eventual labor of the abandoned children in the agricultural economy of the region. Authorities in Paris chose certain areas because of the tradition of wet nursing there, like the Morvan, and it was easier to recruit women because of the groundwork already set. At least since the eighteenth century *meneurs* and *recommandaresses* had recruited women from specific regions to be wet nurses for the *non*abandoned babies of Paris. *Meneurs* brought women to wet-nursing agencies in Paris, where members of the artisan, working, and middle-class families selected their wet nurses. *Meneurs* then took the wet nurses and Parisian babies back to the country. The administrators of the Hospice in Paris made use of this already existing system. Recruitment of wet nurses from the same areas both for private individuals and for the Hospice did not, however, last long. Generally there was little overlap as the century progressed, probably because in any given region there were not enough women to supply the needs of both.

Recruitment of wet nurses by the bourgeoisie to nurse at their homes in

Distribution of Wet Nurses in 1830

Legend

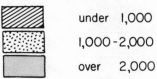

under 1,000

1,000-2,000

over 2,000

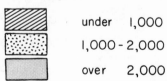

Distribution of Wet Nurses 1866

Legend

▨	under 1,000
▦	1,000 - 2,000
▩	over 2,000

Distribution of Wet Nurses 1886

Legend

under 1,000

1,000 - 2,000

over 2,000

Table 5.1

Number of Abandoned Children of Paris in Each Department, 1820-1886

Department	Distance of Agency From Paris	1820[a]	1830[a]	1856[b]	1866	1868	1872	1874	1876	1880	1886[j,a]
Seine-et-Oise	60km	288									
Oise	82	1,044									
Eure	105	974		57[c]							
Eure-et-Loir	132		260	160[d]	38[c]						
Seine-Inférieur	132	399		82[c]							
Loiret	133	88	220								
Marne	139	118									
Aube	157	63									
Somme	157	2,826	2,828	1,623	1,084	1,005	741	839	845	862	801
Aisne	158	1,248	1,032	1,012	305[f]	202[f]	71[c]	44[d]	24[c]	5[c]	
Loir-et-Cher	185		741	1,508	1,397	1,634	1,409	1,452 –	1,377	1,390	1,093
Yonne	196	1,662	1,176	1,958	2,307	2,287	2,323	2,274	2,214	1,918	1,827
Nord	200	1,788	2,979	2,927	1,687[h]	1,117[h]	733[h,c]	586[h,c]	433[c]	135[c]	12[c]
Sarthe	209		257	737	1,078	1,112	1,330	1,361	1,423	1,497	1,749
Orne	223									641	1,071
Nièvre	230	789	2,194	4,118	6,383	6,796	7,019	7,149	6,645	6,864	6,918
Indre-et-Loire	235		61	130[e]			198	283	281	27	
Pas-de-Calais	265	1,102	1,372	2,987	3,964	3,845	3,411	3,291	3,073	2,788	3,099
Cher	271										
Côte d'Or	282	489	1,054[h]	1,760	2,104	2,455	2,345	2,388	2,251	2,022	1,851
Saône-et-Loire	292	153	646	1,474	1,904	2,175	2,461	2,699	2,628	2,454	2,365
Allier	321				515[d]	1,200	1,688	1,976	2,130	2,820	3,981
Ille-et-Vilaine	355				1,588	1,520	1,821	1,999	2,007	2,120	2,155
Puy-de-Dôme	366						368	448	507	565	437[i]

Table 5.1

Number of Abandoned Children of Paris in Each Department, 1820-1886

Department	Distance of Agency From Paris	1820[a]	1830[a]	1856[b]	1866	1868	1872	1874	1876	1880	1886[j,a]
Divers (incl. Colonies Agricoles and Special Hospitals)			981		58	100	111	149	124	78	17
TOTAL		13,031	16,030	20,533	24,432	25,486	26,029	26,938	25,962	26,186	26,939

aSource: Dupoux, *Sur les pas de Monsieur Vincent*, pp. 269-273.
bSource: *Rapps. Anns.*, 1856-1880.
cAll foundlings aged 12-21.
dAll foundlings aged 4-21.
eAll foundlings aged 6-21.
fMost foundlings aged 12-21.
gMost foundlings aged 4 years.
hMost foundlings aged 8-21.
iData for 1885.
jNo data are included for the years after 1886 since the statistics for those years include the *moralement abandonnés*, those children not abandoned at the Hospice but who were abused or neglected and who came under the jurisdiction of l'Assistance Publique after 1889.

Paris continued, and increasing numbers of artisan and working-class women sent their children out to nurse. The individuals and nursing agencies concentrated on recruiting women close to Paris, and the Hospice sought those further away. In the beginning of the century some areas, such as the Eure-et-Loir, supplied wet nurses for both the abandoned and nonabandoned of Paris alike. By the 1880s the Eure-et-Loire supplied many wet nurses for families of Paris, but none for the foundlings. In general, in the 1880s *meneurs* and *meneuses* (*recommandaresses*) still recruited wet nurses for the private and municipal wet-nursing agencies. They sought the wet nurses from the Nièvre, Saône-et-Loire, the Loiret, Sarthe, Eure-et-Loir and the Loir-et-Cher. [44] With the exception of the departments of the Loiret and the Eure-et-Loir, there was some overlap in the choice of departments, though not necessarily the selections of communes, as a source of wet nurses by both Hospice authorities and private or municipal agencies.

Many of these areas had come to rely upon the wet-nursing industry as an important source of income and had done so for several decades. [45] Particular communes that supplied wet nurses were rural, with no major cities, no significant industries or mineral resources, and no cottage craft manufacturers in which women could find regular employment. [46] Wet nursing declined in certain areas and shifted to others according to the nature of the local economy. For example, wet nursing in Cambrai and Avesnes (two areas that took abandoned children) declined as work in sugar beets increased. [47] In Bonnières the waning of wet nursing coincided with the beginning of industrialization of the town. [48] With industrialization, the standard of living may have improved and families were not in such urgent need of cash that they had to take in nurslings. Furthermore, when factories that were willing to hire women were established, many women preferred factory work to wet nursing—if for no other reason than the pay was better.

Looking at the problem from a slightly different perspective, the choice of certain areas for wet nurses was also dependent on the nature of women's work in a particular locale and the demand for foundlings. In the Allier, there was a lack of women's work and a demand for labor—especially that of abandoned children paid in effect by the state. Landlords wanted labor and shifted the cost of acquiring labor onto the state. [49] They sought abandoned children not so much for the income that wet nursing would provide, but for the labor the grown child could contribute. There appears to be an inverse relationship between the existence of cottage crafts and the growth of industry in an area with wet nursing. Wet nursing of abandoned children was a cottage craft in areas where no other employment for women existed and where the eventual labor of the child might be used.

Authorities definitely did not place abandoned children in geographical areas according to the needs of the child. There is no evidence that the wet nurses were better or the climate was healthier further from Paris. It was 1896 before anyone even suggested placing a child in an area beneficial to his or her constitution. At that time Dr. Henri Thulié, chairman and member of the Conseil Général of the Service des Enfants Assistés in the department of the Seine, suggested that delicate children and those subject to respiratory ailments be placed in the plains where the air is milder, and that the more robust or scrofulous or lymphatic child should be placed in the mountains where the air was dry and brisk. [50] Officials, even then, ignored his advice. Children went to plains, marshy, swampy areas, or mountainous areas seemingly at random—depending on the geographical residence of the wet nurses who arrived at the Hospice when the child was ready to be sent out. [51] The director of the Hospice tried to justify this procedure; he argued that it was not always possible to place the children according to the health of the very young child, because that was not always easy to determine. Furthermore, wet nurses were not available at all times in all areas. If the child were kept in the Hospice until a wet nurse from the right area were found, the danger of death in the Hospice increased. [52]

Authorities recruited wet nurses from wherever they could get them. That meant they had to transport the women to Paris to pick up the baby, and they had to transport them back to the countryside again. The nurses' journeys were particularly onerous, especially the return trip with infants in tow. Moreover until the advent of the railroads, the farther from Paris, the more hazardous the journey.

Transportation of Wet Nurses

Prior to 1820, the wagons that transported the wet nurses to Paris and back with the foundlings did not have to conform to any specifications in structure, size, or design. In 1820, in an effort to set standards and improve the conditions of transport, the Conseil Général des Hôpitaux et Hospices Civils de Paris began directly to administer and supervise the transportation system of foundlings and wet nurses. The director of the Conseil Général issued a decree setting forth specifications for the wagons already in use, and ordered new wagons constructed according to specific regulations. [53] This decree, like the administrative order of 1819 that substituted agents of the Administration for the *meneurs* in the recruitment of wet nurses, undermined the control *meneurs* had over the wet-nursing business in the countryside. The wagons had been the private property of the *meneurs*, but the newly constructed ones became the property of the Administration.

The specifications of 1820, for the first time, required the wagons to be covered, have a suspension system, be drawn by two horses, and have a floor of planked wood that was to be covered with new straw. Customarily, the wet nurses and infants had scattered themselves helter-skelter on the floor of the wagons, which had been pulled by only one horse and whose floors had been covered with old, moldy straw. It was a very slow, very tortuous journey. After 1820, the women were supposed to be seated on benches along the sides of the wagons with the infants resting in suspended hammocks. [54] As late as 1874, however, wet nurses sat and the infants slept scattered on the straw on the floor of the wagons. [55] Either the wagons did not have the required benches and hammocks, or, as was most likely, the straw-padded floor was more comfortable than the spartan wooden benches for long days' journeys. [56]

The Administration only gradually replaced wagons or carriages open to the sky with covered ones. In the late 1820s, those on the route going to the department of the Nord were still uncovered. [57] Having roofs put on the wagons was not, as might be expected, to protect the wet nurses and babies from the elements but to shield them from the jeers of the spectators and the populace along the route. (Criminals also had been transported in open wagons. When the authorities ordered the change in the transportation of criminals from open to closed wagons around the same time, the reason was similar: not to protect the prisoners from rain, hail, sleet, and snow but from hectoring crowds.)

Surprisingly little change occurred in the horse-drawn vehicular transport of wet nurses and infants after the 1820s. An engraving of 1882 depicts wet nurses and babies entering a rectangular boxlike wagon, almost entirely enclosed. It rested on four, bare metal wheels and it was drawn by two horses.

Another regulation promulgated in the 1820s restricted the *meneur* to carrying just the wet nurses and the foundlings. [58] He was forbidden to carry farm produce, strangers, or other travelers in the same wagons as the wet nurses and the babies. This rule was probably honored more in the breach than in the observance. Throughout the first half of the century *meneurs* continued to carry merchandise along with the babies and the wet nurses. The director of the Administration empowered the *préposés* to reprimand the drivers for infraction of the rules; if they repeated the offense, the drivers were to lose their jobs. Apples, wheat,

17) Wagon transporting the wet nurses from the Hospice des Enfants Trouvés in Paris. *Voiture servant au transport des nourrices de l'Hospice des Enfants Trouvés de Paris.* Engraving of Henri Pottin, 1820-1864.

18) The departure of the wet nurses for the provinces. Signed "W.I." and titled *Un départ de nourrices pour la province—Aux enfants assistés.* (1880-1890?).

pigs, and goats, however, were carried in the wagons along with the infants and wet nurses, and travelers between the city and the country

179

became illegal passengers. [59] The wagons were vans of convoy; to make money, the *meneurs* transported any cargo they could. After the 1820s the *meneur* ceased being an independent entrepreneur, and he merely drove the government-owned wagon. For this the Administration paid him for each day of the trip.

Each wagonload of wet nurses also had a *surveillante* or supervisor, always a woman, likewise paid by the Administration per day of each trip. Upon departure from the Hospice, the director of the Hospice gave each supervisor a *feuille de départ* (departure list), which included the name of each infant and the wet nurse to whom the child belonged, the *livrets* (booklets on which was to be inscribed all relevant data pertaining to the child) of each infant, and a list of instructions. She kept all of these papers in a box which she turned over to the *préposé* or *sous-inspecteur* upon her arrival in the *arrondissement* or commune of the department. [60] The supervisor's job was to keep a watchful eye on the driver and the wet nurses and to report any infractions of the rules to either the director of the Hospice or to the field representative. The supervisor was responsible for seeing that each wet nurse had the assigned baby and kept that baby, without exchanges.

Initially the wife, daughter, or other relative of the *meneur*, or a special friend of the wet nurses, served as the supervisor. But a wife or other relative of the driver was unlikely to report an infraction committed by him, and in 1826 a regulation forbade the employment of any relative of the driver or the wet nurses as supervisor. [61] Henceforth, the *préposés* appointed supervisors who were required to be respected women in the commune who demonstrated good morality and could read and write. A director's repeated admonition to the *préposés* to choose the supervisors wisely suggests that administrators suspected unreported abuses in the transport system. [62] Whether to save the money normally spent on the supervisor, or to ensure greater compliance with regulations and care of the wet nurses and babies, a nun from the Hospice sometimes performed the role of supervisor as one of her acts of charity. The Administration always reserved the right to send back and dismiss any driver or lay supervisor if there were well-founded complaints. *Surveillantes* accused *meneurs* of mistreating the wet nurses, of drinking wine excessively, of making wet nurses walk long distances along the road if the *meneur* wanted to lighten the load, and of carrying farm produce, merchandise, and strangers. [63] The supervision and inspection of the transportation of *enfants assistés* remained inadequate or rudimentary for most of the century. Nevertheless, such attempts at regulation of child welfare in the public sector preceded any regulations of the wet-nursing business handled by private registries. [64]

The trip of the wet nurses and their return with the infants in the wagons took place in all months and in all seasons. The estimated distance traveled by the horse-drawn wagons was forty to forty-eight kilometers per day. At this rate, a two-hundred-kilometer journey took four to five days; many nurses' trips often took five to six days each way since the average distance of their houses from Paris could exceed two hundred kilometers. During the journey between Paris and the provinces, the wet nurses stopped once during the day to wash, change, and feed the infants. They spent the nights at inns or hospices along the route. The Administration instructed the *meneurs* to drive only from sunup to sundown, but the one extensive inspection of conditions and practices along the route indicates that the *meneur* stopped for the night at 7:45 P.M. during the month of November—considerably after sundown.[65]

Upon arrival at the inn, the wet nurses fed, cleaned and changed the infants. They often dried the diapers, which had been wet during the day, at the stove or fireplace. The diapers were not washed; a lack of cleanliness, even by nineteenth-century standards, prevailed. The wet nurses sought places near the stove so they could warm themselves, but at an inn that also housed workers the wet nurses usually lost any competition for places of warmth.[66] Furthermore, the workers mocked and ridiculed the wet nurses, who found it difficult to nurse their babies with any degree of modesty or privacy. Soup provided at the inn, paid for by the Hospice, constituted the evening meal for the women. Aside from the ration of four pounds of bread provided for the entire journey when they left the Hospice, it was their only meal during the day. During the night, the wet nurses usually slept two in a bed, but in one inn there were five beds for twelve wet nurses. In some places the infants slept in hammocks, in others in the same beds with the wet nurses; at one inn they slept on bunches of straw over which a mattresslike covering was spread. The room where they slept, summer or winter, had neither a fireplace nor a stove.[67] At 4:30 A.M. the wet nurses arose and again washed, changed, and fed the infants, but the wet diapers had no chance to dry. Departure was at 6 A.M.—well before sunrise in winter. The wet nurses and their babies were on the road for approximately thirteen hours a day in wagons that were cold in winter and hot in summer.

Roads were often deplorable, and sometimes no more than rudimentary paths, so that nurses and their charges bumped along for twelve to fourteen hours on each day of the trip. The road system had been built to serve the government and the cities; it lacked a supporting network of secondary thoroughfares.[68] Since children were not sent to the cities but to rural communes, the secondary road system was of prime importance.

181

As Eugen Weber has succinctly noted, "Most of the nineteenth century was one consistent moan over the state of the local roads; they were nothing but ruts, sometimes four, five, and six feet deep, damp and miry." Peasants used the roads as part of their fields and dug up mud from them to use on their own fields, piled rocks on them, and plowed over parts of them. In the winter many roads were totally impassable for a person on foot or horse, let alone a carriage. As late as 1858, most of the roads in the Nièvre (where one-fourth of the abandoned children were sent) were "projects or hopes." [69] It was over these roads that the wet nurses traveled, and over them that the field doctors, representatives, and inspectors were supposed to travel when they made their required rounds.

The Administration to some extent recognized difficulties posed by the poor road conditions by giving supplemental payments to the *meneurs* in times of bad conditions. [70] They allotted the *meneurs* extra time during the seasons when the roads were muddy and two horses were insufficient to pull the wagon out of mud holes, and rerouted some trips when conditions were very bad. Extra days were often needed for the journey between Paris and Saint-Calais and Châteaudun when the wagon had to make a detour and go by way of Vendôme, a town further south than either of the two other locales. A regulation took into account the bad road conditions by allowing an extraordinary payment to the *meneur* when the wagon could not be pulled by two horses even when all the wet nurses descended and walked. [71]

Not until the 1880s did rural road conditions improve, but by then the railroads, not *meneur*-driven wagons, transported most wet nurses to and from Paris. The advent of railroads in 1846, indeed, drastically changed the transport of babies and wet nurses during the second half of the century as the rail network became more widespread. Rail travel brought about a substantial reduction in travel time. The trip from Paris to Saint-Calais in the Sarthe and to Avallon in the Yonne, which by horse-drawn wagon had taken four to five days, took only seven to eight hours by train in 1860. [72] As the length of travel time decreased the Administration began recruiting wet nurses from further away—Ille-et-Vilaine, Allier, and Saône-et-Loire—all three to four hundred kilometers from Paris. The railroads reached new sources of wet nurses and new markets for babies.

Despite the shortening of the journey, the travel by railroad was not an unmitigated blessing. The nurses and the babies traveled at half-fare in third-class cars. These cars were unheated, open, and uncovered, so that they were in many ways similar to the pre-1820 horse-drawn carriages and to the freight cars of 1960.[73] It was in these that the wet nurses and infants traveled, "like animals."[74] In the 1850s the government decreed that third-class cars be covered and heated, which should have improved travel conditions. But the order apparently went unheeded, for in 1880 the government officials repeated the order. By the end of the decade, all new third-class cars finally were covered.[75]

After 1861, by an agreement with the Compagnie de Chemin de Fer, the wet nurses and their charges could travel second class for the price of third-class tickets if there were a full complement of ten wet nurses to fill a compartment. When more than ten but fewer than twenty traveled together, the difference between ten and the number in the shipment had to travel third class.[76] It is not possible to judge how frequently second-class rail transport was used.

Of necessity *meneurs* continued to serve areas untouched by the railroad. In locations where the railroad prevailed, the *meneur* still transported the wet nurses and the babies to and from the station and the Hospice in Paris, and to and from the rural railroad station and the branch office where the field representative was located. Blois, Saint-Calais, and Vendôme, for example, were all branch offices but the railroad only went as far as Blois. The wet nurses had to travel in the horse-drawn wagons, driven by the *meneurs*, from Blois to Vendôme or Saint-Calais, generally a one-day trip.[77]

At the end of the journey, whether by horse-drawn carriage or by railroad, each wet nurse was not deposited at her home but at the branch office in the *arrondissement*. The office was sometimes almost fifty kilometers from the residence of the wet nurse. The women walked in rain and in 30°C (86°F) heat, carrying both the infant and the layette. In 1826 an inspector demanded that the wagon deposit the wet nurses not at the *préposé's* office but as close to their houses as possible to prevent their walking great distances with their bundles.[78] His request went unheeded until 1851, when the Administration in Paris issued a decree that the wet nurses be deposited at their homes whenever possible. If they lived more than four kilometers from the branch office of the *sous-inspecteur* where they were deposited, the decree mandated that the *sous-inspecteur* was to assure places for the women on public carriages which could take them much closer to their homes. Since money was always an obstacle in providing care for the abandoned children, the director of the Hospice agreed to reimburse the departments for the cost of public transportation.[79] Nevertheless, two years later, the director of l'Assistance Publique found it necessary to reiterate that the duty of the *sous-inspecteurs* included seeing that the women were deposited as close as possible to their home.[80] Thus, more than twenty-five years after an inspector first recommended this procedure, wet nurses finally were taken to within a few kilometers of home.

Despite these conditions, many babies survived this arduous journey. But the nurses could not care for the infants properly and exposure to weather made their continued health problematic. Some surely died. The *meneurs* were instructed to list those who died on the margin of the departure sheet; but never do the record books list an infant dying *en route*. It is not clear whether the wet nurse could keep the first trimester payment if the child died before reaching the destination.[81] If the wet nurses were not allowed to keep the money they may have taken better care of the infant *en route* so as to ensure the child's survival, or the records may have been inexact and indicate that all lived so that the person concerned could keep the money.

Upon the arrival of the wet nurses and the babies in each *arrondissement*, the field representative confirmed the identity of each baby by checking the number on the *livrets* for each infant against the necklaces that were affixed to the babies at the Hospice. The field representative then checked the departure list to make sure that the right baby was with the wet nurse to whom he or she belonged. Assuming that all identifications were correct, the wet nurse then trudged off to her home. Following confirmation of the identities by the field representative, the doctor examined each child for syphilis; those with the disease were not to be wet nursed, but fed artificially. After the doctor's examinations, the *curé* and the mayor of the parish and commune were notified of the arrival of the children and of the women who received them. Thus, the abandoned child began his or her stay with the wet nurse or foster parent. But, who were the wet nurses? Why did they take abandoned babies? Why did they endure the hardships of the long trip to Paris?

The Wet Nurses' Backgrounds

As mercenary wet-nursing fulfilled particular economic needs of the geographical areas from which the Administration recruited the nurses, so too did taking nurslings fulfill particular economic needs of the individual women and their families. Despite the income the nurslings provided and the labor the child later supplied if it lived, women were reluctant to nurse abandoned children. In contrast to the lack of women to nurse abandoned babies, surprisingly the supply of wet nurses for individual bourgeois, artisan, and working-class families exceeded the demand during most of the nineteenth century. According to Faÿ-Sallois, many wet nurses who came to Paris seeking a baby were unable to get a nursling. [82] The discrepancy in the market of wet nurses in the private and public sectors arose in some degree from an inequality in wages.

The wet nurses for the abandoned children received very low salaries. Although they increased periodically during the century, wages seemed always insufficient. [83] In 1821 wet nurses received eighty-four francs for the first year of the child's life, or 7 francs per month. In addition, if the child survived until his or her first birthday with the same wet nurse, that women was awarded an additional thirty francs. Each increase in salary led to a slight ease in recruitment, but the effect was always short-lived. The increases may have been insignificant, for even with them wet nurses hired by the state for the abandoned children received less than those hired privately. Those recruited through the municipal Direction des Nourrices, received 20 francs per month by 1866. [84] At the same time those hired to nurse the foundlings received 12 francs a month. All wet nurses' wages were considerably lower than those of a poorly paid domestic or day laborer. Women in factories around the 1860s received an average of two francs a day for work; at that wage they would only have to work ten days to earn twenty francs. A factory worker earned in six days what a state-paid wet nurse received in a month. In the last quarter of the century, wages of foundlings' wet nurses increased again to eighteen francs per month in 1876, to twenty-five francs a month in 1888 and to twenty-eight francs per month in 1902. Even at that level, the salary was much lower than the wages of a textile worker earning 3.50 francs a day, who needed to work only slightly more than seven days to earn twenty-five francs per month.

The low wages meant that wet nursing only attracted women who had no other occupation available to them. Moreover, among those who supplemented the family income in this way, many may have preferred not to wet nurse the abandoned children of Paris. In the Morvan, where women had a reputation for being superior wet nurses, they could, and did, get far better salaries as wet nurses at the homes of the bourgeoisie in Paris. [85] Only those rural families with a sufficient degree of comfort, however, could spare women from farm work to reside in Paris for a year or two. Other women, less well off, took children of the bourgeoisie into their own houses in preference to abandoned children. [86] The bourgeoisie paid more than did l'Assistance Publique and the Service des Enfants Assistés.

In addition to low salary, other deterrents contributed to the reluctance of women to nurse abandoned children. Prior to 1874 there were relatively few restrictions placed on, requirements for, regulations concerning, or medical and other inspections of wet nurses who worked for private individuals. Only the Service des Enfants Assistés supervised the care of the infants and their wet nurses. Many women may have preferred not to submit themselves to periodic examinations and inspections. The length and rigors of the trip to Paris to collect an abandoned child may also have deterred wet nurses seeking employment. They spent ten to fifteen days in an uncomfortable wagon and another two days in the Hospice. This constituted half a month away from home, her own family, and farm. Even though she was paid for her time and journey, the discomfort of the trip coupled with a peasant woman's dislike of alien surroundings undoubtedly made recruitment difficult. Even during the winter, when farm work lessened and women could be spared, wet nurses for abandoned infants remained in short supply.[87] Fear of disease—specifically, venereal disease—increased problems of recruitment. The least problem or untoward incident regarding a wet nurse and her foundling had great repercussions in the region.[88] If one wet nurse contracted syphilis from a child, other women in the area balked at nursing the foundlings.

Recruitment after 1870 was complicated by demographic changes in France. First, a decrease in the birth rate led to fewer lactating mothers and, hence, fewer women in the pool from which wet nurses were drawn. Furthermore, after 1885, at least in the Avallonnais and Morvan, the relative economic well-being of the population in the area improved, and many women no longer needed so desperately the meager income that nursing an infant represented.[89] It may be more than a coincidence that, at the same time, bottle feeding was beginning to become safe and widespread so as to lessen the dependence on wet nurses for the abandoned infants.

Perhaps more important in recruiting wet nurses than any tangible deterrent was the problem of job status. Raising an abandoned child was popularly referred to as *élevage humain* ("élevage" commonly denotes stock raising and breeding) and the wet nurses as a *vaches à lait* (milk cows).[90] Few people considered wet nursing a noble calling, nor was taking an abandoned child to wet-nurse thought of as an altruistic act. Quite the contrary. Had it not been considered worthy of derision, the populace would not have mocked the wet nurses who traveled through town in open wagons.

Despite the difficulties and problems, the Administration and its agents managed to recruit wet nurses for the abandoned babies of Paris. In view of all these deterrents, why, then, did women agree to serve as wet nurses for the state? The socioeconomic strata or milieu from which the wet nurses came help explain their motives for taking abandoned children. For the most part, wet nurses were women from the poorest farms in villages several kilometers from the main city of their *arrondissement* or province. [91] When the directors of the Hospice questioned the field representatives as to the economic comfort of the wet nurses or foster mothers, their reply invariably was "none." [92] Moreover, when the wet nurses arrived at the Hospice during winter, they did not have the necessary clothing to protect themselves from the cold. In 1861, the director ordered ten coats to be given to the supervisor of each wagonload of wet nurses for use by the women traveling to and from the country in the wagon. [93]

Another argument which supports the contention that the wet nurses were from the poorest rural segments of society is that the payment to them was so meager as to only attract those who were in dire need. [94] The general investigation of 1849 reported that:

the wages for the wet nurse and the allowance for the [older] *enfant trouvé* are much too small and this aid is not given for a long enough time. It follows that the farmers slightly well off do not wish to take charge of such a nursling. As a result, most of these unhappy infants fall to the most impoverished and often the most depraved class who only take them to exploit them. [95]

It might seem that the smaller the farms, the poorer the farmers and the greater the number of available wet nurses. But just the opposite was also true: in the Avallonnais, the larger the property holdings in a region, the more wet nurses there were. Wherever the plots of owned farmland were small or wherever small-scale sharecropping prevailed, the women not only had to take care of the household but also had to help out with milking, chicken raising, truck gardening, and the like; but where the property holdings were relatively large, most men tended to work for wages, (as journeymen, agricultural workers, and butchers) and their wives had few opportunities outside the home. Traditionally, women had been vital contributors to the family economy, either by their labor in the fields or farmyards, or by their wages from cottage industry or other employment. When the economy of the area was such that women could not work in factories or mining, and there were no cottage industries, or landlords instituted a change in agricultural production that undermined the labor of sharecropper and tenant farming women, the wives engaged in mercenary motherhood. In short, suckling children provided work for farmhands' and rural laborers' wives. [96]

Generalizing across the population at large from which wet nurses

187

came can be misleading. Each locale had its own peculiarities, and not all regions fit the general pattern. In Avallon, sharecroppers in large land-holding areas contributed to the population of the wet nurses. Here, as in other areas, wet nurses came from poor peasant families having little or no land on which to support themselves. In the Nivernais, small tenant farmers contributed wet nurses. In the Allier, sharecroppers welcomed the foundlings for their eventual agricultural labor.[97] In all instances, accepting an abandoned child for money provided by the state was a strategy for survival: an essential contribution to the family income immediately, and a future farm laborer for a family's economic health later. In some cases, the immediate need for income was so great that taking in a nursling was necessary even for a family in which the wife also participated in farm labor. In general, wet nursing was the occupation of last resort for the poor, the incompetent, or the indigent—the lowest socioeconomic levels of rural society.

Initially, wages to the wet nurses were important. The 144 francs a wet nurse earned for keeping an infant during the baby's first year was a significant addition to the family income, since a family of four required 500 francs per year to support itself.[98] Even if the nursling died in less than half a year, 50 francs still represented one-tenth of their necessary income. In addition to their earnings they received clothing and medical attention for the infant. If they nursed the baby, expenditure for food was minimal or zero. Their wages were pure profit. But these wages paid to the wet nurses and foster parents decreased as the child got older. The Administration paid significantly more money during the first two years of a child's life. The payments then gradually decreased over the next five years, at which point they fell sharply again, followed by another gradual decrease until the child reached his thirteenth birthday. At this time regular payments to the foster parents stopped. If the foster parents kept a child for the full twelve years, the Administration rewarded them with a 50-franc bonus. Both administrators and foster parents expected that the foundling's labor in the foster parents' home and farm would compensate for the shelter and food provided.

Taking a foundling was eventually a means of getting another hand on the farm, and obtaining the labor of another person without paying for it. In rural France where "children were hands, hence wealth," a seven-year-old foundling worked regularly as a farm laborer, sometimes alongside the farmer's own children. Wet nurses or foster parents were not permitted a preference for male or female foundlings. They had to take the child they were given at the Hospice. There was no philanthropy involved in taking an abandoned child. "Philanthropy was a luxury that they [peasants] were not permitted."[99] It is entirely possible, however, that real and reciprocal affection formed between the children and their foster parents—although that development formed little part of the state's desire to place the abandoned children of Paris with families in the countryside.

Conclusion: Objects of the System

The system that developed for the farming out of babies abandoned in Paris was fraught with problems and potential for abuse. Wet nurses, especially good ones, were difficult to recruit throughout the century; yet officials relied on them because they had no better alternative for caring for the infants. Authorities in Paris found it even more difficult to recruit wet nurses to feed the infants in the Hospice, and housing all wet nurses in Paris would have been an additional expense. The Administration would have had to provide food for the women and shelter for both women and infants. The physical facilities were already strained and could not possibly accommodate more wet nurses and ten times as many children. Just as important as the economic motive for sending the babies to wet nurses in the countryside was the social one. The sheer number of babies abandoned, and the lack of safe and sanitary artificial feeding, made the Hospice environment fatal. Sending the babies to wet nurses was both economical, and also resolved the conflict between state responsibility for the welfare of its citizens and belief in the socialization of abandoned children by a family.

Difficulty in recruiting wet nurses indicates that too few women were willing to take the job—and not without reason. They had to submit to medical examinations, travel to Paris in uncomfortable wagons along deeply rutted roads, receive babies whom they had no choice in selecting, and then allow another five days for the trip home. This involved spending almost two weeks away from home in alien, unpleasant surroundings. They also shared society's beliefs and fears that the babies had inherited the vices and illnesses of their mothers—specifically sphyilis. Furthermore, the Administration paid the women as little as possible. Government wages for wet nursing were lower than for any other occupation, including nursing the babies of artisan and working-class families.

Many women nursed the foundlings in spite of all the misery. Those who did came from the lowest strata of rural society and had no opportunity for other regular employment. Either there were no cottage crafts, or factories did not hire women. Generally, whatever work was available in the areas where they lived was seasonal and irregular. The economic survival of the family depended upon the extra income which these women could only earn by the sale of their milk. For the wet nurses' biological children, the addition of a foundling to the family may have meant premature weaning with a possibly higher mortality rate for them, although this has not be conclusively demonstrated. Wet nursing disappeared as other means of employment for women became available. The process of industrialization, which sometimes included the hiring of women, contributed to the demise of the special cottage industry of wet nursing. Fortunately, the waning of wet nursing coincided with the development of pasteurization and a change in the system of caring for abandoned infants.

The Administration created an interlocking bureaucracy of local field representatives and doctors, national inspectors, and local and departmental participants in the process of placing and supervising the children—a system that, in theory at least, provided good, if not optimal, care for the *enfants assistés*. About four times a year, government-employed officials visited the homes of the rural poor who had taken foundlings. In this way they could recommend and insist upon specific practices, such as the use of cribs, fireplace screens, and the proper time for infant weaning. In some areas where one out of five homes had a Parisian foundling, this allowed state officials to enter one-fifth of all the homes in the area to inspect, recommend practices, and even report back to Paris. By inspecting wet nurses and foster families, the state could supervise in order to exercise authority over the poor, as Donzelot suggests they did.

Under modern conditions and where child labor is needed, children are the wealth of a country. But the abandoned children of Paris were only grudgingly received by state and departmental officials. They were the passive objects of the system, subject to the planning and maneuvering of all who participated in their care. Not only were the children spread out among the wet nurses and foster parents in the countryside, but fiscal and administrative responsibility for their care was spread as well. No one wished to shoulder complete responsibility. They were shuffled around as the national budget, the economy of a region, and the financial needs of the rural labor force dictated. In this entire apparatus, officials tried to ensure that women who took the children were lactating so that the infants might have a chance to survive. Some authorities expressed concern for their well-being, but rarely did such considerations assume top priority—at least during the first three-quarters of the nineteenth century.

Public welfare for the abandoned children epitomized the interaction between the state and rural family. Placement of the Parisian abandoned babies with wet nurses or foster parents in the countryside fulfilled the needs of the families who accepted them and of the state and departments that were obligated to feed them and preserve their lives. The Administration had taken over the system that had evolved over centuries, and modified it. This system, on paper, assured that the children abandoned in the capital were given at least a chance for survival.

CHAPTER SIX

Chez la Nourrice

State policy toward abandoned children reflects the increasing involvement of public assistance in their lives, and in the lives of the women who raised them. Reformers of the July Monarchy viewed the babies as a potentially dangerous part of the "social question." Shifting this population from the city to the wet nurses in the country was philosophically compatible with the prevalent view that rural life and country air were more beneficial to the children than the corrupt city. Furthermore, bureaucrats saw the wet-nursing system as a means to repopulate the countryside, countering the continued rural migration to Paris. [1] The wet-nursing system was expedient from the point of view of the administrators who had not developed the facilities or means to keep the abandoned children in Paris. It also aided rural women who needed the income and eventual labor from the children. The system allowed for parentless children to be raised in a family milieu and provided an environment for the babies' survival that was better than that of the Hospice.

The Second Empire witnessed the first signs of any concern for the abandoned children themselves. Officials of this time, much more than those of the July Monarchy, made efforts to take care of those abandoned. They aimed to reduce the infant mortality and to increase government authority in the countryside. The state took a more active role in supervising the children *chez la nourrice* (at the home of the wet nurse). During the Third Republic the state extended its influence into the lives of the foundlings and their wet nurses in an effort to protect the children.

Nowhere did public policy have a stronger impact on the family than through the wet-nursing system of public welfare for the wards of the state. The result was, as Donzelot says, a "policing of families," but not always to the detriment of the children. For half the century officials paid little overt attention to the needs of the children, yet the success of any social welfare program must be measured, at least in part, by how it affected its recipients—in this case the infants—and how they fared under it. Their survival, in a large measure, depended on the wet nurse and conditions of life in her home.

Enfants Perdus — *Infant Mortality*

Infant mortality most accurately reflects the success of child care under the state-run system of social welfare for abandoned children. Throughout the nineteenth century, between sixty and seventy-five percent of all deaths of abandoned children, whether in the Hospice, *en route*, or in wet nurse-foster parent households, occurred in infancy—that is, before they reached their first birthday* (see table 6.1). The proportion who died during the first year remained relatively constant, with minor fluctuations until 1880 and then slightly declined. As many as three-quarters of all children who had been abandoned at the beginning of the century died during their first twelve months of life; roughly two-thirds died in infancy in the third quarter of the century (except for the war years of 1870-71); as many as one-third died in infancy by the end of the century (see table 6.2 and figures 6 and 7). More specific generalizations, however, cannot easily be made, because it is impossible to obtain consistent data and to fix accurate ratios year by year. Record keeping varied in both accuracy and thoroughness during the century—even to the number of deaths, where the deaths occurred, and at what age (the high proportion of infant deaths in 1843 and 1844 can be traced to errors in the recorded data).

Infant mortality in the Hospice and with wet nurses in the country are strikingly different: at first glance, the death ratio with wet nurses is more than double that in the Hospice. One might erroneously conclude

---

* Infant mortality is, by definition, death during the first twelve months of life. Throughout this chapter, unless specified otherwise, the mortality figures are given in percentages, or ratios computed by the number of deaths in the numerator and the population from which they are drawn in the denominator. The mortality figures are not mortality rates in the technical sense; they are not invariably based on deaths per thousand of the population for the entire year. Given the nature of the data, infant mortality rates for the abandoned children were not always possible to compute; therefore, for the sake of consistency ratios are used.

Table 6.1

Proportion of All Deaths of Abandoned Children Aged 0-12 Years
Which Occurred in First Twelve Months of Life (in percentages, 1820-1890)

Year	Deaths	Year	Deaths
1820	73.4	1867	76.4
1821	68.3	1868	73.2
1822	65.3	1869	70.1
—		—	
—		—	
—			
1843	90.5	1873	66.4
1844	92.5	1874	68.6
—		1875	78.0
—		1876	61.9
—		1877	56.7
1854	52.0	1878	70.6
1855	48.0	1879	65.1
1856	64.3	1880	60.9
1857	69.5	1881	65.9
—		1882	68.5
—		1883	66.2
—		1884	65.0
1863	64.0	1885	55.4
1864	73.0	—	
1865	75.0	—	
1866	75.0	—	
		1890	55.6

Source: Pre-1843 data are computed from raw data located in AN F[20] 282[39-44].
Post-1843 data are derived from *Rapps. Anns.*, 1854-.

Note: This percentage is computed by dividing the total number of deaths of infants in the first twelve months of life by the total number of deaths of abandoned children aged 0-12 years.

that the wet-nursing system was more detrimental to the lives of the children than was Hospice care. Just the opposite is true: infant feeding or staying in the Hospice was far more detrimental to the lives of the children than was wet nursing. The issue is the length of time that the children are at risk of dying. Assume that a child either dies in the Hospice or leaves after ten days. If twenty percent, or 200 infants per thousand die in the Hospice, that is 200 deaths per thousand *per ten days*. Infant mortality, however, is usually understood to be *per year* of life at risk. If the rate of 200 per thousand in the first ten days continued to a full year, the infant death rate would be greater than 999 per thousand per year.[2] Of course, infant mortality is much higher in the first month after birth than later in the year; moreover, a few children came back from the country and died in the Hospice. Consequently, this progression based on 200 per thousand per ten days is not entirely accurate. For most of the century, the

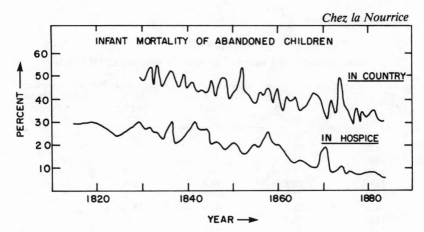

INFANT MORTALITY OF ABANDONED CHILDREN

IN COUNTRY

IN HOSPICE

PERCENT →

YEAR →

Fig. 6

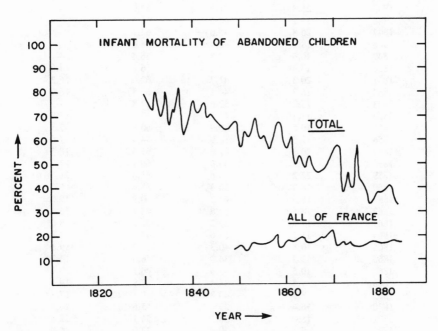

INFANT MORTALITY OF ABANDONED CHILDREN

TOTAL

ALL OF FRANCE

PERCENT →

YEAR →

Fig. 7

195

Table 6.2

Infant Mortality of Abandoned Children (in percentages, 1815-1885)

Year	Died in the Hospice (A)	Died in the Country (B)	Total Deaths (C)	Infant Mortality In France
1815	28.5	—	—	—
1820	28.9	—	—	—
1825	23.3	—	—	—
1830	28.9	49.3	78.2	—
1831	26.8	46.8	73.6	—
1832	27.1	51.8	78.8	—
1833	25.1	43.4	68.5	—
1834	24.9	54.1	79.0	—
1835	22.2	43.7	65.8	—
1836	26.1	45.3	71.4	—
1837	29.6	51.0	80.6	—
1838	19.1	49.0	61.1	—
1839	21.0	44.0	65.0	—
1840	24.6	49.9	74.5	—
1841	25.6	44.5	70.1	—
1842	28.6	46.6	75.2	—
1843	26.1	42.7	68.8	—
1844	26.5	43.1	69.6	—
1845	26.3	41.6	67.9	—
1846	19.1	46.3	65.5	—
1847	20.8	40.0	62.1	—
1848	18.2	46.4	64.6	—
1849	16.6	49.8	66.4	—
1850	17.3	39.2	56.6	14.6
1851	20.3	41.7	62.0	16.3
1852	16.7	44.1	60.8	16.2
1853	15.2	52.6	67.8	14.9
1854	17.7	41.8	59.5	17.9
1855	19.6	40.9	60.8	17.5
1856	17.5	36.9	54.4	17.0
1857	20.3	41.2	61.5	18.5
1858	25.5	40.6	66.1	17.7
1859	22.2	43.6	65.8	21.5
1860	18.9	36.4	55.4	15.0
1861	18.6	42.2	60.8	19.0
1862	14.5	33.8	48.3	16.3
1863	11.8	39.2	51.0	18.0
1864	11.1	38.0	47.8	17.3
1865	10.8	40.3	51.2	19.1
1866	12.2	34.3	46.6	16.2
1867	10.5	35.6	46.1	17.1
1868	9.5	38.4	47.9	19.1
1869	8.3	40.8	49.1	17.7
1870	16.4	39.3	55.6	20.1
1871	18.0	38.1	56.1	22.8
1872	7.1	29.9	37.0	15.9

Table 6.2

Infant Mortality of Abandoned Children (in percentages, 1815-1885)

Year	Died in the Hospice (A)	Died in the Country (B)	Total Deaths (C)	Infant Mortality In France
1873	7.2	37.6	44.9	17.8
1874	6.7	31.7	38.3	15.9
1875	9.1	47.1	56.2	17.0
1876	5.7	35.0	40.6	16.6
1877	7.7	32.1	39.8	15.7
1878	5.9	27.1	33.0	16.9
1879	5.6	29.1	34.7	15.8
1880	6.2	31.8	38.0	17.9
1881	6.9	30.8	37.7	16.6
1882	6.9	32.5	39.4	16.5
1883	6.9	30.3	37.2	16.5
1884	4.3	28.1	32.4	17.7
1885				16.1

Source: *Rapps. Anns.*, 1885; B. R. Mitchell, *European Historical Statistics*, p. 163.
Note: The figures in columns A, B, and C correspond to ratios in which the denominator is the number of abandoned children admitted to the Hospice each year. The numerators differ. For column A, the numerator is the number who died in the Hospice; for column B it is the number of those who died with the wet nurses. Each entry in column C is simply the sum of the entries in columns A and B for that year. These percentages are inflated since the denominator is consistently those abandoned in one year—most of whom were infants—while the numerator consists of children who died at any age and were abandoned in any year but happened to die in any one year. While inflated, the data have the effect of being internally consistent and showing trends which no other set of data does. Furthermore, since over sixty-five percent of all deaths of abandoned babies occurred in the first twelve months of life and since over seventy percent of children were abandoned before their first birthday, the data present a reasonably accurate picture of comparative infant mortality.

rate of infant mortality with the wet nurses of approximately forty-five percent per year is probably slightly less than half the rate of mortality in the Hospice, taking into consideration not only the amount of time at risk of dying but also the declining risk of dying as infants aged. Infants, therefore, fared better with wet nurses than in the Hospice. Still, the mortality ratio for abandoned children is extraordinarily high, especially since the infant mortality rate for all of France was just under twenty percent.

The mortality rate for the abandoned children of Paris is substantially higher than that of the population of France as a whole—and, indeed, higher than the gross figures seem to indicate. The data for all of France include the abandoned children of Paris and are based on deaths per live births. Thus, not only do the high figures for abandoned children raise

197

the overall rate for France, but the data for all France include newborns in the first hours to first few days of life—a population essentially excluded from the mortality rates for abandoned children. The abandoned babies were at least one to two days old at the time of abandonment; after mid-century, they were generally seven to nine days old. This difference in base age of two populations (that at risk in all of France and that of the abandoned children) makes the higher mortality rate for *enfants trouvés* even more striking. Indeed, if the two populations were identical, the difference between the mortality of infants in France and of the abandoned infants of Paris would be even greater. As it is, the raw data—data that are very difficult to adjust for these differences—yield a mortality rate for the abandoned children of Paris more than three times as high as that for all babies in France from birth to the end of the first year of life. [3] Rather than calling the abandoned children of Paris *enfants trouvés*, one reformer referred to them as *enfants perdus*. [4]

Children who were abandoned in Paris and sent to a wet nurse in Avallon are representative of the total population of abandoned children. Copious data are available for Avallon. Although comparable information is available for no other region, there is no reason to believe that the children sent to Avallon were any different from abandoned children sent elsewhere. Children's placement in any given region depended entirely upon where the wet nurses came from at the time that the babies were ready to leave the Hospice. [5]

Only between one-fourth and one-third of children abandoned in Paris and sent to Avallon died before their first birthday (see table 6.3 and figure 8). These babies were roughly the same age when they arrived in Avallon as were those sent to other parts of the country. The lower infant mortality of children sent to Avallon compared with children who went to other parts of France is due in part to the method of computation, and, in part to the competence of the well-reputed wet nurses in the Morvan and Avallonnais. Although there are annual fluctuations in the percentage of infant mortality due to the small number of infants in Avallon, general trends in infant deaths there parallel those in other areas of France. After 1850 the ratios of infants who died never again reach the one-third which it had been earlier in the century, and there is a parallel decline in 1885 and 1890.

The Avallon data permit the computation, by decade, of the percentage of all children who left the Hospice and died before they were twelve months old and an analysis of the relationship between the ages at which the children left the Hospice and their likelihood of dying (see tables 6.4 and 6.5). The highest infant mortality in Avallon occurred in the years

Table 6.3

Infant Mortality of Babies Abandoned in Paris
and Sent to Avallon (in percentages, 1815-1890)[a]

Year	Mortality[b]	Year	Mortality[b]	Year	Mortality[b]
1815	—	1839	33.9	1863	25.3
1816	—	1840	27.2	1864	14.9
1817	—	1841	32.3	1865	22.6
1818	—	1842	34.8	1866	15.2
1819	29.8	1843	35.6	1867	13.6
1820	14.5	1844	34.0	1868	17.5
1821	16.5	1845	34.0	1869	19.6
1822	25.1	1846	32.6	1870	25.9
1823	14.5	1847	27.9	1871	20.0
1824	18.8	1848	33.0	1872	19.4
1825	15.8	1849	39.6	1873	16.7
1826	30.2	1850	20.2	1874	24.1
1827	17.1	1851	24.0	1875	20.0
1828	23.4	1852	20.7	1876	19.6
1829	26.3	1853	12.9	1877	23.4
1830	26.7	1854	23.5	1878	18.4
1831	27.0	1855	10.3	1879	27.5
1832	22.4	1856	21.8	1880	24.5
1833	22.2	1857	26.1	1881	21.6
1834	35.3	1858	23.7	1882	28.9
1835	20.9	1859	22.4	1883	24.4
1836	30.9	1860	19.7	1884	28.0
1837	25.0	1861	26.2	1885	13.7
1838	26.1	1862	22.7	1890	12.0

Sources: E. Blin, "Les enfants assistés de la Seine dans l'Avallonnais, 1819 à 1906. –Etudes statistiques," 2 vols. (Mss. 1907) 2:6.
[a]These figures are age specific: number of deaths under 1 year/number of children under 1 year. These figures are based on the total number of abandoned children under 12 months who died in a given year computed against the total number of abandoned children under 12 months who *existed* during that year. Both populations include children alive from the prior year, plus the new admissions during the current year. By this method, some abandoned children are counted twice—both when admitted and when existent during the next year. This ratio is therefore lower than absolutely accurate.
[b]*Excludes* the very youngest and those who died in the Hospice. Includes only those who survived the first few days of abandonment to be sent out to a wet nurse.

from 1841 to 1851.* This period included the famine years of 1846 to 1848. Another upsurge in infant mortality occurred in the years from 1874 to 1885, another era of economic crisis. The infant mortality for all of France during these years, however, did not appreciably increase,

* The data are available only in eleven-year aggregates, hence an eleven-year span is used rather than the customary ten.

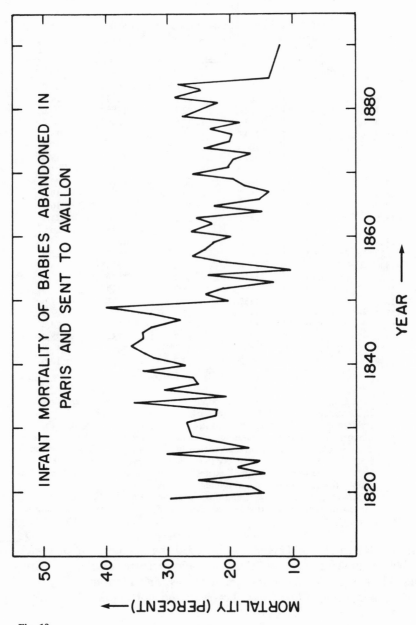

Fig. 10

which it should have were the agricultural crises a cause of mortality of French infants. Agricultural and economic crises may have contributed to abandoned infant mortality more than to infant mortality among children in general, since foundlings were housed among the poorest segments of the rural population. An undernourished nursing woman would have less milk and milk deficient in nutrients, thus contributing to the malnutrition and possible death of the foundling. Abandoned children were, quite likely, fed last and therefore least; hence, they were the ones who suffered most severely and became mortality statistics.

In Avallon the mortality of abandoned infants declined from over forty percent in the first half of the century to less than twenty percent at the end—from three times the mortality ratio of infants in all of France to approximate parity. Throughout the century, children who were less than ten days old when they arrived in Avallon had the highest rate of death. Thus, it might seem that the decline in infant mortality was in part a measure of the increase in the average median age at abandonment over the century. Focusing on infants who were from fifteen to ninety days old upon arrival at the wet nurses will control for this increase in the age of abandonment. As in the entire population of infants sent to Avallon, there is a general decrease in the mortality ratio over the century, except for relative increases, very pronounced in the 1841-1851 and 1874-1884 periods (see table 6.6).

The infant mortality ratios may be understood by not looking at the 1840s and the 1870s-1880s as an *increase* in mortality, but rather looking at the subsequent decades as a *decrease* in mortality. The decline of more than ten percent from the 1840s to the 1850s was due in part to the bad economic conditions of the mid-to-late 1840s and subsequent improvements just after mid-century. More significant, however, were the greater restrictions placed on admissions in 1852 and the limitation of admissions to the Hospice of children over eight days old if they had been born in the Maison d'Accouchement—about forty percent of those abandoned. These restrictions were enforced for the better part of two decades. They had the effect of reducing the number of children under nine days old, thereby eliminating many in the age bracket most vulnerable to death at any stage of infancy, especially if they had been born very small and therefore very weak. Perhaps more importantly, those admitted after eight days had presumably been nursed and cared for by their mothers with milk of just the right "age." The children would have benefited from immunities to certain diseases transmitted with their mothers' milk. In the 1840s, seventy percent of the children were under ten days old, whereas in the 1850s only thirty-seven percent

Table 6.4

Infant Mortality (under 12 months) by Decade (in percentages, 1819-1900)

Decade	Abandoned Children of Paris Sent to Avallon[a]	All Children Abandoned in Paris[b]	All Infants in France[c]
1819-1829	36.		15.4
1830-1840	45.		17.4
1841-1851	47.		16.5
1852-1862	34.		
1850-1860*			17.2
1874-1884	38.		
1875-1879		35.	
1870-1880			16.6
1880-1885		33.	
1885-1895	20.		
1880-1890			16.6
1896-1906	19.		
1890-1900			16.2

Sources: [a]Blin, "Avallon," 2:58-59. A precise number of the percent of children abandoned in any give time period who died before reaching their first birthday can be achieved by:

Taking the number of deaths under 12 months in a given time period.

Adding the number of deaths of children abandoned in that time period who died the next year but before their first birthday.

Subtracting the number of deaths under 12 months in that time period of children who were abandoned the year *before* the time period but survived into the time period and then died, but before their first birthday.

If the numbers added and subtracted (which are unknown) are small compared to the number of deaths under one year, a best estimate percentage may be computed by simply using the number of deaths under 12 months, dividing by the number of abandoned under 12 months, all during the extended time period. This formula provides the best possible level of accuracy if the time period is in five or ten year intervals. The data (for abandoned children) in table 6.4 are computed by this method. Blin presents the data in eleven-year aggregates, hence an eleven-year group is used rather than the customary ten.

[b]Data are from the *Rapps. Anns.*, 1880 and 1885 and the ratios are computed as above.

[c]B. R. Mitchell *European Historical Statistics*, (New York, 1975), p. 128.

*Data are not available for the 1860s.

were. Since those of nine days or younger had the highest mortality rate, it seems reasonable to look at the 1850s as a decline due to a higher average age of arrival in Avallon. Considering only deaths of children from fifteen to ninety days old controls for this higher age of admission, and the proportion of infant deaths by decade shows similar trends as when the week-old babies are considered. Even though the increased age of babies when abandoned contributed to a slight decline in mortality, it is not the only reason for this decline.

In a similar manner, although 1874-1884 did see an increase in infant mortality, it might be more readily understood if we look at the period

Table 6.5

Difference in Mortality According to the Age at Which the Children Abandoned in Paris Arrived in Avallon, 1819-1906

Number of Days Old		1819-1829	1830-1840	1841-1851	1852-1862	1863-1873	1874-1884	1885-1895	1896-1906	Total	Average
0- 4	Number Arrived	705	492	461	90	137	41	31	32	1989	
	Number Died	251	243	211	39	50	15	6	8	823	
	Percent Died	36	49	46	43	37	37	20	25		41.4
5- 9	Number Arrived	463	504	470	139	78	33	62	21	1770	
	Number Died	174	230	240	50	28	12	10	3	747	
	Percent Died	38	46	51	36	36	36	16	14		42.4
10- 14	Number Arrived	82	80	75	100	54	79	154	125	749	
	Number Died	27	33	26	37	25	42	33	22	267	
	Percent Died	33	41	35	37	46	53	21	18		35.6
15- 30	Number Arrived	49	47	46	105	75	43	69	61	495	
	Number Died	22	17	25	35	22	21	16	16	174	
	Percent Died	45	36	54	33	29	49	23	26		32.2
31- 90	Number Arrived	60	61	63	59	50	47	56	72	468	
	Number Died	25	21	35	18	18	14	14	17	162	
	Percent Died	42	34	56	31	36	30	25	24		34.6
91-180	Number Arrived	21	32	37	39	36	29	35	62	291	
	Number Died	11	6	18	16	7	10	6	9	92	
	Percent Died	52	19	49	41	19	34	17	15		31.6
181-365	Number Arrived	44	51	57	90	132	59	63	61	557	
	Number Died	8	15	12	16	21	13	7	6	104	
	Percent Died	18	29	21	18	16	22	11	10		18.7
TOTAL PER YEAR	Number Arrived	1424	1267	1209	622	562	331	470	434	6319	
	Number Died	518	567	567	211	171	127	92	81	2413	
	Percent Died	36	45	47	34	30	38	20	19		38.2

Source: Blin, "Avallon," 2:64-67. Data available only in eleven-year groups.

Table 6.6

Mortality of 15- to 90-Day-Old Infants in Avallon, 1819-1901

Year	Number Abandoned	Number Died	Percentage of Deaths
1819-1829	109	47	43.1
1830-1840	108	38	35.2
1841-1851	103	60	58.3
1852-1862	164	53	32.3
1863-1873	125	39	31.2
1874-1884	90	35	38.9
1885-1895	124	30	24.2
1896-1901	133	33	24.8

Source: Blin, "Avallon," 2:65-67.

beginning in 1885 as one of ever-decreasing mortality of newborns due to technological improvements in hygiene and medicine, and increased supervision, inspection and medical care of the wet nurses and their foundlings. After the increases in mortality during the decades of 1840 and 1870, the percentage of deaths goes below what it had been before.

A breakdown of infant mortality by sex reveals that in all decades except 1821-1829 and 1885-1895 the mortality of boys under age one is from six to eight percent greater than that for girls. During the two periods when the mortality ratio is greater for girls the difference is only two to four percent.[6] The wet nurses did not obviously favor the boys. In nineteenth-century France boys died at a higher rate than did girls, and abandoned children were no exception.

The infant mortality ratio for abandoned children of Paris was approximately triple that for France as a whole, but was closer to that of other infants sent out to wet nurse by families through private and municipal bureaus. In the Morvan, where both abandoned and nonabandoned children were nursed, Ardouin-Dumazet claimed a thirty-three percent mortality ratio of *enfants assistés* compared with a sixty-five to seventy percent mortality ratio for infants belonging to Parisian families.[7] The thirty-three percent is similar to the mortality ratio of abandoned children in Avallon that year, but the sixty-five to seventy percent mortality of others seems very high. Sussman has placed the mortality ratio for children sent out to nurse by the Paris Bureau des Nourrices between 1831 and 1874 much lower—between twenty-six and forty-one percent. He has shown that, by decade, the mortality for infants placed by the Paris municipal bureau actually increased. For the decade of the 1830s, the mortality ratio was 26.3 percent; for the 1840s it was 32.4 percent; it was 30.3 percent for the period of the 1850s, 33.8

percent for the decade of the 1860s, and 41.6 percent for the years 1871 to 1874. [8] In contrast, the mortality of those abandoned and placed by the Hospice remained relatively stable and then decreased slightly in the same time period (see tables 6.2, 6.3 and 6.4). In general, the percent of the abandoned infants who died in the country was marginally higher than for the wet-nursed, nonabandoned babies until the 1870s. In the 1860s the death ratio for the abandoned infants was thirty-eight percent—only five percent more than for the nonabandoned. In the period of 1871 to 1874, the mortality ratio for the abandoned babies was 34.3 percent—actually lower than that for the nonabandoned wet-nursed. The mortality of more than one-third of the babies abandoned (more than half when considered together with those who died in the Hospice) is tragically high. What were the causes of this excessive mortality of abandoned children and the reasons for its eventual decline?

Effect of Travel on Mortality

The strenuous trip from Paris to the wet nurses' homes was not significant in accounting for the substantial difference in the death ratios between abandoned children and all the children of France. Although both the length of time spent traveling and the deaths of abandoned infants decreased over the century, they did not always do so during the same time periods or in the same proportions. [9]

From 1819 to 1844, the trip from Paris to Avallon took four to five days. During those twenty-five years, sixteen percent of the infants died within one month of their arrival, and forty-two percent of the children died during their first year. The mortality of infants for that first year of life ranged from thirty-six to forty-seven percent, and this variation was unrelated to the time spent on the trip from Paris to Avallon. During the next five years, the trip took twenty-seven to twenty-eight hours by wagon with a *relais de poste*, and twenty-one percent of the infants died during the first month after arrival. Thus, as the travel time shortened toward mid-century, the mortality ratio actually increased. Travel time, therefore, did not have a dominant influence on mortality.

In 1850, a combination of railroad and wagon travel effectively reduced the travel time by half, to twelve or thirteen hours. Only fourteen percent of the infants died within the first month of residence in Avallon. From 1851 to 1861, the overall rate of infant mortality for abandoned children declined; the decrease in travel time perhaps affected the decline but probably not. After 1861, the more widespread use of the railroad reduced the travel time to ten hours. By 1874 it was to seven hours, which was the norm until the end of the century. From 1861 to 1863, thirteen percent of the children died within one month after arrival; that figure declined again to ten percent from 1874 to 1906. Once travel time was reduced to less than half a day, there was a decline in deaths of abandoned children within the first month after arrival in Avallon, which was the same as the first month of life. Once the nurses and babies reached Avallon, however, they still had to travel as much as a whole day to their villages and homes. It was not likely therefore, that this decline in mortality was highly attributable to a reduction in travel time.

The season in which the foundlings journeyed from Paris to Avallon slightly affected their life expectancy. Inspectors believed that sudden and great changes in temperature led to an increase of mortality in young infants. They noted that of the ten or twelve infants sent from Paris in the same day, from half to three-fourths died within a month of their arrival when the weather had been marked by "brusque variations in the atmosphere," most common in the summer.[10] Their perception was exaggerated. A breakdown of infant mortality within the first month after arrival in Avallon reveals only little seasonal variations: the summer was a slightly more precarious season for children under thirty days of age to travel, and the winter was a slightly more dangerous time for those over thirty days. The differences in mortality according to the season of travel is, however, minimal.

Regardless of season or mode of transportation, children who left the Hospice under thirty days of age had an almost ten percent greater chance of dying during their first month in the country, than those who left after they were one month old. The trip probably had little to do with their deaths. It is far more likely that those who died early in infancy were born weak and sickly and had inadequate care since birth. For many, the age of abandonment and age of leaving the Hospice only determined *where* they died (Paris or Avallon) rather than the rate at which they died. The rigors of the trip and new surroundings may only have hastened their death, or contributed to their death where in optimal conditions they might have lived.

Living Conditions Chez la Nourrice: *Housing and Hygiene*

For the first half of the century there are very few reliable statistics on the causes of infant mortality. Death certificates for children who had died in the country were completed by the doctors and filed with the mayors of the communes. Unfortunately, they are not readily available, but it is not essential to know the causes of death assigned by local physicians. Some conclusions about several possible causes of infant mortality can be made based on the conditions *chez la nourrice*: housing, hygiene, clothing, food, inspection, and medical care.

Abandoned children sent from Paris entered homes with conditions typical of those of most of the children of rural France. Only the level of poverty distinguished housing conditions of the abandoned children and those of the rest of the population. Inasmuch as the wet nurses came from among the poorest segments of the peasant population, their housing was rudimentary. Fortunately, housing, water supply, road systems, living conditions and daily habits among the peasant population of the Morvan, Avallonnais, and the Nivernais, where approximately one-third of the abandoned children ended up, have been well documented. [11]

Houses generally consisted of one unventilated room, approximately fifteen feet by twenty-two feet by just over six feet. [12] Because of the door and window tax (not abolished until 1917) and the costs of construction, most rural houses had the fewest possible number of openings. Indeed, most of the daytime interior light came from the doorway. Dwellings with at most one window accounted for one-third of the taxable structures in 1831-1832, one-fourth in 1871, and one-fifth in 1893. Houses with few apertures were, moreover, easier to heat—a major consideration with fuel quite scarce throughout the century. [13]

Housing conditions varied little from one part of France to another. In the Nivernais alone, where more than one-quarter of all abandoned children of Paris lived, the houses were low, damp, had dirt floors, and were poorly aired. [14] In the neighboring Morvan, they were windowless thatched huts of timber. [15] In the Nord, they were *"caves humides."* [16] Not necessarily damp cellars, although possibly partially below ground, they certainly had dirt floors and perhaps also dirt walls. Sun, light, and air were all shunned, perhaps because in constructing houses these also represented drafts, leaks, and insects. As it was, most houses lacked adequate clasps and latches on the windows and doors.

Conditions changed in the countryside only after 1875. Timbered houses gave way to those of stone (in the Morvan) and thatched roofs were replaced by those of slate and tile. Second stories were added to some houses and were a sign of increased wealth and status. These improvements were a result of technological advances, the increasing availability of limestone and cement, and modernized transportation that brought these materials to all regions. [17] Thus, even houses that were homemade or constructed by workmen of little skill became tighter—less damp and less drafty, but also more filled with dead air.

The fireplace, used for both heating and cooking, was the focal point of the interior of an otherwise cold, dark, and damp house. In the poorer households without chimney ventilation, the smoke of the fireplace exited through the door, which was left open for that purpose. In some households the fireplaces were open without a *garde-feu*, a screen. Even though one of the requirements for the *certificat d'allaitement* of a wet nurse specified that her fireplace have a *garde-feu*, there is no way of knowing how many nurses had a screen, or the extent to which the authorities enforced its use. Given the frequency of burned children,[18] *gardes-feu*, if available, were not always used.

Interior furnishings were also rudimentary. A wooden bed with a straw mattress and feather comforter—all enclosed by heavy curtains—constituted the main item of furniture. Old and young children as well as the sick, the healthy, and the aged slept together on this one bed. In this manner all shared the warmth of the others' bodies as well as their diseases. At most one sheet covered the bed and this was only washed about once or twice a year. In addition to the one bed, the room contained a wooden table and benches, a cabinet for pans and plates, and one or more troughs (one to be used for kneading dough).

Certificats d'allaitement stipulated that the wet nurse had to provide a crib or cradle for the infant. In the course of the century, wicker baskets on legs (a type of bassinet) replaced wooden cradles. Wooden cradles had the main disadvantage of housing insects, which frequently bit the babies. Wicker baskets did not harbor so many bugs, and they were more mobile, so the nurses could rock the infants. It is not known how many families provided cradles for the infants, nor whether they were used, when available, by the foundlings. Some foundlings slept with the family in the one big bed and some on straw mattresses in a dark, dank corner of the room. According to one report in 1838, the infants slept "on a little straw or on a board in a corner of the hut open to all comers and no one was there to watch them."[19] It is possible that the wet nurse's own child, if she had one, used the cradle and the foundling slept on the straw.

Vermin were a fact of life. Straw mattresses, whether of old or new material, harbored bedbugs, lice, and disease vectors of all kinds. Folklore featured the acceptance of lice, scabies, and parasites; witness the saying: "Good day and a good year, with lice by the handful."[20] Dogs and chickens also had the run of the house,[21] and pigs with "their slops fermenting in buckets" shared the living quarters.[22] Occasionally, wild pigs came into the house, and, if a nursling were all alone, the pigs could attack the baby. The poor even welcomed cattle in the house since they provided warmth.[23]

Animals of all sizes also contributed fecal matter to mix with the dirt on the floors. Young children, prone to put anything into their mouths, ingested this polluted soil. Parasitic tapeworms and roundworms in the children were the results, leading to malnutrition, internal bleeding, trichinosis, general intestinal disorders, and even death. Whenever the dirt floors were swept, the debris added to the dungheaps that were adjacent to the houses.[24] "Piles of manure stood guard outside the doorways."[25] The air in and around the houses must have been heavy with smoke and the smell of dung, especially in the summer months.

The water supply in many parts of the country was inadequate and egregiously pathogenic. In the Nivernais, for example, only half of the townships had adequate cisterns, wells were too few, and many were uncovered. The shallower wells of the district became low in the summer, and a peasant's nearest water supply sometimes was half a kilometer or more away.[26] Even the private fountains and ponds ran dry during the hottest days of summer, and the lack of upkeep and cleansing led to an accumulation of sludge and muddy water. In general, water was scarce, dirty and unpalatable.[27]

Animals and people used the same water, which was contaminated by the many manure piles in each village. Furthermore, hemp was steeped in the same water that was used for drinking. The river Nièvre was a virtual sewer, and most well water was not much better. As late as 1890 the Conseil d'Hygiène reported:

> At Moulins-Engilbert, in 1889, the Coulon spring was "covered by a small courtyard that contains a manure pile, a stable, a pigsty, and privies," and the river was also contaminated by latrines. "As soon as the first hot weather arrives, and water becomes scarce, fecal matter forms a black pulp that gives off a noxious odor and usually mingles with the water in a number of wells." [In addition] . . . many villages still had cemeteries that provoked seepage into water fountains and wells. At Saint-Parize-le-Châtal, the cemetery was located on unstable permeable soil and "directly overlooked the laundry tubs and fountains several meters below." At Tammay, the way the cemetery was placed acted as a veritable filter, for the liquids produced by the decomposing bodies . . . ran through a part of the town and in summer slowly drained, open to the air and the sun, into the river at the place used for watering animals and doing the laundry.[28]

Health officials did not acknowledge contagion from contaminated water as a source of typhoid fever until about 1887. This, in part, explains the general indifference toward polluted water and the refusal of the mayors and local notables to vote the necessary tax increase to improve the quality and the quantity of the water.

Owing to the obvious inadequacy of the water available, most rural women did laundry only on rare occasions. Peasants wore clothing until it was so dirty and sweat-saturated that it stuck to their bodies. They then removed it, piling it in a heap in the hut to await the next laundering session. In Brittany, at the turn of the century, women did laundry twice a year—in spring and fall. [29] To have washed clothes more frequently would have meant a great hardship. In some areas the clothes were beaten with stones while in a stream and then laid out in the fields to dry; in others, clothes were scrubbed in common laundry tubs, for which proprietors charged high fees. The fee, coupled with the long drying time for the air-dried clothes, made the procedure slow and expensive. The poor wet nurses had little money to spare on laundry; furthermore, they could not spare their small quantity of clothing for several days while it was washed and dried. [30]

Whether for the wet nurse's own child or a foundling, the lack of laundry meant that bedding and diapers were not washed. Most likely, "ces agents putrides" [31] were just air dried, whenever possible, and were otherwise re-used damp. Infant fecal matter, which was never fully cleaned out of the diapers, was added to the dung heap outside the door. Diaper rash, giving way to open, festering sores, must have been a common phenomenon unless the babies were kept with bare bottoms.

Personal hygiene was virtually unknown. People did not wash themselves any more than they washed their clothes and linens. They did not even wash their hands and face regularly. Baths with soap were unknown; soap was too expensive. Furthermore, the peasants believed that a bath would give a child a cold. [32] A contemporary proverb even condoned dirty children: "The dirtier the children, the better they grow." [33] Since "questions of cleanliness and income can not be separated," [34] abandoned children who went to families with the lowest incomes also must have been the dirtiest.

Living Conditions Chez la Nourrice: *Clothing*

When the abandoned children first arrived at their wet nurses' homes, they often had more clothing than the wet nurse's children had. Infants left the Hospice in a full set of swaddling clothes, accompanied by a minimal, but complete, layette (see table 6.7). Wet nurses had no responsibility for supplying clothing for their charges; the Hospice in Paris provided the Parisian foundlings' clothing from birth through age twelve, in yearly installments. Remarkably little change occurred in the amount, type, and distribution of clothes over the century. The Hospice, through the services of the field representatives, distributed the children's clothing once a year. These outfits were to last until the representative delivered the next bundle of clothes from Paris. If a child died, the field representatives were to repossess the clothes and either send them back to Paris or redistribute them among other abandoned children within their areas of jurisdiction.

The Hospice provided the first augmentation of infant clothing in 1847, but by 1860 the quantity of clothes had decreased, probably in order to compensate for the increased expense of the bedding that the Hospice had begun to provide sometime after 1850 and discontinued sometime before 1872. The provision of bedding was probably made in the interest of the infants' well-being, given the state of the wet nurses' own furnishings. But, since the wet nurses often had to walk the last several kilometers to their homes, straw bedding, in addition to the infant, and the standard layette, was burdensome to carry. Officials, too, may have been concerned about who benefited from the bedding—the foundling for whom it was intended or the wet nurse's own child, to whom the mother was bound to be more attached.

Even though the diaper allowance doubled between 1822 and 1885, the paucity of diapers that the Hospice provided seems alarmingly low, especially in light of the infrequency of doing laundry and the annual replacement provisions. Actually, the wet nurses changed the infants at the most three times a day. Skirts or dresses without diapers or underpants were worn by both sexes until age five or six in some areas and age three in others.[35] Skirts on a toddler obviated the need for many diapers, especially since the floors of the house were of mud and could absorb accidents. The Hospice provided the last set of diapers when the children were two years old, at which time they received two. Children were evidently toilet trained by their third birthday—a schedule quite similar to that for infants in twentieth-century America.

Child welfare authorities placed particular emphasis on head covering for the protection of the health of the children. A large number and variety of hats and bonnets made up the layette and first set of clothing for the children. In the belief that vermin in the head were a sign of health, women in the Morvan never washed the bonnets or the children's hair. By the end of the nineteenth century, however, some women and health officials had come to believe that the bonnets contributed to the formation of black scabs on the scalp.[36]

Swaddling clothes were *de rigueur* throughout the first half of the century, for abandoned children at least up to twelve months. This restraint of infants' movements, while detrimental to their general development and specifically to their large and small motor coordination, also effec-

Table 6.7

Clothing Provided to Abandoned Infants, 1822-1860

Clothing	1822[a] Layette	1822[a] 1ère vêture†	1849[b] Layette	1849[b] 1ère vêture†	1860[c] Layette	1860[c] 1ère vêture†	1872[d] Layette	1872[d] 1ère* vêture	1885[d] Layette	1885[d] 1ère* vêture
diapers	9	2	12	2	6	2	6 new 6 old	6	12 new 6 old	10
swaddling clothes (*langes*) (wool)	2	2	2	2	2	2	2		2	
swaddling clothes (*langes*) (cotton)	2		3		2	2	2	3	2	3
undershirts (*chemise à brassière*)	4						4	3	6	4
woolen undershirts (*brassières*)	2		2	4	2		2	1	3	1
cotton undershirts						3	2	2	2	2
Cotton shirts (*chemise en toile*)	4	4	4		4					
cap, wool (*calote*)	1			1				1		1
hoods (*béquins*)	4	4	4	4	4	2	4	2	4	2
bonnets, calico	2	2	2	2	2	2	2		3	
small shawl (*fichu en toile*)	4	4	4	4	2	2	4		4	
blanket (*couverture*), wool	1		1		1		1	1	1	1
dress, cotton				2		1				
dress, wool						1				
stockings, wool	2		2	2		2				
stockings, cotton						2				

212

Table 6.7

Clothing Provided to Abandoned Infants, 1822-1860

Clothing	1822[a] Layette	1ère vêture	1849[b] Layette	1ère vêture	1860[c] Layette	1ère vêture	1872[d] Layette	1ère* vêture	1885[d] Layette	1ère* vêture
petticoat (*jupon*)		1								
blouse (*corsage*)		1								
shoes (*souliers*)		1		1		1				
pillow cases					2					
mattress (double)					2					
cradle cover of cotton					1					

Sources: [a]AAP Foss. 647₆. [b]deWatteville, *Rapport*, (1849). [c]*Enquête*, (1860). [d]*Rapps. Anns.*, 1872, 1885.
†Provided at end of 1st year.
*Provided at 7 months and to last until the child was 15 months.

tively prevented the infants from crawling. The infants thus required little supervision and were less accident-prone. Swaddling also prevented the infants from scratching themselves; babies' fingernails may have been quite long since there was a belief in some regions, such as the Avallonnais, that cutting a baby's fingernails prevented learning to talk and made the child a thief. [37]

As early as 1856, officials realized that the layettes and first-year clothing that they sent for the infants were too limited and that children should not be swaddled after they could crawl. [38] To reduce swaddling, the Administration provided the children with dresses of cotton and wool as well as stockings and shoes in the package containing the first-year clothing. In Avallon, toward the end of the century, the wet nurses swaddled the infants only for their first few months of life, and swaddling clothes gave way to dresses after the children could move about. In some communes, wet nurses only swaddled the lower body, leaving the arms free. [39] This practice let the baby move his arms and upper body, but not creep around the house. The wet nurses probably used swaddling clothes provided, especially in the winter months, but none of the evidence suggests that the children were kept in them all the time. In the summer months, both infants and young children quite likely wore nothing from the waist down, a custom still common in some parts of rural France today.

The clothes for children over twelve months of age were even more meager than those for the infants. [40] In addition to an annual allotment of three shirts, the Administration provided the children with the minimal number of essentials: dresses, pants, vests, socks, blouse, bonnets, petticoat, handkerchief, shoes and stockings. In 1849, boys received their first long pants at age five, and in 1860, at age three. In Brittany at the turn of the century, boys wore skirts until age five or six, when they received one pair of long pants [41] The Administration provided the abandoned children with two sets of some items such as pants, dresses, and vests; one of each garment was of wool for winter and one was of cotton for the summer.

Problems abounded within the system of supplying the clothes for the children. Many complaints from foster mothers and from field representatives focused on clothes that should better suit the needs of the children. [42] The clothing allotment, moreover, often failed to arrive when it was due or expected. Absurdly, the clothes the Hospice sent for any child of a given age was of one size—that is, a package for a child seven years old consisted of garments of one standard size. No account was made for the fact that different children of the same age might be a dif-

214

ferent size or that children grow irregularly throughout a year. Thus, the clothes were too small for some children and too large for others, and they were not replaced as needed before the year was up if the child either outgrew the clothes or wore them out. Shoes were of a poor quality and it was not unusual for a child to wear out one pair of them in a week.[43] Shoes and socks, like clothing, were not replaced when outgrown or worn out.

Wet nurses or foster parents had little recourse in cases where the clothing did not fit or was inappropriate for the children. They could always try to exchange the clothes by giving them back to the field representative in return for clothes of the correct size. However, this involved the foster parent traveling often the better part of a day to the field office, or waiting for the field representative to make his trimestral visit. A supply of clothing existed at the storehouse in the field office, but if the size needed was not available, the field representative would have to request it from Paris. It then took at least a month and could take as long as a trimester for it to arrive, if at all.[44]

Several inspectors suggested to central officials that the foster parents themselves make the clothes for the children, claiming that the women were willing to do so if they got paid for it.[45] But this suggestion was never adopted. While some foster parents, on their own initiative, may have made or altered the clothes for the foundlings if the garments failed to arrive from the Hospice when needed, or if they were inappropriately sized, many probably did not.[46] That the women did not make the clothes, or would do so only for money, speaks to the extreme poverty of these women, who probably could neither afford the material nor the time to sew. It also could indicate a lack of maternal love for the children, if those who had the means failed to dress the children properly despite inadequate shipments from the Hospice. Only in the 1870s and 1880s, when the Administration allocated increased amounts of clothing and sent it at more frequent intervals, were some of the problems of inappropriate clothing alleviated.

The field representatives accused the foster mothers of using the foundlings' clothes for their own children. As a result of these accusations, the Administration instructed them to check the foundlings' clothes at each visit to make sure that the women used the clothes for the child intended.[47] They most often reported the woolen blankets missing. They believed that the wet nurses used the blankets for their own children, or else sold them.[48] While the quantity of clothes for the abandoned children may seem meager to us, it was probably more than belonged to the wet nurse's own child. Otherwise why would she ap-

215

propriate blankets and other items for her own? What l'Assistance Publique provided for the foundlings was perhaps no better and no worse than most other children received during the century. In fact, they may have been better than those items children would have received had they stayed with their mothers, and possibly better than the peasants in the countryside were accustomed to supplying for their own children.

The shelter and clothing of a Parisian foundling, while dirty and meager, differed little from what was typical for the chidren of the rural poor who took them in. Only in attentive care and nourishment, the two basics of life, was the foundling deprived.

Living Conditions Chez la Nourrice: *Attention and Neglect*

Wet nurses neither had the time nor the inclination to give the infants the constant surveillance and attention that one associates with infant care in the twentieth century. It must be borne in mind, however, that the concept of nurturing care was not part of the peasant culture for about the first three-quarters of the nineteenth century. In actuality wet nurses frequently left infants and children alone all day. When an inspector made his rounds during the harvest season, he found all inhabitants of the villages employed in the fields from morning to night. Only the children who were still too young to work remained "at home." The inspector's reports never mentioned the elderly.[49] In view of the level of poverty, the wet nurses' parents or other older generation relatives may have died or have had to work in the fields alongside the younger, more able-bodied members of the family.

In some areas of contemporary Asia and Africa mothers take the nurslings with them, shelter the infants in some shade, and nurse the children when necessary. There is no evidence of this type of practice among the wet nurses, however, in nineteenth-century France. Wet nurses apparently left the nurslings in the house all day, either alone or in the care of an older child who was often not more than six years old and thus still too young for labor in the fields.[50] Wet nurses who left the foundlings alone in the house, probably treated their own children in a similar manner. The six year old who was left alone to watch the baby was just as neglected! Before she took a foundling she might have taken her own children to the field with her or stayed near the house with her own baby. Now she had no need to do either, because the older child could stay and look after the infant. Moreover, since the wet nurse could always receive another foundling (with the accompanying payments to her), she probably neglected the "little Parisian" more than her own children. This neglect contributed to a number of deaths by accidents, but only to a very small proportion of total deaths.

Based on fragmentary evidence primarily from Avallon and Saint-Calais, burns and suffocation by smoke and smoldering straw did not occur very often but occurred more frequently than any other accidental cause of death throughout the century.[51] Such deaths point to a high incidence of fire in rural homes or to the lack of supervision of the children. Infants were swaddled in layers of heavy cloth, and since they were rarely changed, at least the inner layers would be wet or damp. On a cold day, the infant may have been placed on a pile of straw near the fireplace. A spark or ember could have flown from the fire and landed on the straw. The mud or dirt floors of the house as well as the straw were presumably damp. It would have taken quite some time for the straw to ignite. The time required for damp diapers and swaddling clothes to reach a burning point would have been even longer.[52] Death of children from burns and smoke indicates neglect for extended periods of time, and this seems extraordinary during the winter months when there was little to do outside.

Children's burns not only resulted from sparks from fireplaces. Some mothers, and presumably some wet nurses, put hot bricks in the cradle or next to the infants. Infants often died of burns, either directly from the bricks or from smoldering straw as a result of excessively hot bricks.[53] Death by smoke inhalation and suffocation would probably occur in a shorter time than death from burns. It nevertheless signaled neglect of the child. Toddlers died of burns, probably because they wandered too close to the fire when unattended and their clothing caught fire. Death by drowning occurred among children under five years when they fell into rivers or stagnant pools.[54] Deaths by accident accounted for only a small percentage (estimated at under five percent) of infant deaths. By far the leading cause of infant deaths was diarrhea and gastroenteritis. Both of these are due to lack of care in the feeding of the children.

Living Conditions Chez la Nourrice: *Food*

Infant deaths due to diarrhea, dehydration, and gastroenteritis were as prevalent at the beginning of the century as at the end, although detailed data exist only for the last three decades of the century (see table 6.8). Deaths from diseases of the digestive tract accounted for almost half of all infant deaths, and most of these reflect inadequate nourishment. Other causes of death due to disease ranged from pneumonia to childhood maladies like measles. *Athrepsie*, or cellular hardening, the most widespread cause of infant mortality in the Hospice, barely received mention as a cause of death in the countryside. Perhaps it affected only those less than a few days or weeks old; perhaps it was diagnosed and recorded as a gastrointestinal disease since diarrhea is a precondition of cellular hardening.[55] The latter seems more probable.

Table 6.8

Mortality by Disease: Infants Abandoned in Paris
and Sent to Avallon (in percentages, 1874-1906)

	1874-1875	1885-1895	1896-1906
Diarhea, Gastro-Intestinal Diseases	44.5	37.1	44.3
Pneumonia, Lung-Respiratory Diseases	12.5	9.3	10.0
Maladies of Nervous System	11.7	18.5	20.3
Cellular Hardening (*athrepsie*)	3.1	2.0	—
General Sickness (Including Grippe, Diphtheria, Measles & Syphilis)	21.1	26.0	17.0

Source: Blin, "Avallon," 2:42-50.

The proportion of deaths from diarrhea and diseases of the intestinal tract seems overwhelming, but comparing the causes of death of the abandoned children under age one with a larger population puts it in perspective. Throughout the century, diarrhea was the most common cause of infant mortality. In Paris of 1837, diarrhea of young children was the third most common cause of death for the entire population of the city;[56] and in the United States in 1910, diarrhea and gastrointestinal diseases were the most prevalent causes of infant mortality and were the causes of twenty-eight percent of all deaths of children under one year.[57] In England as well, gastrointestinal disorders were the leading cause of infant mortality. Abandoned infants just succumbed in greater proportions, in large measure due to their weakened condition and the likelihood that they were fed artificially.

Ideally, wet nurses breast-fed newborn foundlings until they reached their first dentition—in other words, until infants reached nine to eighteen months of age. This initial breast-feeding was crucial, since infants frequently arrived at the wet nurse with distended stomachs and thin faces, crying from malnutrition.[58] The advantages of breast-feeding over artificial feeding were legion. Not only was it less costly, but it was also life preserving for the infants. Recent studies in immunology show that modern "formula lacks certain proteins that serve to protect the breast-fed infant from infection." Furthermore, human milk has immunological properties; lactoferrin, lymphocytes, and macrophages all

218

protect infants from intestinal, viral, and bacterial infections. In addition, human milk contains an immunoglobulin, IgA, which is "an excellent source of protection against gastroenteritis, a major cause of death among infants." [59] Babies who were breast-fed most likely were the ones who survived, for nineteenth century "formulas" were not even as potentially good for infants as modern ones might be. All scientific studies demonstrate that breast-fed infants in all time periods and climates have lower death rates than infants fed on substitutes; specifically, differences have been found in death rates from intestinal and respiratory infections in which an immunological response is critical. Historians have found that "the areas where breast-feeding is customary experience considerably lower levels of infant mortality than areas where it is avoided," and the availability of a "pathogen-free" milk supply either in fresh, condensed or dried form to replace contaminated milk, coincided with a decrease in infant mortality. [60] In rural nineteenth-century France sanitation and medical care were rudimentary and the protection afforded by breast-feeding was essential.

The best of wet nurses undoubtedly breast-fed the infants, but less regularly than middle-class women do in the Unites States today. They nursed the infants three times a day at the most: in the morning, before going to work in the fields; at noon, returning to the house to feed; and again at night, after finishing work on the land. Indeed, if the wet nurse worked in the fields she might have skipped the noon feeding, especially in the critical planting and harvesting seasons, [61] and may have been much too tired at night to nurse. In the winter, work or poor diet might have made adequate nursing difficult.

Even with the best intentions, a wet nurse may not have been able to nurse successfully due to the symptoms of poverty: fatigue, improper diet, and economic need. As experts have found in third-world countries today, "many undernourished . . . women are physically unable to breast-feed, and . . . others are too preoccupied with the basics of survival to find the time to do so." [62] Such may well have been the situation in nineteenth-century France. Wet nurses, either from insouciance or from inability to nurse, substituted various liquids of dubious nutritional value for their breast milk, the most shocking of which was *le biberon dormant* (the sleeping bottle), which was a mixture of a distillate of poppies, probably a form of opium, given to infants in order to keep them quiet. [63] More often, the wet nurses used a type of pacifier, called a *sucette*, which consisted of rag soaked in a mixture of wine, milk or water, and flour or cereals upon which the infant sucked. Undoubtedly this wet rag fell on the floor from time to time, where it picked up dirt and then went back into the infant's mouth. Giving *sucettes* to infants began on the trip from Paris to the countryside and continued in the wet nurses' homes, despite the administrators' instructions to field representatives and doctors not to tolerate the practice. [64] *Sucettes* may have contributed to thrush and thereby to the deaths of infants from intestinal infection. Some nineteenth-century medical personnel considered thrush a disease of the digestive tract, since it was a mouth disease. Thrush was not a cause of death in itself but rather a contributing factor. The white, pimple-like sores on the inside of the mouth characteristic of this disease made nursing painful to the baby and often coincided with intestinal upset.

Resorting to *sucettes* as pacifiers was not only expedient because the wet nurses were absent from their homes all day or physically unable to breast-fed, but also necessary because many women may have been responsible for feeding multiple nurslings at one time. Multiple nurslings resulted in part from the wet nurse not weaning her own child before taking an abandoned infant. While it is theoretically possible for a woman to breast-feed more than one infant successfully, to do so her own diet must have sufficient nutrients and she must have adequate rest. Poor rural peasants were hardly able to fulfill these criteria. Because of the shortage of wet nurses for abandoned babies, the inadequate inspection, and the abuses in the system, some wet nurses had several nurslings. [65] The director of the Hospice must have condoned sending more than one newborn to the same wet nurse, for examples of this practice occasionally appear on the record books of the Hospice throughout the century. [66] In cases of multiple nurslings, wet nurses likely gave preference to their natural children; if the foundlings did not receive supplemental feedings they would waste away little by little from malnutrition until they died. [67]

Artificial feeding was widespread. It ranged from supplemental feedings to a complete regimen of water, cow's or goat's milk, cereals, breads, and bouillon. A complete diet predominantly or exclusively comprised of these foods given before the first birthday, when a child could not digest such foodstuffs even under the most hygienic of conditions, was detrimental to the health and life of a child. Recognizing that many wet nurses would not breast-feed the foundlings, Mme. Elisabeth Celnart wrote a manual for wet nurses in which she instructed them in the proper formulas for infant feeding. [68] Such a manual seems very well and good; however, almost all of the wet nurses were illiterate. Furthermore, they had set ideas and superstitions of their own. Even if the instructions were read to them, as was supposedly done during their overnight stay in the Hospice, it is unlikely that they would follow them. [69]

Celnart recommended formulas consisting of three parts cow's or goat's milk to two parts weak bouillon, theoretically a close imitation of human milk. The manual warns against using pure cow's milk until the child was six or seven months old. Goat's milk was preferable to cow's milk, and the recipe recommended the addition of a little sugar in an unspecified amount to make the formula more palatable and more natural. Celnart also suggested that women whose milk was weak supplement the infants' diet with some sugar or sugar water. [70]

Recognizing that many wet nurses were completely "dry" the manual further instructed women without any milk on how to get it started again. [71] This procedure included a diet rich in vegetables, consumption of pure water, and frequent nursing; few women who took an abandoned child would have had the time, energy, income, or inclination to attempt such a program for starting lactation. Most women surely found it far simpler to feed the child *bouillie*. If a child died, a wet nurse could always reapply to the Hospice for replacement.

Perhaps these guidelines were better than none at all. For the *nourrices* who tried to follow them, these formulas may have been better than what they would have done on their own. The formulas were certainly better than *sucettes*, but the manual shows a certain naïveté about conditions *chez la nourrice*. For example, sugar water, rather than having a beneficial effect, would have had a deleterious effect on the health of the baby. The water supply in the rural areas which housed abandoned babies was impure at best, and would have had pernicious effects on the infants unless boiled so that the impurities were removed. Would the wet nurses have taken the time and effort to do that? In any event, sugar may have been too expensive a commodity for most peasants to feed a Parisian foundling. Many wet nurses cut the cow's or goat's milk with rice or barley water, or with water mixed with wheat flour, thus making a liquid pap or *bouillie*. [72] Such pap constituted a semiliquid formula that wet nurses commonly fed to infants. Women also cut the milk with various infusions of herbs. [73] In areas where cows had plentiful, rich milk, such as Normandy, infants were raised on pure cow's milk. [74] Whether the formula consisted of undiluted cow's milk, or a mixture of milk cut with irritating liquids, water, bouillon, or just plain *bouillie*, it was generally not easily digestible to a newborn.

Perhaps as great a problem as the contents of artificial feeding was the way the formulas were handled. It is likely that they would have been standing for some time exposed to all the germs of the hut, where insects abounded and animals roamed freely. During the warm summer months it probably soured and the germs multiplied rapidly. Spoilage of milk was a factor in infant mortality. Between 1874 and 1906, half of the infant deaths in Avallon from diarrhea occurred in the four months from June to September when the heat fostered bacterial growth in the milk. Studies of infant mortality show the greatest proportion of infant deaths—especially those of babies sent out to wet nurse—occurred in the summer months. Some attribute this high mortality from July through September to employment of women in the fields and subsequent neglect of the nursling. [75] It is equally probable, however, that while neglect contributed to infant mortality, so did spoilage of milk in the heat of the summer. Deaths of infants from diarrhea, intestinal disorders or dehydration definitely could result from premature weaning or the feeding of solid food that was contaminated, spoiled, or had too much salt or solid content. [76]

Infants did not have to be fed formula from birth to die from diarrhea. Even if wet nurses initially breast-fed the infants, it is likely that they weaned them early, at the age of five to six months. This was commonly done for both foundlings and the wet nurses' own children. [77] Wet nurses took an abandoned infant when their own baby was from four to nine months old. They would breast-feed the foundling until that baby was about five months old, and then go to the Hospice for another infant. When they received their second foundling, their milk would not be more than fifteen months old. The wet nurse's own child, the first foundling, and soon the second foundling would be fed artifically after they were about five months old. [78] At that age they would be given cow's milk, sometimes diluted, and *bouillie*.

When not breast-feeding the babies, some mothers fed them drop by drop from a spoon, or directly from a cup, or by *biberon*. Few wet nurses had the patience or time to feed a baby drop by drop from a spoon. Those fed from a cup were offered the same germ-ridden mixture that those fed from a spoon were given. Newborns fed from a cup, however, may have suffered more indigestion since they could not swallow the huge gulps of liquid received that way. Only babies of at least five months are able to drink from a cup satisfactorily. In areas such as Normandy, where feeding an infant with cow's milk was prevalent, special little jugs called *petit pots* existed just to hold the milk for the babies.

Except in Normandy, the *biberon* prevailed as the main method of artificial feeding. The cleanliness of the bottle left much to be desired. The wood bottles were porous, and the milk or *bouillie* mixture inside the cylinder was absorbed by the wood and lingered there, turning sour over the days, weeks, and months that the *biberon* was in use. Furthermore, milk that the baby did not drink remained at the bottom of the *biberon* until the next feeding, when the wet nurse would add new milk to it; sometimes the baby would just consume old milk from the last feeding.[79] Diseases of the digestive tract resulting in death were "especially prevalent among the babies raised *au biberon*."[80] Metal and glass *biberons* came into greater use in the late 1870s and may have been effective in reducing the incidence of death by diseases of the digestive tract connected with artificial feeding.[81] For the abandoned infants, premature weaning and subsequent artificial feeding by the wet nurses contributed to weanling diarrhea and death.

Weaned and older children who survived the pernicious effects of the *biberon, bouillie,* and premature feeding of solid foods, consumed food that reflected the nourishment of the peasants of the regions to which they were sent. Bread constituted the staple of the diet, but at least in the Nivernais, that bread "contained sawdust, starch, and toxic salts; cooking salt was mixed with plaster, dirt, . . . saltpeter, [and] even arsenic oxide." The copper utensils, improperly cared for, and used with acidic foods like vinegar, "kept the body in a permanent toxic state, predisposing the digestive system to the most serious consequences in case of disease."[82] Besides bread, the diet of the rural poor featured a thin soup; they ate virtually no meat. Only on rare occasions did the soup even contain animal fat. The peasants and their children were vegetarians not by conviction but from poverty. Poverty also regulated their consumption of liquids. Peasants drank little or no wine,and they often diluted what little wine they did consume.[83] The abandoned children drank no wine either, except for those times when the wet nurses wished to take advantage of its soporific effect.

Nourishment, or the lack thereof, did not directly affect the mortality of children over one year. Those who survived infancy must have had iron stomachs. Most older children did not die of digestive tract diseases. Respiratory diseases were the major cause of death for children between one and five years of age. In the period from 1874 to 1906, twenty-nine percent of the deaths of children between one and five years of age were due to respiratory or lung diseases, whereas diseases of the digestive tract accounted for only seventeen percent. Miscellaneous diseases accounted for thirty-two percent of all deaths in this age bracket.[84]

For children of the five to twenty year age bracket, diseases classified as "general" or "divers" accounted for half the deaths. These diseases included syphilis, grippe, diphtheria, croup, measles, typhoid, typhus, and tuberculosis. Diseases of the nervous system (encephalitis, meningitis, convulsions) ranked second as a cause of death, and diseases of the circulatory and respiratory systems were the third and fourth most prevalent causes of death. Diseases of the digestive apparatus fell to the fifth most commonly cited cause of death for those over twelve months. A more detailed breakdown of diseases is not practical since nosography changed during the century. For example, in 1878 Dr. Parrot attributed many cases of pneumonia to a complication of measles, and many cases of broncho-pneumonia had been formerly cited as tuberculosis or syphilis. [85]

Survival of any abandoned children was miraculous considering that their mothers had been undernourished and had received no prenatal care. Even today, the incidence of premature births and high infant mortality is great among young, poor women such as these. Some mothers may have attempted abortion or been syphilitic, and may have abandoned the babies in a weakened, sickly, and sometimes moribund condition. Wet nurses who received them did not always breast-feed them, and frequently neglected them. Moreover, doctors, field representatives, and inspectors were also negligent in their supervision of the children *chez la nourrice.*

Inspection and Medical Care Chez la Nourrice

The responsibility for seeing that the foundlings received the proper food, clothing, shelter, and medical attention at the homes of foster parents belonged to the field representative—the *préposé* or *sous-inspecteur*—and to the doctor of that commune in the employ of the Administration for abandoned children.

Before 1877 the field representative was to visit each foster parent every three months to see if the child were alive, in good health, dressed properly, and provided with an identification necklace and *livret*, and if the home of the foster parent were clean. If he were satisfied with these conditions, he paid the foster parent for the trimester. The field representative was not supposed to announce his visits, so that the foster parents would not expect him or prepare in any special way for inspection. Since visitations coincided with times when the payments were due, however, foster parents could generally anticipate the arrival of the *préposés*. When the health of the infant was at risk, the field representative, in cooperation with the doctor, sometimes recommended a change of foster parent. This occurred about a dozen times over the century in Saint-Calais (Sarthe) when the *préposé* was particularly zealous in the performance of his duties. [86]

In many cases the *préposé* did not visit at all, but required the wet nurses to come to him with their children in order to claim their money. Obviously, at such times the wet nurse would have fed, cleaned, and properly dressed the child, but the *préposé* then had no way of knowing conditions in the home or what other clothing was being used for whom. Not only were the field representatives negligent of their duties, but their superiors, the inspectors, were sometimes negligent as well. Many saw their duties exclusively as administrators; therefore some never visited the children, nor even thought to do so. [87] The field representatives and inspectors defended their negligence by complaining that the roads were poor and permitted only slow travel, either by foot or by horse, when they were not altogether impassable. Houses in some areas were far from one another, and field representatives stated that distances to be covered were too great for them to visit each child at the wet nurse each trimester. [88] Consequently, they asked the wet nurses to come to them to pick up their payments.

The average number of children within the jurisdiction of any one field representative was 865 although some had as many as 1500. [89] The children ranged in age from newborn to twelve years old. With 865 children to supervise, the field representative would have to visit an average of more than ten children per working day, assuming he did not work on Sundays. Given his other duties, such as recruitment of wet nurses, record keeping, and the travel distances and times, he might have had legitimate reasons for failure to execute his duties. Failure to visit the children did not always go unnoticed by the Administration in Paris. The director of l'Assistance Publique ordered the removal of one field representative at Saint-Calais for failure to visit all of the 821 children under his supervision. [90]

Negligence by the doctors, which seems to have been even more prevalent than that of the field representatives, was less excusable. Doctors had much more responsibility for the well-being, welfare, health, and lives of the foundlings, and they had fewer children in their care. The number of children under the supervision of any one doctor was not very great by modern standards. In mid-century there were from 22 children per doctor to 175 per doctor, with an average of 73. These included children of all ages from the newborns, whom he was to visit frequently, to the twelve year olds whom he visited less often. By the 1880s the ratio of children to doctor was an average of 101 per doctor. [91] The average number of children under any one doctor's care was higher than in mid-century, but by the 1880s transportation and road conditions had improved somewhat and made visitations easier.

One hundred children per doctor was a very light load, if these children were their only patients. But the doctors quite likely had other duties and practices. Doctors were not full-time, salaried staff of

225

l'Assistance Publique but were paid *per capita*, according to the number of foundlings within their jurisdiction. Doctors received between two hundred and five hundred francs annually from l'Assistance Publique for services rendered. Since the annual wages of laborers in Paris were between two and three hundred francs and physicians presumably had a higher income than did laborers, it follows that doctors who served the foundlings of l'Assistance Publique had their own private practice, hospital appointments, or other welfare duties. [92] Treating the abandoned children may well have been their lowest order of priority, since it probably was their least remunerative task.

Upon the arrival of each foundling in their district, doctors were supposed to check for syphilis, the symptoms of which may have appeared in the four or five days since the child left the Hospice. The doctors were to prescribe artificial feeding for syphilitic babies in order to prevent contagion. During the first three months of care the doctors were responsible for vaccinating each child. The records show little vaccination in the countryside. [93] Either the doctors were grossly negligent in their duties, or the record keeping was haphazard and incomplete.

During the children's stay in the country, the doctors were to supervise the health care of the abandoned children, including their feeding, from birth to twelve years of age—or later if the child had a chronic ailment. The doctors supposedly accompanied the field representatives on their rounds and inspected the health of the children, the wet nurses' milk, and recommended either weaning or continuation of nursing. They also prescribed medicines and treatment for the sick children of all ages. In cases of a chronic ailment, they recommended either keeping the children with the foster parents or, occasionally, sending a child back to the Hospice or another hospital in Paris. After 1875, when the Administration of l'Assistance Publique established special hospitals for specific maladies or infirmities of the abandoned children, the doctors were to recommend sending the children to one of them when necessary. [94] If children were infirm, the foster mother was entitled to extra payments and the doctor was responsible for determining the extent of infirmity and whether or not an extra payment to the foster mother was necessary. No one could change foster parent or wet nurse without the doctor's consent. If they exercised all their duties, doctors were a powerful force for change in the countryside.

Throughout the century, wet nurses, foster parents and local authorities constantly complained that the doctors, out of apathy, negligence, willful neglect, or preoccupation with other duties, did not visit the children regularly as they were supposed to, nor did they come when summoned for a sick child. [95] Although the prescribed level of care the doctors were supposed to give increased over the century, it never, in any decade, attained that standard.

In the 1820s and 1830s, doctors in some areas did not respond to foster parents' notification of a sick child, did not visit the children when sick, or, if they did visit, did not respond with alacrity. Doctors visited the children not when most needed but whenever most convenient, generally timing their visits (if they visited at all) for those days when they made their rounds in the communes. In some instances foster parents complained that they had to go to doctors not attached to the Service des Enfants Trouvés to get emergency care for a sick child, and often private doctors refused their services. [96] Doctors in the service frequently demanded that the foster parents make office visits with any sick children. If a foster parent chose not to bring the child, the doctor asked for a description of the illness. In these instances the foster parent probably did not see the doctor herself but described the illness to someone else, who in turn relayed that information to the doctor. Reporting an illness of a child in this fashion had many drawbacks. Not only could the descriptions of the symptoms change in the relay of the message, but foster parents were unskilled in knowing what symptoms to describe. Based on the inexact or vague reports of the women, the doctors prescribed treatment and gave certain medicines—an uncertain diagnostic and treatment procedure at best. [97]

Doctors, on their part, defended their nonvisitation of the children by stating that the foster parents did not notify them of an illness until the disease had progressed, often beyond cure. [98] They also complained about the impossibility of visiting all the children to whom they had to minister—some because they had too many children assigned to their care, others because they were charged with communes very far from their residences and had to travel too far.

Throughout the 1820s and 1830s the only response of the Admininstration in Paris apparently was to impose the responsibility for the medical service more clearly on the *préposés*. Administrators enjoined the *préposés* to see that the doctors carried out their duties with "exactitude and zeal" and instructed doctors to see the children more regularly and to go without delay to any wet nurse who sought them. The *préposés*, in other words, were charged with enforcing adequate medical care. [99] In response to the doctors' complaints, the Administration urged the *préposés* to establish more carefully the area of jurisdiction of each doctor so that the distances involved would be reasonable and that the number of children under the supervision of any doctor in the *arron-*

dissement was not excessive. [100] Although the *préposé* under these regulations was ultimately responsible for the performance of the doctors, no *préposé* seems to have forced the resignation of, or replaced any, doctors during these two decades. It is likely that officials could not easily replace a deficient doctor.

Complaints continued and, in the 1840s the Administration limited the term of the doctors to three years, subject to renewal upon the recommendation of the *sous-inspecteur* and inspector. [101] It was easier for the *sous-inspecteurs* and the Administration not to renew a contract than to ask for a resignation or fire a doctor. As a possible result, in the 1850s there were fewer complaints of doctors failing to visit children and fewer doctors were replaced at the end of their term for failure to fulfill their duties. [102] The administrators in Paris could remove a doctor, upon the recommendation of the *sous-inspecteurs* and inspectors. Negligence by the doctors was still significant enough in the 1850s for the director of the Service des Enfants Assistés to state publicly that not all doctors were negligent and engaged in malpractice and that those who were, were being removed. [103] The 1850s was also the beginning of increasing societal and government concern for the children.

All of the changes were of little avail, for by the 1870s the lack of visitation by the doctors and their neglect of the children still provided the substance of many complaints. Dr. A.-T. Brochard was one of the most outspoken critics of the Administration. As a doctor, not attached to the Service in Paris, he visited the abandoned children and charged the Administration with deliberately overlooking the lack of child visitation by the doctors. He alleged that the Administration preferred minimal visitation. If the doctor did not inspect and visit, more children would die, and a higher incidence of death meant reduced Administration expenditures. [104] There may have been some validity to this harsh attack.

The criticisms of Dr. Brochard, coupled with a growing change in attitudes may have had some effect, for a major change occurred in 1877. The director of l'Assistance Publique decreed that doctors were to visit all infants under twelve months of age at least once a month. They were paid per visit, instead of per child per year as they had been paid in the past, thus encouraging the doctors to visit the children more frequently. Doctors obeyed Mammon more than Hippocrates. By the 1880s complaints were rare, and there was some praise for the zeal of the doctors; conditions had improved, as did the lives and health of the children.

Part of the liability for poor medical care of the abandoned children rests with the doctors themselves in their failure to make their rounds.

228

But providing care for the chidren was far from simple. The system of health care delivery reflected the times. For the foster parents, money was not an obstacle to proper medical attention, since the Administration bore all the expenses for medical care and medicines. But communication was difficult due to the great distances between the doctor and the foster parents and to the poor conditions of the roads. Foster parents could not conveniently notify a doctor of a sick child nor bring the child to the doctor. It was up to the doctor to visit regularly and frequently.

Foster parents themselves share responsibility for the lack of proper medical care of abandoned children because of their many superstitious beliefs surrounding childhood diseases and cures, coupled with their great mistrust of doctors. [105] They often summoned the doctors only as a last resort; even when the doctors came, the foster parents did not always follow instructions. They tended to misuse or disregard medication given by the doctor, and instead relied on folk remedies. [106] Perhaps if the doctors had visited the children regularly, they would have been able to instruct the foster parents, supervise treatment and build a bond of trust between doctor and parent.

Superstition ruled the day *chez la nourrice*, and collections of prayers and home remedies for various diseases were almost as numerous as the diseases themselves. Examples abound. Children with the skin disease *dartre* (the slang was *diètre*) were made to drink rain water which had collected in the rocks, and then the scabby crusts were washed with such water. In the Morvan, the Rocher de Ste. Diètrine in the commune of St. Germain-des-Champs was believed to have special powers. Women left an offering on the rock there to Ste. Diètre—to the profit of a neighboring farmer. Since *dartre* consists of scabs on the skin, attributable to a herpes virus, it is unlikely that the waters did much good, unless as a cleanser. The foster parents probably did not try to "cure" the black scabs and crusts from the head of infants, since to remove them would, it was thought, make the child an idiot. By the 1890s the scabs were not so positively regarded. [107]

Home remedies for other ailments were worse than the diseases themselves. To treat the swelling of lymph glands, the children were made to drink water which was left in a pail to which a horse or ass had come to drink. To ensure that teething was not too painful, wet nurses believed in rubbing the gums of a baby with hare brain. Some preventive medicine was almost as bad. If a child stepped on a nail, it was common practice to cleanse the sore with urine. The preventive measure for sore throats was perhaps the most innocuous, consisting of only putting a pinch of wax in a sachet and hanging it on a child. If a child were very ill, the foster parent dipped the shirt of the sick child into the fountain of St. Mark—not to wash it, but to get a prognosis. If the shirt maintained a dry spot, there was a cure; if it got wet throughout, the child would die. [108] By such measures, many a foster parent avoided an "unnecessary" visit to or from the doctor, and perhaps hastened the child's death.

Country women generally postponed calling a doctor until their complete arsenal of home remedies was exhausted. Perhaps the foster parents believed that if the child got sick, it was their fault, so they were reluctant to submit their error to the critical eye of a doctor or a neighbor; perhaps they feared that the doctor would take a sick or infirm baby away from them because they were bad custodians, thus causing the loss of an additional source of income as well as some status in the wet-nursing community. Or, conversely and more likely, they had little faith in the ability of the doctors to cure the child.

Medical care improved toward the end of the century, both because of new medical knowledge (germ theory of disease, pasteurization of milk, diphtheria vaccine) of the 1880s and because of the periodic medical visits to the wet nurses during the first year of the foundling's lives. By these monthly visits, the wet nurses and the doctors became acquainted. Toward the end of the century wet nurses may have had empirical evidence that doctors' visits were worthwhile; the patient might actually heal. Earlier, summoning a doctor may not have been such a rational act if they saw that a doctor could not do much and the child died anyway. When the doctors came regularly and something nevertheless happened to the babies, the wet nurses could feel that the doctors, not they, were culpable. Therefore, the wet nurses were more prone to summon a doctor when the first symptoms appeared. The child benefited.

Greater influence of doctors began in 1877. Doctors began to be paid on the basis of prescribed monthly visits to the children, and, by then, the improved road conditions in the 1880s made regular doctors' and inspectors' visits to the wet nurses more feasible. Had medicine continued to be as primitive as it had been earlier in the century, increased visitation by doctors might not have amounted to much. But by the 1870s and 1880s doctors brought new medical information and concepts of hygiene to the peasants in rural France. Since the tenure for state-paid doctors was for three years, many newly appointed physicians were recently trained. Thus, they could spread more advanced concepts of hygiene in the countryside, such as the necessity of boiling water to remove con-

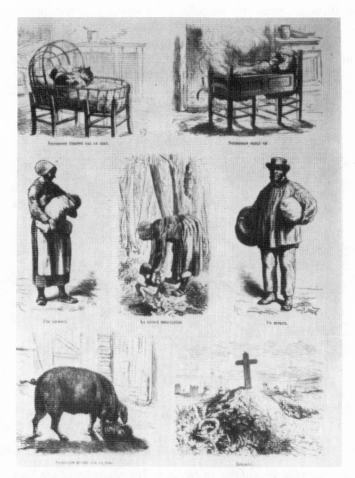

19) *La mortalité des enfants en bas age*—The Mortality of the Very Young Children. From *L'Illustration*, December 12, 1874.

tamination and the substitution of metal bottle feeding for other types of artificial feeding.

Other health-related changes of the 1880s and 1890s markedly improved the care babies received *chez la nourrice*. Pasteurization provided uncontaminated cow's milk. Living conditions also began to be transformed. Some new houses were of two stories, and some new one-level dwellings were larger. In both, animals no longer roamed freely. In the late 1880s, doctors and scientists learned that typhoid fever was a water-

231

borne disease caused by bacteria. The ensuing public projects that drained many swamps led to a marked decrease in its incidence. Moreover, l'Assistance Publique established hospitals for the chronically sick and incurable. Ill and infirm children could now be sent to them, either for cure, or custodial care. The influence of the doctors was dramatic, and not to the detriment of the children. The intervention of doctors was critical in saving the lives of many.

20) *La mortalité des enfants en bas âge*—The Mortality of the Very Young Children. From *L'Illustration*, December 12, 1874.

Conclusion: Improved Conditions

How successful was the social welfare system for abandoned infants after they left the Hospice? Mortality *chez la nourrice* until the 1880s was two to three times greater than infant mortality in all of France, and it was marginally greater than that for infants sent out to wet nurses by their own mothers during the nineteenth century. For half the century, the survival rate of abandoned children with all the supposed medical care and inspection was no better than for those placed with a wet nurse without follow-up care through a municipal bureau. From the 1860s through the 1870s, however, mortality among both the abandoned and nonabandoned with wet nurses was almost equal. From the beginning to the end of the century, approximately one-half to three-fourths of all abandoned infants died during their first twelve months of life, and their deaths were partly due to general conditions of life with the wet nurses.

In terms of housing and hygiene, the Parisian foundlings had an environment neither better nor worse than many peasant children in the countryside. Even though these conditions did not bode well for keeping people disease free, such conditions, common among the rural poor, were unlikely to have selectively contributed to the deaths of abandoned babies, unless, of course, they were especially vulnerable at birth. If, through lack of prenatal care and proper delivery, they were born premature and weak, they might have been more likely to succumb to rudimentary housing, inadequate sanitation, and nonexistent hygiene.

Improper feeding was the leading cause of infant mortality. Most babies died from diarrhea and diseases of the gastrointestinal tract brought about by premature weaning and artificial feeding of contaminated milk. Many wet nurses were too impoverished, or too concerned with their other work and source of income, to have the will or ability to successfully nurse a foundling. Some often neglected the baby with the resultant malnourishment and death of the infant. For the wet nurses, as for the natal mothers, children were of necessity subordinated to the economic needs of the family.

Conditions surrounding the lives of abandoned children in the countryside were not, after all, static. Administrative reforms throughout the century, in the 1850s, and especially again in the last three decades of the century reflect other changes: advances in medical knowledge and procedures, new attitudes toward children, the growth of social welfare support personnel, and a general improvement in peasant living standards in some parts of France. In the 1880s, with the prescribed and executed frequent visits of doctors and inspectors, the French state looked at the supervision and care of its wards in a family as the means to exert their approved ideals. Behind these late nineteenth-century efforts lay a political and theoretical history, as well as earlier attempts and practices to influence family behavior—at least as it affected the abandoned children. Toward the end of the century many of the state's efforts succeeded where others had failed because of increased state centralization and commitment at the same time that medical advances fostered real change. Field representatives and doctors, as public assistance employees, served the state in influencing rural, poor families who housed abandoned children. The doctors' involvement in family life carried forth the middle-class ideas of cleanliness, orderliness, and a more child-oriented family life—much to the benefit of the children.

Upper-class and bourgeois attitudes toward children prevalent in the 1790s may have taken a century to filter down to the rural peasant families; they really took hold only after the influence of doctors and state officials increased in the 1880s. Generally, recognition and practice of good hygiene, increased visits by doctors and inspectors, and improvements in housing, drainage, and roads, all led to massive changes in the countryside with a resultant decline in the mortality of abandoned children *chez la nourrice.*

The most difficult factors to evaluate in the care the wet nurses gave the children are psychological. Emotional neglect of the children and maternal deprivation—defined by Bowlby as insufficient interaction between a child and a mother figure—may have contributed to the high infant mortality. Twentieth-century investigations in both France and the United States reveal that infants who are deprived of maternal warmth and physical contact may not survive without some physical, emotional, or developmental impairment. In some cases, severe maternal deprivation may result in the death of the child. René Spitz reported in 1945 that many of the children admitted to orphanages and foundling homes in Baltimore died within a year even though they received adequate food, clothing and shelter; the babies were not handled, cuddled, or spoken to. [109]

To what extent outright neglect and maternal (or human) deprivation may have contributed to infant death when added to disease, malnutrition, inadequate shelter and the like is also impossible to determine. It is probable that by the end of the century, increased nurturing of children—less emotional neglect—combined with all the other changes decreased the risk of death for infants *chez la nourrice.* Throughout the century more abandoned children did survive infancy and young childhood with a wet nurse. Once past infancy, and especially after age five, their chances of continued survival substantially improved. But the lives they led were far from easy.

CHAPTER SEVEN

Survivors: The Older Children and Young Adults

Older abandoned children were, in some ways, in a precarious position in society even though they had survived infancy. In the views of nineteenth-century social critics, teenage abandoned children posed a threat to the established social order. Many believed that the children, after becoming young adults, would become juvenile delinquents, vagrants, and beggars. Lenard Berlanstein noted that nineteenth-century "reformers were unanimous in associating the problem children with broken and overburdened families." Even modern scholars have been prone to condemn them. Theodore Zeldin implied they were "idiots and subnormal people."[1] The *enfants assistés* of l'Assistance Publique in Paris constituted an important and large subset of this group of problem children. Authorities acted to alleviate the perceived threat to society posed by their existence. State provisions for the older children reflected these attitudes. In turn, the children's lives were circumscribed by these policies.

With the creation of l'Assistance Publique in 1849, the state extended its power and control over the abandoned children. Having taken stringent measures to control admissions of abandoned children, authorities in the Second Empire made efforts to take better care of those admitted. More important, the state in this era of paternalistic social reform began to concentrate more on the older child, whom they viewed as potentially dangerous. Prior to 1852, all direct supervision and authority of any administration over the abandoned children ended when they completed their twelfth year. After that no one had moral, legal, or fiscal responsibility for them. If the foster parents did not want the children, then the teenagers were on their own. In 1852, l'Assistance Publique extended its

235

control and supervision of children up to age twenty-one by assuming legal responsibility and assigning bureaucratic officials the task of enforcing rules and regulations.

French social policy with respect to the surviving abandoned children was fashioned over the century in ways intended to create a docile, economically useful, and politically neutral underclass out of a segment of the population that officials believed would otherwise be an economic drain and a social liability. The state aimed to supervise the children's upbringing and have them, by their labor, repay the state for the costs incurred in their care. Authorities sought to minimize the perceived threat and the problems posed by the children and create model, working-class citizens by four methods: 1) discouraging mothers who wished to reclaim their offspring, 2) keeping children with a "proper" family, specifically foster parents, as long as possible, 3) insisting on secular and religious education, and 4) training the children in a skill, trade, or productive occupation. [2]

Parental Reclamation of the Children

The sparse data available on the identity of the reclaimants—their sex, occupation, or relation to the child—indicate that most of the parents who sought to claim their abandoned children were mothers, usually illiterate and married. If unmarried at the time of request, they married either the father of the child, or the man with whom they were living, in order to legitimize or legally recognize the child prior to the latter's return. Mothers who reclaimed their children were generally workers, daylaborers, seamstresses, or domestics. [3] Not surprisingly, these were the same occupations as were held by the abandoning mothers. Far from all reclaimants, however, were mothers. During the period from 1845 to 1871, the only years for which complete data are available, the proportion of fathers reclaiming their children increased to about one-fourth. The fathers included an army officer and a pharmacist, as well as artisans and workers. A small fraction, roughly five to ten percent, comprised other relatives—sisters, uncles, aunts, grandparents. [4]

The state made it very difficult for relatives to reclaim abandoned children, and few children were returned to their biological mothers. Authorities were intensely concerned with what they saw as twin threats to the social order—poverty and lack of morality. Any mother who bore an illegitimate child whom she later abandoned exhibited both "evils" and thus was an unfit parent. The state feared that the sins and vices of the mother would be passed on to the child by her bad example and her lack of a stable, married family life. By her poverty, she automatically belonged to the "dangerous classes" of Paris; if her children were returned to her, they would swell the ranks of that social group in the city.

Despite the stated intentions of many mothers at the time of abandonment to reclaim their babies, few made the attempt. Those who did found getting their children back difficult because of the Administration's rules and requirements. To ensure approved socialization and control of the child, the Administration established five criteria which people (usually the mother) had to fulfill. First and foremost, they had to prove maternity or paternity (or other clear proof of kinship). Second, the reclaimant had to show good morality and, third, a stable, married family life. If the mother was the reclaimant she had to be married, preferably to the father of the offspring or, alternatively, to someone who would legally recognize the child. Every reclaimant had to be married. Fourth, the reclaimant had to prove possession of sufficient resources to rear the child, and fifth, had to reimburse the state for all charges incurred in the care of the child from time of abandonment to reclamation.

The last requirement for the return of a child was waived at three periods during the century. In 1821-1822, the Duchesse de Berry donated a fixed sum of money to the state so that mothers who satisfied other criteria could reclaim their children without paying the charges. In 1837-1838 the Duchesse d'Orléans made a bequest of 10,000 francs, and in 1853 Napoleon III donated a fixed sum of money for the free return of abandoned children to their parents who sought them. [5] In all three cases, the donations were to commemorate a happy personal family event such as a birth of a son or a marriage. The money applied to the abandoned children in all of France; Paris received its proportionate share. Even during periods of suspension of the repayment requirement, many parents who sought to reclaim their children were not able or permitted to do so. In 1837 to 1838, and in 1853, authorities granted less than half the Parisian requests for the return of the children. [6] Prior to the return of any child, the Administration conducted an investigation of the reclaiming relative that included a visit to her residence as well as an examination of her habits and marital status. They rejected some claims because the mothers were too indigent to keep a child, their conduct was judged immoral, their residence was inexact, or they were not married. [7] In a great number of cases a parent was not able to reclaim a child because the child was dead. During most of the century, under two percent returned to their parents each year (see table 7.1).

Table 7.1

Abandoned Children of Paris Who Returned to Parents, 1816-1895

Year	Number of children returned	Percent returned	Year	Number of children returned	Percent returned	Year	Number of children returned	Percent returned
1816	93	.8	1840	116	.8	1864	475	2.2
1817	73	.6	1841	122	.9	1865	409	2.0
1818	97	.8	1842	—	—	1866	496	2.1
1819	56	.5	1843	128	.5	1867	510	2.5
1820	96	.7	1844	179	.8	1868	585	2.5
1821	95	.8	1845	184	.8	1869	600	2.9
1822	107	.9	1846	213	1.0	1870	461	—
1823	101	.8	1847	198	.9	1871	444	—
1824	127	.9	1848	287	1.3	1872	783	—
1825	113	.8	1849	266	1.2	1873	559	—
1826	113	.8	1850	313	1.4	1874	580	—
1827	114	.8	1851	285	1.2	1875	566	—
1828	116	.7	1852	261	1.1	1876	423	—
1829	92	.6	1853	460	2.2	1877	240	—
1830	98	.6	1854	246	1.4	1878	316	—
1831	112	.7	1855	261	1.5	1879	285	—
1832	131	.8	1856	306	1.4	1880	275	—
1833	163	1.0	1857	329	1.6	1881	329	—
1834	162	1.0	1858	328	1.5	1882	221	—
1835	158	1.0	1859	391	1.9	1883	247	—
1836	153	.9	1860	313	1.4	1884	208	—
1837	315	1.9	1861	308	1.4	1885	233	—
1838	163	1.0	1862	292	1.3	1890	228	—
1839	161	1.1	1863	424	1.8	1895	458	—

Source: *Rapps. Anns.*, 1852-1900; AN F[15] 146-147.

238

Data do not permit a breakdown as to age or sex of the reclaimed children except for the years from 1845 to 1870 when the data were classified by sex, and Hospice records are available. For those years, there was no significant difference in the number of boys or girls returned to their parents. In some months and years there were more boys returned and for others more girls.

The motives of the parents for seeking their children are related to the reasons for abandoning them. Many mothers, when seeking their children, stated that they had abandoned the infant because they had been unemployed and too poor to take care of the baby. Now that they were married and both she and her husband were working she could afford to keep her child. Married mothers requesting the return of legitimate abandoned children also stated that poverty or imprisonment of the child's father had necessitated abandonment. With the husband out of prison and working they could afford to rear the child. These are typical justifications for abandonment and acceptable reasons for return of the children. One woman, however, had a different story. In 1853 she requested the return of a daughter born and abandoned in 1849. She said that her mother-in-law had taken the infant from her because she believed that the baby was the result of an adulterous affair. The mother had been trying to see her infant for four years, but since her last baby was born she had been ill and in bed "almost always." Her husband was a *bijoutier journalier* (journeyman jeweler) and they could not repay the state for all costs. She would offer her daughter food and legal status (*état*). As she said, "I am a good mother and I have suffered." The girl was returned. The mother may have waited until 1853 to request the child because return was free that year.[8]

The age of the child upon request for return might also have had a bearing on the parents' (or other relatives') motives for wanting the child back. Social commentators at the end of the century, interested in protecting the children, suggested that the children taken back who were over the age of twelve would be exploited by the parents as a source of income and profit.[9] The children at that age could work and earn an income which they would contribute to the parents, or the parents could even appropriate the money which the child had saved from prior work. In mid-century, slightly more children returned to their parents during the farming and harvest season, between May and October, (sixty percent) than during the other six months. There was an even split between boys and girls and almost all were under six years of age, with many under three years old. Many parents reclaimed their children within a few weeks of abandonment. This is as true of the infants as the older children. In the case of demand for return of infants, it seems likely that the mother had second thoughts about abandonment, and perhaps reconsidered the proffered aid. The older children reclaimed were generally those brought in to the Hospice by the police or other intermediaries. Some parents came soon to get their children. On the whole, parents sought and requested very few of the total population of abandoned children.

Not only did rules and regulations deter women from seeking the children whom they had abandoned, but society's reprobation and scorn toward unwed mothers who abandoned their babies may have led receptionists and administrators to speak to mothers harshly, intimidating them and discouraging further action. Mothers had to make repeated visits to the office of the director of l'Assistance Publique during normal working hours and thus lost pay which they could ill afford to relinquish. Furthermore, once at the director's headquarters she may have been subject to harrassment. Authorities did not make it easy for women to go in search of their children. [10]

The state successfully discouraged the return of children to their parents. In apparent contradiction to the middle-class belief in the sanctity of the biological family ties, and with seemingly nary a care for reuniting children with parents, state officials left the socialization of the abandoned children in the hands of the foster parents.

Children and Young Adults with Their Foster Parents

To the bureaucrats, foster parents in rural areas of France provided the proper family environment for raising foundlings. Abandoned children stayed with the same foster parents in the countryside as long as it was feasible, at least until age twelve or thirteen. [11] To encourage foster parents to keep their charges, the Administration paid a bonus to the wet nurses whose foundlings survived their first birthday, and awarded an additional bonus of fifty francs to foster parents who kept and cared for children until they reached the end of their twelfth year. In cases when the foster parents received the child after infancy, bonus payments were prorated when the foster parents had cared for a child for less than the full twelve years. [12]

Wages to wet nurses (those who cared for children under twelve months of age) increased fourfold during the century. These wages were not meant to underwrite the costs of rearing an infant since those were nonexistent if the woman breast-fed the baby, but rather were probably designed to compensate the wet nurse for the loss of her labor in the family economy. Wages to foster parents (those who took care of weaned and older children) increased only three times during the century (see table 7.2). The payments were not to recompense foster parents entirely for the upkeep of the children; rather, the children were expected to contribute by their labor.

Table 7.2

Payments to the Foster Parents in Francs per Child per Month, 1819-1902

Age of Child	1819	1855	1862	1876	1882	1888	1902
0 - 1 yr.	7	12	15	18	18	25	28
1 - 2 yrs.	6	10	10	15	15	20	20
2 - 4 yrs.	5	8	8	12	12	15	15
4 - 7 yrs.	5	7	7	8	10	13	13
7 -12 yrs.	4	6	6	7	10	13	13

Source: Dupoux, *Sur les pas de Monsieur Vincent*, p. 238.

The older a child, the smaller the monthly payments to the foster parent. At first glance, this would seem to counteract the extra payments for foster parents to keep the children. The rationale for the decreasing payments to the foster parents was the belief that the older the child, the more labor he or she could do around the farm. The children were to earn their keep and contribute to the income of the family, and in that way more than compensate for the decrease in payments. Children were wealth for the families who lived by their work more than by their capital. This was especially true of children above the age of six; by that time, they had supposedly reached the age of reason and had become an economic asset rather than a liability. [13] By the 1880s, however, a change in attitudes is evidenced by the scale of payments. Officials considered those between ages seven and twelve to be at a similar stage of development to those between four and seven years old. They were capable of some work, but not yet an economic asset since the 1882 education law mandated that children through their thirteenth year spend part of their days in school. Boys between seven and twelve years old generally worked as field hands, plowboys, or swineherders when not attending school. Girls were employed as keepers of sheep, goats and chickens, and as general domestic help, which often included the care of younger children.

When staying with the same foster parents was not possible, children changed families, some several times during the first years—from infancy to age twelve. Such children did not, however, first go back to the Hospice for reassignment; generally the field representative placed them with another family in the same village. Although sometimes altered family circumstances prevented the continuation of a foundling in a family, that change almost always resulted from the foster parents' desire not to keep them. Truly mercenary foster parents who gave a child up at the end of the first year could keep the whole of the first year payment. That meant they received the relatively high first-year wages, collected the bonus, and then returned the baby in the anticipation of receiving another newborn for whom they would also be paid the maximum amount. Foster parents frequently relinquished their charges at age four or seven, evidently because the children's labor was not needed, and the payments were insufficient to warrant keeping the children. Some foster parents refused to keep the children because the youngsters allegedly were lazy or thieves. [14] The Administration sometimes ordered a change of foster parents for incompetence. For example, in 1843, thirty children in Saint-Calais changed foster parents because an inspector reported that the children lacked care, begged, and never went to school, and that the foster parents exhibited bad conduct, immorality, or were even too poor to keep the foundlings. [15] This happened rarely, since child neglect and even abuse were not punishable crimes and were seldom reported.

The situation for the abandoned children changed drastically when they attained age twelve. While they continued as wards of the state, and the director of l'Assistance Publique continued as their guardian until they reached the age of twenty-one, all payment for their upkeep ceased at the end of their twelfth year, and they were no longer welcomed or accepted at the Hospice. Foster parents received nothing more for keeping them beyond the fifty franc bonus. All inspection of the care and treatment meted out to the young people, however minimal it may have been, stopped. Field representatives were supposed to supervise the children within their jurisdiction who were over the age of twelve, but most authorities had no record or knowledge of the housing or even the existence of the teenagers. Since payments to the foster parents had stopped, field representatives no longer found it necessary to visit the foster parents even each trimester as they had. Since no money was involved, these abandoned children over age twelve did not even appear on the record books. At that age they were in effect abandoned for a second time—this time not just by their mother but also by l'Assistance Publique. [16] This was true before 1850, less so after 1852, and still less true after 1882.

Before 1852, teenagers were free to leave their foster parents of their own accord, or they could be turned out of their house. Since the foster parents were the only family the children had known, many probably elected to remain with them unless they had been severely mistreated. Of course, only if the foster parents agreed, could the young person stay. Since children represented "hands," foster parents probably encouraged the children to stay if they had work that needed to be done, particularly if the family sharecropped and could use an extra field hand to bring in more wages. After 1852, adolescents were less free to wander about on their own, and the Administration placed them in jobs or apprenticeship positions if the foster parents could not, or would not, keep them. By the 1880s, social welfare policies provided training, institutional care, or employment for those teenagers turned out by their foster families.

The relationship between children and foster parents was not necessarily devoid of affection. Use of the foundlings' labor did not preclude real and reciprocal attachment between foster parents and children; hard work was part of daily family life among the rural poor. Not requiring such work of foundlings would have set them apart even more from the life of their foster families. Only if the foundlings worked so that the other members did not have to labor quite as hard would the foundlings have been exploited. Sometimes the foster parents may have grown attached to the child, so the child was as welcome to stay and work as the foster parents' own, even after payments stopped. Field representatives had stated that there was evidence of attachment in many cases where foster parents kept a child for several years—usually since infancy—and the child was not repeatedly moved from one family to another. Foster families, however, kept some adolescents who could not work to earn their keep, and with whom there may not have been bonds of affection. These were the infirm or disabled.

Incurably Infirm or Disabled Children and Young Adults

The Administration preferred that, no matter what their age, children who were incurably infirm or disabled (a relatively low percentage of all the abandoned who survived) spend their time in the countryside with foster parents rather than in a hospital or other institution. Prior to 1853, there were no regular provisions for either infirm children or those over twelve years old—whether disabled or not—although special arrangement could be made. In Saint-Calais the foster parents of a nineteen-year-old girl with a shoulder ailment, for example, sent her back to the Hospice in Paris. The director of the Hospice returned her to Saint-Calais as incurable, and he instructed the *préposé* to return her to her foster parents and give them a supplemental payment. If they refused, the director insisted that the *préposé* find a new family to take her.[18] After 1853, the Administration provided for those of all ages who were unable to work by awarding extra payments to the foster parents, in compensation for the loss of the child's labor if they would agree to keep such children. They usually agreed, although in many cases not out of any great love for the child. Repeated requests for more money and threats to send the children back if the Administration did not make sufficiently large payments to the foster parents indicate that the foster

243

families only kept the children if they received extra money. They could not afford to keep them otherwise.

To secure an extra payment for an incapacitated child, the foster parent had the doctor in charge of the abandoned children in the area examine the child. He then filed a report stating the youngster's infirmity and requested an extra payment for the foster parent. The Administration occasionally complained that there were too many requests made by a particular doctor at a particular time, especially for compensation to a foster parent for a child with urinary incontinence. In the majority of cases, however, the foster parent was paid. Payments ranged from 1 to 9 francs extra per month, depending on the disability of the child. The average monthly payment was 4 francs, or 50 francs a year.[19] It was probably enough to cover food and some clothing. The Administration took care of medical expenses. All extra compensation to the foster parents for a youngster's infirmity were made for twelve months, renewable for another year upon a new certificate from the doctor.

In cases where a child had more than one disability, the foster parents frequently demanded double payments, but this request was not always honored. In a typical instance of a denied request, a woman who received 4 francs extra per month for a deaf-mute, asked for an additional 4 francs when, at age five years, the child also proved incontinent.[20] Other denials of requests for extra compensation occurred in the cases when a foster parent had already received the 50 francs at the end of a child's twelfth year. In such instances the foster parents were not always entitled to extra payment for the chronically disabled teenager. There are no records as to how many foster parents who were denied extra payment actually kept the children.

The total percentage of abandoned children in the under twenty-one year age bracket for whom the foster parents received extra payments never exceeded 8.6 percent of the total, and was over 7 percent only for the years 1871, 1875, and 1880 (see tables 7.3 and 7.4). Given the circumstances of the birth of the children and the type of care many received, this percentage seems low. The data may not represent the total number of infirm children and only indicate those for whom the foster parents received extra payment. Presumably, most foster parents sought the money to which they were entitled. It is quite possible, however, that the state refused the payments and authorities did not recognize a disability where one existed. Concepts of abused or battered children are modern, and many children with permanent burn marks, bruises, or even lameness may not have been reported and no extra indemnity sought by

244

or awarded to the foster parents if such children could still work. Therefore, the percentages of disabilities reported are slightly lower than the amount of infirmities the children actually suffered.

Young adults over twenty-one ceased to be wards of the state and l'Assistance Publique no longer had any responsibility for them. Nevertheless, after mid-century it provided for the maintenance with foster parents of those who were incurably infirm or incapacitated and therefore could not live alone or seek employment. The number of young adults disabled or infirm so as to warrant extra payments to their foster families was very low—approximately three to four hundred (see table 7.5).

Some minor problems of interpretation are inherent in the data; they do not present a complete picture of all infirmities that the abandoned children suffered. If the infirmity or disease was mild or curable in less than a year, no extra payments were awarded. Nor do the data include those hospitalized for short periods of time. Children afflicted with ringworm—an ailment prevalent throughout the century and affecting 250 abandoned children in 1894—for example, were hospitalized in a special sanitorium, Berck-sur-Mer, which had been developed just for treating this ailment.[21] Treatment was short term, the state paid hospital costs and the foster parents received no extra payment. If, by some chance, children had ailments for which the foster parents did not request extra payment, those cases also are not reflected in the data. Moreover, children often had more than one infirmity and this does not show up on the tables. For example, some children had both rickets and were incontinent, or they were classified as idiots and also scrofulous or deaf.[22] There is no way of ascertaining under which infirmity any child was listed.

The rates for some ailments and diseases are constant over the century, while others show a decline after 1880-1885 (see tables 7.3, 7.4 and 7.5). The incidence of epilepsy, paralysis, deafness, and muteness remained relatively constant over the years, and these are disorders little affected by advances in medical care. All other infirmities decreased after the 1880s, which suggests that hygiene and medical treatment improved after that time and resulted in a decline in the incidence of disabling diseases. Rickets, incontinence, and constitutional weakness were the most common disablements for which the Administration paid the foster parents for children under twelve. The incidence of these afflictions, however, was very low—about one percent for each disease out of the total population of abandoned children in that age group. As the children got

245

Table 7.3

Infirm Children under 12 Years of Age For Whom Foster Parents Received Extra Payments, 1856-1900
(Number and Percent of all Abandoned Children Under 12 Years)

Infirmities	1856		1866		1871		1875		1880		1885		1890		1895		1900	
	No.	%	No.	%	No.	%	No.	%	No.	%	No.	%	No.	%	No.	%	No.	%
Deaf and/or Mute	6	.04	8	.05	16	.10	11	.07	14	.10	22	.13	14	.07	13	.05	23	.07
Eye Diseases	25	.18	58	.37	85	.51	95	.62	84	.61	44	.27	51	.25	38	.14	29	.09
Epilepsy	14	.10	13	.08	15	.09	30	.20	16	.12	21	.13	18	.09	10	.04	20	.07
Mental Deficiency	39	.28	20	.13	62	.37	33	.22	29	.21	24	.15	20	.10	23	.09	33	.11
Paralysis	21	.15	17	.11	33	.20	23	.15	27	.20	18	.11	14	.07	27	.10	18	.06
Rickets	156	1.10	173	1.10	265	1.60	262	1.70	256	1.90	117	.71	0	0.00	31	.12	38	.12
Scrofula	68	.49	77	.50	150	.91	98	.64	146	1.10	83	.50	190	.92	14	.05	10	.03
Incontinence	112	.81	115	.74	244	1.50	284	1.90	268	2.00	94	.57	73	.35	41	.15	85	.28
Phthisis, TB, Lung Diseases	2	.01	6	.04	5	.03	2	.01	11	.08	6	.04	5	.02	8	.03	15	.05
Syphilis	1	.01	3	.02	24	.14	18	.12	19	.14	8	.05	16	.08	7	.03	10	.03
Skin Diseases	24	.17	23	.15	45	.27	38	.25	36	.26	26	.16	13	.06	10	.04	24	.08
Gibbosity (Humpback Deformation)	11	.08	46	.30	8	.05	51	.33	52	.39	37	.22	29	.14	21	.08	21	.07
Constitutional Weakness	51	.37	92	.59	176	1.1	93	.61	153	1.10	51	.31	21	.10	22	.08	49	.16
Other			23	.15	116	.70	85	.55	75	.55	101	.61	21	.10	18	.07	26	.08
TOTAL	530	3.80	674	4.30	1243	7.50	1123	7.30	1186	8.60	652	4.00	464	2.30	283	1.1	401	1.30

Source: *Rapps. Anns.*, 1856-1900.

Note: Percentage is based on the number of abandoned children at these ages.
Data exist only for the years 1856-1900 since prior to 1853 there were no regular provisions for the infirm or disabled and there is no information on the disabilities of children.

246

Table 7.4

Infirm Children 12 to 21 Years of Age For Whom Foster Parents Received Extra Payments, 1856-1900
(Number and Percent of All Abandoned Children in this Age Group)

Infirmities	1856 No.	1856 %	1866 No.	1866 %	1871 No.	1871 %	1875 No.	1875 %	1880 No.	1880 %	1885 No.	1885 %	1890 No.	1890 %	1895 No.	1895 %	1900 No.	1900 %
Deaf and/or Mute	7	.10	13	.14	14	.16	16	.14	24	.19	7	.07	15	.07	25	.09	22	.07
Eye Diseases	60	.89	59	.64	56	.62	60	.54	110	.88	38	.38	55	.27	59	.22	40	.13
Epilepsy	18	.27	24	.26	6	.07	19	.17	22	.18	25	.25	39	.19	26	.10	57	.19
Mental Deficiency	43	.64	61	.66	73	.81	69	.62	74	.59	42	.41	61	.30	54	.20	70	.23
Paralysis	24	.36	33	.36	47	.52	22	.20	21	.17	44	.43	13	.06	26	.10	42	.14
Rickets	87	1.30	06	1.20	97	1.30	94	.84	132	1.10	53	.52	0	0.00	40	.15	37	.12
Scrofula	86	1.30	47	.51	113	1.30	74	.66	105	.84	46	.45	156	.76	26	.10	29	.09
Incontinence	51	.76	58	.63	83	.93	120	1.10	102	.82	46	.45	29	.14	26	.10	25	.08
Phthisis, TB, Lung Diseases	5	.07	12	.13	7	.08	8	.07	20	.16	12	.12	23	.11	20	.08	37	.12
Syphilis	0	0.00	0	0.00	0	0.	2	.02	3	.02	8	.08	0	0.00	0	0.00	0	0.00
Skin Diseases	8	.12	16	.17	15	.17	21	.19	20	.16	4	.04	5	.02	3	.01	8	.03
Gibbosity (Humpback Deformation)	38	.56	74	.80	15	.17	91	.81	74	.59	41	.40	64	.31	76	.29	118	.38
Constitutional Weakness	54	.80	61	.66	73	.81	44	.39	103	.83	42	.41	92	.45	94	.36	173	.56
Other	0	0.00	33	.36	109	1.20	48	.43	73	.59	76	.75	29	.14	42	.16	115	.37
TOTAL	481	7.10	597	6.50	708	7.90	688	6.20	883	7.10	484	4.80	581	6.50	517	4.80	773	5.30

Source: *Rapps. Anns.*, 1856-1900.

Note: Percentage is based on the number of abandoned children at these ages.

Data exist only for the years 1856-1900 since prior to 1853 there were no regular provisions for the infirm or disabled and there is no information on the disabilities of children.

247

Table 7.5

Infirm Children over 21 Years of Age For Whom Foster Parents Received Extra Payments, 1856-1900
(Number and Percent of Those Over 21)

Infirmities	1856 No.	1856 %	1866 No.	1866 %	1871 No.	1871 %	1875 No.	1875 %	1880 No.	1880 %	1885 No.	1885 %	1890 No.	1890 %	1895 No.	1895 %	1900 No.	1900 %
Deaf and/or Mute	9	3.4	8	2.6	16	4.5	16	5.0	14	4.2	17	5.2	17	5.1	18	4.7	24	5.5
Eye Diseases	34	12.9	64	20.6	52	14.9	61	19.0	64	19.0	69	21.2	76	22.8	97	25.2	106	24.1
Epilepsy	21	8.0	17	5.5	19	5.5	12	3.7	16	4.7	27	8.3	17	5.1	26	6.8	24	5.5
Mental Deficiency	49	18.6	48	15.4	46	13.2	62	19.3	70	20.8	45	13.8	77	23.1	80	20.8	81	18.4
Paralysis	20	7.6	25	8.0	25	7.2	31	9.7	30	8.9	39	12.0	25	7.5	39	10.1	30	6.8
Rickets	47	17.8	33	10.6	65	18.7	36	11.2	32	9.5	17	5.2	0	0.00	21	5.5	23	5.2
Scrofula	31	11.7	28	9.0	35	10.1	11	3.4	23	6.8	22	6.7	41	12.3	12	3.1	13	3.0
Incontinence	16	6.1	3	.96	1	.29	0	0.00	6	1.8	7	2.1	1	.3	0	0.00	1	.23
Phthisis, TB, Lung Diseases	3	1.10	3	.96	2	.57	8	2.50	5	1.50	3	.92	6	1.80	10	2.60	19	4.30
Syphilis	0	0.00	1	.32	1	.29	0	0.00	0	0.00	0	0.00	2	.60	2	.52	2	.45
Skin Diseases	1	.38	5	1.60	1	.29	1	.31	1	.30	0	0.00	1	.30	1	.26	4	.91
Gibbosity (Humpback Deformation)	26	9.8	31	10.0	8	2.3	65	20.2	57	16.9	28	8.6	43	12.9	48	12.5	56	12.7
Constitutional Weakness	13	4.9	19	6.1	8	2.3	3	.93	4	1.2	1	.31	8	2.4	2	.52	8	1.8
Other	0	0.00	26	8.4	71	20.4	15	4.7	15	4.5	51	15.6	20	6.0	29	7.5	49	11.1
Total	264	100.00	311	100.00	348	100.00	321	100.00	337	100.00	326	100.00	334	100.00	385	100.00	440	100.00

Source: *Rapps. Anns.*, 1856-1900.
Note: Data exist only for the years 1856-1900 since prior to 1853 there were no regular provisions for the infirm, disabled or those over twenty-one years old and there is no information of the disabilities of the young adults. All *enfants assistés* over age 21 for whom foster parents received any money were infirm or disabled.

older, reports of scrofula and eye diseases (particularly blindness) increased. Mental deficiency was not very common among children under twenty-one.

These infirmities reveal much about the care of the children at the wet nurses and foster parents. Rickets, the most prevalent problem, was caused by a lack of Vitamin D, supplied in milk and activated by sunlight. Data on the incidence of rickets among abandoned children suggest that at least one percent of surviving babies received inadequate amounts of milk, were kept inside dark, damp houses, and rarely went out into the sunlight during the years of bone development. Incontinence, the other abnormality with a high incidence of occurrence, may be due to bladder or urinary tract infection, a birth defect in the urethra, or it may be psychological in origin stemming from emotional insecurity. Accidents accounted for only a small proportion of reported disabilities (they appear in the three tables as "deformations" and "other"). The most prevalent accidents were burns, broken limbs resulting in deformity, the loss of limbs, and broken, mangled or lost hands—injuries that occurred when caught in machinery were the child worked.

For young adults over age twenty-one, eye diseases (predominantly blindness), deformations, and "idiocy" were the most common disabilities that warranted payments to the foster parents to encourage their keeping the young adult. The eye disease could have been "xerophthalmia, a sight disease that in its advanced stage is known as nutritional blindness. Associated with malnutrition and caused by a deficiency of vitamin A, the disease strikes children between the ages of six months and six years."[24] By age twenty the person would be blind. "Idiocy" could originate in gestation and birth, but malnutrition and emotional neglect also lead to mental deficiency. Generally, as a result of inadequate diet, many young adults were retarded physiologically. Women rarely began to menstruate before eighteen, and in many villages there was not a single man of military stature.[25] But this was true of both the native children of the villages and the Parisian foundlings sent there.

Despite the type of treatment the children received, and their general neglect, the incidence of serious disability is low. This is in part explained by the high mortality rate. Only the hardiest survived. Those who survived infancy and young adulthood apparently did so with little permanent infirmity, illness, or incapacitation. Most were able to work and contribute to the family economy before they left their foster parents. Throughout the century, but increasingly after the 1880s, the lives of abandoned children with their foster parents were neither ones of the dependent chronically ill nor filled with pure, unadulterated work. The law required, among other things, that foster parents send their charges to school.

Secular and Religious Education

The Administration tried to ensure the education of children in the care of foster parents. Officials believed that a primary school education would prevent crime and moral vices and make the children better workers and citizens; thus they would become less of a burden to society. Incentives to education increased as the century progressed. In 1835, Guizot, France's minister of Public Instruction, notified the *préposés* that male abandoned children over eight years old were to be admitted free to the public primary schools, and the communes were to provide free books and materials to these children just as they did for the indigent of the area.[26] The Administration declared, in 1841, that it would do everything in its power to establish schools in those communes with large numbers of abandoned children from Paris so that education would be given to all, especially the poor and wards of the state.[27] At the same time, the Administration encouraged the foster parents to send the children to school. Foster parents, however, were reluctant to part with the labor of their charges, especially the valuable labor of older children who were needed in the fields. In fact, some foster parents sought the abandoned children so that they would have someone to work in the fields while their biological children took advantage of schooling.[28] In addition, commune officials and instructors agreed only reluctantly to educate the *enfants assistés*. In dispensing free education, the commune gave preference to its own indigents; instructors, not paid specifically to educate the abandoned, therefore neglected them.

To overcome the resistance of foster parents to sending the children to school, in 1841 the Administration instituted policies to compensate the foster parents with a monetary supplement of 20 francs if the children went to primary school for three years and also received religious instruction.[29] In the 1840s, the foster parents received an education supplement only if they sent the children for the entire school year. Excessive absence meant the foster parent forfeited all supplementary payment. The first time that a child missed more than ten days of classes per month, the foster parent would lose the entire payment for the month. The second time that a child missed more than ten days in a month the foster parent would forfeit all extra compensation for sending a child to school.[30] This regulation must have had little, if any, positive effect. If a child missed more than twenty days during the first two months, there was no further educational supplement, no matter how often the foster parent sent the child to school. Thus, there was no incentive to keep a child in school, and many foster parents must have ceased sending the children.

School attendance lagged; children attended irregularly and were absent especially when there was work to be done in the field. Accordingly, in 1850 new regulations were issued. For the first time the Administration requested that foster parents send the children to school starting when they were six years old rather than eight. There were two theories behind this change. Six-year-olds were less valuable as field hands than eight-year-olds, so that if education began at six, children might receive at least two years of schooling. In addition, education was viewed as improving morals and as encouraging proper work habits and good behavior. Thus, the earlier the child received such training the better.

Starting in 1850, the Administration paid foster parents according to the number of days a child attended school. The older the child, and the more days he spent in school, the higher the monthly compensation to the foster parents. This measure was designed to serve as an incentive for foster parents to keep children in school all year, not just for the days when there was little work to be done around the farm. If a child attended fewer than one hundred and fifty days, the foster parents received no money.[31] Furthermore, foster parents received less money for children ages six to eight than they did for those over eight on the theory that foster parents deserved increased compensation for the loss of the more valuable labor of the older child.

Instructors and the commune also received monetary incentives to teach the *enfants assistés*, starting with regulations of 1844 and 1847 which required the Administration to reimburse them for each day an abandoned child spent in school.[32] For children aged eight to twelve who went to school, regulations required the instructors to keep grade sheets and attendance lists which were open to inspection by the field representatives or inspectors. If a child were absent more than ten days a month, the instructor would receive, at most, half his allotted pay, Instructors' payments varied according to the age of the children in school. For children age six to eight, instructors received 50 centimes per month; for children eight to twelve they were paid double that amount.

Clothing distributed to the abandoned children was all alike in style and quantity and was allocated annually until the child was eight. In an effort to promote school attendance even more, the Administration ordered new sets of clothes for the children's eighth birthday so they could go to school sufficiently clad. Then, children did not receive another clothing allotment for another three years. Clothing was frequently the wrong size when it arrived and almost certainly too small, not to mention threadbare, by the end of the third year of use. Not only did the fit of the clothing leave much to be desired, but the quantity seemed inadequate for three years of school and work. There is almost no evidence of foster parents dressing the abandoned children in clothes out of uniform.[33] Starting in 1869, the Administration allocated the clothing annually after the seventh year, and except for shirts (3), pants and dresses (2), the quantity of clothing doubled and included two pairs of shoes, extra vests, skirts, and socks. Their clothes set the children apart and revealed their status to the world. They were ridiculed and mocked by others in school, and scorned for having been abandoned.

C'est sur le « bâtard » que, enfant, le bourgeois a déjà jeté sa première pierre.

21) "C'est sur le 'bâtard' que, enfant, le bourgeois a déjà jeté sa premiere pierre." Drawing by Couturier for *L'Assiette au beurre*, no. 89, December 13, 1902 titled "Les Filles-Mères".

Conditions seem not to have changed much between the 1850s and 1870. An inspection of 1870 revealed that instructors refused to teach the *enfants assistés* who entered their classes and refused to give them materials and books. Some were just given a corner of a desk. The youngest and least advanced sat on a bench with no books, supplies, or desk, and had nothing to do.[34]

Regulations enacted in 1882, making primary school attendance not only free but compulsory for boys and girls, constituted the major educational reform of the century. Obligatory attendance at school until age thirteen led l'Assistance Publique to compensate the foster parents an extra ten francs per month for the loss of the child's labor (see table 7.2) and, in 1885, to send the children new winter coats at their seventh and tenth birthdays. If the children received a certificate of completion, all those involved in the education process received a bonus: the foster parents received 50 francs, the instructors received 10 francs, and the child received 10 francs, which was deposited in his or her name in a savings account. The payment was not negligible, since 50 francs was close to a month's wages for a working woman.

A large percentage of children attended school from time to time despite all the reluctance of the foster parents to send them and the instructors to teach them (see table 7.6). These attendance figures are inflated, however, since they include all children who went to any class at any time, even those who only saw the inside of the school for one day and never returned. Furthermore, some entries were falsified on the school registers so that foster parents and teachers were paid who had no right to the payment.[35] The data do not indicate how many children attended daily and regularly. In 1885, almost one hundred percent of those aged six to thirteen attended school—at least once!

Table 7.6

Number and Percent of Abandoned Children who
Attended Primary School, 1857-1885

| Year | Number of Children 6-12 Years | | Percent |
	Those who should have gone to school	Those who attended classes	
1857	7,919	5,443	68.7
—			
1862	8,577	6,434	75.0
1863	7,996	6,763	84.6
1864	7,628	6,518	85.4
1865	7,459	6,535	87.6
1866	8,468	7,528	88.9
1867	8,512	7,416	87.1
1868	8,145	6,672	81.9
—			
1875	10,387	7,911	76.2
—			
1880	9,555	7,532	78.8
—			
1885	9,272	9,235	99.6

Source: *Rapps. Anns.*, 1857-1885.

More relevant figures about the extent of primary education at the end of the century are those that exclusively enumerate children who attended school on a regular basis frequently enough to pass the tests required to receive a certificate of completion of primary school. The numbers increase consistently from 1886. The increase is due, in part, to the inclusion of the *moralement abandonnés* among the data (see table 7.7). The data reflect the delayed effect of the institution of compulsory education in 1882, taking several years for the children to earn a certificate. The total number of children eligible to receive certificates is unknown. As a result accurate percentages are impossible to compute, but adequate estimates are obtainable.[36] Roughly one-third or less of those eligible to receive certificates did so. Literacy rates, the best measure of education, are unfortunately unavailable for the abandoned children.

Table 7.7

Number of *Enfants Assistés* of Paris who Received
Certificates of Completion of Primary School, 1886-1895

1886	147
1887	137
1888	99
1889	171
1890	224
1891	285
1892	334
1893	339
1894	343
1895	450

Source: *Rapps. Anns.*, 1886-1895.

The Administration considered the religious instruction of the abandoned children as important as the secular. Accordingly, it encouraged foster parents to send the children for such training for two years, from age ten to twelve, and to have the children receive their Communion. Monetary supplements provided the added incentive for foster parents to give their charges some religion. Despite this stimulus, attendance at church classes was no more regular than at primary school. Data for religious education are similar to those for primary education; the numbers are inflated and do not truly reflect the quantity of spiritual education received. The Administration recorded roughly seventy-five to eighty percent as having attended at least one class—but maybe only one—in religious instruction. Unfortunately, there are no records as to whether or not the children took their First Communion, or were confirmed.

Both the parish priests and the Administration complained of the lack of religious education for these children. The Administration blamed the priests for neglecting the abandoned children within their parishes. Around mid-century, some administrators claimed that the priests were so negligent of their duties that the Hospice was forced to recall the children to Paris so they could take their First Communion and Confirmation.[37] The parish priests in turn blamed the foster parents for not sending the children to them. They complained that the foster parents had no religion themselves and were only interested in profiting from the child's labor.[38] Time spent with the priest was time spent away from duties on the farm.

The lack of religious education of the abandoned children might indicate their lack of integration into both the family of the foster parents and into the community as a whole. Perhaps some local priests felt that these *enfants assistés* were not really part of their parish, merely temporary outsiders. It is probable that the foster parents did not subscribe to the ideas of reformers and bureaucrats that the abandoned children must be educated to become law-abiding, moral citizens—at least not at the expense of their labor. The Administration of l'Assistance Publique placed so much emphasis on education, and even perhaps inflated its figures to show the country that their wards were receiving an adequate education, because officials believed that the moral education provided by primary and religious schools would make the children better workers and citizens and prevent crime and moral vices.[39]

To expand educational opportunity for the abandoned children, in 1834, one leading reformer, Benoiston de Châteauneuf, proposed saving a space for abandoned children in a college in each department where those children were abandoned. He advocated careers of talent open to abandoned children.[40] His proposal was ignored, but on a few occasions during the century an abandoned child was admitted to higher education. In Saint-Calais, a boy, born and abandoned in 1847, was admitted to the Ecole Normale de Mans in 1865.[41] This was a rare and isolated case, but probably not the only one. Finally, in 1897, the Conseil Général de la Seine established a scholarship at the Ecole des Beaux Arts in Paris to be awarded annually to a former abandoned child.[42] Abandoned children—as well as their "milk brothers and sisters"—rarely continued their formal education beyond their twelfth or thirteenth year. There was almost no opportunity for them to pursue an occupation other than that of an agricultural laborer, factory worker, artisan, or domestic.

Vocational Training, Agricultural Labor, and Apprenticeship

Vocational training for children over age thirteen was quite different from an academic education. Consistent with the new attitudes of the 1880s, in 1882 l'Assistance Publique began instituting formal training of abandoned children in special schools. This training expanded greatly in the 1890s with the admission of the *moralement abandonnés* to the service.

In 1882, both the Ecole d'Alembert and Ecole le Nôtre opened as vocational training schools for boys. The Ecole d'Alembert, occupying the site and buildings of a former prison in the department of the Seine-et-Marne, was run by l'Assistance Publique of Paris for a maximum of 110 boys. The school consisted of workshops for typography, printing, and cabinet making. The boys spent four years at apprenticeship in this school and then l'Assistance Publique placed them in the private sector. The Ecole le Nôtre differed from the Ecole d'Alembert in that its maximum capacity was only fifty boys, of a minimum age of fourteen, and it required that the boys have a certificate of primary education prior to admission. This school specialized in horticulture, and the boys spent three years at the school prior to placement in agriculture and horticulture. Boys at both schools were able and encouraged to spend vacation periods with their foster parents. After 1889, the two institutions had wings set aside for the *moralement abandonnés*. [43]

Institutional vocational training for girls began on a miniscule scale in the 1850s and 1860s. The Ecole d'Accouchement in Paris each year took at least one abandoned girl as a student to train her to be a midwife. As the century progressed, and especially in the 1880s, many more than one were admitted each year to that school. [44]

These institutions served only a minority of abandoned children. Most youths after their twelfth year spent their time on the farms of their foster parents, if they could use the labor of the child. If not, the Administration frequently placed these adolescents on other farms, as often as possible in the same area as that of the foster parents. Administrators and politicians had become concerned with the declining population of the rural areas, and employment of children on the farms was an attempt to repopulate these areas and to increase agricultural production. [45] In 1860 there were 44,000 abandoned children engaged in agricultural labor in France. [46] Since most of the children had Parisian or other urban mothers, this represents an out-migration from an urban to a rural area.

Most, but not all youths from ages twelve to twenty-one served as agricultural laborers. Starting in 1852, the director placed many in apprenticeship positions with artisans, generally in the same village as that of the foster parents, or else in the main town of the area. Boys were apprenticed to wooden clog, shoe and boot makers, masons, day-laborers, hair dressers, woodworkers, nailsmiths, tailors, gardeners, and wheelwrights, among others. Girls found places primarily as domestics, although some served as dressmakers or embroiderers, or worked as linen maids. At the end of the century, of a sample of 580 abandoned boys not engaged in agriculture, the highest proportion were domestic servants (twelve percent) followed by shoe and boot makers (nine percent), railroad employees (nine percent), blacksmiths, tailors, and miners (seven percent each). In the sample of 942 abandoned girls not employed in agriculture, by far the leading occupation was that of domestic servant (eighty-four percent), followed by seamstresses (at nine percent). These were traditional occupations for working-class youths. There were a few boys in nontraditional occupations such as pharmacists, notary clerks, teachers, and typographers (one percent or less in each). A few girls worked as nurses, sales girls or *employées du commerce* (less than one percent in each).[47]

No matter what trade teenage abandoned children followed, the Administration placed them under the tutelage of a master or patron—as an apprentice under contract. This placement, in theory, occurred from the 1850s, but there are no records as to precisely what percentage of abandoned children over twelve the Administration placed in apprenticeship, how many stayed with their foster parents, and with how many the state simply lost all contact.

Contracts for the placement of abandoned children were drawn up by the patron and the director of l'Assistance Publique. They lasted from three to six years, depending on the agreement worked out between the director and the patron. The adolescent had virtually no voice in the terms of the agreement. In theory, the director of l'Assistance Publique placed the youth with a farmer or artisan according to the teenager's physical constitution, intelligence, and disposition.[48] In placing these youths, the parish priests, mayors, and field representatives who supposedly knew the children, served as advisors to the director, who was the legal guardian over all abandoned children aged twelve to twenty-one. Verbal contractual agreements were the rule in placement of children as farm laborers until 1875, when written agreements became the practice. Until that time, written contracts of apprenticeship occurred only when the youth was placed in industry. Even then, there was no requirement that salaries be stipulated in writing, and often they were not. After 1875, all contracts and salary stipulations were to be in writing for factory, artisan, and farm laborers. [49]

Salary and payment for jobs performed by abandoned children varied with the department. In some areas, payment to the children started with their twelfth year; in others it was later. [50] Children were to work in return for their room and board, but in most situations they were entitled to payment for good conduct and good work. The abandoned children serving as apprentices or as farm workers were entitled to keep that money which the director of l'Assistance Publique deemed indispensible to their needs. Extra earnings immediately went into savings accounts in the children's names, to be used as a dowry or nest-egg when the person reached majority or married. Thus, the state enforced thrift, and provided for the children's futures.

Officials of l'Assistance Publique could not always know the correct placement of each child, and there was no supervision or inspection of the sites where the children were placed. It stands to reason that many children were unhappy or unsuitable in their positions and left. Some placed themselves with another master or patron, often without the intervention or interference of l'Assistance Publique. The second, and subsequent positions, were frequently in the same trade as the first one. [51] The Administration learned of such placements only if the child or the patron reported it to the Hospice or to the director of l'Assistance Publique, as they often did. If children found positions for themselves in the countryside where they had been reared, it was probable that the *sous-inspecteurs* or inspectors knew and reported it. Sometimes teenagers left their position in the country and went to Paris in search of a new one. The Administration generally allowed them to stay if the apprenticeship or job was appropriate. If, however, children left their initial position and found a new one for themselves in a department where l'Assistance Publique had no jurisdiction, the Administration considered them runaways and ordered their return to their previous place. In one such instance a sixteen-year-old boy from Saint-Calais in the department of the Sarthe left his position and found a job with a miller in Orne, a neighboring department. The miller and the mayor of the town in Orne liked the lad and wanted him to stay. The boy refused to leave the miller willingly and the miller refused to part with him. His return, however, was ordered by the justice of the peace and all obeyed the rules. The boy returned to the Sarthe to the commune in which he had been reared, and to the control of the government representatives. [52]

Not all young people who left their first position found new ones for themselves. Some returned to their foster parents, and some to the Hospice, either of their own accord, or unwillingly when the police picked them up and brought them there. When young people quit their positions, they were without resources; often they wandered the streets of Paris and the roads of the countryside or went in search of employment that suited them. Police often picked up boys as vagabonds and girls as prostitutes. Some charges may have been correct, but quite likely many were merely homeless waifs without family, resources, or a place to go. The Administration usually found new positions for them.

To the Administration, a less desirable alternative to placing individual teenagers with private masters was placing them in groups in workshops or factories. Several manufacturers requested ten to twenty youngsters to work for them. There was a two-pronged criticism of such group employment of the youngsters. Moralists thought that groups of foundling youths living together without the socializing and controlling influence of a family would encourage their "natural" vices. Others criticized the conditions to which the youths were subjected. Visitors to the sites reported children sleeping in unheated and unventilated attics, eating meager and inadequate food rations, and subject to physical abuse.[53] Such group placement of *enfants assistés* seems to have been rare.

No matter what the placement of a youth over twelve—whether with a farmer, with a tradesman or artisan in the countryside or in Paris, or in a factory or workshop—there was no regular system of inspection and no supervision. When the young adults complained about treatment and conditions of life and work, or when the masters complained about the youths' laziness or inclination to steal, it was one person's word against another's. There was no protection of the children and no assurances that they would be treated humanely. The situation was similar for other, nonabandoned, workers. Lenard Berlanstein has provided a picture of the lives of working-class boys who were not considered deviants, and who indeed may be considered typical of a certain class of workers in the capital. A comparison of the apprenticeship situations of the boys he describes and those of the *enfants assistés* reveals striking similarities. Berlanstein reported that "three-quarters of the contractual arrangements between boys and their masters broke down, and one-fifth ran away."[54] While the records for abandoned youths do not permit us that degree of exactness, they do indicate that large numbers of youths begged the Administration for a change of placement and even more broke the contract, ran away, and actively searched a new placement for themselves.[55] Masters accused both the working-class boys and the *en-*

fants assistés of tendencies toward vagrancy, lack of responsibility, and laziness. From the boys' point of view, abuses by the masters were similar—a lack of nourishment (one meal a day, which was usually meatless) and physical mistreatment. Exploitation of the adolescents' labor seems clear in both cases. Masters or patrons kept an apprenticed *assisté* as long as such a child could be used; there was no mention of "training" the person. If Berlanstein's descriptions of the apprenticeship experiences of boys in Paris can be taken as typical, then there is little material difference between the abandoned children's experiences as apprentices and those of working-class youths of Paris in general during the nineteenth century. There is one crucial difference: working-class youths in general had families on whom they could fall back;[56] the abandoned children did not.

The state successfully discouraged parental reclamation of the children, kept the children with foster parents as much as possible and for as long as possible, provided for their primary and religious education, and enabled some to learn a trade and get a job. This multifaceted social welfare system for the children was designed to create hardworking, law-abiding and predominantly rural citizens. Military service, marriage, and the extent of moral deviancy are three criteria by which to measure the success.[57]

Military Service

According to the Decree of 1811, all male abandoned children and poor orphans, upon their twelfth birthday, were to serve in the navy as a means of repaying the debt they owed to the state for their care. The interest in these children for military duty was inspired by the demand for 7,000 new recruits in that year.[58] The twelve-year-olds were to serve as *mousses* (ships' boys). For the first year in which the Decree was in effect, 526 boys from the department of the Seine served as *mousses*. Several years later, the minister of the navy refused to take all the orphans and abandoned boys. He did not want the boys with "bad inclinations" or bad conduct to be sent to him as a form of correction. He preferred to select them according to ability, intelligence, good dispositions, and good and regular habits—characteristics he believed lacking in the abandoned boys.[59]

By mid-century, officials again argued that the abandoned boys owed a debt to the state for raising them and therefore should serve in the military. As a result, after 1849, the *enfants assistés* served as conscripts in the military just as everyone else. Abandoned boys from this date on were listed on the census of their commune and were subject to the draft when their turn came, along with all the other boys from the commune where they lived. The resulting numbers recruited each year by conscription and the number who volunteered seem low (see table 7.8). Unfortunately, data are not available for the years prior to 1875.

Table 7.8

Number of Abandoned Children of Paris Entering Military Service, 1875-1895

Year	Number of Conscripts	Number of Volunteers
1875	458	22
1876	566	not available
1877	531	14
1878	425	38
1879	512	54
1880	570	21
1885	717	31
1890	678	24
1895	571	39

Source: *Rapps. Anns.*, 1875-1895.

During the years from 1875 to 1895, between 7,000 and 9,000 abandoned children were above the age of twelve. Roughly half were young men. Thus, those conscripted were drawn from roughly 3,500 to 4,500 eligible men. The numbers conscripted were approximately eight to eighteen percent of those eligible. Contrary to the provisions of the Decree of 1811, most abandoned boys did not enter military service. Not even all those chosen by the *tirage* (drawing or draft) served. On rare occasions, those picked for the draft were already serving after having volunteered. [60] A larger portion were unfit—as many as thirty-nine percent of all the abandoned boys in all of France who were chosen for the draft were found to be unfit. This figure compares with twenty-six percent for the rest of the population. A more accurate comparison is with young men of the *arrondissements* where the *assistés* grew up. On the average, 27.7 percent of the *assistés* from Paris were unfit compared with 15.4 percent of their "milk brothers." This differential of twelve percent is the average for all the areas where the *asistés* lived, although it varied from near zero at Saint-Calais (where a high of forty-five percent were unfit) to a twenty-seven percent difference at Alençon and Bethune. [61] Those who failed to qualify for service were either too small or weak, or had an infirmity or debility.

261

Marriage

Marriage was possible, and indeed desirable, for the *enfants assistés*. In order to marry before they reached their majority, they needed the consent of their legal guardian—the director of l'Assistance Publique. Very few married before their twenty-first birthday; of those who did, most were young women (see table 7.9). This is not surprising since the average age of marriage for women in France was in the mid twenties, and for men in the late twenties.

Table 7.9

Number of Consents for Marriage given by l'Assistance Publique, 1874-1895

Year	Number
1874	75
1875	111
1876	99
1877	82
1878	73
1879	94
1880	125
1885	127
1890	99
1895	110

Source: *Rapps. Anns.*, 1874-1895.

As in the rest of society, a trousseau or dowry was common upon marriage. For the abandoned, this came from three sources: clothing allotment, personal savings, and special funds. When a young girl reached her twelfth birthday, she received her final allotment of clothing from the Administration. This was intended to suffice as her trousseau, but was only slightly more than the regular amount received in her preceeding year. Her dowry generally came from her own savings. If she worked as a seamstress or domestic, a certain portion of her wages were set aside in a special savings for her until she married or turned twenty-one. If she stayed with her foster parents, they were under no obligation to set aside something for her dowry. Sometimes, however, the foster parents used the 50 franc bonus that they received if they kept a child until her twelfth birthday as a dowry for the girls—a clear indication of consideration, and even possible affection, for the girl.

Funds permitting, l'Assistance Publique provided a dowry consisting of 100 to 150 francs to each girl upon her marriage. Most money for these dowries came from donations and legacies from benefactors.

Funds donated or bequeathed in wills as gifts to the Hospice des Enfants Assistés were to be used by children of either sex "who have exhibited good behavior and have a good disposition." [62] Other gifts were more specific, such as for boys entering a certain trade, or for girls marrying or "taking the veil." Some were very specific and could be called "conscience money." Much of it came from men who earmarked it for girls fitting particular physical descriptions and born in a certain year. In some cases, a specific child is named to receive the money when she turned twenty-one. For example, a man left 6,000 francs for a specific girl, Cyprienne-Françoise, upon her twenty-first birthday. He stated that he had committed an indiscretion when he was twenty-one, and the offspring was a girl by that name who had been abandoned by the mother. [63]

Marriage to a foundling was held in low esteem. In *François le Champi*, by George Sand, a young girl whose parents owned property was in love with François, the foundling. Her friends exclaimed to her, "What, Mariette, a girl of your status marrying a foundling! You would henceforth be called by the name of Madame La Fraise! He has no surname other than that. I would be ashamed for you, my poor friend." [64] But marriage prospects for a female foundling were often similar to others of her class. Rigolette, in *Mystères de Paris*, explained, "I ought only to think of marrying some workman. I am an *enfant trouvé*—I possess nothing except my small room and my good courage." [65]

While early in the century parents did not want their children to marry a foundling, by 1885 attitudes seemed to have changed. The director of the agency of the Administration at Chateau-Chinon would write, "People no longer fear marrying their daughters to an *enfant trouvé*." [66] People normally married within their village. If one-fourth of those eligible for marriage in a particular village had been abandoned children (as was frequently the case) parents often either had to condone marriage to such a person or else reconcile themselves to a marriage to someone outside their village. As the number of adult *assistés* increased, and as people realized that most were not dangerous, much of the earlier prejudice may have diminished. Some of the young women who had been foundlings married well to sons of farmers or landowners. In general, the young women wed farmers, cultivators, landowners, wine growers, day-laborers, and artisans such as barrel makers. Most of their husbands came from the same department as the women and some from the same village. [67] There are few marriage records available for young men who had been foundlings, since most appeared to marry after age twenty-one and hence beyond the control of the Administration.

In terms of military service and marriage, young adults who had been abandoned resembled others of a similar socioeconomic group. Reformers still perceived the abandoned children as potential, if not actual, delinquents and hence dangerous. They believed that the children were not born delinquent, but only with a "tendency toward crime," which exhibited itself in specific stages of the child's development: up to age twelve the children were seen as usually docile and orderly; from twelve to fourteen, certain "perversities" became apparent; after age fourteen, "bad instincts reveal themselves" and often the "instinct to rob becomes very developed."[68] Laziness and vagabondage were the forms of deviant behavior most frequently attributed to boys, while thieving and sexual licentiousness were attributed to the girls.[69] To some extent, government officials predicated their policies on ideology rather than on real problems.

Deviant and Criminal Behavior

Authorities attributed begging, thieving, vagrancy, and licentiousness to abandoned children and took measures to prevent such behavior and punish it when it occurred. Begging seems to have been a far greater problem at the beginning of the century than at the end. It was not entirely an act of the abandoned children, but involved complicity by the foster parent. It must have been widespread, since numerous proposals on how to end it appeared in the 1840s, all centering around the concept of paying the foster parent more, especially in the winter, to avoid begging during those months.[70] *Préposés* were often the ones who suggested paying the foster parents more on the condition that the children in their charge not beg.[71] Concern with begging ebbed during the second half of the century as the Administration increased payment to the foster parents for children under twelve and also provided for teenagers. At this time, concern with other forms of bad behavior increased.

Youths who exhibited "criminal deviancy" did not have the same life styles as the norm. The children who were lazy, who robbed, or who ran away suffered one of four consequences of their behavior: they changed their place of employment or foster parent, they were sent to a *colonie agricole* (prison farm or reformatory), they went before a tribunal and faced the possibility of prison, or they ran away and were not apprehended.

The number of those who ran away and were never caught was very small—generally less than one-tenth of one percent of abandoned children aged seven to twelve (see table 7.10). This low percentage does not represent all runaways, but just those who successfully evaded authorities. The Administration aimed to keep the children under the surveillance of the field representative. Evidently they succeeded to a great extent, especially after 1860. Many who ran away were found on neighboring farms, in the nearby town, or in Paris. Some runaways came back to the Hospice of their own accord and sought shelter there. Probably they had nowhere else to go, and at least they were aware that the administrators at the Hospice were responsible for them. The police picked up others under suspicion of prostitution or as beggars and vagrants. After apprehension, the youths were either immediately released to the Administration or were taken to the *dépôt* of the prefect of police and from there taken back to the Hospice. The director of the Hospice permitted some of the youths to remain in the institution under his supervision as *filles* or *garçons de service* (orderlies, nurses' aids, general helpers). Most of them he either sent to new foster parents in the same *arrondissement* of the department where they had originally lived, or to a new employer under a new contract of apprenticeship. [72]

Table 7.10

Abandoned Children of Paris Who Evaded the Authorities and Escaped, 1843-1875

Year	Number	Percent	Year	Number	Percent
1843	20	.09	1859	46	—
1844	17	.08	1860	50	.2
1845	10	.05	1861	14	—
1846	22	.10	1862	1	.01
1847	41	.2	1863	4	.05
1848	19	.09	1864	5	.06
1849	11	.05	1865	3	.04
1850	19	.09	1866	1	.01
1851	8	—	1867	—	—
1852	23	—	1868	—	—
1853	—	—	1869	4	.05
1854	31	—	1870	2	—
1855	30	.1	1871	4	—
1856	—	—	1872	5	—
1857	—	—	1873	3	—
1858	—	—	1874	4	—
			1875	1	.009

Source: Computed from *Rapps. Anns.*, 1852-1860. The data in the Report of 1852 are cumulated from 1842. The years above are the only years for which data are available.

Note: The percentages are based on the number of abandoned children aged six to twelve. Unfortunately, that number is known only for the years given.
"—" = missing data, although for the years 1867 and 1868 there is reason to believe that the number is 0.

265

Some foster parents and employers requested that their charges be sent back to Paris because the behavior of the youths did not conform to their wishes. Of the girls whom they sent back, most were over twelve years old and usually accused of being unwilling to work, incorrigible, doing as they pleased, engaging in misconduct, or being quarrelsome or licentious. The boys whom the foster parents or patron returned were usually accused of laziness, refusal to work, and "bad conduct." [73] For all those children who committed minor infractions, the director found new positions. For the years 1855 and 1865 foster parents sent back to the Hospice approximately 400 children of unspecified ages. This number represents approximately two to three percent of the abandoned children. Only some of these children had behavior problems. In 1849, the only year where complete data exist, only 1.4 percent of children of all ages were sent back to the Hospice for these minor infractions of social standards [74] that would appear to be normal teenage behavior by twentieth-century American standards.

The Administration sent those whose infractions were major (theft, repeated vagrancy, vagabondage, or assault) to a *colonie agricole* or to *la Roquette* or *la Madeleine* (prisons for young offenders). The Administration could do this under the paternal authority invested in the director of l'Assistance Publique. In nineteenth-century France, if a father could not control his children (usually his sons) he could put them in an institution—not as criminals but under the title of parental correction. The director sometimes exercised this right. [75]

The young offenders who committed the most serious crimes came before a police tribunal, and it was the foster parents or the patrons of apprentices who initiated such proceedings. The most common offense was theft. Most of the abandoned children had no lawyer, and the inspectors wrote to the director to intercede in the *assistés'* behalf, which he usually did. Scattered data indicate that fewer than an average of thirty *enfants assistés* of Paris per year (or less than .7 percent) were sentenced before a tribunal and placed in prison (see table 7.11). Prison term was between three and six months for theft. There was only one reported case of assault, and none of a more serious nature. [76] In 1860, in all of France, only 2.23 percent of young offenders in prisons were abandoned children. [77] It appears, however, that in the same year there was one young prisoner out of every 350 *enfants assistés* while for the rest of the population the odds were one in seven hundred. A breakdown for 1849 of abandoned children in Paris, aged twelve to twenty-one, reveals that there were 130 "vicious" or bad youths out of 9,000 or one in sixty-eight. [78] Not all of these were sent to prison. While the prisons were not filled with abandoned children, proportionately more turned up on the roles as juvenile delinquents than in the population at large. This proportion is even greater considering that the population at large includes abandoned children. A high proportion of delinquents is not surprising considering the low socioeconomic level and lack of stable home life for the *enfants assistés*. The data for the population at large, however, are not precisely comparable, since they include those of all socioeconomic groups, and not just the lower ones.

Table 7.11

Abandoned Children between the Ages of 12 and 21 Who Were Placed in Prison[a]
1857-1870

Year	Number	Percent
1857	30	.7
1867	28	.5
1868	33	.6
1869	22	.4
1870	14	.3

Source: Computed from *Rapps. Anns.*, 1857-1870. The years above are the only years for which data are available.

[a]These are the number who entered prison in a given year, not the total number of *assistés* residing in prison during that year.

The question is not why there was such a high proportion of the *assistés* in the prison, but given their background, life styles, and treatment received, why there were so few of them. The major reason for so few abandoned children in correctional institutions was the efforts to keep them out. When an abandoned youth caused trouble, the foster parent or master sought to get rid of such a child and immediately reported the youth. The Administration usually took the youth away and placed him or her with another foster parent or master. Administrators were more inclined to find a new placement for troublesome youths than to put them in an institution. It was far less expensive to keep the children out of institutions since the Administration had to pay about one franc per day for each child incarcerated. Cost was an important consideration. Only those over sixteen whom authorities judged "incorrigible," repeat offenders, or "a great embarassment" to the Administration went to prison. [79] More likely the Administration sent young offenders to *colonies agricoles*.

Colonies agricoles functioned as alternatives to imprisonment for the abandoned boys deemed too incorrigible to live and work for foster parents or masters. Convents or *ouvroirs* (a type of workhouse) served a

267

similar function for the girls. In the 1840s private church-affiliated charities founded the first *colonies* and *ouvroirs* for youths from ages eight to twenty. The aim of the founders and advocates of the *colonies* was twofold. They wanted the *colonies agricoles* to instill morals and teach a trade and proper work habits to lazy, unruly and depraved children, and at the same time make farm lands more productive by putting into use lands which had not been cultivated. They also felt that the *colonies* would be economically self-sufficient and self-supported by the sale of the produce of the land and the work of the children. Thus, they would spare the local and state governments as well as the Administration some of the expense for the care of these children. [80]

At the *colonies*, the delinquent boys spent their time receiving religious instruction and doing agricultural work. The girls in the *ouvroirs* also had religious instruction, but rather than agricultural work they spent their time repairing linen, sewing, and doing laundry. Subject to strict discipline and servitude in these reform schools, the young adults in *colonies* or *ouvroirs* often responded by running away or by becoming mediocre workers. Nevertheless, despite the harshness of the regime, some girls willingly went to these institutions and preferred them to placement with a master. [81]

Many *colonies agricoles* existed only for a few years. They were for the abandoned children and nonabandoned alike; few children under the age of twelve went there. In 1860, in all of France there were eighteen *colonies* housing 600 *enfants assistés*. This is only 1.4 percent of the 44,000 *assistés* engaged in agriculture in the same year. The numbers of Paris' abandoned children who went to *colonies agricoles* or *ouvroirs* was also very small, indicating relatively few incarcerated juvenile delinquents (see table 7.12). As one nineteenth-century social critic stated, "Vice, crime and ignorance hardly recruited more victims among *enfants assistés* than among the rest of the population." [82] This may be true but it is difficult to prove. L'Assistance Publique conducted its own discipline and punishment of its abandoned youths through the supervisory and police functions of its directors and field representatives. In this way they managed to keep many of the *assistés* out of correctional institutions.

From 1835, there were elaborate plans made to send the *enfants assistés* to *colonies agricoles* in Algeria. Those planning such ventures stressed the need for a population in Algeria attached to the soil. Abandoned children were just the ones to go, since there were no parental ties or hopes of inheritance to hold them in France. The children sent there would become *citoyens français d'Afrique* (French citizens of Africa). The boys would receive military training and the girls agricultural train-

Table 7.12

Numbers of Abandoned Children of Paris in *Colonies Agricoles* or *Ouvroirs*, 1852-1885

Year	Boys	Girls	Total	Number per 1,000 abandoned children aged 12 to 21
1852	not available		142	not available
1853	106	66	172	22
1854	24	40	64	17
1856	71	58	129	14 or 26[a]
1857	110	32	142	16 or 35[b]
—				
—				
—				
1875	41	72	113	not available
1885	81	109	190	not available

Source: *Rapps. Anns.*, 1852-1885. Within the annual reports, the data vary from one table to another and between the tables and the texts. The years above are the only years for which data are available.
[a]The number of children aged 12 to 21 is not accurate.
[b]The number of children actually in *colonies agricoles* is not accurate.

ing. In 1851, one hundred boys were sent to Bouffarik, Algeria. The project was a failure; some children escaped, others died. The remaining children were sent back to France. In 1889 there was a new attempt at colonization of Algeria with abandoned children. That, too, failed.[83]

One form of "social deviance" which occurred only among women was becoming an unwed mother. A common assumption of the nineteenth century was that abandoned female children grew up to be libertines, unwed mothers, and prostitutes; the three were often equated. Gabriel Latour, writing in 1872, best expressed this bias:

If she [the abandoned girl] is pretty, that is to say she is doomed to prostitution; the young men in the village consider her as a prey who is not able to escape them. There is no father, mother, or brother to protect her. She cannot benefit from the lessons of personal experience of the mother who abandoned her. She may struggle for a moment against the obsessions with which she will be overwhelmed, but like her mother, she will succumb. As her mother, she will give birth to unfortunate little beings whom she will not have the courage to raise.[84]

It cannot be denied that there were unwed mothers among the abandoned of Paris, but unfortunately there are no data available which would allow us to compare the frequency of illegitimate births among women abandoned as children with that of the population as a whole.

269

The small number of pregnant women sent back to the Hospice and the few cases of unwed mothers found in the records of Saint-Calais and Avallon suggest that the problem was not very widespread, especially not among the young women who were under age twenty-one and hence still wards of the state. [85] The problem may have been greater among women over twenty-one.

Not every woman who had an illegitimate child was engaged in vice. Almost all had served as domestics in the same department where their foster parents had raised them, and the possibility existed that they had been "seduced" or raped by their employer. In one case, a twenty-year-old woman openly blamed the pregnancy on her employer. While he did not admit his guilt, he agreed to pay the young girl 300 francs—but only after the inspector threatened to put the affair before the police tribunal. [86] An illegitimate birth may have been the result of a liaison between two people of similar age and occupation, as had been common among the nonabandoned population. In one instance, the girl was engaged to marry the father of the child, but his family's objection to her prevented the marriage. There was only one recorded case in Saint-Calais of an unwed mother who demonstrated repeated bad conduct and "licentiousness." More commonly, the unwed mother was said to be suffering from "idiocy." [87] While mentally retarded women are easy prey to seducers, to some nineteenth-century people one sign of "idiocy" might have been a willingness of a woman to engage in pre-marital sex with one or numerous partners. "Idiocy" was vague and undefined.

It was the practice of the Administration that if any ward became pregnant while living in the provinces, she was to stay on location to have the baby. This, they believed, lessened the chances of her abandoning the child. To facilitate home birth in the country, the Administration paid the midwife, the foster parents if they permitted the new mother to stay, and the unwed mother if she kept the child. [88]

Unwed mothers who themselves had been abandoned at birth, occasionally arrived at the Hospice with their illegitimate child, whom they chose to abandon; sometimes they arrived pregnant in Paris to give birth at the Maison d'Accouchement and then abandon the baby. In most instances, if a formerly abandoned mother chose to abandon her child, the Administration required that she stay at the Hospice as a *nourrice sédentaire*. Second-generation abandoned children occurred with higher frequency after 1865. This was probably due to the higher survival rate of first-generation abandoned children. Less than two percent of abandoned children per year were second-generation *assistés*.

Most female *enfants assistés* did not become prostitutes. Whereas, in

1838, one-fourth of all prostitutes had been born out of wedlock, that is not to say they had been abandoned. Among the registered prostitutes of Paris in selected years during the 1830s, there were only forty-one (or 1.8 percent) formerly abandoned children.[89] In 1860, in all of France there were only 537 registered prostitutes who had been abandoned children compared with 13,674 who had never been an *assisté*. Thus, only 3.8 percent of all registered prostitutes had been abandoned girls. From another point of view, however, it appears that one out of 366 abandoned girls were prostitutes while the ratio was one in 1200 for nonabandoned girls.[90] In short, it was approximately four times as likely for an abandoned girl to become a prostitute as for a girl from the population at large. But in the case of prostitutes as with the juvenile delinquents, comparisons with the population at large are not precise. The population at large, as well as including the abandoned, also includes women of *all* socioeconomic groups, not just the working-class groups from which the abandoned children, and presumably most prostitutes came. The question then becomes, why so few? As with the young men, the Administration sought to keep its wayward children out of institutions, and those included *maisons de tolerance* (houses of prostitution) as well as police registration; *ouvroirs* or foster parents in the countryside were preferable. Furthermore, these data refer only to registered prostitutes. There is no statistical measurement of clandestine prostitution. Changing attitudes toward prostitution and its changing nature during the century led to a decline in the houses of prostitution and an increase in houses of rendezvous and in clandestine prostitution.[91] Thus, data on prostitution are not as straightforward to interpret as one would wish. As their mothers before them, many abandoned girls served as domestics or worked in the garment trade. As with their mothers, there is no accurate way of knowing how many of them turned to prostitution to supplement their income or as a result of a prior seduction. Social welfare for the abandoned children, however, was designed to ensure that the children did not grow up as immoral as their mothers allegedly were.

Conclusion: Bonds of Affection

The treatment of the surviving foundlings reflected the attitudes and political natures of the three major regimes of the century. Officials of the July Monarchy essentially ignored the abandoned children after infancy—perhaps that is because so few infants survived. Officials of that regime were more concerned with preventing abandonment. In keeping

271

with the prevalent attitudes and policies of the Second Empire, the administrators of l'Assistance Publique took a more paternal and supervisory role in the treatment of its older wards. They assumed full legal responsibility for assuring that the older children were not a burden to society. They had the authority to try to make sure that the youths went to school, worked, and behaved themselves but were often lax in the exercise of it. In the eyes of officials, the children owed society a debt for raising them, and as young adults they had to work and contribute to the economy as a way of repaying that debt. The Administration attempted to use its own resources and personnel to control the children as much as possible. When some youths proved too incorrigible for the system, they were placed in *colonies agricoles* or *ouvroirs*. It is not accidental that reformatories for controlling the youths flourished during this period. Officials of the Third Republic aimed to achieve the same goals as those of the Second Empire—raising the *assistés* to be hard-working, law-abiding citizens. Their methods differed slightly. Republicans deemphasized policing of the youths and emphasized education and protection. The officials made primary school attendance compulsory, established vocational training schools for some *assistés*, and more consistently supervised the youths' placement as farm workers, apprentices, or laborers. Throughout the second half of the century, officials hoped to prevent deviance by supervision and education.

To control the abandoned children and diminish the perceived threat, authorities primarily relied on the rural foster parents, with whom most abandoned children lived until they reached their majority, to socialize the youngsters and put them to work. Furthermore, authorities encouraged secular and religious education to enable the children to become law-abiding, hard-working citizens, and hence less of a burden on society. To compensate the foster parents for the loss of the child's labor, the Administration paid them if they sent the *assistés* to school. For children over twelve, the director established apprenticeship positions in order for the children to work and learn a trade. Finally, boys were subject to the military draft. In all this, it was the aim of the authorities to keep these thousands of children out of Paris and in the countryside, where they would be under the influence of surrogate families and the power of the Administration.

Abandoned children had a greater propensity for crime and delinquency and they were more apt to become social deviants than was the population at large. Proportionately more *enfants assistés* were on the roles as juvenile delinquents or prostitutes than the rest of the population. But the difference may not be as great if the *assistés* are compared with those of their own socioeconomic group where problems of crime and delinquency might be greater than in the entire population which includes children of all socioeconomic groups. The middle classes' fears that all the abandoned children would become deviants or criminals were somewhat exaggerated. The numbers and percentages of juvenile delinquents among the abandoned children of Paris are extremely small. The Administration succeeded in controlling them without resorting to correctional institutions. Likewise, the percentage of children suffering from mental or physical incapacitation is low. Perhaps, this is because those few who survived infancy were among the strongest. Many went to school, at least once, and after the mid-1880s a few received certificates of completion of primary school. Some were apprenticed and many found employment. Most became agricultural workers and stayed and married in the same area in which they grew up.

By the end of the nineteenth century the surviving abandoned children of Paris differed only marginally from others of similar age and socioeconomic level in terms of education, occupation, military service, encounters with the law and general morals. They were neither all social deviants as authorities had feared, nor model, working-class citizens as was the goal of the state system. This was due in part to the successes and failures of the Administrations' programs, and in part to the fact that these children were not quite as dangerous as authorities believed. The abandoned children may have differed from others in the lack of a committed family on whom to rely for support, both emotional and financial. This resulted in the instability of their lives, and the lack of a family with the concomitant emotional development and attachment which their own, or long-term adoptive family would offer.

Some contemporary sociologists believe that children need warm, nurturing, loving fathers or mothers, and indicate that those children who do not receive nurturant care are unable to form emotional attachment. They can be found, as adults, in a wide variety of deviant settings: mental hospitals, prisons, slums, prostitution. Sociologists also indicate, however, that a large number of men and women who suffer "diseases of non-attachment" are neither violent nor crime-oriented; they simply are indifferent to life and devoid of human attachments. They may also show intellectual impairment in conceptualization and language development.[92] By implication, if children do not receive parental love they will grow up to be societal misfits.

The abandoned children were first rejected by their biological mothers and then "adopted" by foster mothers who took them principally for the money and the eventual labor the child would bring. Love for the children was not an avowed reason either for taking an abandoned child, or for the authorities awarding a child to a woman. An arrangement so devoid of obvious affection does not appear to bode well for the abandoned. That so few appeared in institutions can be explained only in part by the propensity of officials to keep them out.

It is impossible to say with certainty how much affection the children received from their foster parents; nevertheless speculation is possible. Authorities had sometimes hoped that affection would develop and indeed, by nineteenth-century rural-poor standards several times it did. There are a few instances were the *assistés* would not go back to their biological mothers when they asked for them because of ties to their foster parents, and their foster parents did not want to part with them. There are more numerous cases of *assistés* coming back to their foster parents because they were unhappy in their apprenticeships. Some returned after military service. At maturity, when youths were legally able to leave their foster families, most either did not, or else stayed in the same village where they were raised. Foster parents also occasionally demonstrated affection for their charges. Sometimes when the children were placed in apprenticeship the foster mother would come regularly with food and clothing. Such evidence is flimsy and sparse; most dates from after the 1870s. But, even when foster parents professed attachment to the youths, they never intended to leave them an inheritance. [93] Nevertheless, some bonds of affection undoubtedly developed when children stayed with one family from infancy, in a manner similar to a long-term adoptive relationship. In part, it might account for the relatively low percentage of deviant youths.

Lack of bonds of affection does not necessarily lead to social deviance. Indifference to life and withdrawal, common symptoms of "diseases of non-attachment" may not have put an abandoned youth in a correctional institution in nineteenth-century France. Withdrawn people, unable to form strong permanent attachments as a result of emotional neglect during childhood, are not necessarily criminals, especially not in their adolescent years. The scars from being unwanted children might likely become apparent only in adulthood. [94] Abandoned adolescents went to school, worked and lived only slightly more difficult lives than their "milk brothers and sisters." Given the precarious economic situation of the rural poor and the necessity of hard work, parents may not have had the time, energy or inclination to demonstrate affection to *any* children. Perhaps in a society where demonstrating love and maternal attention is not a regular part of family life, the absence of it does not make the children social misfits. Neglect is a relative term. Violence tends to occur when some people see themselves at a disadvantage in relation to others. It is possible that many abandoned youths did not fare much worse than those around them. For these many reasons most *assistés* were not placed in prisons or other institutions.

As Michel Foucault has argued, officials sought to remove undesirables from society and to use hospitals, hospices, and prisons as effective vehicles for the control and isolation of deviant members of society—the criminal, the insane, or the incurable.[95] The abandoned children were potential deviants of society. But they were not locked up, as actual deviants were. There was always the hope of saving them. The foster family proved to be the selected milieu to educate the children and to teach them to be productive, law-abiding citizens. The system took the children out of Paris and out of sight, effectively confining them as well as isolating them from one another. The family atmosphere in which they were placed was to provide their proper socialization and control. At the same time the state, through its agents—field inspectors, doctors, foster parents, and administrative personnel—assumed legal responsibility for its citizens. Unfortunately for the children, the system had only very limited success. Such a high proportion of the children died, and many became infirm or deviant. Most lived and worked among the rural poor, but we can not say with certainty what emotional and physical scars the survivors wore.

General Conclusion

Abandoned children, far from constituting an atypical, minor part of nineteenth-century French society, were part of the very fabric of that culture, of the life styles of the poor, and of state social welfare policies toward families and children. An analysis of the life and death of abandoned children, and social welfare practices pertaining to them, contributes in a broad sense to an understanding of the working-class family, both as a perceived institution and a reality. It becomes readily apparent that children were valued as part of an economic workforce, and expected to be socially invisible along with the rest of the "dangerous" poor. Using abandoned children as a case study of the working-class family, in order to peel away the "dangerous" label given them by middle-class bureaucrats, leads to the discovery of what indeed their lives were really like—how they lived, what they ate, what they wore, their diseases and afflictions, and the quality of their affective lives.

Abandoned children differed from those of the rest of the population in two crucial aspects. First, their mortality rate was much higher than that of the population at large. Second, those who survived did not have the psychological and emotional advantage of a stable family life. By all other measures—clothes, shelter, education, occupation, and social deviancy—they differed little from the children of a similar socioeconomic class of the population. Among both urban and rural poor families, children were not objects of tender loving care, at least not through the 1850s. Tender buds of affection toward children appeared in the 1860s, only to flower in the 1880s. In general, family life among the poor was governed by economic circumstances.

A mother's abandonment of her child was itself a result of economic

276

reality, not lack of humanity or love. Child abandonment was not a form of pathological behavior on the mother's part, but rather a radical solution to the social, psychological, and above all economic pressures the women faced. Mothering is a set of practices shaped by circumstance (primarily economic) but also by medical knowledge, pedagogical theory, and state policy. Most of the women who abandoned their children were barely surviving on the brink of destitution. They were in many ways representative of those in a similar socioeconomic level in the rest of the population. They differed from these others only in that they had a child whom the economic and social circumstances of their lives made it impossible for them to keep. They abandoned the baby, because to keep the infant meant loss of job, income, and maybe even life for them and the child. Perhaps leaving the infant at the foundling home was the ultimate act of love for the child. Mothers could close their eyes to the likelihood of death for the children, and believe that the infants would be better off with wet nurses than with them. At least the mothers spared themselves the sight of watching their babies die slowly of hunger. Abandonment was a socially acceptable means to cope with an unwelcome child in an era without safe birth control or abortion, and without an effective program of aid to dependent children. The state provided the facilities to receive the children and found the wet nurses to care for the babies whom the mothers gave up.

Focusing carefully on the care of abandoned children with wet nurses and foster mothers leads to a clearer picture of peasant family life in rural France—an area in which blurred outlines and hazy impressions have long been common. There is a tendency to romanticize the rural, pre-industrial, log-cabin "good old days," but that image is not accurate. A glimpse of their housing and hygiene shows us that the peasants were really in dire straits, barely surviving in one dark, damp room. Close examination of the nourishment of abandoned children indicates how fragile their lives were. Scrutinizing the illnesses, infirmities, and causes of death of the abandoned children reveals much about the effect of undernourishment and unsanitary living conditions on the health of the poor. Death by diarrhea is no surprise. Nonabandoned children lived in the same surroundings, among the same people with the same attitudes toward children. The lives of peasant children, and of privately wet-nursed infants could not have been very much better than those of the Parisian foundlings. Tender protection of the young was not part of the culture of the rural poor. Many similarities existed between the living conditions of the abandoned children and of the peasants' own offspring. Examining l'Assistance Publique's clothing provisions for the children, for example, reveals what authorities considered minimal but normal. Feeding and child care manuals prepared for the wet nurses, although they can not be assumed to reflect practices precisely, do show what was regarded as normative, prescribed behavior, at least for all children sent out to wet-nurse. In the absence of the proper biological family, foster parents had the vital role of raising the abandoned children to be proper law-abiding French citizens.

In this study of familial care for abandoned children, men were only in the background, as husbands of wet nurses and foster mothers. Men are apparently nonexistent because they were missing from the thoughts of the French bureaucrats. Their absence reflects the middle-class bureaucratic vision and understanding of the French family and the needs of "every child." In short, for the middle-class child as well as the *enfant abandonné*, childhood was a time divided into three stages of seven years each. For the child's first seven years, the French middle-class male bureaucrats viewed women as the sole nurturers. They did not recognize a role for men in childrearing. In the specific instance of foster parents, officials dealt exclusively with the women. During the next seven years, when a child was expected to perform certain tasks, men made an inconspicuous appearance. The last seven years, until the child reached majority, was a time of training for the proper roles in adult life. At this time the girls remained with the women, primarily in domestic activities, but the boys were with the men. The men, however, were not discussed or described except as having a trade to which the abandoned children were assigned. What the absence of men from the vocabulary of the bureaucrats and from the lives of the foundlings says about the French family life in the nineteenth century remains to be further explored. A study of the foundlings indicates that male officials viewed the raising of children as the proper sphere for women—not men.

A view of the working-class and rural French family is only one, albeit an important part of this study. The other is the effect of public policy on the family. The politics of social welfare increasingly affected the poor. Authorities spent much of the nineteenth century trying to curtail abandonment and to encourage mothers to keep their babies. Not until the latter part of the century did growing public concern over industrialization, urbanization, disease, lack of hygiene, and a shortage of labor lead to long-needed significant improvements in the treatment of foundlings. These improvements coincided with increasing state supervision of their lives.

The treatment of abandoned children can be seen as a paradigm of state efforts to encourage middle-class standards of good parenting.

After 1850, and especially during the last quarter of the century, doctors and state officials tried to prescribe and regulate morals, marriage, cleanliness, infant feeding, and child employment. They regulated child abandonment by deciding which mothers should be allowed to give up their children and which should be offered aid. By taking care of abandoned children, by establishing criteria for wet nurses and supervising foster parents, and by providing the children with the barest essentials for life, the state engaged in social welfare and exercised some control over that "dangerous" group of society's pariahs. The growth of social welfare practices for the children introduced government officials into the private lives of the lower-class families who either relinquished a baby or accepted the abandoned child. These officials were a force of behavior change among the poor—just that very group whose behavior the authorities in Paris wanted to modify.

Government intervention in decision making about family matters may be viewed as a deprivation of personal freedom and individual liberty. In the case of the abandoned children, however, it was not detrimental to them. In fact, the supervision of doctors and other state officials late in the century increased the life expectancy of the infants, and in many ways bettered their lives. The result of French public child welfare policies may indeed have been the prolongation of the lives and the stabilization and education of a certain segment of society. But evidence for the nineteenth century indicates that officials pursued such policies to minimize the cost to society and to the government, and eventually to improve the lives of the recipients so they would be less of a threat and economic burden.

Throughout the century the system functioned imperfectly and was fraught with problems. Mercenary wet nurses and foster parents, and unscrupulous inspectors, doctors and other officials contributed to the neglect and perhaps deaths of many infants. For three-fourths of the century, the lives and well-being of the children were low priority items on the budget and agenda of state officials. They did not allocate sufficient funds nor keep a watchful eye on their charges. Nevertheless, the French national government took the initiative and responsibility in caring for its weakest and most dependent citizens at a time when other nations were leaving the task to private charity and local initiative. Given prevailing conditions in nineteenth-century France such as widespread poverty, the state of medical knowledge, the mentalities of the urban and rural poor, and the basic assumptions that family life was crucial and bastardy morally sinful, the French approaches to the problem of abandoned children were consistent. Alterations in state policy, economic

279

developments, cultural outlooks, and attitudes toward children and the family contributed to changes in child welfare practices during the century.

Public welfare policies of the late nineteenth century evolved from a political and theoretical history. The programs of the last few decades of the century succeeded because of increased state centralization, power and commitment. Republican forms of government and far-reaching expansion of national responsibility for the welfare of the deserving poor were more than mere coincidental developments in nineteenth-century France. The First Republic ideologically had advocated public responsibility for a most private part of society—the family and children—but it was unable to act on its ideals. It could only provide the theoretical underpinnings to future legislation and policy. Successive monarchies tried to ignore the problems posed by the thousands of abandoned children. When that proved difficult, they aimed to curtail the numbers receiving social welfare and thus limit expenses. Reformers and social economists of the time condemned the alleged vices of the abandoning mothers. They desired to improve the morality of these women, in particular, and the working classes from which they came, in general, but at a minimum cost to the government.

The Second Republic witnessed a reopening of debates on the state's responsibility for the destitute (among them the abandoned). The ideals of the First Republic reverberated in the debate halls at mid-century. Reformers and government officials created no new, encompassing legislation, but implemented the state's moral obligation to these people by the creation of l'Assistance Publique of Paris. Officials designed this governmental organization to administer to the abandoned and the insane. The bureaucratic, administrative, and medical officials of l'Assistance Publique oversaw all provisions for the abandoned of Paris. The problems associated with abandoned children could no longer be hidden in an office of a subdivision of the Ministry of Interior. The Second Republic gave full recognition to their existence, and the state took more responsibility for their maintenance.

The designers of the Second Empire built on the foundation laid by previous regimes and assumed more control of the abandoned and the families who had moral and social responsibility for raising them. The officials did this through their field representatives and doctors, and by more stringent requirements for wet nurses. After fifty years, for virtually the first time, concern was expressed for preserving the lives and securing the welfare of the children. Authorities deemed the welfare of the abandoned important only so the children could contribute to the

280

economy by their labor as part of the numerically diminishing rural labor force. At the same time that the Second Empire officials were taking more administrative control, they delegated some responsibility, particularly fiscal, to the departments in which the children had been abandoned.

The ideology of the First Republic was put into practice a century later by the Third Republic. During the 1880s, the well-being of the children was of increasing interest. Bureaucratic inspection of and medical attention to both the abandoned children and their foster families increased, and the education and training of the children became important. Rather than attempt to limit those dependent on welfare, the state, for the first time, acted to increase the numbers of those receiving financial and social aid. Officials followed the principle that the state, through its employees (doctors, teachers, inspectors, judges) and through institutions such as schools and special hospitals, could better form and mold model working-class citizens than could derelict, single-parent, and hence "immoral" families. Creating obedient workers was not the only motive for intervening in their private lives. During the Third Republic, for the first time, the children and those who abandoned them were seen not as social deviants, but as the victims of society; as such, the state had the responsibility to protect them. It took one hundred years for the realization of the ideals of the First Republic, but the Third Republic marked the beginning of modern attitudes toward children, their role in the family and the state, and the state's function in assuring their well-being.

Appendix A

DECRET DU 19 JANVIER 1811, CONCERNANT LES ENFANTS TROUVÉS OU ABANDONNÉS ET LES ORPHELINS PAUVRES.

Titre Premier

Article Premier.—Les enfants dont l'éducation est confiée à la charité publique sont: 1° les enfants trouvés; 2° les enfants abandonnés; 3° les orphelins pauvres.

Titre II

Des enfants trouvés

Art. 2.—Les enfants trouvés sont ceux qui nés de pères et de mères inconnus, ont été trouvés dans un lieu quelconque ou portés dans les hospices destinés à les recevoir.

Art. 3.—Dans chaque hospice destiné a recevoir des enfants trouvés il y aura un tour ou ils devront être exposés.

Art. 4—Il y aura, au plus, dans chaque arrondissement, un hospice où les enfants trouvés pourront être reçus.

Des registres constateront, jour par jour, leur arrivée, leur sexe, leur âge apparent et décriront les marques naturelles et les langes qui peuvent servir à les faire connaître.

Titre III

Des enfants abandonnés et orphelins pauvres

Art. 5.—Les enfants abandonnés sont ceux, qui, nés de pères et du

282

mères connus, et d'abord élevés par eux ou par d'autres personnes à leur décharge, en sont délaissés sans qu'on sache ce que les pères et mères sont devenus, ou sans qu'on puisse recourir à eux.

Art. 6—Les orphelins sont ceux qui, n'ayant ni père ni mère, n'ont aucun moyen d'existence.

Titre IV

De l'éducation des enfants trouvés, abandonnés et orphelins pauvres

Art. 7.—Les enfants trouvés nouveau-nés seront mis en nourrice aussitôt que faire se pourra. Jusque là, ils seront nourris au biberon, ou même au moyen de nourrices résidant dans l'éstablissement. S'ils sont sevrés, ou susceptibles de l'être, ils seront également mis en nourrice ou en sevrage.

Art. 8.—Ces enfants recevront une layette, ils resteront en nourrice ou en sevrage jusqu'à l'âge de 6 ans.

Art. 9.—A six ans, tous les enfants seront, autant que faire se pourra, mis en pension chez des cultivateurs ou des artisans. Le prix de la pension décroîtra chaque année jusqu'à l'âge de douze ans, époque à laquelle les enfants mâles en état de servir seront mis à la disposition du ministre de la Marine.

Art. 10.—Les enfants qui ne pourront être mis en pension, les estropiés, les infirmes, seront élevés dans l'hospice: ils seront occupés dans des ateliers, à des travaux qui ne soient pas au-dessus de leur âge.

Titre V

Des dépenses des enfants trouvés, abandonnés et orphelins

Art. 11.—Les hospices désignés pour recevoir les enfants trouvés sont chargés de la fourniture des layettes et de toutes les dépenses intérieures relatives à la nourriture et à l'éducation des enfants.

Art. 12.—Nous accordons une somme annuelle de 4 millions pour contribuer au paiement des mois de nourrices et des pensions des enfants trouvés et des enfants abandonnés.

S'il arrivait, après la répartition de cette somme, qu'il y eut insuffisance, il y sera pourvu par les hospices, au moyen de leurs revenus, ou d'allocations sur les fonds des communes.

Art. 13.—Les mois de nourrices et les pensions ne pourront être payés que sur des certificats des maires des communes où seront les enfants. Les maires attesteront chaque mois les avoir vus.

Art. 14.—Les commissions administratives des hospices feront visiter, au moins deux fois l'année, chaque enfant, soit par un commissaire spécial, soit par les médecins ou chirurgiens vaccinateurs ou des épidémies.

Titre VI

De la tutelle et de la seconde éducation des enfants trouvés et des enfants abandonnés

Art. 15.—Les enfants trouvés et les enfants abandonnés sont sous la tutelle des commisions administratives des hospices conformément aux règlements existants.

Un membre de cette commission est spécialement chargé de cette tutelle.

Art. 16.—Les dits enfants, élevés à la charge de l'Etat, sont entièrement à sa disposition et quand le ministre de la Marine en dispose, la tutelle des commissions administratives cesse.

Art. 17.—Les enfants ayant accompli l'âge de douze ans, desquels l'Etat n'aura pas autrement disposé, seront, autant que faire se pourra, mis en apprentissage; les garçons chez des laboureurs ou artisans; les filles chez des ménagères, des couturières ou autres ouvrières ou dans des fabriques et manufactures.

Art. 18.—Les contrats d'apprentissage ne stipuleront aucune somme en faveur ni du maître ni de l'apprenti, mais ils garantiront au maître les services gratuits de l'apprenti, jusqu'à un âge qui ne pourra excéder vingt-cinq ans, et a l'apprenti, la nourriture, l'entretien et le logement.

Art. 19.—L'appel à l'armée, comme conscrit, fera cesser les obligations de l'apprenti.

Art. 20.—Ceux des enfants qui ne pourraient être mis en apprentissage, les estropiés, les infirmes, qu'on ne trouverait point à placer hors de l'hospice, y resteront à la charge de chaque hospice.

Des ateliers seront établis pour les occuper.

Titre VII

De la reconnaissance et de la réclamation des enfants trouvés et des enfants abandonnés

Art. 21.—Il n'est rien changé aux règles relatives à la reconnaissance et à la reclamation des enfants trouvés et des enfants abandonnés; mais avant d'exercer aucun droit, les parents devront, s'ils en ont les moyens, rembourser toutes les dépenses faites par l'administration publique ou les hospices; et dans aucun cas, un enfant dont l'Etat aurait disposé ne pourra être soustrait aux obligations qui lui ont été imposées.

Titre VIII

Dispositions générales

Art. 22.—Notre ministre de l'Intérieur nous proposera avant le 1er janvier 1812, des règlements d'administration publique qui seront discutés en notre Conseil d'Etat. Ces règlements détermineront pour chaque département le nombre des hospices où seront reçus les enfants trouvés et tout ce qui est relatif a leur administration quant à ce, notamment un mode de revue des enfants existants et de payement des mois de nourrices ou pensions.

Art. 23.—Les individus qui seraient convaincus d'avoir exposé des enfants, ceux qui feraient habitude de les transporter dans les hospices, seront punis conformément aux lois.

Art. 24.—Notre ministre de la Marine nous présentera incessamment un projet de décret tendant: 1° à organiser son action sur les enfants dont il est parlé aux articles précédents; 2° à régler la manière d'employer sans délai ceux qui, au 1er janvier dernier, ont atteint l'âge de 12 ans.

Appendix B

*DELIBERATION OF 25 JANUARY 1837. MEASURES ADOPTED
BY THE ADMINISTRATION TO DECREASE AND PREVENT
ABANDONMENT.*

Article 1

Aucun Enfant ne sera, sous quelque prétexte que ce soit, admis à
l'Hospice des Enfants-Trouvés que dans les cas, sous les conditions et
dans les formes prévues par les dispositions de la Loi du 20 september
1792, et du Décret du 19 janvier 1811.

Article 2

A cet effet, aucun Enfant ne sera reçu que sur le vu du procès-verbal
d'un Commissaire de police, constatant que l'Enfant a été exposé ou
délaissé, ainsi qu'il est dit aux Art. 2, 3 et 5 du Décret du 19 janvier 1811.

Le Procès-verbal sera visé par M. le Préfet de Police; toutefois les
Commissaires de police pourront, pour la conservation des Enfants, les
faire recevoir provisoirement à l'Hospice, en attendant le visa de M. le
Préfet.

Article 3

Le Registre-matricule, sur lequel sont inscrits les Enfants apportés à
l'Hospice, sera visé, chaque semaine, par le Membre de la Commission
administrative chargé de l'Hospice.

Article 4

Les femmes enceintes ne seront admises à la Maison d'Accouchement, qu'autant qu'elles prendront l'engagement de nourrir, pendant quelques jours, dans l'Etablissement, et d'emporter, à leur sortie, l'Enfant dont elles seront accouchées.

Article 5

Il n'y aura, pour l'allaitement, d'exception que pour les femmes qui seraient jugées, par le médecin, hors d'état de nourir ou de continuer à nourrir leur Enfant.

Il pourra être accordé, sur la fondation Montyon, des secours aux femmes qui continueront à nourrir leur Enfant, ou qui en prendront soin.

Article 6

Les mesures qui précèdent sont applicables, dans tout leur contenu, aux femmes qui vont accoucher dans les Établissements placés sous la surveillance du Conseil.

Article 7

Il sera rendu compte au Conseil, à l'expiration de chaque mois, du résultat des Dispositions ci-dessus prescrites.

Article 8

Il sera écrit une Circulaire aux Accoucheurs, Sages-Femmes, et généralement aux personnes qui s'occupent des Accouchements, pour leur rappeler les règles prescrites par les Lois et Réglements sur l'admission des enfants, et les peines portées par le Code, contre l'abandon et le délaissement des enfants.

Article 9

M. le Préfet de la Seine sera prié d'écrire a MM. ses Collègues des Départements de Seine-et-Oise, Seine-et-Marne, d'Eure-et-Loir, de l'Eure et de l'Yonne, pour les informer des conditions d'admission a l'Hospice des Enfants-Trouvés ou Abandonnés.

Article 10

M. le Préfet de Police sera prié de donner a MM. les Commissaires de police et aux autres Agents de son Administration les Instructions pour l'exécution des dispositions ci-dessus.

Notes

Notes to Chapter One
Social Problems and Social Welfare Until the Restoration

1. Bernard-Benoît Remacle, *Des hospices d'enfants trouvés en Europe et principalement en France dupuis leur origine jusqu'à nos jours* (Paris, 1838), p. 34; Philippe Ariès, *Centuries of Childhood: A Social History of Family Life,* trans. Robert Baldick (New York, 1962), pp. 21, 102, 151, 189, 238, 321; and Jean-Louis Flandrin, "L'attitute à l'égard du petit enfant et les conduits sexuelles dans la civilisation occidental," in *Enfant et sociétés: Annales de démographie historique* (Paris, 1973), p. 173. Ariès discusses the middle- and upper-class families; in those families age seven marked the beginning of school.

2. Maxime DuCamp, *Paris, ses organes, ses fonctions et sa vie dans la seconde moitié du XIXᵉ siècle,* 6 vols. (Paris, 1869-1875), 4: 199-200. I am responsible for all translations from French to English in quotations included in this book.

3. Albert Dupoux, *Sur les pas de Monsieur Vincent: Trois cents ans d'histoire parisienne de l'enfance abandonnée* (Paris, 1958), p. 19, and "Les enfants trouvés et abandonnés: Aperçu historique," *Revue de l'Assistance Publique à Paris* [hereafter *RAP*] 21 (1953), p. 68; Léon Lallemand, *Histoire des enfants abandonnés et délaissés: Étude sur la protection de l'enfance aux divers époques de la civilisation* (Paris, 1885), pp. 125-140; and Claude Delasselle, *Les enfants trouvés à Paris au XVIII siècle,* D.E.S. Lettres (Nanterre, 1966), p. 53.

4. Ernest Semichon, *Histoire des enfants abandonnés depuis l'antiquité jusqu'à nos jours* (Paris, 1880), pp. 90-100.

5. Jean Imbert, *Les hôpitaux en France* (Paris, 1958), p. 24.

6. Dupoux, *Sur les pas de Monsieur Vincent,* p. 20.

7. Ibid., p. 21.

8. Semichon, *Histoire des enfants abandonnés,* p. 95.

9. Jean-François Terme and J.-B Monfalcon, *Histoire statistique et morale des enfants trouvés* (Paris, 1837), p. 89.

10. DuCamp, *Paris, ses organes, ses fonctions et sa vie,* 4:202.

11. Ariès, *Centuries of Childhood,* Parts I and III.

12. Jean-Louis Flandrin, *Families in Former Times: Kinship, Household and Sexuality*, trans. by Richard Southern (Cambridge, 1979), p. 184.

13. Cissie Fairchilds, *Poverty and Charity in Aix-en-Provence, 1640-1789* (Baltimore, 1976), chap. 2 passim.

14. This institution was originally called the Hôpital des Enfants Trouvés, in 1801 it was the Hospice des Enfants Trouvés, in 1860 its name changed to Hospice des Enfants Assistés. It is now the Hôpital de Saint Vincent-de-Paul.

15. Terme and Monfalcon, *Histoire des enfants trouvés*, p. 101. The relationship between the number of abandonments and the ease with which a child could be abandoned is relevant to the nineteenth century as well.

16. Dupoux, *Sur les pas de Monsieur Vincent*, p. 66.

17. Jacques Dehaussy, *L'assistance publique à l'enfance: Les enfants abandonnés*, Thèse (Paris, 1948), p. 20.

18. A. Poitrineau, "Aspects de la crise des justices seigneuriales," *Revue historique de droit français et etranger* 39 (1961), p. 564.

19. In 1656 the Hôpital Général was created. This was not a specific hospital but a central administrative body. Under the Hôpital Général there were originally five hospitals for the deserving poor and vagabonds in Paris. The Hôpital des Enfants Trouvés was added in 1670, and Enfants Rouges and Saint Esprit in 1680. The separate revenues of the individual hospitals were insufficient, and under the Hôpital Général funds could be better raised and distributed. Medical equipment, baked goods, wine, supplies and staff were all apportioned to each individual hôpital by the central administration as the needs of each required.

20. Semichon, *Histoire des enfants abandonnés*, p. 132.

21. Ibid., ch. 10; and Camille Bloch and Alexandre Tuetey, eds. *Procès-verbaux et rapports de Comité de Mendicité de la Constituante, 1790-1791* (Paris, 1911).

22. Delasselle, *Les enfants trouvés*, p. 49.

23. Ibid., p. 69.

24. Flandrin, *Families in Former Times*, pp. 191, 192, 215.

25. For a complete discussion of this topic, see Flandrin, *Families in Former Times;* Cissie Fairchilds, "Female Sexual Attitudes and the Rise of Illegitimacy: A Case Study," *Journal of Interdisciplinary History* 8 (Spring 1978), pp. 627-667; idem. *Poverty and Charity*; Peter Laslett, Karla Oosterveen and Richard M. Smith, *Bastardy and Its Comparative History* (Cambridge, 1980); Edward L. Shorter, *The Making of the Modern Family* (New York, 1975); Louise A. Tilly and Joan W. Scott, *Women, Work, and Family* (New York, 1978); Joan W. Scott and Louise A. Tilly, "Women's Work and the Family in Nineteenth-Century Europe," in Charles Rosenberg, ed., *The Family in History* (Philadelphia, 1975); and Louise A. Tilly, Joan W. Scott and Miriam Cohen, "Women's Work and European Fertility Patterns," *Journal of Interdisciplinary History* 6 (Winter 1976), pp. 447-476.

26. Delasselle, *Les enfants trouvés*, p. 70.

27. Micheline Baulant, "Grain Prices in Paris, 1431-1788," in Marc Ferro,

ed., *Social Historians in Contemporary France: Essays from Annales* (New York, 1972), p. 40.

28. Ibid., p. 41; and Delasselle, *Les enfants trouvés*, p. 71.

29. Fairchilds, *Poverty and Charity*, p. 73; and Olwen H. Hufton, *The Poor of Eighteenth-Century France, 1750-1789* (Oxford, 1974), pp. 326-347. I am grateful to Olwen Hufton for much of the detail on the eighteenth century.

30. Claude Delasselle, "Abandoned Children in Eighteenth-Century Paris," in Robert Forster and Orest Ranum, eds., *Deviants and the Abandoned in French Society* (Baltimore, 1978), p. 49. In 1772 there were 7,676 admissions to the Hôpital des Enfants Trouvés in Paris. In 1773 that number decreased by more than 1000 to a little more than 6,000. After a slight rise in subsequent years to about 6,500, the number admitted fell in 1779 to about 5,800.

31. Dupoux, "Les enfants trouvés et abandonnés," *RAP* 25 (1953), p. 770.

32. Wet nursing of babies—breast-feeding the infant of another women for profit—was common during the eighteenth and nineteenth centuries. Upper-class urban mothers customarily hired country women to feed their babies. Middle-class and artisan women sent their babies to women in the surrounding countryside who nursed the infants. For a complete discussion of wet nursing the nonabandoned babies of urban mothers, see Elisabeth Badinter, *Mother Love: Myth and Reality. Motherhood in Modern History* (New York, 1981); and George D. Sussman, *Selling Mothers' Milk: The Wet-Nursing Business in France, 1715-1914* (Urbana, Ill., 1982).

33. Camille Bloch, *L'assistance et l'Etat en France à la veille de la Revolution* (Paris, 1908), pp. 105-106.

34. Dupoux, "Les enfants trouvés et abandonnés," *RAP* 25 (1953), p. 774.

35. Ibid.

36. Eugen Weber, *Peasants into Frenchmen, The Modernization of Rural France, 1870-1914* (Stanford, Calif., 1976), pp. 1-114; and Joseph Marie de Gerando, *De la bienfaisance publique*, 4 vols. (Paris, 1838), vol. 2.

37. Dupoux, "Les enfants trouvés et abandonnés," *RAP* 25 (1953), pp. 870, 871, 877; (The regulation of 1761 is also given verbatim in Bloch, *L'assistance et l'Etat*, p. 112.)

38. Bloch, *L'assistance et l'Etat*, pp. 112-116. Information for this entire paragraph is found in this source.

39. Fairchilds, *Poverty and Charity*, p. 146.

40. Dehaussy, *L'assistance publique*, p. 40.

41. Bloch and Tuetey, *Procès verbaux et rapports du comité de Mendicité*. Also see the Report of the Comité de Mendicité in Bloch, *L'assistance et l'Etat*, pp. 112-116.

42. DuCamp, *Paris, ses organes, ses fonctions et sa vie*, 4: 207.

43. Dupoux, "Les enfants trouvés et abandonnés," *RAP* 33 (1955), pp. 60-61.

44. Bloch, *L'assistance et l'Etat*, p. 112.

45. Dupoux, *Sur les pas de Monsieur Vincent*, pp. 144-149.

46. Dupoux, "Les enfants trouvés et abandonnés," *RAP* 38 (1955), p. 574. All

provisions of the Maternity Code have been quoted from this article.

47. Erwin H. Ackerknecht, M.D., *Medicine at the Paris Hospital, 1794-1848* (Baltimore, 1967); and F. Campbell Stewart, M.D., *The Hospitals and Surgeons of Paris: An Historical and Statistical Account of the Civil Hospitals of Paris* (New York, 1843).

48. See Appendix A for all the articles of the Decree of 1811.

49. Remacle, *Des hospices d'enfants trouvés*, p. 76.

"Ceux qui délaissent en un lieu solitaire un enfant au-dessous de l'âge de sept ans, ceux qui donnent l'ordre de l'exposer ainsi, si l'ordre est exécuté, sont passibles d'un emprisonnement de six mois à deux ans et d'une amende de 16 francs à 200 francs" (Art. 349, Code pénal).

50. Semichon, *Histoire des enfants abandonnés* p. 228. Remacle, *Des hospices d'enfants trouvés*, p. 76, contains the relevant sections of the Penal Code. Remacle describes the *tour* as being in direct violation of Articles 348 and 352 of the Penal Code.

"Ceux qui portent à l'hospice un enfant au-dessous de sept ans, qui leur a été confié pour qu'ils en prissent soin ou pour toute autre cause, sont punis d'un emprisonnement de six semaines à six mois et d'une amende de 16 francs à 50 francs. (Art. 348, Code pénal.) Si l'éxposition a lieu dans un endroit non solitaire, la peine est de trois mois à un an d'emprisonnement et de 16 francs à 100 francs d'amende" (Art. 352, Code Pénal).

51. Seine (Departement de la) L'Assistance Publique, Administration générale de, Marescot de Thilleul, *L'Assistance publique à Paris: Ses bienfaiteurs et sa fortune mobilière*, vol. 1; *Hôpitaux et hospices* (Paris, 1904), pp. 491-545.

52. Dupoux, *Sur les pas de Monsieur Vincent*, ch. 9.

53. Hufton, *The Poor of Eighteenth-Century France* p. 335.

Notes to Chapter Two
Attitudes and Public Policy Toward the Family

1. A major source for demographic data and for information on public opinion and public policy is the series of annual reports, published since 1852, of l'Assistance Publique—Division of Enfants Assistés: Administration Générale de l'Assistance Publique à Paris, *Rapport à Monsieur le Préfet de la Seine sur la situation du service des enfants assistés et provision des dépenses pour 1852* (Paris, 1852-) [hereafter they will be cited as *Rapps. Anns.* in addition to the year that the report covers (not the year in which the report was published)].

2. Archives de l'Assistance Publique, Fosseyeux Collection [hereafter AAP, Foss.] *Instructions sur le service des préposés à la surveillance des enfants trouvés du département de la Seine placés dans les départements, 1819 and 1823.* AAP, Foss. 647.

Liasse 647 contains seven large packets, five of which are entitled *l'Assistance à l'enfance-Agence de Saint-Calais (Sarthe). Circulaires et Correspondance, 1819-1885.* Two packets contain *Documents d'Archives, après 1814—Hospice Saint Vincent-de-Paul.*

3. Emile Laurent, *L'état actual de la question des enfants assistés à propos de la récente loi sur la protection des enfants du premier âge* (Paris, 1876), p. 14.

4. Rachel G. Fuchs, "Child Abandonment in Nineteenth-Century France: Institutional Care and Public Policy," (Ph.D dissertation, Indiana University, 1980), Introduction and chap. 2.

5. H.-A. Frégier, *Des classes dangereuses de la population dans les grandes villes et des moyens de les rendre meilleures*, 2 vols. (Paris, 1840), 1:9. For a detailed discussion of criminal behavior and the moral economists, see Thomas J. Duesterberg, "Criminology and the Social Order in Nineteenth-Century France," (Ph.D dissertation, Indiana University, 1979), chap. 2. passim.

6. de Gerando, *De la bienfaisance publique*, vol 2, passim.

7. In the 1830s there was an increase in the numbers of abandoned children in France with an accompanying increase in expenses for individual departments and communes as well as for the state. As a result, by the end of that decade there were numerous debates on the causes of abandonment and the means to be used to prevent abandonment. There were attempts to change the law of 1811 which were unsuccessful, so reformers issued circulars, decrees and orders. In addition to works cited previously see de Gasparin, Ministre de l'intérieur, *Rapport au Roi sur les établissements du bienfaisance, les hôpitaux et les hospices,* April 5, 1837, and Valdruche, *Rapports à M. le Ministre de l'intérieur, et au Conseil général des Hospices relatif au service des enfants trouvés dans le département de la Seine, suivi de documents officiels* (Paris, 1838). In addition, the F¹⁵ series—specifically, F¹⁵ 3622 and F¹⁵ 3896–3898—of the Archives Nationales [hereafter AN] contains reports, letters, and *procès verbaux* directed to the subject. The C series contains *procès verbaux* of legislative debates. For the 1830s see AN C789, 912 and 994. (AN C1039 is invaluable for attitudes in the 1850s).

During the 1830s, for the first and only time during the century, there was an active press campaign for reform, and criticism of governmental policies and procedures. See *Journal des débats*, December 7, 1837, *Le Courrier français, Le Constitutionnel,* and *Journal du commerce,* as well as *Revue des deux mondes.*

See also Remacle, *Des hospices d'enfants trouvés*, p. 200; and Terme and Monfalcon, *Histoire des enfants trouvés*, p. 197. "In the big industrial cities and among the working classes, mothers and fathers detach themselves from their newborns with a most deplorable ease, and find it infinitely more convenient and more profitable to bring their children to a hospice and forget them than to take care of them"; Terme and Monfalcon, *Histoire des enfants trouvés*, p. 197.

8. Moniteur Universal, 209, Monday, October 26, 1835.

9. Ministre de l'intérieur—Enfants Assistés, *Enquête générale ouverte en 1860 dans les 86 départements de l'Empire. Rapport de la Commission instituée le 10 October 1861 par arrêté de S. Exc. le Ministre de l'intérieur* (Paris, 1862), [hereafter *Enquête (1860)*].

10. AN C787 Letter from the Mayor of Corbeil to Alphonse de Lamartine December 3, 1838, AN C787.

11. Journal des débats, December 7, 1837.

12. This belief was most commonly held by the Catholic clergymen, such as

293

those writing in the *Annales de la charité* (a Catholic periodical founded in 1844 and published under this title until 1860 when the name was changed to *Revue d'économie chrétienne*). See Lemercier, "Des enfants trouvés," *Annales de la charité* 11 (1855), pp. 201-229; Adolphe-Henri (Abbé) Gaillard, *Recherches administratives, statistiques et morales sur les enfants trouvés, les enfants naturels et les orphelins en France et dans plusieurs autres pays de l'Europe* (Paris, 1837) [hereafter *Recherche sur les enfants trouvés*]; Alphonse de Lamartine in AN C1039, March, 1853, and *Discours sur les enfants trouvés*, (Prononcé le 30 avril 1838 à la Société de Morale Chrétienne) (Paris, 1838).

13. Dehaussy, *L'assistance publique à l'enfance*, p. 79.

14. Lamartine, *Discours sur les enfants trouvés*; and Abbé Gaillard, *Recherches sur les enfants trouvés*.

15. Terme and Monfalcon, *Histoire des enfants trouvés*, pp. 196-203; See also AAP Foss. 707⁵*Memoire sur les enfants abandonnés à l'Hospice de la Maternité de Paris*, from the Curé of St. Julien du Senlis, n.d. (roughly 1829-1830). He felt that the *grands ateliers* of the large manufacturing establishments, with the free mixing of both sexes and the absence of religious education led to illegitimacy and abandonment.

16. Terme and Monfalcon, *Histoire des enfants trouvés*, p. 196.

17. Aninard, *Le problème de l'enfance délaissée* (Montpellier, 1929), p. 14. Fully to test the hypothesis that industrialization and urbanization led to a dislocation of the working-class family entails comparing urban industrial areas with rural agricultural ones. Such dislocations perhaps can be evidenced by the numbers and ratios of abandoned children, but child abandonment is not, in and of itself, a valid indicator. Since industrialization and urbanization are processes and are not well-defined events, correlations over time would have to be devised to measure the existence, and the possible effect, of dislocations. Furthermore, these processes also affected the countryside, leading to a decline in the rural population and perhaps an occupational shift such as a decline in domestic service in rural areas. In the nineteenth century, as in the eighteenth, illegitimacy and abandonment were rural as well as urban problems. Baron Adolphe deWatteville du Grabe pointed out the rural as well as urban nature of the problem. deWatteville, *Statistique des établissements et services de bienfaisance. Rapport à M. le Ministre de l'intérieur sur la situation administrative, morale et financière du services des enfants trouvés et abandonnés en France.* [hereafter *Rapport*, (1849)]. (Paris, 1849). But it was the rural *poor* areas that contributed heavily to the numbers of abandoned children. Perhaps, it was the people too poor to marry who produced the illegitimate abandoned children. Or, perhaps, in the poor areas the young girls would be sent out to work, either as domestics or *ouvrières*, and as such would be seduced or "taken advantage of" by their employers.

18. Terme and Monfalcon, *Histoire des enfants trouvés*, p. 189.

19. Le Courrier Français, November 9, 1835; Le Constitutionnel, October 29, 1835.

20. Frégier, *Des classes dangereuses*, 2:48, 220-230.

21. Donzelot, *The Policing of Families*, p. 32.

22. See Appendix B. Deliberations of January 25, 1837, Article 4.

23. Journal des débats, December 7, 1837.

24. Remacle, *Des hospices d'enfants trouvés*, p. 183; *Enquête*, (1860), and de Watteville, *Rapport*, (1849). This was also the opinion of De Nervaux, director of the Administration générale de l'Assistance publique. He felt, however, that the administration should be less tolerant; *Rapps. Anns.*, 1874, p. 11.

25. Remacle, *Des hospices d'enfants trouvés*, p. 228.

26. Debates of the Corps Législatif, AN C1039. See especially the session of March, 1835.

27. Donzelot, *The Policing of Families*, p. 23.

28. Circular from G. Delessert, Préfet de Police to the Commissaires de Police de la Ville de Paris (1838) [hereafter Police Circular, 1838]; Archives de la Préfecture de Police [hereafter APP] D B/70; and Lamartine, *Discours sur les enfants trouvés*; and in AN C1039.

29. Ibid.; and Prosper Blin, *La condition des enfants trouvés et abandonnés dans le droit français ancien et actuel* (Paris, 1909), p. 114.

30. A. Legoyt, "De l'assistance des enfants en France," *Journal de la société de statistique de Paris* 5 (1864), pp. 286-287.

31. Lee Shai Weissbach, "Child Labor Reform under the Second Empire," (Paper presented at the Ninety-Sixth Annual Meeting of the American Historical Association held December 29, 1981, in Los Angeles, California).

32. Donzelot, *The Policing of Families*, p. 10.

33. No author named, *Annales de la charité* 11 (1855), p. 647.

34. Dr. Télephe P. Desmartis, *Enfants trouvés—suppression des tours—Saint Vincent-de-Paul abandonné par ses disciples* (Bordeaux, 1862), p. 7; and Montalembert in the session of the *Corps Législatif* of March 18, 1853, AN C1039.

35. AN C1039, Dupont, in session of March 31, 1853. The only teenagers in the Hospice were those returned from foster parents because of illness, infirmity, or bad conduct. The teenagers stayed in the Hospice only until the director found new placement for them.

36. David H. Pinckney, *Napoleon III and the Rebuilding of Paris* (Princeton, N. J., 1958), p. 154.

37. Donzelot has used the term "tutelary apparatus" to describe the network of social welfare teams. See Donzelot, *The Policing of Families*, pp. 96-168. For a detailed analysis of attitudes toward children see also Maurice Crubellier, *L'enfance et la jeunesse dans la société française, 1800-1950* (Paris, 1979).

38. Donzelot, *The Policing of Families*, pp. 96-97.

39. Pierre Guillaume and Jean-Pierre Poussou, *Démographie historique* (Paris, 1970), p. 279.

40. Théophile Roussel, Assemblée nationale, Année 1874, Annexe au procès-verbal de la séance du 9 juin 1874, *Rapport fait au nom de la commission chargée d'examiner la proposition de loi de M. Théophile Roussel, relative à la protection des enfants du premier âge, et en particulier des nourrissons* (Versailles, 1875) and *Documents de la commission relative à la protection de l'enfance* (Sénat, Session 1882) 3 vols., 1882-1883; see *Journal de débats*, December 22, 1874, for an article

in praise of the Loi Roussel as a means of decreasing the mortality of newborns.

41. Victor Toursch, "L'enfant français à la fin du XIXᵉ siècle d'après ses principaux romanciers," in *Enfant et sociétés: Annales démographie historique* (Paris, 1973), p. 304. For a complete discussion of childhood in France see Crubellier, *L'enfance et la jeunesse dans la société française* and Ariès, *Centuries of Childhood*.

42. For a complete discussion of wet nursing, see Fanny Faÿ-Sallois, *Les nourrices à Paris au XIXᵉ siècle* (Paris, 1980); and George Sussman, "The End of the Wet-Nursing Business in France, 1874-914," *Journal of Family History* 2 (1977), pp. 237-258; and "The Wet-Nursing Business in Nineteenth-Century France," *French Historical Studies* 9 (1975), pp. 304-328.

43. The above discussion is based on the analysis in Crubellier, *L'enfance et la jeunesse.*

44. Semichon, *Histoire des enfants abandonnés*, p. 2.

45. Ibid., p. 3.

46. André-Théodore Brochard (Dr.), *La vérité sur les enfants trouvés, Avec une lettre de M. le Comte Alfred de la Guéronnière* (Paris, 1876), p. 130.

47. Ibid., pp. 160-161.

48. Dupoux, *Sur les pas de Monsieur Vincent*, pp. 310-317.

49. As quoted in Donzelot, *The Policing of Families*, pp. 83-84.

50. Donzelot, *The Policing of Families*, p. 82-83.

51. G. P. Gooch, *The Second Empire* (London, 1960), pp. 154-160; and Weissbach, "Child Labor Reform under the Second Empire."

52. Donzelot, *The Policing of Families*, p. 80-83, and Dupoux, *Sur les pas de Monsieur Vincent*, p. 329.

Notes to Chapter Three
Mothers and Their Babies

1. Remacle, *Des hospices d'enfants trouvés*, p. 200; and Terme and Monfalcon, *Histoire des enfants trouvés*, p. 197.

2. Eugène Sue, *Martin, l'enfant trouvé ou les mémoirs d'un valet de chambre* (Brussels, 1846-47), trans. [not named], *Martin, the Foundling: A Romance,* Dicks English Library, no. 6 (London, 1927), p. 79.

3. Edward Shorter, *The Making of the Modern Family* (New York, 1975), p. 169.

4. Elisabeth Badinter, *Mother Love: Myth and Reality* (New York, 1981), p. 50.

5. Shorter, *The Making of the Modern Family*, pp. 169, 174; and Badinter, *Mother Love*, p. 50.

6. Jean-Jacques Rousseau, *Les confessions*, ed. Jacques Voisine (Paris, 1964), pp. 423-424.

7. The data for this study come primarily from two sources. The first is the *Registres d'Admission*, the dossiers of the children, and several other record books of the *Hospice des Enfants Assistés* housed in the Archives de Paris et de

l'Ancien Département de la Seine [hereafter AP]. These record books contain relatively complete information on the abandoned children themselves, but they are less complete for demographic data on the mothers.

The children, when admitted, were numbered and inscribed sequentially in the *Registres d'Admission*. From these *Registres*, a random selection of abandoned children has been made of 150 subjects per year for twelve years: 1820, 1825, 1830, 1835, 1840, 1845, 1850, 1855, 1860, 1865, 1870 and 1873. The year 1873 was the last one open to researchers in 1977, so 1873 was sampled instead of 1875. All the *Registres d'Admission* of the sample years contained detailed demographic data on the abandoned child, but only the registers of 1820, 1825, 1870, and 1873 have information on the age, place and birth, residence at the time of abandonment, and occupation of each mother. By using 1820 and 1825 for the beginning of the century and 1870 and 1873 for the end, I have been able to make fairly direct comparisons for the changes across time, but I have had to fill in information for the middle years of the century from a second source—the published annual reports of the division of *enfants assistés* of l'Assistance Publique: *Administration générale de l'Assistance publique à Paris, Rapport à Monsieur le préfet de la Seine sur la situation du service des enfants assistés et provision des dépenses pour 1852* (Paris, 1852-) [hereafter *Rapps. Anns.* and the year that the report covers]. These annual reports have aggregate statistics for the entire population of abandoned children, but the reports of certain years have more complete data than others; e.g., the reports for the 1860s are the most comprehensive.

N.B. The name of the *Hospice des Enfants Trouvés* was changed in mid-century to the *Hospice des Enfants Assistés*. It is the same institution.

8. Marvin Harris, "Why Men Dominate Women," *New York Times Magazine*, November 13, 1977, p. 119.

9. Personal communication from George Alter, July 25, 1981. Complete data are in France, Bureau de la Statistique générale, statistique de la France, *Statistique annuel 1871-1906*. For illegitimate infants the ratio is frequently 101-103 boys born per 100 girls.

10. $t = 0.52$, which is not significant even at the fifty percent confidence level. Available data only permit correlations by sex between abandonment in Paris and live births in that city for the years 1817-1850. During these years there is no significant difference in the proportion of boys abandoned when compared with the proportion of boys born in Paris. For the later years, 1856-1881, data permit comparisons between the number of boys born in the department of the Seine and the number of boys abandoned. There is no significant difference in the ratio of boys to girls abandoned when compared with the proportion of each sex born in that department.

11. Data for the number of boys abandoned come from three sources: For the years 1815 to 1851, plus 1844, from AN F[15] 144-149; for 1845 to 1850, from AN F[15] 282[39]; and, for all other years, from *Rapps. Anns.*, 1852-. The data for the number of boys and girls born in Paris, the department of Seine, and in France come from the *Recherches statistiques sur la Ville de Paris; Statistique générale de*

297

la France; France, *Census Reports*, 1855 1-3 no. 27, pp. 436-437; Institut National de la Statistique et des études économiques, *Annuaire statistique de la France* (Paris, 1879); and Statistique de la France, *Statistique annuel*. The total percent of boys born in France was 51.4339 compared with the total percent of boys born in Paris at 50.8400. The standard deviation is 0.94 and t = 6.32 which is significant with less than 0.005 probability of chance.

12. Weber, *Peasants into Frenchmen* pp. 172-173.

13. William L. Langer, "Checks on Population Growth: 1750-1850," *Scientific American*, February 1972, pp. 93-97; and Harris, "Why Men Dominate Women," p. 119.

14. AP. Computed from *Enfants Assistés*, Etiquette jaune, *Registres d'Admission*, and *Decisions d'abandon*. The increase is not due to an increase in literacy but to new admissions policies which required a name. The *Decisions d'abandon* are records which exist only for the period from 1862 to 1873 and the only ones that specifically give the marital status of the mother.

15. Legitimacy status data are deduced from AP *Enfants Assistés, Registres d'Admission*.

16. Data were collected from declarations made on *Registres d'Admission* and computed by a series of cross-tabulations.

17. Eugène Sue, *Mystères de Paris* (Paris, 1842-1843). The following edition has been used: Jean-Jacques Pauvert, ed. (Paris, 1963).

18. Derived from A. Boicervoise, *Rapport au Conseil général des Hospices de Paris sur le service des enfants trouvés du département de la Seine* (Paris, 1845); and frequency distributions from a sample from AP *Enfants Assistés, Registres d'Admission*.

19. APP D B/70. *Police Circular*, (1838).

20. Ibid.

21. Dupoux, *Sur les pas de Monsieur Vincent*; and Boicervoise, *Rapport au Conseil général des Hospices*; and Valdruche, *Rapport au Ministre de l'intérieur et au Conseil général des Hospices relatif aux enfants trouvés dans le département de la Seine, suivi de documents officials* (Paris, 1831).

22. Dupoux, *Sur les pas de Monsieur Vincent*, p. 211; and *Rapps. Anns.*, 1852. After 1838, although the number of babies abandoned did not decrease, the number of babies born at the Maison d'Accouchement increased by 1,000. Of the 3,500 or so mothers admitted each year, after 1838 almost 2,000 of them kept their babies, some with aid and some without. This compares with fewer than 800 who kept their babies before 1837. Thus, although 500 fewer mothers who gave birth in Accouchement abandoned their babies after 1838 the decrease cannot be conclusively tied to the program of aid to unwed mothers. What did happen was that more women chose to give birth in Accouchement and proportionally more kept their babies upon leaving. Boicervoise, *Rapport au Conseil général des Hospices*. It is entirely possible that these mothers abandoned their babies after leaving the hospital.

23. Appendix B. Circular of 1837. This was the date of the beginning of the

Bureau ouvert for admissions; and Dupoux, *Sur les pas de Monsieur Vincent*, p. 210. The specific questions asked were:

What is your name? Where do you live? What is the name of the child? Has he been baptized? Vaccinated? Do you know the parents? What are their names? Where do they live? What do they do? Are you the parent? Do you know anything at all about the mother? What do you know about her?

The following questions applied if the abandoner was the parent:

Are you married? Why aren't you married? Do you live with the father of the child? Will the father of the child give you aid? Why doesn't he take responsibility for the child? Would you ask him to? Could one take steps in this matter to advantage? Would you like someone to approach him?

The questions then got more specific as to the socioeconomic status of the mother and her reasons for abandonment:

What is your civil status? What is your job? How much do you earn per day? Do you have any other resources? Do you have other children? Are they with you? Has anyone advised you to place your child at the Hospice? Who gave you this advice? Is this the first child you have abandoned? Do you know that you will no longer be able to see the child? Do you know that you will not know where the child is placed? Do you know that you will not be able to have any news of the child without first paying 30 francs and paying 30 francs each time you seek news of the child? Do you know that the child will be sent far from here and placed with people who will not be much better off than you and who naturally will not give the child the tenderness that you will be able to give him? Do you know that whatever the solicitude of the administration the child will never fare as well as with you?

And finally:

Do you see your family? Are you on bad terms with them? Can they take care of your child? If you don't see your family, would you like someone to help you reconcile with them? Would you like to engage someone to take care of your infant? Do you know the provisions of the Penal Code which punishes abandonment and exposure of children?

24. Rapps. Anns., 1853.
25. Boicervoise, *Rapport au Conseil général des Hospices*, p. 5; and Remacle, *Rapport à M. le ministre secrétaire d'Etat de l'intèrieur concernant les infanticides et les mort-nés dans leur relation avec la question des enfants trouvés* (Paris, 1845).

26. Davenne, the director of l'Assistance Publique, reported that if a mother refused to give her name and address, the child was refused, except in very urgent cases; AN C1039 *Procès verbaux* (1853). On the other hand, Dupoux has claimed that "neither the bulletin of birth nor the responses to the interrogation seemed to have been an absolute condition of admission. In the interest of the child, one made exception to that requirement." Dupoux, *Sur les pas de Monsieur Vincent*, p. 213. There was apparently some leeway in what was judged a very "urgent" condition.

27. Rapps. Anns., 1869.

28. AAP Foss. 647₇ Report of René Lafabrèque (1878); APP *Police Circular*, (1838).

29. AAP Foss. 647₇ Report of Armand Husson, Director of the Hospice des Enfants Assistés to the Conseil général des Hospices.

30. Rapps. Anns., 1869.

31. DuCamp, *Paris, ses organes, ses fonctions et sa vie*, 4: 125-126. The layette for an infant who received aid in the 1860s differed little: 1 lange de laine; 2 langes de coton; 2 brassières d'indienne; 4 brassières de coton; 4 fichus de coton; 8 couches de toile. AAP Foss. 33, n.d. but probably 1861 or later.

32. AAP Foss. 647₇ Notes in response to the Report of the Principle Inspector, (1883).

33. AAP Foss. 647₇ letter from Peyron, Director of the Administration générale de l'Assistance Publique to Valdruche, Director of the Hospice des Enfants Assistés (1887).

34. APP D B/70. Circular from the Prefecture of Police to the Inspectors of Police of the City of Paris (1886).

35. J.S. Chasteland and R. Pressat, "La nuptialité des générations françaises depuis un siècle," *Population* 2 (1962). The average age for first marriage for women in 1820-1825 was 26.1, and in 1870-1873 was 24.3. We can assume that the first child arrived shortly thereafter. Unfortunately, the sources supply no information as to whether the women were abandoning first-born children or subseqent children. The *Rapport Annuel* for 1854 states that one-third of the mothers who gave birth in the *Maison d'Accouchement* (*Maternité*) in that year and abandoned the baby had done it before. For this group, it was not their first abandonment, nor their first child. If 1854 is fairly typical then there was a reasonable proportion of women who had abandoned at least two children. Nevertheless, these women could still have been in their early twenties at the time of the birth of their first child. See also Statistique de la France, 2ⁿᵈ Série.

36. Jeanne Gaillard, *Paris, la ville: 1852-1870* (Lille, 1976), p. 221.

37. Edward Shorter, "Female Emancipation, Birth Control and Fertility in European History," *American Historical Review* 78 (1973), pp. 605-640. "The typical French or German girl would have started menstruating towards sixteen or seventeen around the mid-eighteenth century." Edward Shorter, *The Making of the Modern Family* (New York, 1977), p. 86. Shorter computed the average age of menarche in France from 1800 to 1849 at 15.7; from 1850 to 1899 at 15.1, pp.

293-294. Other scholars have put the age of menarche at 18. See, for example, Guy Thuillier, "Water Supplies in Nineteenth Century Nivernais," in Robert Forster and Orest Ranum, eds., *Food and Drink in History, Selections from the Annales: Economies, Sociétés, Civilisations*, vol. 5, trans. Elborg Forster and Patricia M. Ranum (Baltimore, 1979), pp. 109-125. The most accurate assessment and discussion of the onset of menarche in nineteenth century France can be found in Edward Shorter, "Sur l'âge des premières règles en France, 1750-1950," *Annales: ESC* (May-June, 1981), pp. 497-503.

38. Hugo, *Les Misérables*, vol. 1; and Honoré de Balzac, *Cousine Bette*, trans. Marion Ayton Crawford (Great Britain, 1976), pp. 19-20.

39. Derived from Boicervoise, *Rapport au Conseil général des Hospices*, (1845). Data for 1854 to 1876 are derived from *Rapports annuels* for those years. Of the 2,000 cases of abandonment taken from the random sample of the *Registres d'Admission*, not one mother gave "fille publique" as an occupation.

40. Alain Corbin, *Les filles de noce depuis la seconde moitié du XIXe siècle* (Paris, 1978), p. 79; and Elizabeth Weston, "Prostitution in Paris in the Later Nineteenth Century: A Study in Social and Political Ideology," (Ph.D dissertation, SUNY Buffalo, 1979), p. 52. For an excellent discussion on the relationship between domestic service and prostitution, see Weston, pp. 55-57.

41. Weston, "Prostitution in Paris," pp. 64-65.

42. Louise Tilly, Joan W. Scott, and Miriam Cohen, "Women's Work and European Fertility Patterns," *Journal of Interdisciplinary History* 6, no. 3 (Winter 1976), pp. 447-476.

43. Theresa McBride, *The Domestic Revolution and the Modernisation of Household Service in England and France, 1820-1920* (New York, 1976), p. 14.

44. Weston, "Prostitution in Paris," p. 32.

45. Louis Chevalier, *La formation de la population Parisienne au XIXe siècle* (Paris, 1950), p. 40, 45. The population of Paris that was born in other departments is, 1861: 58.65 percent; 1866: 61.05 percent; 1872: 57.22 percent.

46. Chevalier, *La formation de la population Parisienne*, p. 285.

47. Boicervoise, *Rapport au Conseil général des Hospices*, p. 88.

48. AAP Foss. 647₇ Report of the Prefect of Police (Pietri) to the Inspectors of Police of the suburbs and to the Mayors of the rural communes of the department of the Seine. Paris, August 30, 1852.

49. AAP Foss. 647₅. See also AP *Enfants Assistés, Decision d'abandon*.

50. Chevalier, *Formation de la population Parisienne*; and Philippe Ariès, *Histoire des populations françaises* (Paris, 1971). Ariès mentions the 3d, 4th, and 8th (ancien) *arrondissements* as densely populated with workers; ibid., p. 148. See also Gaillard, *Paris, la ville*. Balzac in *l'Interdiction* refers to the (ancien) 12 *arrondissement* as the most "miserable," those from which are "thrown most of the *marmots* to the *tour* of *Enfants Trouvés*." Balzac, as quoted in Adeline Daumard, "Une source d'histoire sociale: L'enregistrement des mutations par décès. Le XIIe arrondissement de Paris en 1820 et 1847," *Revue d'histoire economique et sociale* 35, no. 1 (1957), pp. 52-76.

51. Louis Chevalier, *Laboring Classes and Dangerous Classes in Paris during the First Half of the Nineteenth Century*, trans. Frank Jellinek (New York, 1973), p. 485.

52. Chevalier, *Formation de la population Parisienne*, p. 83.

53. Daumard, "Une source d'histoire sociale," pp. 52-75.

54. René Lafabrèque, "Des enfants trouvés à Paris," *Annales de démographie internationale* 2 (1878), p. 249.

55. McBride, *The Domestic Revolution*, p. 51.

56. Joan W. Scott and Louise A. Tilly, "Women's Work and the Family in Nineteenth-Century Europe," *Comparative Studies in Society and History* 17 (1975), pp. 36-64.
Seduction of unwilling women does not make good romantic ballad material. In the *chansons* of the nineteenth century the theme is repeated that young girls lose their virtue to a lover. While she may have been seduced by her lover, she enjoyed premarital sex of her own free will. In the ballads, the girl and her lover were separated by the girl's parents, or the lover leaves the girl. If the girl is pregnant, she is not welcome in her parent's house. *Chants et chansons populaires de la France* (Paris, 1859). Many writers of the time, however, spoke of seduction of girls, especially by their employers. De Watteville (1849) writes of the seduction of domestics by their masters. Remacle (1853) refers to women too weak to resist seduction, abandoned by family and the world. She is dishonored. The implication is that someone had dishonored her, not that she was the active partner. Desloges goes one step further and refers to young girls assaulted by men. See de Watteville, *Rapport*, (1849), p. 8-13; Desloges, *Des enfants trouvés, des femmes publiques et des moyens à employer pour diminuer le nombre* (Paris, 1836), p. 21; and B.-B. Remacle, Corps Législatif, Session 1853. Annexe au procès verbal de la Séance du 30 avril 1853. *Rapport fait au nom de la Commission chargée d'examiner le projet de loi concernant les enfants trouvés et abandonnés et les orphelins pauvres confiés à l'Assistance publique*, p. 34.

57. AN F[15] 1888. These letters were written in behalf of mothers requesting the return of their children. They may indicate what was considered the appropriate excuse for abandonment and one which would warrant the return of the child.

58. AP *Enfants Assistés, Registres d'Admission*, Etiquette jaune pp. 206-207, 1820.

59. AN F[15] 1902. Correspondence between Peligot as administrator of the Hospitals and Hospices and Mlle. Herbert, a mother who had abandoned her baby and sought his return, September or October 1825. The letters were not written by the mothers themselves, but on their behalf. Most of the mothers were probably illiterate. Some of the letters indicate that premarital intercourse with avowed intent to marry was accepted by this segment of the population. This is confirmed by many of the *chansons* and ballads of the time. Lafabrèque wrote of an unmarried woman who abandoned her child, as one who had been promised marriage but abandoned by her lover. She is "a poor being without a family and always without a moral sense." *Des enfants assistés*, p. 248. Almost all mothers

who gave birth in the Maison d'Accouchement and abandoned their children stated that they had been abandoned by the father of their child. *Rapps. Anns.*, 1854. That so many women stated abandonment by the father of the child speaks to the loneliness, gullibility, and desperate need to be with someone who promised marriage that was experienced by working women living alone in Paris.

60. *Rapps. Anns.*, 1868.

61. For some early years I have used the prepared table "Mouvement de la proportion des abandons comparés aux naissances dans le département de la Seine," *Rapps. Anns.*, 1874, pp. 18-19. For the years possible, I have verified the data in the prepared table, which is quite accurate. For most years through 1865 I have used *Statistique de la France* 1ᵉ série, 13 vols; 2ᵉsérie vols. 3-4, 10-11, 18,20 (Paris and Strasbourg, 1835-1873). For post-1870 data I have used Bureau de la statistique générale, Statistique de la France, *Statistique annuel*, 36 vols. (Strasbourg, 1871-1906). The number of children abandoned each year has been divided by the number of live births in the department of the Seine. The number of live births in the department of the Seine is used rather than the number of live births in Paris alone because the Hospice de Enfants Assistés in Paris was the foundling home for the entire department.

62. Jean Fourastié, *Documents pour l'histoire et la théorie des prix* (Paris, 1958), pp. 79-80. The price index has been used rather than the *prix courant*. The *prix réel* is the price corrected for wages and is the same as the price index; Ernest Labrousse, Romano F. Ruggiero, G. Dreyfus, *Le prix du froment en France au temps de la monnaie stable (1725-1913)* (Paris, 1970), pp. 190-191. The average mean price has been used. Cost of living indices in Paris are from Jeanne Singer-Kerel, *Coût de la vie à Paris de 1840 à 1954* (Paris, 1861), p. 104; Šee also B. R. Mitchell, *European Historical Statistics, 1750-1970* (New York, 1975), pp. 6-7; and Fourastié, *Théorie des prix*, pp. 10-12.

63. The illegitimacy ratio in Paris is computed from Remacle, *Rapport . . . concernant infanticides*, Table no. 5. For the data on the number of illegitimate births in the department of the Seine, the figures were from René Lafabrèque, *De la mortalité du premier âge et du légitimations* (Nancy, 1882), p. 5, and from *Statistique de la France* and *Statistique annuel*.

64. Pierre Emile Levasseur, *La population française: Histoire de la population avant 1789 et démographie de la France comparée à celle des autres nations au XIXᵉsiècle*, 3 vols. (Paris, 1889), 2:34. Most data are derived from *Statistique de la France* and *Statistique annuel*.

65. *Enquête*, (1860); and de Watteville, *Rapport*, (1849).

66. In 1837 a circular from Delessert, Prefect of Police to the midwives (APP D B/70), spoke out against the practice of midwives who, for a sum of money, brought the infant to be abandoned. It also give instructions to the midwives on how to encourage mothers to keep the babies. Mothers had confidence in the midwife; therefore, midwives should persuade the mothers not to abandon the infants.

Further evidence that midwives brought babies is found in letters to the

Minister of Interior, May 18, 1837, complaining about the midwife bringing babies and omitting the name of the mother. The report of 1845 by Boicervoise states that most infants abandoned at the *tour* were left by the midwives or upon their advice. "Les abandons au Tour doivent, presque tous, être imputés aux conseils, nous dirons plus, aux suggestions des Sages-Femmes, qui se chargent de porter les enfants a l'Hospice moyennant au salaire de 10, de 15, de 20 et même de 50 francs, salarie d'autant plus élevé qu'elles ont pu exagérer les difficulties imaginaires de ce mode d'abandon, qui devient pour les Sages-Femmes une industrie lucrative," Boicervoise, *Rapport au Conseil général des Hospices*, p. 21. See also APP D B/70; Boicervoise, "Quelques reflexions au sujet du projet de loi relatif aux enfants trouvés, abandonnés et orphelins presenté à l'Assemblée législative au nom de la Commission de l'Assistance publique dans sa séance du 22 mars 1850," *Revue municipale* (1850), p. 8.

In 1860 midwives were still advising mothers to abandon the infant, and the midwives were still bringing the infant to the Hospice. See deWatteville, *Rapport au Ministre de l'intérieur sur la situation administrative morale et financière des enfants trouvés* (Paris, 1860), p. 30.

67. AP VD[4] 4972-4980.

68. Gaillard, *Paris, la ville, passim*; and Patrick Kay Bidelman, "The Feminist Movement in France: The Formative Years, 1858 to 1889," (Ph.D dissertation, Michigan State University, 1975), chap. 2.

69. APP D B/70. Circular to the Inspectors of Police of the city of Paris from G. Delessert, the Prefect of Police, Paris, November 1, 1838. Frégier mentions that male workers earn 40 sous per day and women workers earn 20 sous. H. A. Frégier, *Des classes dangereuses*, p. 101; and Léon Lallemand, *La question des enfants abandonnés et délaissés au XIXe siècle* (Paris, 1885), p. 197.

70. Jules Simon, *L'ouvrière* (Paris, 1861), p. 282.

71. Weston, "Prostitution in Paris," p. 35; and Simon, *L'ouvrière*, p. 282.

72. John W. Shaffer, "Family, Class, and Young Women: Occupational Expectations in Nineteenth-Century Paris," in Robert Wheaton and Tamara Hareven, eds. *The Family and Sexuality in French History* (Philadelphia, 1980), p. 183.

73. Jeanne Singer-Kerel, *Coût de la vie à Paris de 1840 à 1954* (Paris, 1961).

74. McBride, *The Domestic Revolution*, p. 60.

75. Lafabrèque, *Des enfants trouvés*, p. 26. According to J. Gailllard's figures on wages for an earlier period, this estimate of Lafabrèque is high. Gaillard's figures for wages of 75 centimes to one franc coincide with those of Frégier who wrote that working women, during the first half of the century, received 20 sous (1 franc). There is an obvious discrepancy. Both Lafabrèque and Gaillard used salaries of *ouvrières*. There was a difference between the wages of one type of work and another. Perhaps Lafabrèque used salaries only of better-paid workers; or perhaps some wages did increase twofold during the century. According to the *Statistique annuel* the average daily wage of a woman working in one of the garment trades rose from 2.12 francs in 1853 to almost 3 francs in 1884. This slight

increase in wages might account for the decrease in the rate of child abandonment. However, the increase in wages would be reflected in the price index of bread and there is no correlation between the economic index and child abandonment for the later years. If the well-paid worker of whom Lafabrèque wrote could not afford to keep her child, how could the poorer women? See Frégier, *Classes dangereuses*; and Gaillard, *Paris, la ville.*

76. Lafabrèque, *Des enfants trouvés*, p. 26.

77. Brochard, *La vérité sur les enfants trouvés*, pp. 160-161.

78. AP *Enfants Assistés, Registres d'Admission*; and AN F¹⁵ 1889-1904.

79. Angus McLaren, "Abortion in France: Women and the Regulation of Family, 1800-1914," *French Historical Studies* 9, no. 3 (Spring 1978), p. 462.

80. P. Brouardel, *L'avortement* (Paris, 1901), pp. 123-163.

81. Brochard, *La vérité sur les enfants trouvés*, pp. 158-161.

82. Ibid., p. 161.

83. *Enquête*, (1860), p. 108.

84. *Rapps. Anns.*, 1877-1885.

85. Lallemand, *La question des enfants abandonnés*, p. 185. Lallemand cites the data of Lévasseur.

86. Boicervoise, *Rapport au Conseil général des Hospices*, table no. 2.

87. AP, VIII Arrondissement, Ville de Paris, Actes de Naissance, 5 juin-31 decembre 1869, no. 29.

88. *Rapps. Anns.*, 1878. This report was submitted by Michael Moring. The difference in tone and attitude between this report and the one of 1874 is striking. By 1878 there is a growing interest in the welfare of the children and Moring professed interest in them.

89. *Rapps. Anns.*, 1875-1890. For a study of the practice of sending infants out to wet nurse, and the wet-nursing business see George D. Sussman, "The Wet-Nursing Business in Nineteenth-Century France," *French Historical Studies*, 9 (Fall 1975), pp. 304-328.

90. *Rapps. Anns.*, 1874-1900.

91. AP *Enfants Assistés, Registres d'Admission*, 1860-1873.

92. AN F¹⁵ 1886 to 1904 contain several letters requesting admission for such a child. Sometimes the letter is from an older sister, sometimes from the mother or father of the child, and sometimes from a neighbor or relative. See also AAP Foss. 565, *Registre sur lequel est transcrite les correspondance envoyées par cet établissement—Hospice des Orphelins*. Also AP *Enfants Assistés, Correspondance*, and *Registre de Correspondance*.

93. AN F¹⁵ 1886-1904; AAP Foss. 565; AP *Enfants Assistés, Correspondance* and *Registre de Correspondance*; and Hugo, *Les Misérables*.

94. AP *Enfants Assistés, Registres d'Admission.*

95. We cannot here address the question of why the proportion of illegitimate births in the department of the Seine declined and then remained stable at approximately twenty-four percent of total live births. Analysis of the effects of marriage age and rates, prevalence of sexual intercourse outside of marriage, at-

titudes, ease of abandonment, and the relative size of "a sub-society of the illegitimacy-prone" on the illegitimacy rate must be left to other studies. For example see Peter Laslett and Karla Oosterveen, "Long-Term Trends in Bastardy in England," *Population Studies* 27 no. 2 (July 1973), pp. 255-286.

96. Shorter, *Making of the Modern Family*, pp. 193-196.

Notes to Chapter Four
In the Hospice

1. In 1859 the name had been changed from Hospice des Enfants Trouvés to Hospice des Enfants Assistés; to be consistent, starting with this chapter the name Hospice des Enfants Assistés appears for all references to the institution, whatever the date.

2. Marescot de Thilleul, *L'assistance publique à Paris: Ses bienfaiteurs*, vol. 1, pp. 491-499.

3. Joseph Bouchardy, *Les enfants trouvés*, in *Magasin Théatral*, 34 (Paris, n.d.).

4. AP *Registres d'Admission*. One infant, however, bore the surname "Inconnu" in the correspondence between the Hospice and the Agency of Saint-Calais, AAP Foss. 647₂.

5. Dupoux, *Sur les pas de Monsieur Vincent*, p. 228.

6. APP D B/70. Montalivet, Chief of the 1st Division, Bureau of the Administration générale, Minister of Interior, Circular of June 30, 1812. See also AN F^{15} 1894 for the same circular and AAP Foss. 647₇, Letter of the prefect of the Seine to the mayor of the 12th *arrondissement* of Paris, August 10, 1812; and AAP Foss. 647₆, 1823.

7. APP D B/70 Minister of Interior to the Prefect of Police.

8. Dupoux, *Sur les pas de Monsieur Vincent*, p. 227.

9. AN F^{15} 2531. For the decree of 1817 see AN F^{15} 1886. I have seen and handled the necklaces and this description is partially based on my observations.

10. Dupoux, *Sur les pas de Monsieur Vincent*, ch. 2.

11. *Rapps. Anns.*, 1869, p. 23.

12. AAP Foss. 647₂, Letter from Boicervoise, director of the Division of Enfants Trouvés of the Administration générale to *préposé* at Saint-Calais, September 1847.

13. AN F^{15} 3869, Letter from the Conseil Général of the Meuse, 1842.

14. Adolphe-Henri Gaillard (Abbé), *Recherches administratives, statistiques et morales sur les enfants trouvés, les enfants naturels et les orphelins en France et dans plusieurs autres pays de l'Europe* (Paris, 1837); and Bernard-Benoît Remacle, Corps Législatif. Session 1853. *Annexe au procès verbal de la Séance du 30 avril 1853. Rapport fait au nom de la Commission chargée d'examiner le projet de loi concernant les enfants trouvés et abandonnés et les orphelins pauvres confiés a l'Assistance publique* (Paris, 1853). Also in AN C1039.

15. Dupoux, *Sur les pas de Monsieur Vincent*, p. 287.

16. Alphonse Gabriel Haussonville (Vicomte d'), *L'enfance à Paris* (Paris, 1879), p. 33.

17. AAP Foss. 15.

18. Dupoux, *Sur les pas de Monsieur Vincent*, p. 278. The precise dimensions of the *crèche* were 30 meters long, by 10 meters wide, by 7 meters high. The volume was 2,000 cubic meters.

19. DuCamp, *Paris, ses organes, ses fonctions et sa vie*, 4:220.

20. Shorter, *The Making of the Modern Family*, p. 170.

21. Dupoux, *Sur les pas de Monsieur Vincent*, pp. 286-287.

22. AN AD XIX I 157, *Enquête*, (1860), p. 82.

23. DuCamp, *Paris, ses organes, ses fonctions et sa vie*, 4:220; and F. Campbell Stewart, M.D., *The Hospitals and Surgeons of Paris: An Historical and Statistical Account of the Civil Hospitals of Paris* (New York, 1843).

24. *Rapps. Anns.*, 1852-1890. The number of children existing on December 31 of any given year ranged from 190 to 426.

25. Dupoux, *Sur les pas de Monsieur Vincent*, p. 286. See also Dr. F. S. Ratier, *Coup d'oeil sur les cliniques médicales de la faculté de médecine et des hôpitaux civils de Paris* (Paris, 1830); and A.-B. Marfan, "Documents sur l'histoire de l'Hospice des Enfants Assistés de Paris," *Le Nourrisson*, Septembre 1930; and J. Parrot, "La nourricerie de l'Hospice des Enfants Assistés," *Bulletin de l'Académie de Médecine*, 2ᵉ serie (1882), pp. 839-853; "Les maladies des enfants," *France médical* 21 (Paris, 1874), pp. 408, 441, 513, 537; "Clinique des maladies de l'enfant," *Ann. de démog.* 3, (Paris, 1879), pp. 473-482; and articles and discussions by Drs. Marjolin and Parrot in the *Bulletin de l'Académie de Médecine* 11 (Paris, 1882).

26. Dupoux, *Sur les pas de Monsieur Vincent*, chap. 9; AAP Foss. 647₆; and René Lafabrèque, "Notes pour servir à l'étude . . . des enfants assistés," March 28, 1877. Mss in AAP. The precise dimensions were: medical infirmary, 24.80 m. wide × 7.99 m. long × 3.30 m. high = 644.87 cubic meters; surgical infirmary, 21.80 m. wide × 7.88 m. long × 3.37 m. high = 566 cubic meters; ophthalmology ward, 38.23 m. wide × 3.62 m. long × 3.37 m. high = 467 cubic meters.

27. Dupoux, *Sur les pas de Monsieur Vincent*, p. 280.

28. Ibid., pp. 284-310; and AAP Foss. 11.

29. Dupoux, *Sur les pas de Monsieur Vincent*, p. 287.

30. Ibid., p. 291; and Valdruche, *Rapport au Ministre de l'interieur et au Conseil général des Hospices relatif aux enfants trouvés dans le département de la Seine, suivi de documents officiels* (Paris, 1838).

31. deGerando, *Bienfaisance publique*, vol. 2.

32. Hutinel as quoted in P. Lereboullet, *Paris-Médical*, April 14, 1934. See also Dupoux, *Sur les pas de Monsieur Vincent*, p. 305, who cites Lereboullet.

33. Lafabrèque, "Notes pour servir à l'étude . . . des enfants assistés," 1877.

34. *Bulletin de Académie de Médecine*, 1882, pp. 458-459.

35. Dr. Ratier, quoted in Dupoux, *Sur les pas de Monsieur Vincent*, p. 286.

36. Ibid.

37. Dr. Hutinel, quoted in Dupoux, *Sur les pas de Monsieur Vincent*, p. 305.

38. Gaillard, *Recherches sur les Enfants Trouvés*, p. 173.

39. Dupoux, *Sur les pas de Monsieur vincent*, p. 289.

40. Ruth McClure, *Coram's Children: The London Foundling Hospital in the Eighteenth Century*, (New Haven: 1981), chaps. 13 and 15.

41. DuCamp, *Paris, ses organes, ses fonctions et sa vie*, 4:222; Haussonville, *L'enfance à Paris*, p. 33; and Dupoux, *Sur les pas de Monsieur Vincent*, p. 287.

42. AP *Enfants Assistés, Tables des Réintegrations*; and AAP Foss. 647$_2$, Memoranda from the *préposés* at Saint-Calais to the directors of the Hospice.

43. DuCamp, *Paris, ses organes, ses fonctions, et sa vie*, 4:222.

44. Haussonville, *L'enfance à Paris*, p. 34.

45. AAP Foss 647$_2$, Memoranda from the director of the Hospice to the *préposés* at Saint-Calais.

46. Lafabrèque, "Notes pour servir à l'étude . . . des enfants assistés."

47. Armand Husson, *Etude sur les hôpitaux, considérés sous le rapport de leur construction, de la distribution de leurs bâtiments, de l'ameublement, de l'hygiène et du service des salles des malades, Administration générale de l'Assistance publique à Paris* (Paris, 1862), pp. 312, 554. Husson's data for this may be incorrect. He stated that the *nourrices sédentaires* received an added portion of twenty decagrams of roast meat. This would be a lot of meat and not consistent with other provisions. Twenty decagrams is 200 grams—the equivalent of seven ounces.

48. AAP Foss. 647$_3$, Letter from Eugène Ory, Director of the Hospice to the *sous-inspector* at Saint-Calais.

49. Ibid.

50. deGerando, *Bienfaisance publique*, 4:360.

51. AAP Foss. 647$_5$, Letter from Ory, Director of the Hospice to the *sous-inspector* at Vendôme.

52. Dr. Ratier as quoted in Dupoux, *Sur les pas de Monsieur Vincent*, p. 286-289; Husson, *Etude sur les hôpitaux*, pp. 311-313; Marfan, Académie de Médicine, *Bulletin*, 1882, p. 475; and AAP Foss. 647$_7$. Dr. Baron complained about the quantity and quality of *nourrices sédentaires*.

53. AAP Foss. 647$_7$.

54. Note from Boicervoise in AAP Foss. 647$_7$. Boicervoise at that time was *Directeur de l'Administration générale des Hôpitaux, Hospices civils et secours à domicile de Paris*, in charge of the division for *enfants trouvés*.

55. Dr. Ratier, quoted in Dupoux, *Sur les pas de Monsieur Vincent*, p. 287.

56. Ibid.

57. Hutinel quoted in Dupoux, *Sur les pas de Monsieur Vincent*, p. 305.

58. M. Guéniot, in Académie de Médicine, *Bulletin*, 2nd Series, 11 (Paris, 1882), p. 475.

59. Dr. Parrot, "La Nourricerie," pp. 839-853.

60. A Boudard, *Guide pratique de la chèvre nourrice du pointe de vue de l'allaitement des nouveau nés et de la syphilis constitutionelle* (Paris, 1879).

61. Austury, "Paul Bert," *Nouvelle Revue*, ser. 4, 27 (1933), p. 242, as quoted

in Evelyn Martha Acomb, *French Laic Laws* (New York, 1941), p. 45.

62. Dr. Parrot, "La Nourricerie," pp. 839-853; see also Dr. Tarnier, "L'allaitement artificiel des nouveau-nés," *Bulletin de l'académie de médicine*, (1882) pp. 1075-1089.

63. Unfortunately, the data for the Hospice mortality rate are imprecise, particularly with respect to the population involved. For the years 1824-1887 the data may or may not include the very few temporarily deposited at the Hospice *en dépôt*; for 1815-1823 and 1868-1900, the data are exclusively for those officially registered as definitively abandoned. The mortality data, moreover, refer to those who died during a particular year, not to those abandoned who died in the year of abandonment or to those abandoned in a given year who subsequently died in the Hospice. The short duration of a child's stay, however, means the carry-over from year to year was relatively small. Occasionally, abandoned children who had been with a wet nurse in the country were sent back to the Hospice because they were ill and then died in the Hospice. For example, a child admitted in 1831 may have become ill and died in 1833, and thus shows up in the mortality figures for 1833. This happened rarely, because the administration preferred to have sick children stay in the provinces and go to a hospital there. Thus, although the mortality statistics include all those who died in the Hospice during a given year, regardless of the year of abandonment, the number who died in the year following their abandonment because they were in the Hospice over New Year or who returned and died is so small as to be insignificant in terms of the overall number of deaths reported.

The laicization of 1885 could not have had much effect on the mortality rate since only a very few Sisters were replaced by lay personnel, who may have been neither better nor worse trained than the Sisters.

64. McClure, *Coram's Children*, pp. 250, 251, 261.

65. Dupoux, *Sur les pas de Monsieur Vincent*, p. 289. I am indebted to Robert A. Hannemann, M.D. for this discussion of *athrepsie* and *endurcissement du tissu cellulaire*.

66. Dr. Parrot in *Rapps. Anns.*, 1978.

67. McBride, *The Domestic Revolution*, p. 52.

68. Margaret Llewelyn Davies, ed. *Maternity: Letters from Working-Women*; collected by the Women's Cooperative Guild (1915; reprint ed., New York, 1978).

69. *Enquête*, (1860).

70. AAP Foss. 647₇, 1861.

71. Benoiston de Châteauneuf, *Considérations sur les enfants trouvés* (Paris, 1924), p. 72.

72. Haussonville, *L'enfance à Paris*, p. 39.

Notes to Chapter Five
Spreading the Wealth

1. *Enquête*, (1860); AAP Foss. 15; and Dupoux, *Sur les pas de Monsieur Vincent*, p. 206.

2. The Administration Générale included a Directeur Général and a Conseil Général. In 1859 *enfants trouvés* officially became *enfants assistés*.

3. The Ministry of Interior still had national responsibility for the children.

4. AAP Foss. 647₆ Report of November 27, 1826.

5. AAP Foss. 647₆ Circular from the *Conseil général des Hospices chargé de la surveillance du service des enfants trouvés* to the *sous-préfet* of the Seine, May 19, 1819.

6. Ibid.; and AAP Foss. 647₆.

7. AAP Foss. 647₆ *Instructions*, (1823); AAP Foss. 647₂; and AAP Foss. 688¹ *Instructions sur le service des enfants trouvés, abandonnés, et orphelins placés à la compagne* (Paris, 1852). [Hereafter *Instructions*, (1852)].

8. AAP Foss. 647₃ Husson to Desnoyers, *sous-inspecteur* at Saint-Calais, October 11, 1861; and AAP Foss. 647₇ Report of Peligot, June 15, 1824.

9. Dupoux, *Sur les pas de Monsieur Vincent*, p. 259.

10. deWatteville, *Rapport*, (1849).

11. Brochard, *Vérité sur les enfants trouvés*, p. 299; and A.-T. Brochard, *Les nourrissons, les enfants trouvés et les animaux* (Lyon, 1871).

12. AAP Foss. 647₇ Circular from Peligot to *Inspecteurs*, March 25, 1822. There was a consensus of opinion that inspections were neither done well nor thorough and were not carried out by trained personnel. See also deWatteville, *Rapport*, (1849); *Enquête*, (1860); AN C 1039; and AN F¹⁵ 148.

13. AAP Foss. 647₆ Letter from *préposé* at Saint-Calais.

14. AAP Foss. 647₁, *Instructions*, (1819). In all the documents and literature throughout the nineteenth century, the word used to refer to the doctors for the *enfants assistés* is *médecin*. According to the records, *officiers de santé* were not employed in the Service de Santé des Enfants Trouvés.

15. This is surmised from the correspondence between doctors who were seeking the post and the Administration in Paris. AAP Foss. 647₁, ₆, ₇; and AN F¹⁵ 3897.

16. AAP Foss. 647₂.

17. *Instructions*, (1852); Dupoux mentions that the date of the change in payment to the doctors was 1857. Dupoux, *Sur les pas de Monsieur Vincent*, p. 241.

18. Alain Morel, "Power and Ideology in the Village Community of Picardy: Past and Present," in Robert Forster and Orest Ranum, eds., *Rural Society in France*, Selections from the *Annales: Economies, Sociétés, Civilisations*, trans. Elborg Forster and Patricia Ranum (Baltimore, 1977), p. 112.

19. Evelyn Bernette Ackerman, *Village on the Seine: Tradition and Change in Bonnières, 1815-1914* (New York, 1978), p. 132.

20. *Instructions*, (1823); and *Instructions*, (1852).

21. AAP Foss. 647₁ Letter from Peligot as *Administrateur des Hôpitaux et Hospices* to M. Brochard, *préposé* at Saint-Calais, November 9, 1825. These women were mainly *nourrices sédentaires*.

22. *Instructions*, (1852).

23. The first medical examination was by the doctor of l'Assistance Publique,

the second by the doctor of the commune, and the third by the doctor of the Hospice when she arrived there to pick up a baby.

24. Sussman, "The Wet-Nursing Business in Nineteenth-Century France," p. 318.

25. AAP Foss. 647[1], 1883.

26. AAP Foss. 647[7] circular from the *Conseil général des Hôpitaux et Hospices* to mayors, 1832.

27. AAP Foss. 647[4] Circular on the role of the mayors, from Boicervoise to Sornet, *préposé* at Château-Renault, 1847.

28. AAP Foss. 647[1] Circular from Jourdan to *préposés*, August 2, 1834; AAP Foss. 647[2] Letter from Davenne to Gaudry, *préposé* at Saint-Calais; *Rapps. Anns.*, 1857; and AAP Foss. 647[6] Report of *Inspection* of 1826.

29. AAP Foss. 647[1] Circular from Jourdan to *préposés*, August 2, 1834; It is impossible to determine the extent of the reluctance of the mayors.

30. *Instructions*, (1823); and *Instructions*, (1852). "Age of milk" meant how long she had been lactating. A woman who had been lactating between six and fifteen months had given birth between six and fifteen months prior to seeking a nursling.

31. AAP Foss. 647[1-7]; See especially the correspondence between the *préposés* and *sous-inspecteurs* at Saint-Calais with the administrators of l'Assistance Publique and with the director of the Hospice, AAP Foss. 647[1-5]; AAP Foss. 647[7] Circular from Peligot to *préposés*, January 10, 1826; and AAP Foss. 647[1] Circular from Jourdan to *préposés*, August 2, 1834.

32. AAP Foss. 647[5] Letter from Lafabrèque, 1878.

33. AAP Foss. 647[1] Circular of 1844.

34. AAP Foss. 647[1, 6, 7].

35. AAP Foss. 647[1] Letter from the Director of the Hospice to the *préposé* at Saint-Calais, 1833.

36. AAP Foss. 647[3] Letter from the Director of the Hospice to the *sous-inspecteur* at Saint-Calais, 1857.

37. AAP Foss. 647[1] Circular from Peligot to *préposés*, February, 1827 and another similar circular in 1832.

38. AAP Foss. 647[2] Letter to *sous-inspecteur* at Saint-Calais, 1853.

39. Remacle, *Des hospices d'enfants trouvés*, pp. 274-277.

40. Emile Laurent, *L'Etat actuel de la question des Enfants Assistés à propos de la recente loi sur la protection des enfants du premier âge* (Paris, 1876), p. 14.

41. AAP Foss. 647[6] Report of *Inspection* of 1826; and AN F[15] 1887.

42. AAP Foss. 647[1, 2, 6] Correspondence between administrators in Paris and the *préposés* at Saint-Calais. See also Foss. 647[6] Memorandum to Sornet, *préposé* at Château-Renault, January 23, 1836.

43. AAP Foss. 647[6] Letter from Davenne to the *préposé* at Saint-Quentin.

44. Sussman, "The End of the Wet-Nursing Business in France," p. 251; and Faÿ-Sallois, *Les nourrices à Paris*, p. 105.

45. Waverly Root, *The Food of France* (New York, 1977), p. 185; and Etienne

311

vandeWalle and Samuel H. Preston, "Mortalité de l'enfance au XIXe siècle à Paris et dans le département de la Seine," *Population* 29 (1974), pp. 89-106.

46. Sussman, "The End of the Wet-Nursing Business in France," p. 249; and James R. Lehning, "Family Life and Wetnursing in a French Village," *Journal of Interdisciplinary History* 12:4 (Spring 1982), pp. 649-650. Lehning suggests that women took fewer nurslings in October because of the "resurgence of silk ribbon-weaving," and a July peak in nurslings coincides with a "slump in the ribbon-weaving industries."

47. Louise A. Tilly, "Individual Lives and Family Strategies in the French Proletariat," in Robert Wheaton and Tamara Hareven, eds., *The Family and Sexuality in French History* (Philadelphia, 1980), p. 203.

48. Ackerman, *Village on the Seine*, p. 67.

49. Nancy Fitch, "Les Petits Parisiens en Provence: The Silent Revolution in the Allier during the Third Republic" (Paper delivered at the Twenty-Seventh Annual Meeting of the Society for French Historical Studies, Bloomington, IN, March 1981), p. 26.

50. Henri Thulié (Dr.), *La surveillance des établissements d'assistance privés.* 1° *Rapport de M. le Directeur de l'Assistance et de l'Hygiène publiques*: H. Monot. 2° *Rapport de M. de Crisenoy.* 3° *Extraits des procès-verbaux des séances du Conseil supérieur de l'Assistance publique* (5-6 mars 1895). 4° *Procès-verbaux des séances de Commission spéciale nommée par le Conseil supérieur.* 5° *Rapport de M. le Dr. Thulié* (Paris, 1896), pp. 96-142.

"Lymphatic" was a general term used to describe a weak, flabby, pale, sluggish infant. "Scrofula" was a "constitutional disease characterized mainly by chronic enlargement and degeneration of the lymphatic glands, especially in the neck. It could affect every tissue in the body and predispose a person to tuberculosis. *The Compact Edition of the Oxford English Dictionary*, s.v. (Oxford, 1971), p. 2684. Sometimes scrofula was marked by ulcerated sores which left scars when healed.

51. AP *Enfants Assistés, Registres d'Admission*. This placement of children (according to which ones were ready to leave the Hospice when any wagons or convoy from any locale arrived) seemingly continued at least through 1873—the last year for which Hospice records were available to scholars.

52. Thulié, *La surveillance*, p. 138; and idem. *Les enfants assistés de la Seine* (Paris, 1887), chaps. 5 and 6.

53. AAP Foss. 83.

54. Benoiston de Châteauneuf, *Considerations sur les enfants trouvés dans les principaux états de l'Europe* (Paris, 1824), p. 72.

55. *Journal Officiel, Senat Débats*, Session of May 24, 1874, p. 3286. Report of Dr. Brochard.

56. AAP 30708 *Conseil général des Hôpitaux et Hospices civils de Paris*, Session, September 6, 1820.

57. AAP Foss. 647⁶ *Rapport d'Agent de surveillance de l'Hospices des Enfants Trouvés chargé d'une inspection des "routes" du Nord*, November 27, 1826.

58. AAP Foss. 647_{1, 6} Circular from Peligot to *préposé* at Saint-Calais, June, 1826.

59. AAP Foss. 647₁ Circulars from Peligot, June 1826 and September 1828 to *préposé* at Saint-Calais and Circular to *préposé* at Saint-Calais, December 10, 1837.

60. Ibid.

61. AAP Foss. 647₁. However Dr. Brochard reports that in 1871 *meneurs, sous-inspecteurs* and *surveillantes* were all related. Brochard, *Vérité sur les enfants trouvés*, p. 299.

62. AAP Foss. 647₂ Letter from Boicervoise, *l'Administrateur des Hôpitaux et Hospice civils et secours à domicile de Paris chargé de la 4ᵉ Division* to M. Boudard, *Préposé de l'Arrondissement de Vendôme*, January, 1847.

63. AAP Foss. 647₁ Circular from Peligot.

64. Victor-Eugène Ardouin-Dumazet, *Voyage en France*, 20 vols. (Paris, 1893-1899), 1:36.

65. AAP Foss. 647⁶ *Rapport d'Agent de surveillance de l'Hospice des Enfants Trouvés chargé d'une inspection des "routes" du Nord*, November 27, 1826.

66. Ibid.

67. Ibid.

68. Weber, *Peasants into Frenchmen*, p. 195.

69. Ibid., pp. 199-200, 203.

70. AAP Foss. 647₁₋₅.

71. AAP Foss. 647₁₋₄; and Foss. 83.

72. AAP Foss. 647₃; and Ernest Blin, "Les enfants assistés de la Seine dans l'Avallonnais, 1819-1906, Etudes statistiques," Mss. 2 vols., 1:146-151 [hereafter Blin, "Avallon"].

73. SNCF, *Histoire des chemins de fer en France* (Paris, 1963), pp. 46, 50, 289-291, chaps. 8 and 11; A. Picard, *Les chemins de fer français* (Paris, 1885), vols. 1 and 6; and Brochard, *Vérité sur les enfants trouvés*, p. 253.

74. Brochard, *Les nourrissons, les enfants trouvés, et les animaux*, p. 9.

75. Picard, *Chemins de fer*, 6:212.

76. AAP Foss. 647₄ Letter of June 27, 1866 from the Director of the Compagnie de Chemin de Fer to Ory, Director of l'Assistance Publique.

77. AAP Foss. 647₄, ₅.

78. AAP Foss. 647⁶.

79. AAP Foss. 647₃ Davenne to Cellenet, *préposé* at Saint-Calais.

80. AAP Foss. 647₂ Circular from Davenne to *sous-inspecteurs*, January 31, 1853.

81. AP *Contrôle du Bureau en campagne*. These record books in which the field representatives were to record all payments to the wet nurses, and the date they were paid in addition to the date of death of the child are incomplete. From these books it is unclear whether the wet nurse got paid for the entire trimester if the child died.

82. Faÿ-Sallois, *Les nourrices à Paris*, p. 60.

83. *Rapps. Anns.*, 1852 and 1873; Blin, "Avallon"; and *Enquête*, (1860), pp. 94-95.

84. Ackerman, *Village on the Seine*, p. 67; and Sussman, "The Wet-Nursing Business in France," p. 321.

85. "What accounted for another Morvan specialty, which enters possibly into

the realm of gastronomy, it is difficult to say, unless it was the emulation of the bovine species by the human. In the last century, the specialty of the women of Morvan became the supplying of wet nurses. Many of them went to the large cities—Lyons, Dijon, Paris, to care for the children whose well-to-do mothers had fallen in with contemporary fashion which decreed that it was not well bred to nurse one's own children. In other cases, babies were sent to the Morvan to be reared there. Baby farming became the most important industry in the Morvan." Root, *The Food of France*, p. 185.

86. Blin, "Avallon," 1:193; and AP *Enfants Assistés, Correspondance Avallon*, 1855.

87. AAP Foss. 647₁ Circular from Jourdan, November 11, 1835.

88. Blin, "Avallon," 1:193-200. In 1835 the *préposé* at Blois complained that an infant infected a wet nurse with syphilis. This was the fourth time this had happened in a year. Therefore, it was hard for him to get his choice of good wetnurses. AP *Enfants Assistés, Dossier* 982.

89. Ibid.

90. Ardouin-Dumazet, *Voyage en France*, 1:39.

91. The *Instructions* of 1823 forbade any nursling from being placed with a person who resided in the town. All correspondence reveals that the women were rural farm women. See also AAP Foss. 647₁₋₇.

92. AAP Foss. 647₁₋₅ Correspondence with field representatives at Saint-Calais.

93. AAP Foss. 647₃ Letter from Husson to Veret, *sous-inspecteur* at Vendôme, October 16, 1861.

94. Blin, "Avallon," 1:165-166.

95. deWatteville, *Rapport*, (1849), p. 20.

96. Blin, "Avallon," 1:15-166; Ackerman, *Village on the Seine*, p. 67; Lehning, "Family Life and Wetnursing," p. 650; and George Sussman, "Parisian Infants and Norman Wet Nurses in the Early Nineteenth Century: A Statistical Study," *Journal of Interdisciplinary History* 7:4 (Spring 1977), pp. 637-653.

97. Fitch, "Les Petits Parisiens," pp. 17-27.

98. Lehning, "Family Life and Wetnursing," p. 650.

99. Eugène Ory, *La protection de l'enfant et de l'adulte* (Paris, 1883), p. 392.

Notes to Chapter Six
Chez La Nourrice

1. Henri Doniol, "Les enfants des hospices et la mise en valeur des terres incultes," extract from *Journal des Economistes*, February 15, 1864, (Paris, 1862), p. 2; and Armand Husson, *Etude sur les hôpitaux considérés sous le rapport de leur construction, de la distribution de leurs bâtiments, de l'ameublement, de l'hygiène et du service des salles des malades* (Paris, 1862), p. 310; and *Enquête*, (1860), p. 156.

2. I am grateful to George Alter for this discussion.

3. For a more complete analysis of the data and the problems involved in computing mortality, see Fuchs, "Abandoned Children in Nineteenth-Century France," (Ph.D dissertation, Indiana University, 1980), chap. 5, pp. 249-257.

4. A.-T. Brochard (Dr.), *Les enfants trouvés à Lyon et à Moscou* (Lyon, 1875), pp. 12-13.

5. Blin, "Avallon," 2:6-27, 82-83; and AP *Enfants Assistés, Registres d'Admission.*

6. Ibid., 2:74-75.

7. Ardouin-Dumazet, *Voyage en France*, 1:36.

8. Sussman, "The Wet-Nursing Business in France," pp. 326-327; and *Selling Mothers' Milk*, pp. 65, 121, 143. Sussman's data represent mortality of all children with a wet nurse, regardless of age of death, length of time with a wet nurse, or years at risk. The two sets of data are not precisely comparable. It is likely, however, that the highest proportion of nurslings died in the first six months with a wet nurse, and that few stayed with a wet nurse for much more than twelve months. There are several possible explanations for the rise in mortality among babies placed with wet nurses through the bureaus. Sussman argues that fewer wet nurses actually breast-fed the infants and more fed the babies artificially, resulting in a higher mortality. But it also became more popular, or necessary, for artisan and working-class mothers to send their babies to wet nurses. This resulted in a change in the make up of the population being nursed. Working-class mothers may not have been able to pay very much and as a result could not afford to hire good nurses. In addition, the babies of these women may have been weaker at birth due to poorer prenatal care. An increased demand for wet nurses could have put a strain on the market, resulting in the employment of marginal nurses—such as the abandoned children had all along.

9. Blin, "Avallon," 1:81-87, 2:92-100.

10. Ibid. 2:83.

11. For the Nivernais see Guy Thuillier, "Water Supplies in Nineteenth-Century Nivernais," in Robert Forster and Orest Ranum, eds., *Food and Drink in History*, Selections from the *Annales: Economies, Sociétés, Civilisations*, vol. 5, trans. Elborg Forster and Patricia M. Ranum (Baltimore, 1979), pp. 109-125. For the Morvan, see Weber, *Peasants into Frenchmen* pp. 115-292 and Blin, "Avallon," vol. 1. John Shaffer shows that the Morvan is really part of the greater Nivernais. John W. Shaffer, *Family and Farm: Agrarian Change and Household Organization in the Loire Valley* (Albany, 1982), pp. 112-116.

12. Weber, *Peasants into Frenchmen*, p. 163.

13. Ibid., pp. 156-157.

14. Thuillier, "Water Supplies in Nineteenth-Century Nivernais," p. 120.

15. Weber, *Peasants into Frenchmen*, pp. 156-157; and Remacle, *Des hospices d'enfants trouvés*, p. 275.

16. AAP Foss. 647₆ Report of *Inspection* of 1826.

17. Weber, *Peasants into Frenchmen*, pp. 159-160.

18. Mme. Elisabeth Celnart, *Manuel des nourrices adoptés par le Conseil*

général des hospices civils de Paris (Paris, 1834) (Pseud. Bayle Mouillard). Celnart stated that burning was the most common accident among the abandoned children. For further duscussion of accidental burning as a cause of death, see below.

19. Remacle, *Des hospices d'enfants trouvés*, p. 275.

20. Weber, *Peasants into Frenchmen*, p. 149.

21. Celnart, *Manuel des nourrices, passim*; Remacle, *Des hospices d'enfants trouvés*, p. 275; and Brochard, *Vérité sur les enfants trouvés*, pp. 9-10.

22. Thuillier, "Water Supplies in Ninetenth-Century Nivernais," p. 120.

23. Weber, *Peasants into Frenchmen*, p. 162.

24. Thuillier, "Water Supplies in Nineteenth-Century Nivernais," p. 110, 118.

25. Weber, *Peasants into Frenchmen*, p. 147. See the illustration in Shaffer, *Family and Farm*, p. 204.

26. Quoted by Thuillier, "Water Supplies in Nineteenth-Century Nivernais," p. 109.

27. Ibid., pp. 109-110, 120.

28. Ibid., p. 118, 120.

29. Pierre-Jakez Hélias, *The Horse of Pride: Life in a Breton Village*, trans. June Guicharnaud (New Haven, 1978), pp. 2-3.

30. Marlière, *Statistique de Clemency*, pp. 120-121, as cited in Thuillier, "Water Supplies in Nineteenth-Century Nivernais," p. 119.

31. *Gazette hébdomadaire de médecine et chirurgie*, 8 (February 20, 1870), p. 123.

32. Blin, "Avallon," 1:28-33.

33. Weber, *Peasants into Frenchmen*, p. 149.

34. Thuillier, "Water Supplies in Nineteenth-Century Nivernais," p. 119.

35. Hélias, *Horse of Pride*, pp. 42, 50; *Rapps. Anns.*, 1860; and *Enquête*, (1860).

36. Blin, "Avallon," 1:28-33.

37. Ibid.

38. *Rapps. Anns.*, 1856, p. 11.

39. Blin, "Avallon," 1:43.

40. After 1872, clothes were given to the wet nurses for the infants when the children were seven months, fifteen months, and two years. The clothes given at seven and fifteen months did not constitute a complete wardrobe but only those items which required replacement at a more frequent interval than one year.

41. Hélias, *Horse of Pride*, pp. 50-51.

42. AAP Foss. 647_{2-6}.

43. AAP Foss. 83 Letter from *agent de surveillance* to Peligot, October 20, 1821.

44. AP *Enfants Assistés, Correspondance Avallon*; and AAP Foss. 647_{1-5}.

45. AAP Foss 647_3 Davenne to Veret, *sous-inspecteur* at Vendôme, August 18, 1858.

46. AAP Foss. 647_{1-5} Circulars from *préposés* relative to complaints of wet nurses.

47. AAP Foss. 642_1 Circular to *préposés* from Peligot, 1829.

48. AAP Foss. 647₁ Circular to *préposés* from Peligot, November 26, 1822.

49. AAP Foss. 647₆ *Rapport sur l'Inspection du Service des Enfants placé dans l'arrondissement d'Arras, n.d.*

50. Ibid.; AAP Foss. 647₂ Letter from Jourdan to *préposé* at Saint-Calais, July 1829 complaining about the lack of time a wet nurse spends with the foundling; and remacle, *Des hospices d'enfants trouvés*, pp. 274-277.

51. Celnart, *Manuel des nourrices*; Brochard, *Vérité sur les enfants trouvés*, p. 7; and AP *Enfants Assistés, Correspondance Avallon*, 1865.

52. A similar argument is made by Barbara A. Hanawalt, "Childrearing Among the Lower Classes of Late Medieval England," *Journal of Interdisciplinary History* 8 (Summer 1977), 1-22. On the other hand, deaths from burns is the second leading cause of accidental death for children in the United States in 1981 (after automobile accidents). Mothers of children who died in a fire usually report that they left the child alone "for just a few minutes." The National Safety Council as reported by news media.

53. André-Théodore Brochard (Dr.), *Ouvrière, mère de famille* (Lyon, 1875), p. 10.

54. AAP Foss. 647₆ Memorandum to M. Sornet, *préposé* at Château-Renault from *Administration des Hôpitaux et Hospices civils chargé de la 2ᵐᵉ division (enfants trouvés)*, January 23, 1836.

55. Correspondence from Robert E. Hannemann, M.D., June 1978.

56. *Journal des débats*, Summer 1873.

57. United States, *Census*, 1910. Diseases of the lungs and other respiratory diseases were the most common cause of death for children in this age bracket.

58. Blin, "Avallon," 1:45.

59. "Science and the Citizen," *Scientific American*, August 1981, p. 68.

60. John Knodel and Etienne vandeWalle, "Breast Feeding, Fertility and Infant Mortality," *Population Studies* 21 (1967), pp. 115, 127; and M. W. Beaver, "Population, Infant Mortality and Milk," *Population Studies* 27, no. 2 (July 1973), p. 254.

61. Gabriel Latour, *Les enfants assistés-L'Assistance publique* (Paris, 1872), p. 11; and Remacle, *Des hospices d'enfants trouvés*, pp. 274-277. Conversely, Celnart warns women not to keep the baby at the breast all day, for then the milk supply would be inadequate. It is conceivable that wet nurses of foundlings would keep the infant at their breast, but that would not necessarily increase the nourishment the baby received.

62. Stephen Solomon, "The Controversy over Infant Formula," *The New York Times, Magazine*, December 6, 1981, p. 92.

63. Blin, "Avallon," 1:29-35.

64. AAP Foss. 647₁₋₄.

65. Brochard has noted that some women had five or more nurslings, and Semichon found women with seven or eight. Brochard, *Verité sur les enfants trouvés*, p. 73; and Semichon, *Histoire des enfants abandonnés*, p. 151. The records at the Archives Nationales contain reports on several wet nurses who had as many as three nursing infants, AN F¹⁵ 1887.

66. AP *Enfants Assistés, Registres d'Admission*, record the names and ad-

dresses of each wet nurse who leaves the Hospice with an infant. There are several instances of the same wet nurse leaving the Hospice with two infants of less than one month of age.

68. Latour, *Enfants assistés*, p. 11.

68. Celnart, *Manuel des nourrices*, p. 56.

69. This was suposed to have been done. Celnart recommends this practice in her introduction but there is no evidence that the *Manuel* was ever read to the wet nurses.

70. Celnart, *Manuel des nourrices*, p. 56.

71. Ibid., p. 53; and Remacle, *Des hospices d'enfants trouvés*, pp. 274-277.

72. Dr. Bourée, Doctor at Chatillon-sur-Seine (Côte d'Or), "Rapport de la Commission permanente de l'hygiène de l'enfance pour l'année 1877," *Bulletin de l'académie de médecine*, 2ᵐᵉ Série, tome VII, (Paris, 1878), in the Session of March 12, 1878, pp. 237-244.

73. George Sussman, personal communication July 1977; and Marie-France Morel, "Ville et campagne dans le discours médical sur la petite enfance au XVIIIᵉ siècle," *Annales: Economies, Sociétés, Civilisations*, 32ᵉ année no. 5, Sept.-Oct. 1977, pp. 1007-1023. Although discussion centers on feeding in the eighteenth century, there is much of relevance to the nineteenth century; also see Blin, "Avallon," 1:29.

74. Armand Husson, Académie impériale de médecine, "Discours sur la mortalité des jeunes enfants," prononcé dans la séance du 23 octobre 1866," (Paris, 1866), p. 8. Extract of the *Bulletin de l'Académie impériale de médecine* 32 (1866), p. 89.

75. Blin, "Avallon," 1:20-46, 2:50-70. George Sussman has shown that in Normandy 31.7 percent of all infant deaths *en nourrice* occurred during the summer months. The highest mortality, however, was in December followed by July and September. Paul Galliano found that the three summer months accounted for 33.7 percent of the years' fatalities to infants sent to a wet nurse. A century later, in Avallon, there is a similar seasonal mortality rate for abandoned infants *chez la nourrice*. Both Sussman and Galliano suggest that the reason for this seasonal mortality of nurslings was the wet nurses' other occupation during these months—farm work. Rose Cheney in studying infant mortality in Philadelphia points to July as the month of highest infant mortality. Peak mortality in July declines with the beginning of bacteriological inspections of milk (1897). See George Sussman, "Parisian Infants and Norman Wet Nurses," p. 647; Paul Galliano, "La mortalité infantile (indigenes et nourrissons) dans la banlieue sud de Paris—la fin du XVIIIᵉ siècle (1774-1794)," *Annales de démographie historique* 1966 (Paris, 1967), pp. 161-164; and Rose Cheney, "Seasonal Patterns of Infant and Child Mortality in Philadelphia," (paper presented at the 1981 Annual Meeting of the Social Science History Association, October 22-24, 1981, Nashville, Tennessee), Tables 1 and 2, Figures 2 and 5.

76. Correspondence from Robert E. Hannemann, M.D., June 1978.

77. Brochard, *Vérité sur les enfants trouvés*, p. 73; and Guérin, in *Gazette hébdomadaire de médecine et de chirurgie*, 6 (February 11, 1870), p. 91.

78. AAP Foss. 647₃ Letter from Husson to Desloges, *sous-inspecteur* at Saint-Calais.
79. Blin, "Avallon," 1:46.
80. Report of Dr. Bourée in *Bulletin de l'académie de médecine*, (1878).
81. *Le Temps*, 1873, 1.9, 4B; and Musée de l'Assistance Publique, storage collection of *biberons* from exhibits.
82. Thuillier, "Water Supplies in Nineteenth-Century Nivernais," p. 115.
83. Weber, *Peasants into Frenchmen*, pp. 132-137.
84. Blin, "Avallon," 2:120-121.
85. *Rapps. Anns.*, 1878.
86. AAP Foss. 647₇ Circular from Peligot to Inspectors, March 25, 1822; Foss. 707₅ n.d. but probably 1829-30; and Foss. 647₁₋₇.
87. Brochard, *Vérité sur les enfants trouvés*, p. 564.
88. AAP Foss. 647₆ Report of *Inspection* of 1826.
89. Husson, *Etude sur les Hôpitaux*, p. 564.
90. Ibid.; and AAP Foss. 647₃.
91. Husson, *Etude sur les hôpitaux*, pp. 563-564; and *Rapps. Anns.*, 1885.
In the literature and government reports the doctors are always called either *médecins* or *docteurs*. We have little reason to believe that the medical personnel who were in charge of *enfants assistés* were other than men with medical degrees.
92. AAP Foss. 647₂ Circular from Davenne to *sous-inspecteur* at Saint-Calais, May 24, 1850 indicated that doctors were affiliated with local hospitals. On the average, there was one doctor for 3,000 people around mid-century. See *Statistique de la France*, 2nd Sèrie, tome xi, p.xcj.
93. AAP Foss. 647₂ Circular from Davenne, *Directeur général de l'Assistance publique* to the doctors in the Service, February 15, 1854; AAP Foss. 647₁ Circular from Jourdan, January 18, 1833; and AP *Enfants Assistés, Registres d'Admission, Contrôles du Bureau en Campagne*.
94. Breck-sur-Mer was established for scrofulous children or those with *teigne* (tinea—a scalp disease). Other hospital-hospices were established for children with specific infirmities. These hospitals housed fewer than one hundred children at any one time, and were initially experimental institutions where doctors would test new cures for the diseases.
95. Brochard, *Vérité sur les enfants trouvés*; AAP Foss. 707₅; and Foss. 647₁₋₅.
96. AAP Foss. 709₇ July 25, 1829.
97. AAP Foss. 707₅ n.d. but probably from 1820 to 1830.
98. Blin, "Avallon," 1:28-35.
99. AAP Foss. 647₁ Peligot to *préposé* at Saint-Calais; and AAP Foss. 647₃ Circular to *préposés* and doctors at Château-Renault from Jourdan 1836.
100. AAP Foss 647₁ Boicervoise as acting director of the Service des Enfants Trouvés to *préposé* at Vendôme, June 22, 1832.
101. AAP Foss. 647₂ Circular from Davenne to all *sous-inspecteurs*. The circular is a notification to doctors that their initial three-year term of appointment was approaching the end. Since the circular is dated 1850, the change in regulations in the Service probably occurred in 1847.

102. AAP Foss. 647$_{2-3}$.
103. *Rapps. Anns.*, 1856.
104. Brochard, *Vérité sur les enfants trouvés*, p. 208.
105. Blin, "Avallon," 1:28-35; Hélias, *Horse of Pride*, pp. 83-85; and Weber, *Peasants into Frenchmen*, pp. 23-29, chaps. 10 and 11 passim.
106. Ardouin-Dumazet, *Voyage en France*, 1:33; and AAP Foss. 709[6] *Memoire de S. Dubourg, préposé* at Château-Thierry to Conseil général des Hospices de Paris, December 4, 1831.
107. Blin, "Avallon," 1:33.
108. Hélias, *Horse of Pride*, pp. 83-84; and Blin, "Avallon," 1:33, 132.
109. John Bowlby, *Maternal Care and Mental Health* (New York, 1966), p. 290; and René Spitz, "Hospitalism: An Inquiry into the Genesis of Psychiatric Conditions in Early Childhood," *Psychoanalytic Study of the Child* 1 (1945), pp. 53-54; and Lytte I. Gardner, "Deprivation Dwarfism," *Scientific American* 227 (July 1972), pp. 76-82.
Spitz cites a seventy percent mortality rate; this is even higher than for the abandoned children of nineteenth-century Paris in general, and lower than that for children in the Hospice alone if the rate of death for five days there is extended to twelve months at risk. The total number of children in Spitz's study is less than 100, so his seventy percent figure may be affected by just a few cases. In a later study (see Mary D. Arnsworth, R. B. Andry, Robert Harlow, et. al. *Deprivation of Maternal Care: A Reassessment of its Effects* (New York, 1966), p. 275) Spitz reported that of the ninety-one institutionalized infant children of whom he had been able to keep track, 37.5 percent died before age two and at age four almost all suffered developmental impairment.

Notes to Chapter Seven
Survivors: The Older Children and Young Adults

1. Theodore Zeldin, *France, 1848-1948: Ambition, Love and Politics*, vol. 1 (Oxford, 1973), p. 142; and Lenard R. Berlanstein, "Vagrants, Beggars and Thieves: Delinquent Boys in Mid-Nineteenth Century Paris," *Journal of Social History* 12 (1979), p. 537.
2. The sections of the Archives of l'Assistance Publique relevant to abandoned children which form a basis for this chapter are by and large reliable. Granted, the *Rapports Annuels* accentuate the successes and deemphasize the failures of each state policy. These reports do contain aggregate data on the population of the abandoned children during a given year. These include the number admitted, number who died, the number in the countryside, and the number in other institutions. When compared with data from the *Registres d'Admission* of the Hospice and other sources of the Archives de la Ville de Paris there is no discrepancy. Much of the data discussed here are culled from the *Rapports Annuels*. These data are supplemented, in the case of deviant children, by the results of the independent general inquiry into the situation of abandoned children taken by the deWatteville commission in 1860. *Enquête*, (1860).

Another set of documents consists of the memoranda that transpired between the field representatives of the Administration at Saint-Calais (Sarthe) and the Administration in Paris. These representatives wanted to get as much money from Paris as possible as well as to rid themselves of troublesome youths. Field representatives could take no action with regard to deviant youths without first consulting Paris. Rather than trying to impress Paris officials with what a fine job they were doing, the field representatives were constantly complaining that Paris did not send them enough money, enough clothing for the children, or relieve them of the burden of troublemakers. This is anecdotal and descriptive material that does not lend itself to quantification.

The record books of the Hospice, especially the *Réintegrations* are the third source. All children who left the *arrondissement* and the area of the field representative where they had originally been placed went back to Paris. These included runaways, children picked up by police, children sent back by foster parent or field representative for health or disciplinary reasons, and those reclaimed by their parents. All children put in hospitals, convents, *colonies agricoles, ouvroirs*, or prisons first passed through the Hospice and as a result their placement was recorded. Likewise, the date they left the institutions was also recorded.

Taken together, the *Rapports Annuels*, the *Réintegrations*, and the correspondence of Saint-Calais, complemented with similar correspondence from Avallon (Yonne) housed in the Archives of Paris, provide systematic and reliable sources for this chapter.

3. AN F^{15} 1888-1890, 1902, 3896; and AAP Foss. 647$_{4, 5}$.

4. *Rapps. Anns.*, 1862-1875; and AP *Enfants Assistés, Réintegrations*, 1845-1865.

5. AN F^{15} 146-7, 1888-1890 3896; and AP VD 508-10.

6. AN F^{15} 146-7.

7. AN F^{15} 3896, July 26, 1853; AP VD 5101 Letter from the Mayor to the prefect of the department of the Seine; and AP *Enfants Assistés, Réintegrations*, 1845-1870.

8. AP *Enfants Assistés, Dossiers, Réintegrations*.

9. Laurent, *L'état actuel des enfants assistés*, p. 41; Jacques Bonzon, *Cent ans de lutte sociale; La législation de l'enfance 1789-1894* (Paris, 1894), p. 103. See AP *Enfants Assistés, Réintegrations*, 1855 and 1865 for the data.

10. In 1977 I had the occasion to telephone the director of l'Assistance Publique for information. A poor telephone connection led the person who spoke with me to believe that I was a mother seeking the return of her child. I kept up the act. In harsh, almost hostile tones I was told that I would have to appear before the director of l'Assistance Publique during specified hours later in the week, fill out multiple forms, and then return at a later date for another interview. The details of the procedure escape me, but I will never forget the tone of voice and the runaround that I was given.

11. It was originally prescribed until the children were twelve years old, but in

1882 when primary education became compulsory for all children until age thirteen, the foundlings were to have stayed with their foster parents until this education was completed.

12. AAP Foss. 647_2 From Boicervoise to the *préposé* at Saint-Calais, March 26, 1821.

13. Jean-Louis Flandrin, 'L'attitude à l'égard du petit enfant et les conduites sexuelles dans la civilisations occidental; structures anciennes et évolution," *Annales de démographie historique* (Paris, 1973), p. 144, 173.

14. Record keeping by the *préposés* varied from area to area and it is not always possible to assess accurately the number of children who changed foster parents, or how many times such changes were made. The evidence suggests that many children stayed with the same foster parent until they were twelve or older, and that many others changed parents several times. AAP Foss. 647_{1-7}; and AP *Registres d'Admission, Contrôle de Bureau en province,* and *Réintegrations.*

15. AAP Foss. 647_2.

16. deWatteville, *Rapport*, (1849); AAP Foss. 647_1 Letter from Jourdan as *Administrateur des Hôpitaux et Hospices* to the *préposé* at Château-Renault, 1831; and Remacle, *Des hospices d'enfants trouvés,* pp. 286-288.

17. AAP Foss. 647_{1-5}.

18. AAP Foss. 647_2 Letters from Boicervoise to Osseaune, *préposé* at Saint-Calais, November 29, 1845.

19. Lists of requests for payments and extra payments made, are in AAP Foss. 647_{2-3} which consist of the correspondence between the *préposés* at Saint-Calais and the *Administrateur général de l'Assistance publique.*

20. AAP Foss. $647_{2, 3}$ Circulars to *préposés* at Saint-Calais.

21. AAP Foss. 647_{2-4}; and *Rapps. Anns.,* 1894.

22. AAP Foss. 647_3 contains lists of all the individuals in Saint-Calais in the mid-century for whom extra payments were made, and the nature of their maladies.

23. W. F. Loomis, "Rickets," *Scientific American,* December 1970, pp. 76-89. Loomis has noted that "ultra-violet radiation is necessary for the synthesis of the hormone (calciferol) that prevents rickets."

24. *New York Times,* May 23, 1982, p. 38.

25. Thuillier, "Water Supplies in Ninetenth-Century Nivernais," pp. 120-121. Shorter estimates that, as a rule, menstruation began by age sixteen. But this may not be true for the young women who had been abandoned. Shorter, "L'âge des premiers règles en France," pp. 501-503.

26. Dupoux, *Sur les pas de Monsieur Vincent,* p. 242.

27. AAP Foss. 647_2 Circular of December 2, 1841.

28. Fitch, "Les Petits Parisiens," p. 30.

29. AAP Foss. 647_2 Circular from *Administrateur des Hôpitaux et Hospices, Chargé de la 4 Division,* to *préposé,* December 4, 1841.

30. AAP Foss. 647_7 *Arrêté du Conseil général des Hospices,* signed by Boicervoise, December 24, 1847.

31. AAP Foss. 647_2 Circular from Davenne, *Directeur de l'Administration général de l'Assistance publique*, October 22, 1850; and AAP Foss. 647_3 Circular from Davenne, November 27, 1857.

32. Dupoux, *Sur les pas de Monsieur Vincent*, chap. 9, passim; and AAP Foss. 647_{1-6}.

33. AAP Foss. 647_{1-5}; and *Rapps. Anns.*, 1852-1905. For details on clothing see above, pp. 210-216.

34. *Rapps. Anns.*, 1879; and AAP Foss. 647_4 Memorandum from Husson to deWalles, *sous-inspecteur* at Saint-Calais, August 2, 1870.

35. AAP Foss. 647_2 Circular from Davenne to *sous-inspecteur*, January 31, 1853.

36. For the year 1895 the total number of school-age children was 15,462. Based on this number, the percentage of those who actually received certificates was 2.9 percent. Those of school age, however, were not all old enough nor had they gone to school long enough to receive a certificate. Children born in 1882 and abandoned in that year would all be old enough to receive certificates by 1895. 2,834 children were abandoned in 1882, of whom approximately seventy percent were newborn, thus 1,984 would have been thirteen years old in 1895. The infant mortality rate was about thirty percent, so subtracting those newborns abandoned in 1882 who likely had died, would leave 1,398 alive and eligible for certificates. The number who received certificates in that year was 450 which is thirty-two percent of 1,393.

37. *Rapps. Anns.*, 1862; Henri Doniol, "Les enfants des hospices et la mise en valeur des terres incultes," *Journal des economistes*, February 15, 1862 (repr. ed., Paris, 1862), p. 3; and AP *Enfants Assistés, Réintegrations*, 1855-1860, show several children taking communion or being confirmed at the Hospices.

38. AN F^{15} 3971, January to March, 1843.

39. Eugène Sue, *Martin, l'enfant trouvé ou les mémoires d'un valet de chambre* (Paris, 1846-47). For specific page references the following English translation has been used; *Martin the Foundling: A Romance* [Dicks English Library, v. VI] (London, 1927), p. 80.

40. Benoiston de Châteauneuf, *Consideration sur les enfants trouvés*, p. 97.

41. AAP Foss. 647_4 Husson to Desforges, *sous-inspecteur* at Saint-Calais, February 9, 1865.

42. Dupoux, *Sur les pas de Monsieur Vincent*, p. 244.

43. D'Alembert had been an *enfant trouvé*. *Rapps. Anns.*, 1880-1900; and Dupoux, *Sur les pas de Monsieur Vincent*, chap. 9, passim.

44. *Rapps. Anns.*, 1852-1900; Dupoux, *Sur les pas de Monsieur Vincent*, chap. 9, passim; and AAP Foss. 647_4 Husson to Desforges, *sous-inspecteur* at Saint-Calais, February 9, 1865.

45. Husson, *Etude sur les hôpitaux*, p. 309, and *Rapps Anns.*, 1857, p. 35.

46. *Enquête*, (1860), p. 125.

47. AP *Enfants Assistés, Contrôle du Bureau en Province, Châteaudun 768* (1855-1863), and *Réintegrations*, 1845-1870. For the end of the century see

Rapps. Anns., 1893, p. 99, and *Rapps. Anns.*, 1900, p. 161. The data in *Réintegrations* do not lend themselves to quantification.

48. *Rapps. Anns.*, 1856.

49. *Rapps. Anns.*, 1875.

50. *Enquête*, (1860).

51. AP *Enfants Assistés*, Case histories gleaned from *Registres d'Admission, Contrôle du Bureau en Province*, and *Réintegrations*, 1841-1875.

52. AAP Foss. 647$_4$.

53. *Rapps. Anns.*, 1865-1890.

54. Lenard R. Berlanstein, "Growing up as Workers in Nineteenth-Century Paris: The Case of the Orphans of the Prince Imperial," *French Historical Studies*, 11 (1980), pp. 365-366.

55. AP *Enfants Assistés, Réintegrations.*

56. Berlanstein, "Growing up as Workers," p. 575.

57. Since unfortunately there are no data at all on the *enfants assistés* after they turned twenty-one, their occupations and life styles as adults remain largely unknown.

58. AN F^{15} 2550, 1812-1816.

59. AN F^{15} 146-147, 1815-1839.

60. AP *Enfants Assistés, Contrôle du Bureau en Province*, 768; and *Rapps. Anns.*, 1856-1900. Terry Strieter commented (Twenty-Seventh Annual Meeting of the Society for French Historical Studies, Bloomington, IN, March 1981) that the French army did not permit illegitimate men to serve as officers. There were no restrictions, however, on accepting illegitimate wards of the state as volunteers, or in drafting them. AAP Foss. 647$_2$.

61. *Enquête*, (1860), p. 146; and *Rapps. Anns.*, 1885, p. 74.

62. Thilleul, *L'assistance publique à Paris: Ses bienfaiteurs*, vol. 1.

63. AN F^{15} 153, 1904; and AAP Foss. 647$_2$.

64. George Sand, *François le Champi* (Paris, n.d.), p. 208. This book first appeared in the *Journal des débats* in 1847-48. Publication was interrupted by the Revolution of 1848 and finished in 1852.

65. Eugène Sue, *Mystères de Paris*, p. 713.

66. Dupoux, *Sur les pas de Monsieur Vincent*, p. 246.

67. *Rapps. Anns.*, 1876; and AAP Foss. 647$_{3, 4, 5}$.

68. *Rapps. Anns.*, 1875; and AP *Enfants Assistés, Correspondance Avallon*, 1865.

69. *Rapps. Anns.*, 1875; AN C 1039; and AAP Foss. 647$_{1-6}$.

70. Sand, *François le Champi*, p. 3; and Louvancour, *Un dernier mot sur les enfants trouvés* (Paris, 1842), p. 2.

71. AAP Foss. 709^6 Memoire de S. Dubourg, *préposé* at Château-Thierry to Conseil général des Hospices de Paris, December 4, 1831.

72. *Rapps. Anns.*, 1852-1880; and AP *Enfants Assistés, Réintegrations.*

73. AAP Foss. 647$_2$ October 18, 1845; AAP Foss 647$_2$ September 24, 1839; AAP Foss. 647$_1$ January 12, 1828; and AP *Enfants Assistés, Correspondance Avallon*, November 25, 1865.

74. *Rapps. Anns.*, 1850; and AP *Enfants Assistés, Réintegrations*, 1855, 1865.
75. Husson, *Etude sur les hôpitaux*, p. 309.
76. AP *Enfants Assistés, Correspondance Avallon*, 1868; *Rapps Anns.*, 1857; AAP Foss. 647₄ April 21, 1865; AAP Foss. 647₃ 1862-1863; and AAP Foss. 647₄ 1865-1868.
77. *Enquête*, (1860), p. 134.
78. Ibid., pp. 140-141; and AAP Foss. 15 (1849).
79. *Rapps. Anns.*, 1871, p. 60.
80. H. Rollet, *Enfance abandonnée: vicieux, insoumis, vagabonds. Colonies agricoles, écoles de reforme et de préservation* (Paris, 1899), p. 19; and *Rapps. Anns.*, 1856-1900.
81. AP *Enfants Assistés, Correspondance Avallon*, 1868.
82. Laurent, *L'état actuel des enfants assistés*, p. 37.
83. AN F¹⁵ 144, Letter to the Minister of Interior, March 29, 1837; and *Rapps. Anns.*, 1853, 1890.
84. Gabriel Latour, *Les enfants assistés-L'assistance publique* (Paris, n.d.), p. 15.
85. AAP Foss. 647₁₋₇; AP *Enfants Assistés, Correspondence Avallon*, 1870, 1873; and AP *Enfants Assistés, Correspondence 777, Réintegrations*.
86. AP *Enfants Assistés, Correspondence Avallon*, October 12, 1865.
87. AAP Foss. 647₄, 1867 and 1869; AP *Enfants Assistés, Correspondance Avallon*, 1870, 1873; and AP *Enfants Assistés, Correspondence 777*.
88. AAP Foss. 647₅ Blondel, *Directeur de l'Administration général de l'Assistance publique* to deWalles, *sous-inspecteur* at Saint-Calais December 14, 1871; and AAP Foss. 647₅ March 3, 1876. There was no mention of payment directly to a midwife, or if the fifty francs paid to the foster parents at the time of the birth of their ward's child was to be used by them to pay the midwife.
89. Remacle, *Des hospices d'enfants trouvés*, p. 398. He is here referring to the statistics of A. J.-B. Parent-Duchâtelet, *De la prostitution dans la ville de Paris* (Paris, 1836). Parent-Duchâtelet's figures, however, only consist of registered prostitutes. They do not include the clandestine prostitutes assumed to exist in large numbers.
90. *Enquête*, (1860).
91. Corbin, *Les filles de noces*, pp. 172 ff.
92. Selma Fraiberg, *Every Child's Birthright: In Defense of Mothering* (New York, 1977), pp. 47, 52-53.
93. AAP Foss. 647₂, ₃ Answers to questionnaires sent to *préposés* and *sous-inspecteurs* from the *Directeur de l'Administration générale de l'Assistance publiques*; Ardouin-Dumazet, *Voyage en France*, 1:36; and *Rapps. Anns.*, 1879-1900.
94. Personal communication from Carla D. Carrol, M.D., Los Angeles, California, December 30, 1981.
95. Michel Foucault, *Madness and Civilization: A History of Insanity in the Age of Reason* (New York, 1973), chap. 2; and idem. *Discipline and Punish: The Birth of the Prison* (New York, 1979), pp. 231-308.

Bibliography

Primary Sources

Archives

Archives de l'Assistance Publique (AAP).
    M. Fosseyeux, ed. *Catalogue des Manuscrits*, 1913.
    Liasse 310   Hôpital des Orphelins.
    Liasse 564   Hospice des Orphelins—Correspondance, 1834-1837.
    Liasse 592   Direction des Nourrices.
    Liasse 647   Assistance à l'Enfance—Agence de Saint-Calais (Sarthe).
                Circulaires et Correspondance, 1819-1885. (5 dossiers).
                Hospice Saint-Vincent-de-Paul. Documents d'Archives,
                après 1814. (2 dossiers).
    Liasses 676-
    690   Enfants Assistés. Circulaires, Rapports, Statistiques.
    Laisses 707-
    710   Enfants trouvés et abandonnés.
Archives de la Préfecture de Police (APP).
    Series D B/61-76 Enfants abandonnés.
    D A/635-693 Enfants delinquant.
Archives de la Ville de Paris et Département de la Seine (AP).
    Series VD⁴   Assistance Publique
                Bureau de Bienfaisance
                Etablissements Hospitaliers
                Oeuvres Charitables
                Sociétés Charitable diverse
                Police Local
                Hygiène Publique et Salubrité
                Médecins, Chirugiens et Sage femmes.

Enfants Assistés
Contrôle de Bureau en province. Cote 715-945.
Decisions d'Abandon, 1862-1873. Cote 144-216.
Envois à la Campagne, 1829-1854. Cote 655-673.
Enfants envoyés en nourrice par département, 1855-1870. Cote 674-683; 713.
Registres d'Admission
Etiquette jaune, 1820-1825. Cote 206-229.
Etiquette blanche, 1830-1873. Cote 1-43.
Réintegrations, 1841-1875. Cote 528-565.
Repertoire des décès, 1832-1876. Cote 567-587, 589, 686-698.
Diverse—Finances et Administration Générale.

Archives Nationales (AN).

Series F — Administration Générale de la France.

F² — 122-143 Affaires diverses AN XII- 1839.

F⁴ — 287-394, 1934-2666 Comptabilité Générale.

F⁸ — 124 Police Sanitaire.

F¹¹ — 1324-1444 Subsistances—Réserve de Paris, 1760-1823.

F¹⁵ — Hospices et Secours.

144-149 Dossiers concernant objects généraux—enfants trouvés.

1883-1943 Enfants trouvés et abandonnés.

2154-2204 Demandes d'admission dans les hospices, IV-1840.

2205-2457 Comptes des Hospices, VII-1844.

2458-2547 Enfants Trouvés 1783-1836.

2548-3622 Secours de toute nature, 1788-1854.

3896-3898 Enfants Trouvés et Assistés—Correspondance,1835-1863.

3916 Correspondance—enfants trouvés, 1846-1864.

F¹⁶ — 3893-9103—Prisons, Colonie Agricole de Mettray.

F¹⁹ — 3969-3972 Cultes—Education des enfants assistés.

F²⁰ — 135-282 Statistique—Statistique générales—enfants assistés, 1835-1860.

Series BB¹⁸ 1162 Versements du Ministère de la Justice—(dossiers on waifs and strays).

Series ADXIX I 157 Enfants Assistés—Enquête de 1860.

Series ADXIX T — Préfecture de la Seine.

Series C Corps Législatif

787 Réponse à l'enquête de Lamartine sur les Enfants Trouvés et leur condition en 1838.

912 Procès-verbaux des délibérations de la Commission de l'Assistance publique sous la Constituante Assemblée.

924 Proposition de création de 50 salles d'asile à Paris.

969   Enquête sur le travail agricole et industrial prescrit par le decret du 25 mai 1848.
994   Conseil d'Etat—Projet de loi sur les Enfants Trouvés, 1851.
1039 Conseil d'Etat—Projet de loi sur les Enfants Trouvés, 1853-54.
2766 Réforme du système pénitentiaire et discours de Lamartine (1836-1838).

Manuscripts

Blin, Ernest. "Les enfants assistés de la Seine dans l'Avallonnais, 1819 à 1906." 2 vols. MSS. AAP.
Lafabrèque, René. "Des enfants trouvés à Paris." 1876. MSS. AAP.
———. "Notes pour servir à l'étude de la question des enfants assistés en France. Démographie figurée." 1878. MSS. AAP.
"Minutes des séances des délibérations du Conseil général des hospices de Paris, 1801 à 1848." 207 vols. MSS. AAP.

Public Documents

France, Assemblée nationale législative. *Rapport et projet de loi sur les enfants trouvés, abandonnés et orphelins*, présentés au nom de la commission d'Assistance publique par M. Armand D. Melun. Séance du 22 mars 1850. Paris: 1850.
———. *Projet de loi sur les enfants trouvés et abandonnés et les orphelins pauvres*. Examiné par le conseil d'état. Séance du 19 juillet 1851. Paris: 1851.
France, Bureau de la statistique générale. Statistique de la France. *Statistique annuelle 1871-1906*. 36 vols.
———. *Statistique de la France*. 1ᵉ sèrie, 13 vols. 2ᵉ sèrie, 21 vols. Paris: Imprimerie royale, nationale, impériale, and Strasbourg: Veuve Berger-Levrault 1835-1873.
France, Chambre des députés. *Contre-enquête sur les enfants trouvés, et rapports des commissions administratives des hospices de France aux questions posées par M. de Lamartine*, mai 1839. Paris: 1839. AN C 787.
France, Corps législatif. *Rapport fait au nom de la commission chargée d'examiner le projet de loi concernant les enfants trouvés et abandonnés et les orphelins pauvres, confiés à l'Assistance publique* par M. Remacle. Annexe au procès-verbal de la séance du 30 avril 1853. AN C 1039.
France, Ministère d'intérieur. Commission des enfants trouvés. *Travaux de la Commission des enfants trouvés instituée le 22 août 1849 par arrêté du ministre de l'intérieur. 3 vols: vol. 1; Procès-verbaux des séances de la Commission—projet de loi. vol. 2; Documents sur les enfants trouvés. vol 3; Tableaux statistique officiels.* Paris: Imprimerie Nationale, 1850.
———. *Rapports à M. le ministre de l'intérieur, et au Conseil général des*

hospices, relatifs au service des enfants trouvés dans le département de la
Seine; suivis de documents officiels. Paris: Huzard, 1838.

———. *Rapports au Conseil général des hospices de Paris sur le service des
enfants trouvés du département de la Seine.* Paris: E. J. Bailly, 1845.

———. *Rapports à M. le ministre de l'intérieur et au Conseil général des
hospices, relatifs au service des enfants trouvés dans le département de la
Seine; suivis de documents officiels.* Paris: Dupont, 1858.

———. *Rapports de MM. les docteurs Lunier et Foville, inspecteurs généraux
des services administratifs sur l'Hospice des enfants assistés de Paris.*
(Mission spéciale du 9 mars 1882.) Paris: 1882.

———. *Rapport adressé au Président de la République sur l'execution de la
loi du 23 décembre 1874 relative à la protection de l'enfant du premier âge,*
par le Ministre d'Intérieur. Paris: Impr. des Journaux Officiels, 1886.

France, Enfants Assistés. *Enquête générale ouverte en 1860 dans les 86 départements de l'Empire. Rapport de la Commission instituée le 10 octobre 1861
par arrêté du ministre de l'intérieur.* Paris: Imprimerie impériale, 1862.
(AN ADXIX I 157).

———. *Renseignements sur le service.* Paris: Impr. du Journal Officiel, 1884.

Seine (Département de la). Administration générale de l'Assistance publique à
Paris. *Budget.* Paris: 1899-1902.

———. *Hospice des enfants trouvés.* Montévrain: Impr. de l'école d'Alembert,
n.d.

———. *Instruction générale sur le service des enfants assistés du département
de la Seine.* Paris; P. Dupont, 1860.

———. *Instruction générale sur le service des enfants assistés du département
de la Seine.* Paris: P. Dupont, 1869.

———. *Instruction sur le service des enfants trouvés, abandonnés et orphelins
placé à la campagne.* Paris: P. Dupont, 1852.

———. *Rapport sur le service des enfants trouvés du département de la Seine,*
présenté par le directeur de l'Administration générale de l'Assistance publique à M. le sénateur, préfet de la Seine. Paris: P. Dupont, 1852-1856.

———. *Rapport sur le service des enfants assistés du département de la Seine,*
présenté par le directeur de l'Administration générale de l'Assistance publique à M. le sénateur, préfet de la Seine. Paris: P. Dupont, 1852-1856.

———. *Rapport de la delegation chargée d'étudier un avant projet de colonisation agricole en Algerie pour les enfants assistés du département de la Seine.*
Paris: P. Dupont, 1883.

———. *Recueil des arrêtés, instructions, et circulaires réglementaires concernant
l'Administration générale de l'Assistance publique à Paris.* Paris: P. Dupont,
1855.

———. Thilleul, Marescot (du). *L'Assistance publique à Paris: Ses bienfaiteurs et sa fortune mobilière.* 2 vols. Paris: 1904.

Seine (Département de la). Conseil général d'administration des hôpitaux et
hospices de Paris. *Extrait des délibérations du Conseil général du département
de la Seine. Séance du 25 octobre 1838.* Paris: Mme. Huzard, 1838.

———. *Rapport au Conseil général des hospices sur le service des enfants trouvés dans le département de la Seine, suivi de documens officiels.* Paris: Mme Huzard, 1838.

———. *Rapports au Conseil général des hospices de Paris sur le service des enfants trouvés du département de la Seine.* Paris: 1845.

———. *Rapports a MM. les members des Conseils généraux. Memoire sur le rétablissement des tours. Precédé du rapport sur la même question prononcé par M. de Goulhot-de-Saint-Germain,* Sénateur, dans la séance du 13 juin 1862, par Leon Valery. Paris: 1862.

———. *Rapport présenté par M. Thulié, au nom de la 3ᵉ commission, sur le services des enfants assistés.* Adopté dans la séance du 26 décembre 1882. Paris: 1883.

Seine (Département de la). Service de la statistique municipale. *Recherches statistiques sur la ville de Paris et le département de la Seine, 1826-1844.* 5 vols. Paris: Imprimerie Royale, 1826-1860.

———. *Annuaire statistique de la ville de Paris.* 1880.

Articles, Books, Journals, and Pamphlets.

Ardouin-Dumazet, Victor-Eugène. *Voyage en France.* 20 vols. (vol. 1) Paris: 1893-1899.

Balzac, Honoré de. *Cousine Bette.* Translated by Marion Ayton Crawford. Great Britain: Penguin Books, 1976.

Burruel, M. "Considérations hygièniques sur le lait vendu à Paris comme substance alimentaire." *Annales d'hygiène publique et de médecine légale* 1 (1829): 404-419.

Batault, Charles. *Du placement et de l'éducation des enfants trouvés.* Paris: 1899.

Benoiston de Châteauneuf, Louis François. *Considérations sur les enfants trouvés dans les principaux états de l'Europe.* (Memoire lu à l'Académie royale des sciences dans sa séance du 11 août 1873) Paris: Chez l'auteur, 1824.

———. *Nouvelles considérations sur les enfants trouvés, suivies des rapports sur l'histoire des enfants trouvés faits à l'Academie des sciences morales et politiques par M. Benoiston de Châteauneuf et à l'Academie française par M. Villemain.* Lyon: 1838.

———. "Sur les enfants trouvés." *Annales d'hygiène publique et de médecine légale* 21 (1839): 88-123.

Béquet, Léon. *Régime et législation de l'assistance publique et privée en France avec le concours de M. Emile Morlot . . . M. Trignant de Beaumont.* Paris: P. Dupont, 1885.

Berenger de la Drome. *Jeunes libérés.* Sociétés de patronage du département de la Seine. Comptes rendus des travaux de la Société pour le patronage des jeunes détenus et des jeunes libérés du département de la Seine, de 1833 à 1844. Paris: A. Henry, 1845.

————. *Société pour le patronage des jeunes libérés du département de la Seine.* Asemblée générale tenue le 12 juin 1836, compte rendu des travaux par M. Bérenger, rapport de M. Pontignac de Villars, exposé financier par M. Roquebert. Paris: A. Henry, 1836.

————. *Société pour le patronage des jeunes libérés du département de la Seine.* Assemblée générale tenue le 9 juillet 1837 compte rendu des travaux par M. Bérenger, rapport de M. Adolphe Chauveau, exposé financier par M. Ternaux. Paris: A. Henry, 1837.

Bertillon, Jacques (Dr.). *Calcul de la mortalité des enfants du premier âge. De la méthode à suivre et des documents à recueillir pour calculer la mortalité des enfants en bas âge et spécialement celle des enfants protégés par la loi du 24 décembre 1874.* Rapport présenté au Conseil supérieur de statistique (deuxième session de 1886). Paris: Impr. Nationale, 1887.

————. *De la dépopulation de la France et des remèdes à y apporter* (Extrait du *Journal de la Société de statistique de Paris*, n° de décembre 1895). Nancy: Berger-Levrault, 1896.

————. "Du Degré d'efficacité de la loi du 24 décembre 1874 (Loi Théophile Roussel)" *Journal de la Société de statistique de Paris* 43 (1902): 389-342.

Blache, (Dr.). "Quelques observations à propos des résultats obtenus par l'application de la Loi Roussel dans le département de la Seine." *l'Union médicale* (1887): 3-10.

Boicervoise, A. *Quelques reflexions au sujet du projet de loi relatif aux enfants trouvés, abandonnés, et orphelins, presenté à l'Assemblée Legislative au nom de la Commission de l'Assistance publique dans sa séance du 22 mars 1850.* (Extrait du *Revue municipale*, 1850). Paris: 1850.

————. *Rapport au Conseil générale des Hospices de Paris sur le service des enfants trouvés du département de la Seine.* Paris: 1845.

Bonde, Amédée. *Etude sur l'enfant. L'exposition et la condition des enfants exposés. De la condition civile des enfants abandonnés et orphelins recueilli par la charité privée ou publique.* Paris: Derenne, 1883.

deBondy, François Marie de Taillepied, (Comte). *Memoire sur la necessité de reviser la législation actuelle concernant les enfants trouvés, abandonnés et orphelins.* Auxerre: Impr. de Gallot Fournier, 1835.

Bonjean, Georges. *Enfants révoltés et parents coupables. Etude sur la désorganisation de la famille et ses conséquences sociales.* Paris: A. Colen, 1895.

————. *Rapport sur la dépopulation des campagnes et l'assistance des enfants abandonnés ou coupables* (Extrait de *l'Annuaire de la Société des agriculteurs de France*, 5 février 1880). Nancy: Berger-Levrault, 1880.

Bonzon, Jacques. *Cent ans de lutte sociale. La législation de l'enfance 1789-1894.* Paris: Librairie Guillaumen et Cie, 1894.

Bouchardy, Joseph. "Les enfants trouvés." In *Magasin théatral*, vol. 34. Paris: Marchant, 1882.

Boucheron, Martial. *Les enfants assistés et la famille.* Paris: Paul Dupont, 1869.

Boudard, A. *Guide pratique de la chèvre nourrice au point de vue de l'allaitement des nouveau nés et de la syphilis constitutionelle.* Paris: Gannat, 1879.

Bourée, (Dr.). "Rapport de la Commssion permanente de l'hygiène de l'enfance pour l'année 1877." *Bulletin de l'Academie de médecine,* 2me sèrie, VII (1878): 237-244.

————. *Rapport au Conseil générale des Hospices de Paris sur le service des enfants trouvés du département de la Seine.* Paris: 1845.

Boys de Loury (Dr.). "Memoire sur des modifications à apporter dans le service de l'administration des nourrices." *Annales d'hygiène publique et de médecine légale* 27 (January 1842): 5-35.

Brochard, André-Théodore (Dr.). *Les enfants trouvés à Lyon et à Moscou.* Lyon: By the author, 1875.

————. *Le guide pratique de la jeune mère, où l'éducation du nouveau nè. Paris: P.-N. Josserand, 1874.*

————. *De l'industrie des nourrices dans la ville de Bordeaux.* Bordeaux Féret, 1867.

————. *De la mortalité des nourrissons en France, specialement dans l'arrondissement de Nogent-le Rotrou (Eure-et-Loir).* Paris: 1866.

————. *Les nourrissons, les enfants trouvés et les animaux.* Lyon: P.-N. Josserand, 1871.

————. *L'ouvrière, mère de famille.* Lyon: P.-N. Josserand, 1875.

————. *La vérité sur les enfants trouvés.* Avec une lettre de M. le Comte Alfred de la Guéronnière. Paris: E. Plon, 1867.

Brueyre, Loys. *De l'éducation des enfants assistés et des enfants moralement abandonnés en France.* (Mémoires et documents scolaires publiés par le musée pédogogique. 2e sèrie, Fascicule n° 46). Paris: Impr. Nationale, 1889.

————. *Utilité d'organiser le patronage de l'Assistance publique, prescrit par l'article 19 de la loi du 5 août 1850 au profit des jeunes détenus libérés. Rapport lu au Comité de défense des enfants traduits en justice.* (Extrait de la *Gazette du Palais*). Paris: 3, Bd du Palais, 1895.

Castelnau, Ph. Boileau de (Dr.). *Des enfants naturels devant la famille et devant la société.* Nimes: 1864.

Celnart, Mme. Elisabeth Félicie. *Manuel des nourrices adopté par le Conseil général des hospices civils de Paris.* (Pseud. Bayle Mouillard). Paris: Renouard, 1834.

Chalvet, P. et Proust, A. *Projet de création d'une ferme nourrice pour un cetain nombre d'enfants.* Paris: Martinet, 1870.

Cherbuliez, A.-E. *Etude sur les causes de la misère, tant morale que physique et sur les moyens d'y porter remède.* Paris: Librairie de Guillaume et Cie, 1853.

Curel, T.M. *Parti a prendre sur la question des enfants trouvés.* Paris: Dupont, 1848.

Curzon, Emmanuel de. *Etudes sur les enfants trouvés au point de vue de la législation, de la morale et de l'économie politique.* Poitiers: Henri Oudin, 1847.

Daru, Charles and Bournat, Victor. *Adoption, éducation, et correction des enfants pauvres, abandonnés, orphelins ou vicieux.* Paris: Ch. Douniol et Cie, 1875.

Demetz, Frédéric-Auguste. *Application du système de Mettray aux colonies d'orphelins et d'enfants trouvés.* Paris: 1850.

Desloges. *Des enfants trouvés, des femmes publiques, et des moyens à employer pour en diminuer le nombre.* Paris: 1836.

Desmartis, Télèphe P. (Dr.). *Enfants trouvés—Suppression des tours—Saint Vincent-de-Paul abandonné par ses disciples.* Bordeaux: 1862.

Desportes, Fernand. *Essai historique sur les enfants naturels.* Paris: 1857.

Doniol, Henri. *Les enfants des hospices et la mise en valeur des terres incultes.* (Extrait du *Journal des économistes*, n° du 15 fèvrier 1862). Paris: Guillaumen et Cie, 1862.

Doublet de Boisthibault. *Memoire sur les enfants trouvés,* Chartres: Garnier, 1841.

Douniol, C. *L'enfant du peuple de Paris.* Paris: 1864.

DuCamp, Maxime. *La charité privée à Paris.* Paris: Librairie Hachette et Cie, 1885.

———. *Paris bienfaisant.* Paris: Librairie Hachette et Cie, 1888.

———. *Paris, ses organes, ses fonctions et sa vie dans la seconde moitié du XIXe siècle.* 6 vols. Paris: Librairie Hachette et Cie, 1869-1875.

Ducarre. *Note sur les enfants trouvés.* Paris: 1875.

Dupin, Claude-François-Etienne. *Histoire de l'administration des secours publics, ou analyse historique de la législation des secours publics.* Paris: 1821.

Esquiros, Alphonse. "Les enfants trouvés." *Revue des deux mondes* 15 janvier et 15 mars 1846.

Frégier, H. A. *Des classes dangereuses de la population dans les grandes villes, et des moyens de les rendre meilleures.* 2 vols. Paris: J.-B. Baillière, 1840.

Gaillard, Adolphe-Henri, (Abbé). *Recherches administratives, statistiques et morales sur les enfants trouvés, les enfants naturels et les orphelins en France et dans plusieurs autres pays de l'Europe.* Paris: Th. Leclerc, 1837.

———. *Résumé de la discussion sur les enfants trouvés et observations sur la loi proposée au corps législatif.* Paris: Parent-Desbarres, 1853.

Gazette hébdomadaire de médecine et chirurgie VIII (February 1870): 91-123.

Gerando, Joseph Marie de, (Baron). *De la bienfaisance publique.* 4 vols. Paris: Jules Renouard, 1839.

Guignard, Charles (Dr.). *Infanticides, faut-il rétablir les tours?* Tours: Mazereau, 1884.

Guillot, Adolphe. *Les prisons de Paris et les prisonniers.* Paris: 1890.

Guyot, L. *Hygiène et protection des enfants du premier âge.* Paris: Baillière, 1878.

Haussonville, Alphonse Gabriel (Vicomte de). *L'enfance à Paris.* Paris: C. Lévy, 1879.

Herpin, J. Ch (de Metz). *Sur le déplacement ou l'écharger des enfants trouvés et la suppression des tours.* Paris: 1838.

Hugo, Victor. *Les Misérables.* 3 vols. Paris: Editions Gallimard, 1973.

Husson, Armand. *Discours sur la mortalité des jeunes enfants, prononcé dans la séance du 23 octobre 1866.* (Extrait du *Bulletin de l'Académie impériale de médecine* 32 ([1866]: 89-116) Paris: J.B. Baillière et fils, 1866.

————. *Discours sur la mortalité des enfants.* Séance du 5 octobre 1869 à l'Académie impériale de médecine. (Extrait de la *Gazette hebdomadaire de médecine et de chirurgie,* 1869) Paris: Impr. de E. Martinet, n.d.

————. Administration générale de l'Assistance publique à Paris. *Etude sur les hôpitaux, considérés sous le rapport de leur construction, de la distribution de leurs bâtiments, de l'ameublement, de l'hygiène et du service des salles de malades.* Paris: Paul Dupont, Imprimeur de l'Administration de l'Assistance Publique, 1862.

————. Administration générale de l'Assistance publique à Paris. *Exposé des progrès et des améliorations réalisés dans les services du 1 janvier au 31 décembre 1867.* Paris: Paul Dupont, 1868.

————. Administration générale de l'Assistance publique à Paris. *Mémoire au Conseil de surveillance sur la proposition de supprimer la direction municipale des nourrices et d'instituer en faveur des familles nécessiteuses des secours spéciaux pour l'allaitement des enfants, suivi d'un mémoire complémentaire et de documents sur le même objet.* Paris: Paul Dupont, 1866.

————. Administration générale de l'Assistance publique à Paris. *Note sur la mortalité des enfants du premier âge nés dans la ville de Paris.* Paris: Paul Dupont, n.d.

————. Administration générale de l'Assistance publique à Paris. *Statistique médicale des hôpitaux.* 4 vols. Paris: Paul Dupont, 1867-1870.

Jacobi, A. *The Raising and Education of Abandoned Children in Europe, with Statistics and General Remarks on that Subject.* New York: 1870.

Labourt, L.-A. *Recherches historiques sur les enfants trouvés.* Arras: DeGeorge, 1845.

Lacroix, J.A. *Enfants abandonnés et du rétablissement des tours.* Lettres pour servir à l'étude de cette question, avec une préface de F. Passy. Paris: 1878.

Lafabrèque, René. "Notes pour servir à l'étude de la question des enfants assistés en France: Des enfants trouvés à Paris." *Annales de demographie internationale* 2 (1878): 27-60, 226-299.

Lagneau, Gustave (Dr.). *Mortalité des enfants assistés en général et de ceux du département de la Seine en particulier.* (Extrait du compte rendu de l'Académie des sciences morales et politiques). Orléans: Colas, 1882.

————. "Remarques sur la natalité et la mortalité des enfants naturels, ainsi que sur la matrimonialité, considérées au point du vue de la recherche de la paternité." *Bulletin de l'Académie de médecine de Paris* 2ᵉ sèrie vii (1878): 870-873.

Lallemand, Léon. *De l'assistance des classes rurales au XIXᵉ siècle.* Paris: A. Picard et Guillaumin, 1889.

————. *Histoire des enfants abandonnés et délaissés: Etude sur la protection de l'enfance aux diverses époques de la civilisation.* Paris: A. Picard et Guillaumin, 1885.

————. *La question des enfants abandonnés et délaissés au XIXe siècle.* Paris: A. Guillaumin et Cie, 1885.

Lamartine, Alphonse de. *Discours sur les enfants trouvés* (prononcé le 30 avril 1828 à la Société de morale christian). Paris: 1838.

LaPaire, Hugues. *Les enfants.* Paris: A. Savine, 1890.

Latour, Gabriel. *Les enfants assistés—L'assistance publique.* Paris: Librairie Démocratique, 1876.

Laurent, Emile. *L'état actuel de la question des enfants assistés à propos de la récente loi sur le protection des enfants du premier âge.* Paris: Guillaumin, 1876.

Levasseur, Emile Pierre. *La population française: Histoire de la population avant 1789 et démographie de la France comparée a celle des autres nations au XIXe siècle.* 3 vols. Paris: Arthur Rousseau, 1889.

Leyval, M. Augustin de. *Observations sur les mesures adoptées dans les départements à l'égard des enfants trouvés.* Paris: 1877.

Ligier, A. *Considérations sur les tours et les conséquences de leur suppression au point de vue de l'hygiène publique.* Paris: 1877.

Louvancour. *Un dernier mot en faveur des enfants trouvés.* Chartres: Garnier, 1841.

Marchand, P.-R. *Sur les enfants trouvés et abandonnés.* Caen: 1841.

Marfan, A.-B. (Dr.). *Traité d'allaitement.* Paris: 1899.

————. *Académie de médecine. Bulletin* (1882): 475.

Marjolin, René (Dr.). *Mémoire de la nécessité du rétablissement des tours.* Paris: 1878.

————. "Rapport sur l'insuffisance des ressources de therapeutique dans les affections chirugicals des enfants pauvres à Paris." *Bulletin et mémoires de la Société de chirurgie de Paris* (1875): 793-830; Discussion (1876): 853, 886.

Melun, Amand de. *Mémoires.* Paris: 1891.

Métérié-Larrey, Dumon. *De l'administration des enfants assistés. Repertoire méthodique de la législation et des instructions ministérielles.* Paris: Berger-Levrault, 1897.

Molènes, Jacques-Denis Gaschon de. *Des enfants trouvés.* Auxerre: Gallot-Fournier, 1837.

Monod, Henri. *Enfants assistés. Rapport au Conseil supérieur de l'Assistance publique. Observations des inspecteurs départementaux sur le projet de loi (Conseil supérieur de l'Assistance publique. Fascicule n°28).* Melun: Impr. administrative, n.d.

————. *Les enfants assistés. Rapport du directeur de l'assistance et de l'hygiène publiques au Ministre de l'Intérieur. Rapports des inspecteurs généraux et des inspectrices générales (Conseil supérieur de l'Assistance publique. Fascicule n° 48).* 2 vols. Melun: Impr. administrative, 1895.

———. *Enfants assistés. Révision de la législation. Rapport. Conseil supérieur de l'Assistance publique. Fascicule n° 23.* Paris: Impr. nouvelle, n.d.

———. *Extension des attributions des inspecteurs des enfants assistés. Rapports de M. H. Monod et du Dr. Thulié (Conseil supérieur de l'Assistance publique Fascicule n° 21).* Paris: Impr. nouvelle, n.d.

Ory, Eugene. *La protection de l'enfant et de l'adulte.* Saint-Etienne: J. Besseyre et Cⁱᵉ, 1883.

Nicole, E. D. A. *La nourricerie de l'hospice des enfants assistés.* Paris: 1891.

Parent-Duchâtelet, Alexandre Jean-Baptiste. *De la prostitution dans la ville de Paris, considerée sous le rapport de l'hygiène publique, de la morale et de l'administration; ouvrage appuyé de documents statistiques puisés dans les archives de la préfecture de police.* 2 vols. 3d. ed. Paris: J.-B. Baillière et fils, 1857.

Paris Cries. The Arts, Trades and Cries of Paris: Taken from Nature: Protrayed in 60 copper-plate engravings. London: James Izzard, 1818.

Parrot, J. "Clinique des maladies de l'enfant." *Annales de démographie* 3 (1879): 473-482.

———. "Leçons sur les maladies du premier âge." *Archives de tocologie* (1878): 283-291.

———. "Les maladies des enfants." *France médicale* 21 (1874): 408, 441, 513, 537.

———. "La nourricerie de l'Hospice des enfants assistés." *Bulletin de l'Académie de médecine,* Paris, n.s. 11 (1882): 839-853.

Paul, Victor. *Réflexions sur les enfants trouvés.* Avignon: Bonnet fils, 1844.

Pocquet du Haut-Jussé, Barthélemy-Ambroise-Marie. *Essai sur l'Assistance publique: Son histoire, ses principes, son organisation actuelle.* Paris: Marescqainé, 1877.

Ratier, F.S. (Dr.). *Coup d'oeil sur les cliniques médicales de la faculté de médecine et des hôpitaux civils de Paris.* Paris: 1830.

Regime alimentaire des hospices civils de Paris. Paris: Mᵐᵉ Huzard, 1817.

Réglement sur le régime alimentaire des hôpitaux et hospices civils de Paris, approuvé par le ministre de l'intérieur le 30 novembre 1841. Paris: E. J. Bailly, 1841.

Remacle, B.-B. Corps législatif. Session 1853. *Annexe au procès-verbal de la séance du 30 avril 1853. Rapport fait au nom de la Commission chargée d'examener le projet de loi concernant les enfants trouvés et abandonnés et les orphelins pauvres confiés à l'Assistance publique.* Paris: 1853.

———. *De l'état des orphelins à leur sortie des hospices; Mémoire lu à l'Académie royale du Gard dans sa séance publique du 29 août 1841.* Aix: Nicote et Aubin, 1861.

———. *Des hospices d'enfants trouvés en Europe, et principalement en France, dupuis leur origine jusqu'a nos jours.* Paris: Treuttel et Wurtz, 1838.

———. *Rapport à M. le ministre secrétaire d'Etat de l'intérieur concernant les infanticides et les morts-nés.* Paris: Impr. Royale, 1845.

————. *Rapport concernant les infanticides et les mort nés dans leur relation avec la question des enfants trouvés.* Paris: 1838.

Robin, E. *Des écoles industrielles et de la protection des enfants insoumis ou abandonnés.* Paris: J. Bonhomu, 1879.

Rollet, H. *Enfance abandonnée: vicieux, insoumis, vagabonds. Colonies agricoles, écoles de reforme et de preservation.* Clermont-Furand: G. Mont-Louis, 1899.

Rousseau, Jean-Jacques, *Les confessions.* Edited by Jacques Voisine. Paris: Editions Garnier Fréres, 1964.

Roussel, Théophile, *Assemblée nationale. Année 1874. Annexe au procès-verbal de la séance du 9 juin 1874. Rapport fait, au nom de la Commission chargée d'éxaminer la proposition de la loi de M. Théophile Roussel, relative à la protection des enfants du premier âge, et en particulier des nourrissons.* Versailles: Cerf et fils, 1874.

————. *Rapport concernant la loi du 23 décembre 1874, présenté à M. le Ministre de l'intérieur.* Paris: A. Wittersheim, 1880.

————. *Rapport concernant la loi du 23 décembre 1874, présenté au nom du Comité supérieur de protection des enfants du premier âge.* Paris: Impr. du Journal officiel, 1882.

————. *Sénat session 1882 n° 151. Protection des enfants abandonnés, délaissés ou maltraités. Annexe du procès verbal de la séance du 25 juillet 1882. I. Rapport fait par M. Roussel. II. Rapport sur les résultats de l'Enquête concernant les orphelinats. III. Note préliminaire sur la protection et éducation des enfants abandonnés.* 3 vols. Paris: Impr. du Sénat, n.d.

Sand, George, "François le Champi." *Journal des débats* (1847-48); reprint ed. Paris: Calman-Levy, n.d. *François the Waif.* Translated by Jane Minot Sedgwick. Boston: Little Brown and Co., 1894.

Semichon, Ernest. *Histoire des enfants abandonnés dupuis l'antiquité jusqu'a nos jours.* Paris: E. Plon et Cie, 1880.

Simon, Jules. *L'ouvrière.* Paris: Hachette, 1861.

Smith, Valentin. *Rapport sur les enfants trouvés.* Paris: 1839.

Stewart, F. Campbell (M.D.). *The Hospitals and Surgeons of Paris: An Historical and Statistical Account of the Civil Hospitals of Paris.* New York: J. and H. G. Langley, 1843.

Strauss, Paul. *Dépopulation et puericulture.* Paris: Fasquelle, 1901.

Sue, Eugène. *Martin, l'enfant trouvé or les mémoires d'un valet de chambre.* Also titled: *Les misères des enfants trouvés.* 4 vols in 2. Paris: l'Administration de Librairie, 1850-51.

————. *Martin, the Foundling: A Romance.* Dicks English Library, vol. 6. London: John Dicks, 1927.

————. *Les mystères de Paris.* Paris: Jean-Jacques Pauvert, 1963.

————. *Mysteries of Paris.* Translated by Charles H. Toun, Esq. New York: Harper and Bros., 1844.

Tarnier. "L'allaitement artificiel des nouveau-nés." *Académie de médecine bulletin* (1882): 1075-1089.

Tenon, Jacques. *Mémoires sur les hôpitaux de Paris.* Paris: Ph. – D Purres, 1788.

Terme, Jean-François and Monfalcon, J.-B. *Histoire des enfants trouvés.* Nouvelle édition revisé, corrigée et augmentée. Paris: Paulin, 1840.

———. *Histoire statistique et morale des enfants trouvés.* Paris: J.-B. Baillière, 1837.

———. *Nouvelles considérations sur les enfants trouvés, suivies des rapports sur l'histoire des enfants trouvés faits à l'Académie des sciences morales et politiques par M. Benoiston de Châteuneuf et à l'Académie française par M. Vellemain.* Lyon: J.-M. Bajat, 1838.

Thulié, Henri (Dr.). *Les enfants assistés de la Seine.* Paris: Bureaux du Progrès médical, 1887.

———. *La surveillance des établissements d'assistance privés. 1. Rapport de M. le directeur de l'Assistance et de l'Hygiène publiques: H. Monod. 2. Rapport de M. de Crisenoy. 3. Extraits des procès-verbaux des séances du Conseil supérieur de l'Assistance publique (5-6 mar 1895). 4. Procès-verbaux des séances de la Commission spéciale nommée par le Conseil supérieur. 5. Rapport de M. le Dr. Thulié.* Melun: Impr. administrative, 1896.

Tourdonnet, A. de (Comte). *Essais sur l'education des enfants pauvres. De l'éducation des enfants assistés par le charité publique.* Paris: Brunet, 1861.

Valdruche. *Rapport au ministre de l'intérieur et au Conseil générale des hospices relatif aux enfants trouvés dans le departement de la Seine, suivi de documents officiels.* Paris: 1838.

Vidal, François. *Des enfants trouvés. Lettre addressée a MM. les members du Conseil générale de la Gironde. Extrait du mémorial Bordelais des 13 et 14 juillet 1840.* Bordeaux: Impr. de Lavigne, 1840.

Villermé, Louis. "Influences des marais sur la vie des enfants." *Annales d'hygiène publique et de médecine légale* 12 (1834): 31-53.

———. "De la mortalité des enfants trouvés." *Annales d'hygiène publique et de médecine légale* 19 (1938).

Wattevile du Grabe, Adolphe (Baron de). *Essai statistique sur les établissements de bienfaisance.* Paris: A. Hévis, 1846.

———. *Du sort des enfants trouvés et de la colonie agricole du Mesnil-Saint-Firmin avec un appendice contenant des documents sur les institutions étrangères et des notes statistiques.* Paris: P. Dupont, 1846.

———. *Statistique des établissements et services de bienfaisance. Rapport à M. le ministre de l'intérieur sur la situation administrative morale et financiére du service des enfants trouvés et abandonnés en France.* Paris: Impr. nationale, 1849.

———. *Statistique des établissements de bienfaisance. Rapport à Son Excellence le ministre de l'intérieur sur l'administration des bureaux de bienfaisance et sur la situation du paupérisme en France.* Paris: Impr. impériale, 1854.

————. *Statistique des établissements de bienfaisance. Rapport à M. le ministre de l'intérieur sur les tours, les abandonnés, les infanticides et les mort-nés de 1826-1854.* Paris. Impr. nationale, 1856.

Secondary Sources

Ackerknecht, Erwin H., M.D. *Medicine at the Paris Hospital, 1799-1848.* Baltimore: Johns Hopkins Press, 1967.

Ackerman, Evelyn Bernette. *Village on the Seine: Tradition and Change in Bonnières, 1815-1914.* Ithaca, N.Y.: Cornell University Press, 1978.

Acomb, Evelyn Martha. *French Laic Laws.* New York: Columbia University Press, 1941.

Anderson, Michael. *Family Structure in Nineteenth-Century Lancashire.* Cambridge, Eng.: The University Press, 1971.

Aninard. *Le problème de l'enfance délaissée.* Thèse. Montpellier: 1921.

Ariès, Philippe. *Centuries of Childhood: A Social History of Family Life.* Translated by Robert Baldick. New York: Vintage Books, 1962.

————. *L'enfant et la vie familiale sous l'ancien regime.* Paris: Librairie Plon, 1960.

————. *Histoire des populations françaises.* Paris: Librairie Plon, 1971.

Armengaud, André. "L'attitude de la société à l'égard de l'enfant au XIXᵉ siècle." *Enfant et sociétés: Annales de démographie historique.* Paris: Mouton, 1973.

————. "Industrialisation et démographie dans la France du XIXᵉ siècle." *Industrialisation en Europe au XIXᵉ siècle.* Lyon: 1970.

————. "Les nourrices de Morvan au XIXᵉ siècle." *Etudes et chroniques de démographie historique.* (1969): 131-193.

Azema, G. *L'état et les enfants abandonnés.* Thèse. Bordeaux, 1930.

Badinter, Elisabeth. *Mother Love: Myth and Reality. Motherhood in Modern History.* New York: Macmillan, 1981.

Bariéty, M.-D. "De l'Hôtel-Dieu de jadis à l'hôpital d'aujourd'hui." *Revue des deux mondes* 5 (1958): 64-76.

Batany, Jean. "Regards sur l'enfance dans la littérature moralisant." *Enfant et sociétés: annales de démographie historique.* Paris: Mouton, 1973.

Baulant, Micheline. "Grain Prices in Paris, 1431-1788." *Social Historians in Contemporary France: Essays from Annales.* Mark Ferro, editor. New York: Harper and Row, 1972.

Beaver, M. W. "Population, Infant Mortality and Milk." *Population Studies* 27 (July 1973): 243-254.

Behlmer, George K. *Child Abuse and Moral Reform in England, 1870-1908.* Stanford, CA: Stanford University Press, 1982.

Berlanstein, Lenard R. "Growing up As Workers in Nineteenth-Century Paris: The Case of the Orphans of the Prince Imperial." *French Historical Studies* 11 (1980): 551-576.

———. "Vagrants, Beggars and Thieves: Delinquent Boys in Mid-Nineteenth Century Paris." *Journal of Social History* 12(Summer 1979): 531-522.

Bernouville, Gaetan. *Un apôtre rural de l'enfance abandonnée. Le Père Gaillard.* Paris: Bonne Presse, 1949.

Bidelman, Patrick Kay. "The Feminist Movement in France: The Formative Years, 1858 to 1889." Ph.D dissertation, Michigan State University, 1975.

Blin, Prosper. *La condition des enfants trouvés et abandonnés dans le Droit français ancien et actuel.* Thèse. Paris: A. Rousseau, 1909.

Bloch, Camille, *L'assistance et l'état en France à la veille de la Revolution.* Paris: 1908.

———. and Alexander Tuetey, eds. *Procès-verbaux et rapports du Comité de Mendicité de la Constituante 1790-1796.* Paris: Imprimerie nationale, 1911.

Block, Maurice. "L'assistance il y a cent ans." *Hôpital et aide sociale de Paris* 8, no. 44 (1967): 165-171; no. 45 (1967): 427-435.

———. "L'assistance il y a cent ans (suite): Enfants assistés." *Hôpital Paris* 10, no. 55 (1969): 127-135.

Bonde, Amedée. *Le domaine des hospices de Paris, depuis la Révolution jusqu'à la Troisième République.* Paris: 1906.

Bourguin, docteur F., Mme. M. and M. Lebas. *Tables générales de la législation sanitaire française, 1790-1955.* 3 vols. Paris: Impr. nationale, 1957.

Bouteiller, Marcelle. "Les types sociaux décrits à propos de l'orphelin dans la littérature 'enfantine' de 1800 à 1890." *Ethnographie* n. ser. 60-61 (1966-67): 16-25.

Bowlby, John. *Maternal Care and Mental Health,* and Ainsworth, Mary D.; Andry, R.G.; Harlow, Robert G.; Lebovici, S.; Mead, Margaret; Prugh, Dane G.; and Wootton, Barbara. *Deprivation of Maternal Care: A Reassessment of its Effects.* New York: Schocken Books, 1966.

Braudel, Fernand and Labrousse, Ernest, eds. *Histoire économique et sociale de la France,* vol. 3: *L'avènement de l'ère industrielle (1789-années 1880).* Paris: Presses Universitaires de France, 1976.

Brouardel, P. *L'avortement.* Paris: J.-B. Baillière et fils, 1901.

Candille, Marcel. "L'admission des malades à l'hôpital à travers les siècles." *Hôpital et aide sociale de Paris* 17 (1962): 635-640.

———. "Evolution des principes d'assistance hospitalière." *Revue de l'Assistance publique, Paris* 9, no. 51 (1958) 43-51; *Revue hospitalière France* n. ser. 23, no. 98 (1958): 207-218.

deCasabianca, Rose-Marie. *Eveil et dévelopement social de la première enfance en situation institutionnelle.* Thèse. Doctorat d'état. University of Paris IV, Paris: 1977.

Ceccaldi, D. *Les institutions sanitaires et sociales.* Paris: Foucher, 1969.

Chamoux, A. "L'enfance abandonnée à Reims à la fin du XVIIIe siècle." *Enfant et sociétés: Annales démographie historique.* Paris: Mouton, 1973.

Charbonneau, Pierre. "Une antique et grande institution française: l'Assistance publique à Paris." *Revue économique française* 89 (1967): 10-24.

Charles, F. "L'évolution de l'assistance à l'enfance." *Les cahiers français d'information*, Paris 240 (1953): 4-8.

Charpentier, Jehanne. *Le droit de l'enfance abandonnée: Son évolution sous l'influence de la psychologie, 1552-1791*. Paris: Presses Universitaires de France, 1967.

Chasteland, J. D. and Pressat, R. "La nuptialité des générations françaises depuis un siècle." *Population* 2 (1962).

Chesnais, J.-C. "La mortalité par accidents in France depuis 1826." *Population 29(1974): 1097-1136*.

Chevalier, Alphonse. "Une vielle question: L'humanisation de l'hôpital au XIXe siècle." *Hôpital et aide sociale de Paris* 8, no. 44 (1967): 225-226.

Chevalier, Louis. *La formation de la population parisienne au XIXe siècle*. Paris: Presses Universitaires de France, 1950.

————. *Le choléra à Paris. Le choléra, la première épidémie du XIXe siècle*. La Roche-sur-Yon: Imprimerie Centrale de l'Ouest, 1958.

————. *Laboring Classes and Dangerous Classes in Paris During the First Half of the Nineteenth Century*. Translated by Frank Jellinek. New York: Howard Fertig, 1973.

Chevillet, Georges. *Les enfants assistés à travers l'histoire*. Paris: 1903.

Clement, Henry. *La dépopulation en France, ses causes et ses remédes d'aprés les travaux les plus récents*. Paris: Librairie Bloud et Cie, 1903.

Clouzet, Maryse (Choisy). *L'amour dans les prisons*. Reportage. Paris: Editions Montaigne, 1930.

Collin, Anatole. "L'inspection des enfants assistés de la Seine. Ses origines, son fonctionnement dans le passé. Son rôle dans l'avenir." *La revue philanthropique* (1906-07): 33-45.

Corbin, Alain. *Les filles de noce depuis le seconde moitié du XIXe siècle*. Paris: Aubier Montaigne, 1978.

Corvisier, A. "La société militaire et l'enfant." pp. 328-343. *Enfant et sociétés. Annales de démographie historique*. Paris: Mouton, 1973.

Cottereau, Alain. *Travail, école, famille: Aspects de la vie des enfants ouvriers à Paris au 19^{éme} siècle*. Mimeograph pre-print from the Centre d'étude des mouvements sociaux, June, 1977.

Crubellier, Maurice. *L'enfance et la jeunesse dans la société française, 1800-1950*. Paris: Armand Colin, 1979.

Daumard, Adeline. "Sur l'histoire sociale du XIXe siècle. Paris et les archives de l'enregistrement." *Annales: Economies, sociétés, civilisations* 13 no. 2 (1958): 289-313.

————. "Quelques remarques sur le logement des Parisiens au XIXe siècle." *Annales de démographie historique* (1975): 49-64.

————. "Une source d'histoire sociale: L'enregistrement des mutations par décès. Le XIIe arrondissement de Paris en 1820 et 1847." *Revue d'histoire économique et sociale* 35, no. 1 (1957): 52-75.

Davies, Margaret Llewelyn, ed. *Maternity: Letters from Working Women*.

Collected by the Women's Cooperative Guild, 1915. Reprint edition. New York: Norton, 1978.

Debré, Robert. *La mortalité infantile et la mortinalité: Résultats de l'enquête poursuivie en France et dans cinq pays d'Europe sous les auspices du Comité d'hygiène de la Société des Nations.* Paris: 1933.

Dehaussy, Jacques. *L'assistance publique à l'enfance. Les enfants abandonnés.* Thèse, droit. Paris: Librairie du Recueil, Sirey, 1948.

Delasselle, Claude. *Les enfants trouvés à Paris au XVIIIᵉ siècle.* Nanterre: D.E.S. lettres, 1966.

———. "Les enfants abandonnés à Paris au XVIIIᵉ siècle." *Annales: économies, sociétés, civilisations* 30 (January-February, 1975): 187-218.

deMause, Lloyd, ed. *The History of Childhood.* New York: Harper Torchbooks, 1975.

Dewaepenaere, Claude Hélène. *L'enfance illégitime dans le département du Nord au XIXᵉ siècle.* Memoire de maîtrise histoire, Lille, III, 1970. Paris: Micro-éditions Hachette, 1973.

Donzelot, Jacques. *The Policing of Families.* Translated by Robert Hurley. New York: Pantheon, 1979.

Dreyfus, Ferdinand. *L'assistance sous la Second République, 1848-1851.* Cornély: De la Bibliothèque d'Histoire Moderne, 1907.

———. *Misères sociales et études historique.* Paris: Société d'Editions Littéraires et Artistiques, 1901.

Duesterberg, Thomas J. *Criminology and the Social Order in Nineteenth-Century France.* Ph.D dissertation, Indiana University, 1979.

Duplessis-le Guélinel, G. *Les mariages en France.* Paris: A. Colin, 1954.

Dupoux, Albert. "Les enfants trouvés et abandonnés: Aperçu historique." *Revue de l'Assistance publique à Paris* 4 (1953), no. 21: 65-74; no. 22: 289-301; no. 23: 397-407; no. 24: 541-554; no. 25: 757-778; no. 26: 869-889; 6 (1955), no. 33: 57-63; no. 34: 147-155; no. 35: 267-273; no. 38: 573-580; 7 (1965), no. 40: 319-325; no. 42: 551-559; no. 43: 645-647.

———. "L'hospice des enfants assistés après 1814." *Annuaire de la Société historique XIVᵉ arrondissement de Paris* (1958): 51-64.

———. *Sur les pas de Monsieur Vincent. Trois cents ans d'histoire parisienne de l'enfance abandonnée.* Paris: Revue de l'Assistance Publique à Paris, 1958.

Fairchilds, Cissie. "Female Sexual Attitudes and the Rise of Illegitimacy: A Case Study." *Journal of Interdisciplinary History* 8(Spring 1978): 627-667.

———. *Poverty and Charity in Aix-en-Provence, 1540-1789.* Baltimore: Johns Hopkins University Press, 1976.

Fédou, Gaston. *L'avortement de sa répression et de sa prévention dans le code de la famille et les lois postérieures.* Villeurbane: Impr. Marquez, 1946.

Flandrin, Jean-Louis. *Les amours paysannes, XVIᵉ-XIXᵉ siècle.* Paris: Editions Gallimard-Julliard, 1975.

———. "L'attitude à l'égard du petit enfant et les conduites sexuelles dans la civilisation occidental: Structures anciennes et évolution." pp. 143-210. *En-*

fant et sociétés: Annales de démographie historique. Paris: Mouton, 1973.
———. *Families in Former Times: Kinship, Household and Sexuality.* Translated by Richard Southern. Cambridge: Cambridge University Press, 1979.

Fohlen, Claude. "Revolution industrielle et travail des enfants." pp. 319-326. *Enfant et sociétés: Annales de démographie historique.* Paris: Mouton, 1973.

Forrest, Alan. *The French Revolution and the Poor.* New York: St. Martin's Press, 1981.

Forster, Robert and Ranum, Orest, eds. *Biology of Man in History. Selections from the Annales: Economies, Sociétés, Civilisations.* Translated by Elborg Forster and Patricia M. Ranum. Baltimore: Johns Hopkins University Press, 1975.

———. *Deviants and the Abandoned in French Society. Selections from the Annales: Economies, Sociétés, Civilisations.* Translated by Elborg Forster and Patricia M. Ranum. Baltimore: Johns Hopkins University Press, 1975.

———. *Family and Society. Selections from the Annales: Economies, Sociétés, Civilisations.* Translated by Elborg Forster and Patricia M. Ranum. Baltimore: Johns Hopkins University Press, 1979.

———, *Food and Drink in History. Selections from the Annales: Economies, Sociétés, Civilisations.* Translated by Elborg Forster and Patricia M. Ranum. Baltimore: Johns Hopkins University Press, 1979.

———. *Rural Society in France. Selections from the Annales: Economies, Sociétés, Civilisations.* Translated by Elborg Forster and Patricia M. Ranum. Baltimore: Johns Hopkins University Press, 1977.

Foucault, Michel. *The Birth of the Clinic: An Archaeology of Medical Perception.* Translated by A. M. Sheridan Smith. New York: Random House, Pantheon Books, 1973; Vintage Books, 1975.

———. *Madness and Civilization: A History of Insanity in the Age of Reason.* Translated by Richard Howard. New York: Random House, 1965; Vintage Books, 1973.

———. *The Order of Things: An Archaeology of the Human Sciences.* Translated by the publisher. New York: Random House, Pantheon Books, 1970; Vintage Books, 1973.

———. *Surveiller et punir: Naissance de la prison.* Paris: Editions Gallimard, 1975, and *Discipline and Punish: The Birth of the Prison.* Translated by Alan Sheridan. New York: Random House, 1979.

Fourastié, Jean. *Documents pour l'histoire et la théorie des prix.* Sèries statistiques réunies et élaborées. Centre d'Etudes Economiques, Recherches sur l'Evolution des Prix en Période de Progrès Technique. Paris: A. Colin, 1958.

Fouillée, Alfred. *La France au point de vue morale.* Paris: F. Alean, 1907.

Fraiberg, Selma. *Every Child's Birthright: In Defense of Mothering.* New York: Basic Books, 1977.

Freud, Anna and Burlangham, Dorothy. *Infants Without Families.* New York: International Universities Press, 1973.

Fuchs, Rachel Ginnis. "Child Abandonment in Nineteenth-Century France:

Institutional Care and Public Policy." Ph.D dissertation, Indiana University, 1980.

———. "Crimes Against Children in Nineteenth-Century France: Child Abuse, *Law and Human Behavior*, 6(January 1983): 237-259.

Gaillac, Henri. *Les maisons de correction, 1830-1945*. Paris: Cujas, 1971.

Gaillard, Jeanne. *Paris, la ville: 1852-1870*. Thèse. Université Lille III. Lille: Atelier Reproduction des Thèses, 1976.

Galliano, Paul. "La mortalité infantile (indigènes et nourrissons) dans la banlieue sud de Paris—la fin du XVIIIe siècle (1774-1794)." *Annales de démographie historique*, 1966. Paris: 1967.

Gardner, Lytte I. "Deprivation Dwarfism." *Scientific American* 227 (July 1972): 76-82.

Gillis, John R. *Youth and History: Tradition and Change in European Age Relations, 1770 to the Present*. New York: Academic Press, 1974.

Gooch, G. P. *The Second Empire*. London: Longman, 1960.

Grylls, David. *Guardians and Angels: Parents and Children in Nineteenth-Century Literature*. United Kingdom: Faber, 1978.

Guelaud-Leridon, Françoise. *Recherches sur la condition féminine dans la société d'aujourd'hui*. Institut national d'études démographiques. Travaux et Documents. Cahier no. 48. Paris: Presses Universitaires de France, 1967.

Guillaume, Pierre and Poussou, Jean-Pierre. *Démographie historique*. Paris: Librairie Armand Colin, 1970.

Harouel, Jean-Louise. *Les ateliers de charité dans la province de Haute-Guyenne*. Paris: Presses Universitaires de France, 1969.

Harris, Marvin. "Why Men Dominate Women." *New York Times Magazine*, November 13, 1977, pp. 46, 115-123.

Hartley, Shirley. *Illegitimacy*. Berkeley and Los Angeles: University of California Press, 1975.

Hatzfeld, Henri. *Du pauperisme à la securité sociale: Essai sur les orgines de la securité sociale en France, 1850-1940*. Paris: A. Colin, 1971.

Hayet, P. E. *Les écoles professionnelles du service des enfants assistés de la Seine: L'Ecole d'Alembert (1882-1909)*. Montévrain (Seine-et-Marne): Impr. d'Alembert, 1910.

Hélias, Pierre-Jakez. *The Horse of Pride: Life in a Breton Village*. Translated by June Guicharnaud. Forword by Laurence Wylie. New Haven: Yale University Press, 1978.

Hilaire, J. *Histoire des institutions publiques et des faits sociaux (XI-XIXe siècles)*. 3d ed. Paris: Sirey, 1976.

Hillairet, Jacques. *Dictionnaire historique des rues de Paris*. Paris: Les Editions de Minuit, 1961.

Hommage à Marcel Reinhard: Sur la population française au XVIIIe et au XIXe siècles. Paris: Société de demographie historique, 1973.

Hufton, Olwen H. *The Poor of Eighteenth-Century France, 1750-1789*. Oxford: Clarendon Press, 1974.

———. "Women and the Family Economy in Eighteenth-Century France." *French Historical Studies* 9(Spring 1975): 1-22.

Hunt, David. *Parents and Children in History: The Psychology of Family Life in Early Modern France.* New York: Basic Books, 1960; Harper Torchbook, 1972.

Hutchings, N. W. "4000 Years of Infant Feeding." *The Chemist and Druggist* (1958): 714-718.

Imbert, Jean. *Les Hôpitaux en France.* Que Sais-je? no. 795. Paris: Presses Universitaires de France, 1958.

Institut national d'études démographiques, cahier no. 35. *La prévention des naissances dans la famille: Ses origines dans les temps modernes.* Paris: Presses Universitaires de France, 1964.

Johnson, Ronald and Medinnus, Gene. *Child Psychology, Behavior and Development.* New York: John Wiley, 1969.

Journet, René and Guy, Robert, *Le mythe du peuple dans 'Les Misérables'.* Paris: Editions Sociales, 1963.

Kessen, William. *The Child.* New York: Wiley, 1965.

Knodel, John and vandeWalle, Etienne. "Breast Feeding, Fertility and Infant Mortality." *Population Studies* 21, no. 2 (September 1967): 109-131.

Kohl, Marvin, ed. *Infanticide and the Value of Life.* New York: Prometheus Books, 1978.

Labrousse, Ernest; Léon, Pierre; Goubert, Pierre; Bouvier, Jean; Carrière, Charles; and Harsin, Paul. *Histoire économique et sociale de la France, tome II: Des derniers temps de l'âge seigneurial aux préludes de l'âge industriel, 1660-1789.* Paris: Presses Universitaires de France, 1970.

Labrousse, Ernest; Romano, Ruggiero; and Dreyfus, F. G., eds. *Le prix du froment en France au temps de la monnaie stable, 1725-1913.* Réédition de grands tableaux statistiques. Paris: S.E.V.P.E.N., 1970.

Lampérière. *La revendication des enfants recueillis par l'Assistance publique.* Thèse. Paris: 1910.

Lang, Maurice. "Noms sous lesquels sont déclarés les enfants trouvés." *L'intermédiaire des chercheurs et curieux* XIV, 159 (June 1964): 631-632.

Langer, William L. "Checks on Population Growth, 1750-1850." *Scientific American* 226 (February 1972): 93-99.

———. "Infanticide: A Historical Survey." *History of Childhood Quarterly* 1 (1974): 353-365.

Laslett, Peter. "Age of Menarche in Europe Since the Eighteenth Century." *Journal of Interdisciplinary History* 2.2 (1971).

———. "L'attitude à l'égard du l'enfant dans l'angleterre du XIXᵉ siècle." *Enfant et sociétés: Annales de démographie historique.* Paris: Mouton, 1973: 313-328.

Laslett, Peter; Oosterveen, Karla; Smith, Richard M. *Bastardy and Its Comparative History.* Cambridge: Cambridge University Press, 1980.

———. and Oosterveen, Karla. "Long-Term Trends in Bastardy in England." *Population Studies* 27, no. 2 (July 1973): 255-286.

Ledé, Fernand. "La protection des enfants du premier âge." *Journal de la Société de statistique de Paris* 63 (1922): 261-301; 64 (1923): 59-68.

Lehning, James R. "Family Life and Wetnursing in a French Village."

Abandoned Children

Journal of Interdisciplinary History 12(Spring, 1982): 645-656.
Levade, Maurice. La délinquance des jeunes enfants en France, 1825-1968. 3 vols. Paris: Editions Cujas, 1974.
Léonard, Madeleine. La protection de l'enfance malheureuse. Les enfants assistés en droit comparé. Thèse, Droit, Rennes. Melun: Impr. administrative, 1938.
Lereboullet, Paris médical. April 24, 1934.
Louis, Paul. La condition ouvrière en France depuis cent ans. Paris: Presses Universitaires de France, 1950.
Lucas, Nettey. Criminal Paris. London: Hurst & Blackett, Ltd., 1926.
Marfan, A.-B. "Documents sur l'histoire de l'Hospice des enfants assistés de Paris." Le nourrisson. September, 1930.
Marion, Marcel. Dictionnaire des institutions de la France aux XVII et XVIIIᵉ siècles. Paris: A. Picard, 1923.
Mazeres, Marie. Saint Vincent-de-Paul et l'assistance aux enfants. Thèse, médecine, Paris, 1941. Paris: Vigot Frères, 1941.
McBride, Theresa. The Domestic Revolution and the Modernization of Household Service in England and France, 1820-1920. New York: Holmes & Meier, 1976.
McClure, Ruth K. Coram's Children: The London Foundling Hospital in the Eighteenth Century. New Haven: Yale University Press, 1981.
McLaren, Angus. "Abortion in France: Women and the Regulation of Family, 1800-1914." French Historical Studies 9(Spring 1978): 461-485.
Mireur, Hippolyte. La syphilis et la prostitution dans leurs rapports avec l'hygiène, la morale et la loi. Paris: Librairie de l'Académie de Médecine, 1875.
Mitchell, B. R. European Historical Statistics, 1750-1970. New York: Columbia University Press, 1975.
Morel, Marie-France and Loux, Françoise. "L'enfance et les saviors sur le corps; pratiques médicales et pratiques populaires dans la France traditionnelle." Ethnologie française 6(1976): 309-324.
Mossé, Armand. L'application des lois relatives à la préservation et à la protection des enfants en danger d'abandon moral. Melun: Impr. Administrative, 1920.
Murton, Marie-Claude. L'enfance abandonnée dans l'Ain pendant la première moitié du XIXᵉ siècle. D.E.S. lettres. Lyon, 1962.
Nadot, Robert. "Evolution de la mortalité infantile indigène en France dans la deuxième moitié du XIXᵉ siècle." Population 25(1970): 49-58.
Perrot, Margueritte. La mode de vie des familles bourgeoises. Paris: A. Colin, 1961.
Peyronnet, Jean Claude. Les enfants trouvés de l'hôpital général de Limoges au XVIIIᵉ siècle: Etude économique et sociale. Paris: Micro-éditions Universitaires Hachette, 1973.
Piacentini, le P. Chronique de l'orphelinat de Saint Michel de Priziac, 1856-1956. Priziac: Impr. de l'Orphelinat, 1956.
Picard, A. Les chemins de fer français. vols. 1 and 6. Paris: J. Rothschild, 1885.

Pinkney, David H. "Migrations to Paris during the Second Empire." *Journal of Modern History* 49(1953): 1-12.

———. *Napoleon III and the Rebuilding of Paris*. Princeton, N.J.: Princeton University Press, 1958.

Poitrineau, A. "Aspects de la crise des justices seigneuriales." *Revue d'histoire de droit français et étranger* 39 (1961).

Pottet, Eugène. *Histoire de Saint-Lazare (1122-1912)*. Paris: Société Française d'Imprimerie et de Librairie, 1912.

Prevost, Eugène. *De la prostitution des enfants: Etude juridique et sociale (Loi du 11 avril 1908)*. Paris: Plon & Nourrit, 1909.

Rabb, Theodore K. and Rotberg, Robert I., eds. *The Family in History: Interdisciplinary Essays*. New York: Harper & Row, 1971; Harper Torchbook, 1973.

Rebeillard, E. *Les enfants assistés: Historique, réglementation*. Paris: Dunod, 1908.

Rhém, Charles. *Les enfants abandonnés*. Thèse. Paris: 1903.

Risler, Marcelle. *La condition des enfants assistés en France de 1818 à 1850. Etude d'administration sociale*. Thèse complementaire. Paris: 1958.

Rochaix, Maurice. *Contribution à l'étude des problémes hospitaliers contemporains. Essai sur l'évolution des questions hospitalières de la fin de l'Ancien Regime à nos jours*. Paris: Federation Hospitalière de France, 1959.

———. "Quelques chiffres sur l'évolution des établissements hospitaliers et leur place dans l'économie nationale." *Revue hospitalière de la France* n. ser. 24, 119 (1959): 934-944.

Rosenberg, Charles, ed. *The Family in History*. Philadelphia: University of Pennsylvania Press, 1975.

Root, Waverly. *The Food of France*. New York: Random House, 1977.

Roussin, Georges. "L'assistance publique à Paris de 1820 à 1945. Aspects de l'évolution de la structure du prix de revient hospitalier." *Hôpital et aide sociale de Paris* vi, 34 (1965): 419-433; vi, 36 (1965): 698-712; vii, 37 (1966): 48-58.

Roussel. *De la lutte contre l'abandon de l'enfant nouveau-né*. Thèse médecine. Nancy: 1929.

Samarin. *Les pupilles de l'Assistance publique et leur condition légale*. Thèse. Paris: 1907.

Sauvigny, Guillaume de Bertier de. *Nouvelle histoire de Paris: La Restauration, 1815-1830*. Paris: Hachette, 1977.

Scott, Joan W. and Tilly, Louise A. "Women's Work and the Family in Nineteenth-Century Europe." *Comparative Studies in Society and History* 17 (1975): 36-64.

Sevrin, Ernest. "Croyances populaires et médecine supranaturelle en Eure-et-Loir au XIXe siècle." *Revue d'histoire de l'Eglise de France* 32 (1946): 264-308.

Shaffer, John W. *Family and Farm: Agrarian Change and Household Organization in the Loire Valley, 1500-1900*. Albany: State University of New York Press, 1982.

————. "Family, Class and Young Women: Occupational Expectations in Nineteenth-Century Paris." *The Family in French History.* Edited by Robert Wheaton and Tamara Hareven. Philadelphia: University of Pennsylvania Press, 1980.

Shorter, Edward L. "Female Emancipation, Birth Control and Fertility in European History." *American Historical Review* 78 (1973): 605-640.

————. *The Making of the Modern Family.* New York: Basic Books, 1977.

————. "Sur l'âge des premières règles en France, 1750-1950." *Annales: ESC* (May-June, 1981): 497-503.

Sicard, Emile. "Notes et hypothèses sur les paternités." *Annales de Normandie* iv, 1 (1954): 3-30.

Singer-Kerel, Jeanne. *Le coût de la vie à Paris de 1840 à 1954.* Paris: A. Colin, 1961.

Sommerville, C. John. *The Rise and Fall of Childhood.* Beverly Hills, CA: Sage Publications, 1982.

Spitz, René. "Hospitalism: An Inquiry into the Genesis of Psychiatric Conditions in Early Childhood." *Psychoanalytic Study of the Child* 1 (1945): 50-55.

Stone, Lawrence. *The Family, Sex and Marriage in England, 1500-1800.* New York: Harper & Row, 1977.

Sussman, George D. "Parisian Infants and Norman Wet Nurses in the Early Nineteenth Century: A Statistical Study." *Journal of Interdisciplinary History* 7(Spring 1977): 637-653.

————. *Selling Mothers' Milk: The Wet-Nursing Business in France, 1715-1914.* Urbana: University of Illinois Press, 1982.

————. "The End of the Wet-Nursing Business in France, 1874-1914." *Journal of Family History* 2(Fall 1977): 237-258.

————. "The Glut of Doctors in Mid-Nineteenth-Century France." *Comparative Studies in Society and History* 19(July 1977): 287-304.

————. "The Wet-Nursing Business in Nineteenth Century France." *French Historical Studies* 9(Fall 1975): 304-328.

————. "The Wet-Nursing Business in Paris, 1769-1876." In Edgar Leon Newman, ed. *Proceedings of the First Annual Meeting of the Western Society for French History.* March 14-15, 1974. University Park: New Mexico State University Press, 1974.

Thuillier, Guy. *Pour une histoire du quotidien au XIXe siècle en Nivernais.* Paris: l'Ecole des Hautes Etudes en Sciences Sociales, 1977.

————. "Water Supplies in Nineteenth-Century Nivernais." *Food and Drink in History. Selections from the Annales: ESC.* Edited by Robert Forster and Orest Ranum. Baltimore: Johns Hopkins University Press, 1979.

Tilly, Louise A. "Individual Lives and Family Strategies in the French Proletariat." *The Family and Sexuality in French History.* Edited by Robert Wheaton and Tamara Hareven. Philadelphia: University of Pennsylvania Press, 1980.

Tilly, Louise A. and Scott, Joan W. *Women, Work and Family.* New York: Holt, Rinehart, Winston, 1978.

Tilly, Louise A.; Scott, Joan W.; and Cohen, Miriam. "Women's Work and European Fertility Patterns." *Journal of Interdisciplinary History* 6(Winter 1976): 447-476.

Toursch, Victor. "L'enfant français à la fin du XIXᵉ siècle d'après ses principaux romanciers." *Enfant et sociétés: Annales de démographie historique.* Paris: Mouton, 1973.

Turin, Y. "Enfants trouvés, colonisation et utopie. Etude d'un comportement social au XIXᵉ siècle." *Revue d'histoire* 496 (1970): 329-356.

Ulmann, Jacques. *Les débuts de la médecine des enfants.* Paris: Palais de la Découverte, n.d.

vandeWalle, Etienne and Preston, Samuel H. "Mortalité de l'enfance au XIXᵉ siècle à Paris et dans le département de la Seine." *Population* 29 (1974): 89-107.

Vidal, Marguerite. *Contribution à l'étude du problème des enfants abandonnés en France.* Thèse, médecine. Paris: Ferenczi, 1939.

Weber, Eugen. *Peasants into Frenchmen: The Modernization of Rural France, 1870-1914.* Stanford, California: Stanford University Press, 1976.

Weston, Elizabeth. "Prostitution in Paris in the Later Nineteenth Century: A Study in Social and Political Ideology." Ph.D dissertation, SUNY Buffalo, 1979.

Wheaton, Robert and Hareven, Tamara, eds. *The Family and Sexuality in French History.* Philadelphia: University of Pennsylvania Press, 1980.

Wooden, Kenneth. *Weeping in the Playtime of Others: America's Incarcerated Children.* New York: McGraw-Hill, 1976.

Zehr, Howard. *Crime and Development of Modern Society: Patterns of Criminality in Nineteenth-Century Germany and France.* Totowa, New Jersey: Rowan and Littlefield, 1976.

Zeldin, Theodore. *France, 1848-1945.* Vol. 1: *Ambition, Love and Politics.* Vol. 2: *Intellect, Taste and Anxiety.* Oxford: Clarendon Press, 1974.

Index

Abandoned children: ages of, when abandoned, 64; attitudes toward, 15-17, 40, 46, 49, 55, 155, 159, 165; bureaucracy developed to accommodate, 156-63, 191n; categories of, 18, 23; clothing for, 47, 85, 124, 125, 210-16, 251; economic role of, 1, 32, 156-57, 188-90, 240-43, 250; financial support for, 2, 7-8, 16-17, 24, 26, 30, 34, 40, 156-58, 281, 293n; gender of, 64, 297n; geographical distribution of, 169-170, 176-77; identification of, 66, 120-23; legitimacy status of, 4, 35, 66, 70-71, 75, 77; institutions for, 9, 31, 34-35, 40 (*See also* Hospice des Enfants *Trouvés*); medical care for, 24, 57, 161-163, 230, 245, 281; numbers of, 8, 10, 12, 70, 77, 106; occupations of, 4, 16, 236, 241, 256-58; responsibility for, assumed by departments, 18-19, 21; responsibility for, assumed by nobility, 3, 5, 8; responsibility for, assumed by state, 18-20, 27, 34, 60, 190; reclamation of, by parents, 20, 236-40; terms used for, 18; transportation of, 12, 14, 34, 40-41, 160, 170, 178, 180. *See also* Adolescents; Child abandonment; Education, of abandoned children; Foster parents; Infants; *Moralement abandonnés*; Mortality, child; Orphans; State policy, toward abandoned children

Abortion, 4-5, 22, 26, 104, 277; abandonment as alternative to, 12, 42, 44; methods for, 103

Académie des Sciences et Politiques, 36-37

Administration Générale des Hôpitaux, Hospices Civils et Secours à domicile de Paris-Service des Enfants Trouvés et Orphelins de Paris, 158-162, 214-215;

field representatives of, 34, 149, 163, 183-84, 214-15; field representatives of, as agents of government policy, 280; field representatives of, duties of, 190, 210, 224-25, 242, 257; policies of, 34, 158-63, 178, 180-82, 189-90, 242-43; wet nurses recruited by, 134, 158, 160, 164-66, 169, 186. *See also Préposés; Meneurs; Sous-inspecteurs*

Adolescence, 49, 51-53. *See also* Adolescents, abandoned

Adolescents, abandoned, 48, 270, 274; deviance among, 264-71 (*see also* Juvenile delinquents); education of, 15, 53; marriage of, 262-64; military service of, 260-61; occupations of 256-60; returned to Hospice, 265-66; state policies toward, 36, 192, 235-36, 242, 256-58. *See also* Abandoned children

Adoption, 25, 29-31

Adults, abandoned children as, 245, 249

Agriculture, 47-48, 256-57

Aid to unwed mothers. *See* Mothers, unwed, aid to

Algeria: plan to colonize with abandoned children, 268-69

Allier, Department of the, 170, 176, 182

"Angel makers." *See* Wet nurses

Apprenticeships, 6, 16; state policy toward, 24, 47, 272; types of, 256-57

Arras, 170

Ariès, Philippe, 6, 25

Artificial feeding: animals' milk used in, 3, 14, 51, 138-39, 220-21; compared to breast-feeding, 51, 218; formulas used in, 136, 218-22; health hazards of, 137-38, 219-20; improvements in, 32, 186, 231; in Hospice, 136-42; methods of, 23, 137-38, 219-23

Assistance Publique, L', 58, 151, 160,

350